Incredible Teachers
Nurturing Children's Social,
Emotional and Academic Competence

INCREDIBLE TEACHERS

Nurturing Children's Social, Emotional, and Academic Competence

CAROLYN WEBSTER-STRATTON, PH.D.

The Incredible Years®
Parents, teachers, and children training series

www.incredibleyears.com

Incredible Teachers
Nurturing Children's Social, Emotional, and Academic Competence

Some chapters were updated and substantially revised from the book *How to Promote Children's Social and Emotional Competence,* published in 1999 by Sage Publishers.

Book design by Janice St. Marie
Cover photos: www.istockphoto.com

Webster-Stratton, Carolyn
Incredible Teachers
Nurturing Children's Social, Emotional, and Academic Competence

Includes bibliographical references.
ISBN 978-1-892222-10-7

Publisher:
Incredible Years®, Inc.
1411 8th Avenue West
Seattle, WA 98119 USA
206-285-7565
www.incredibleyears.com

Printed in USA

ACKNOWLEDGEMENTS

I would like to thank the many teachers who I have worked with over the past 30 years who have taught me so much about their experiences teaching children who may be temperamentally difficult, developmentally delayed or typical. It is their compassion, energy and commitment to help these children not only learn academic skills but also to develop into socially and emotionally competent individuals that has provided the fuel for this book. I would also like to thank the children who have attended Dinosaur School with me at the Parenting Clinic. They have taught me the most and have convinced me that aggression, bullying, peer rejection and ultimately violence can be prevented. Finally, thanks to my colleague Jamila Reid, my friend and colleague in my research and clinical work who has read and commented upon drafts of this revision and provided unfailing support. Also Lisa St. George, director of Incredible Years business, has helped immensely by proofreading, copy editing and working tirelessly with our graphic designer, Janice St. Marie, to make this a reality.

CONTENTS

CHAPTER THREE: The Proactive Teacher ~ Scaffolding the Environment   **95**

CHAPTER FIVE: Spotlight Sunshine on Positive Behavior Growth ~ Importance of Teacher Attention, Encouragement and Praise   189

CHAPTER SIX: Strengthening Positive Behavior ~ Using Incentives to Motivate Students   221

CHAPTER SEVEN: Managing Student Misbehaviors: Ignoring and Redirecting   273

CHAPTER EIGHT: Managing Misbehaviors: Natural and Logical Consequences 305

CHAPTER NINE: Managing Misbehaviors: Time Out to Calm Down 335

PREFACE

As an educational and clinical psychologist for the past 30 years, I have worked extensively with teachers. Yet I am also a parent of two children, who are now adults, and sometimes I felt when they were young that these two roles had little overlap. Like all parents, I was concerned with supporting my children's optimal social and emotional development as well as their academic achievement. Naturally, this involved many conversations with their teachers throughout their school age years—conversations that ideally should always be a two-way exchange. However, there were times when my children's teachers responded to my attempts to talk with them in ways that discouraged collaboration and left me feeling reluctant to try again.

For example, my daughter—a normally lively, self-confident girl—came home from school one day saying, "I'm the dumbest in the class. Everyone but me can read!" I could see that her difficulty learning to read was affecting not only her enjoyment of school and her willingness to participate in class, but also her self-esteem. I felt it was important to talk with her teachers about this issue. But when I called to set up an appointment to meet, something about their response left me with the impression that scheduling a parent meeting was burdensome. Nevertheless, we did meet. My husband and I were told that our daughter was doing fine and that we should stop worrying about her reading. My concerns about the impact on her enthusiasm for school had not been allayed; yet I also began to feel guilty for having needlessly taken up the teacher's time even though as a professional I knew the importance of parent/teacher collaboration. A year later our daughter was diagnosed as having a reading disability. I felt both angry with her teachers for having minimized my concern and incompetent as a parent for not being more effective in communicating my concern and advocating for her needs earlier.

There is no doubt that this experience would have dampened my enthusiasm for collaborating with teachers, were it not for an experience I had the next year with her teachers. One day I received a call from her teacher telling me about something wonderful our daughter had done in class to help some children problem-solve a tricky situation. My husband and I were beaming! A few weeks later her teacher came to watch her baseball game. (I later learned that her teacher attended special events for ALL the students in her classroom.) As a result my daughter was back to her bubbly self in school and we would have done anything for her teachers. My husband and I were so taken with these teachers who we thought were "incredible teachers" that we would sing their praises to whomever would listen. With a few acts of kindness and a commitment to caring, these teachers had bridged the home-school gap in a fundamental way.

RESEARCH BACKGROUND

I have spent the past 30 years developing, evaluating and refining the Incredible Years® (IY) parent, teacher and child training programs designed to both prevent and treat disruptive behavior problems in young children as well as to promote their social and emotional competence and academic readiness. During the first decade of my research I focused on the IY parent training programs designed to help parents manage children with Oppositional Defiant Disorder, Conduct Disorder, Attention Deficit Disorder and internalizing problems (Webster-Stratton & Herman, 2008; Webster-Stratton & Reid, 2010). Our own randomized control group trials as well as others' research have shown that when parents are trained to use effective parenting and discipline skills and to nurture positive relationships their children have increased social and emotional competence, higher self-esteem and fewer aggressive behavior problems in comparison to control children. (See Chapter One for review of some of this research.) However, while parents have been successful in bringing about a more harmonious family life at home, studies have shown there has not necessarily been a corresponding improvement in the children's relationships and behaviors at school. Some of the teachers of the children in my parent training studies reported after the parents' training programs were completed that the students were still defiant, inattentive and disruptive in class and had considerable peer relationship difficulties. Furthermore many teachers reported feeling stressed by the time and energy it took to manage these difficult students in the context of a large classroom of students. They reported feeling inadequately prepared to manage the escalating number of students with behavior problems or for knowing how to provide the necessary emotional and social curriculum (Webster-Stratton, 1998).

Indeed teachers today are presented with more complex classrooms. Increasing numbers of students with English as a second language (National Clearinghouse for English Language Acquisition, 2009) and with emotional, social and behavioral problems are entering school (Brophy, 1996; Conroy, Sutherland et. al, 2009). Furthermore, increased classroom sizes and the inclusion of students receiving special education services in general education classrooms present challenges for teachers working to provide instruction and manage classroom behaviors among diverse learners. In fact, nearly half of new teachers leave the profession within five years, many citing student misbehavior as a primary reason (Ingersoll, 2002). Thus, to fully support teacher efforts in providing effective classroom management practices designed to nurture, encourage, and motivate students with varying developmental abilities and cultural backgrounds, evidence-based teacher classroom management training programs and social and emotional curriculums are needed that are flexible and adaptive to the unique challenges faced by teachers. Moreover, these training programs need to be attentive to the varying backgrounds and experiences of teachers and to the ability to provide teachers with additional consultation and support according to individual classroom needs.

In 1990, the 2nd decade of my professional career, I developed the Incredible Years Teacher Classroom Management Training (IY TCM) program (Webster-Stratton, 1994) designed to reduce the multiple risk factors associated

Training programs and social and emotional curriculums are needed that are flexible and adaptive to the unique challenges faced by teachers.

Both teachers and parents felt less stressed, less adversarial, and more supported when collaborating to provide for the children's needs.

with emotional and social difficulties in young children ages 3 to 8 years and to strengthen emotional and social competence. Indeed it seemed to me that ALL young children could benefit from an education delivered by teachers who effectively managed misbehavior and who emphasized students' effective social skills, emotional literacy and problem-solving as well as their academic achievement. Consequently I began a program of research to evaluate the added effects of training teachers in the IY TCM program delivered in conjunction with the parents receiving the IY Basic Parenting program (Webster-Stratton & Reid, 2007; Webster-Stratton, Reid, & Hammond, 2004). I saw that in our studies this collaboration led to a fundamental change in parent-teacher relationships where each was supporting the other and behavior planning together for the children's individual needs. Our experience indicated that both teachers and parents felt less stressed, less adversarial, and more supported in providing for the children's needs. Our studies showed that when teachers are involved in the training program along with parents, not only did the child's behavior improve, but the whole classroom became more cooperative and there was greater academic engagement (Webster-Stratton & Reid, 2009; Webster-Stratton & Reid, 2007; Webster-Stratton, Reid, & Hammond, 2001a; Webster-Stratton et al., 2004).

I also developed and evaluated a child social, emotional and problem-solving curriculum (aka the IY Dinosaur School curriculum) for training children diagnosed with Oppositional Defiant Disorder or Conduct Disorder (Webster-Stratton, 1990). This program was offered to children while their parents were participating in the parenting program and to some children as an after-school program each week. In two randomized control group treatment studies evaluating the added effects of combining child training with parent training, I found that the children who had participated in Dinosaur School had significantly better problem-solving skills and prosocial behaviors when interacting with their peers in a laboratory and according to independent classroom observations compared with children who got parent training alone and to control children (Webster-Stratton & Hammond, 1997; Webster-Stratton & Reid, 2003; Webster-Stratton, Reid, & Hammond, 2001b; Webster-Stratton et al., 2004). This led me to believe that children who had difficulties with peers at school in addition to behavior problems at home could benefit from a specific curriculum designed to promote what some have called "emotional literacy" (Goleman, 1995) or what I call "social and emotional competence."

Over the past 20 years we have trained many Head Start preschool teachers as well as elementary school teachers of kindergarten through grade 3 students in high risk schools in both the IY TCM program and the Dinosaur Curriculum. Some of these trainings have been targeted as special treatment programs to help students with diagnosed problems and others have been targeted as prevention programs to improve the social and emotional competence of all the students (Webster-Stratton & Reid, 2009; Webster-Stratton & Reid, 2008a, 2008b; Webster-Stratton, Reid, & Stoolmiller, 2008). This book is the direct result of these trainings and research findings and the many ideas shared by the teachers who participated in delivery of these programs. I am indebted to these teachers for teaching me and sharing with me their insights and strategies for promoting children's emotional and social competence. Without their input this book could not have been written.

PURPOSE OF BOOK

This book is the text that accompanies the training for the Incredible Years Teacher Classroom Management Program (IY TCM) and the IY Child Social, Emotional and Problem Solving Curriculum (aka Dinosaur School). It is addressed to teachers of young children (ages 3 to 8 years) with several purposes or principles in mind:

Principle One ~ Promoting Supportive Relationships with Students and Parents

The first principle is to discuss ways teachers can develop supportive relationships with students as well as with their parents and develop collaborative partnerships in order to address their students' educational, social and emotional needs and individual goals. Chapters 1 and 2 address some of the research regarding the impact of teacher-student relationships and teachers and parents working together to support the essential social and emotional skills which provide the foundation for children's successful academic learning. A thread throughout all the chapters includes the topic of teacher-parent partnerships in order to promote learning at home as well as at school. For instance, chapters 3 through 6 discuss how teachers can develop meaningful relationships with their students by involving parents in ongoing dialogues, home-school connected activities, classroom participation, teaching parents coaching strategies and planning home-school incentive programs for helping children overcome difficult problems providing consistency across settings. Chapters 7 through 10 suggest ways teachers can include parents in discipline plans and work together to determine what works best with a particular child's unique temperament, developmental ability and individual goals. Chapters 11, 12 and 13 address ways to include parents in a curriculum designed to promote emotional regulation, emotional literacy, social skills, and problem-solving at school and at home. Chapter 14 specifically addresses interpersonal processes teachers need to have successful team meetings with parents.

This bottom layer of the pyramid provides the foundational scaffolding and nurturing necessary to promote student learning and developmental growth and should be applied liberally.

Principle Two ~ Teachers Using Research-based Classroom Management Strategies

The second purpose of this book is to present a variety of research-based classroom management strategies or tools which teachers can choose from to strengthen children's social, emotional and academic competence. The emotional literacy and social competence of children is considered as having equal importance to academic literacy. The Incredible Years Teaching Pyramid (shown next page) serves as the roadmap for the content and teaching methods discussed. The bottom of the pyramid as depicted in the early chapters focus on tools to encourage students' positive relationships and behaviors and build their confidence, self-esteem, emotional regulation, problem-solving and motivation for learning. This bottom layer of the pyramid provides the foundational scaffolding and nurturing necessary to promote student learning and developmental growth and should be applied liberally. A basic premise of the model is that a positive relationship foundation precedes discipline strategies, and teacher attention to positive behaviors should occur far more frequently in effective classroom environments than attention to negative behaviors. Only when this positive foundation is in place do later aspects higher on the pyramid work. Further up the pyramid the focus

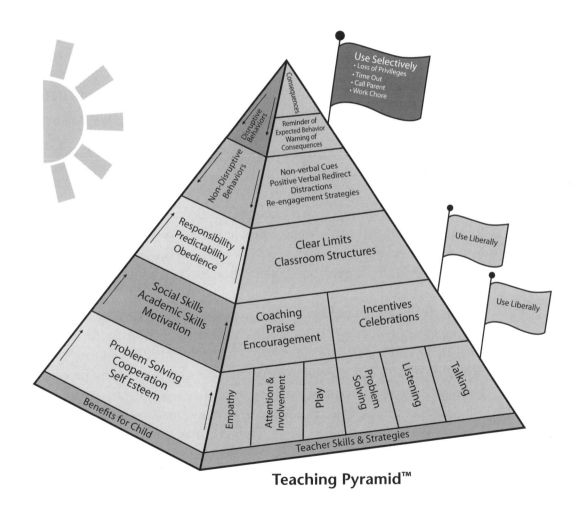

Teaching Pyramid™

is on proactive, nonintrusive classroom strategies such as clear rules, predictable limits, re-engagement strategies, and a clear routine or structure designed to minimize classroom disruption and avoid confrontation, in order to create a smoothly functioning classroom with students taking on increasing responsibility for their behavior. Higher in the pyramid Chapters Eight and Nine focus on more intrusive discipline strategies such as Time Out and loss of privileges required when students are verbally and physically violent. After all these basic classroom management tools have been learned Chapters 11, 12 and 13 go back down the pyramid to present curriculum activities, games and scripts for teaching emotional regulation skills, social skills, and problem-solving. The final Chapters 14 and 15 focus on building teachers' partnerships with parents and teachers managing their own stress by having a colleague support network and working collaboratively with families. The final Chapter integrates all the stategies discussed in the book to show how schools, teachers and parents can build a "bullyproof" environment.

Principle Three ~ Individualization of Students' Learning Goals

The third purpose or theme of this book is to illustrate how teachers can set up individualized programs that address the special social and emotional needs of high risk children. Children may be at higher risk for social, emotional and academic problems because of some biological factors or developmental delays such as learning disabilities, hyperactivity, impulsivity, attention deficit disorder, language and reading delays and highly aggressive behavior. The book takes a developmental perspective helping teachers to choose management strategies that are developmentally appropriate for young children ages 3-10 years. As Piaget (Piaget, 1962; Piaget & Inhelder, 1962) has noted children in the "preoperational stage" of development vacillate in their thinking process between fantasy and reality, lack the cognitive capacity necessary to self-reflect or anticipate consequences, to emotionally self-regulate, or grasp some verbal abstract concepts. They are however driven to explore, to experience, to discover and to establish some independence. The social and emotional small group activities recommended in this book are based on children's ability to learn best from experiential activities designed according to their developmental ability and in conjunction with supportive coaching from teachers.

Some children may be at higher risk for difficulties because of coming from home situations where the adults are unresponsive or abusive, or where the adults are so overwhelmed with their own stresses that they are unable to meet their children's needs. This book shows how teachers can integrate individualized interventions for these high risk children in the mainstream classroom while at the same time enhancing the social and emotional competence of all their students.

Principle Four ~ Teachers Start Nurturing Students Early and Build a Secure Learning Foundation

Over the past 30 years a variety of family and school interventions have been developed to address child conduct problems (Estrada & Pinsof, 1995; Han & Weiss, 2005). In studies evaluating these interventions, results suggest that if intervention occurs early—when the child is still in preschool or early school-age—rather than later, it is more effective and more likely to prevent a chronic pattern from developing. In fact, there is evidence that the younger the child at the time of intervention, the more positive the child's emotional and behavioral adjustment at home and at school (Hindman, Skibbe, Miller, & Zimmerman, 2010; Strain, Steele, Ellis, & Timm, 1982). Therefore it is strategic to offer children interventions as early as possible so as to prevent the development of conduct disorders and keep those children who show early signs of aggression off the spiralling track to delinquency.

One might think of the teaching pyramid described above as similar to teachers' nurturing the growth of a new plant. The teacher's positive relationships with students provides healthy soil necessary for the child's optimal development. As the seed begins to grow the gardener provides regular water, sunshine and puts down stakes to scaffold the plant's growth and prevent it from falling over, and at times

Like the plant,
the earlier the child
receives this nurturing
and support the more
likely it will be strong,
survive weather storms
and be uniquely beautiful.

the plant may need some fertilizer. Similarly an effective teacher, like the gardener, will provide coaching, praise and incentives to support her students' learning. Without this nurturing and scaffolding, like the plant, the student would fail to grow and learn. Finally, the gardener prunes weeds that threaten to cause damage to the plant, just as the teacher sets clear limits and imposes consequences for students' inappropriate behaviors. This discipline is needed to assure the safety of students and an optimal environment for all. Like the plant, the earlier the child receives this nurturing and support the more likely it will be strong, survive weather storms and be uniquely beautiful.

Principle Five ~ Teachers Develop Support Networks

The fifth purpose of this book is to lend support to the efforts of teachers to give more attention to developing the social competence and emotional well being of children. Teachers understand that just as a child's cognitive competence affects his or her ability to learn, a child's social competence and emotional security affects his or her ability to learn. It is my hope that this book will be a useful tool to support this effort. Stable and nurturing teachers who do this emotional and social teaching may be able to provide a buffer for some young children against the impact of parental psychopathology and family stress and may be able to provide support when parents are relatively unavailable to their children. When teachers promote social and emotional competence in children, they help not only the children who are at risk or have behavioral problems, but all students in their classrooms benefit.

This is an important but also stressful undertaking for teachers who are coping with larger classrooms, more academic demands and children with varying developmental and language abilities and family cultural backgrounds. By teachers' involving parents in this endeavor when possible, research has shown that not only will children do better academically but teachers will feel more satisfied because they have the support of parents and recognition from society for the important job they have. In addition to parental support, teachers need support groups from administration and other teachers where they can collaborate on behavior plans, reflect on their approaches, and share strategies for how to help particular students learn. To expand this vision, the nurturing of teachers and recognition of their importance in children's lives will increase their job satisfaction and decrease the likelihood they will drop out.

OTHER BOOKS AND MATERIAL AVAILABLE

The parent, child and teacher training materials with extensive manuals, books and DVDs may be obtained from:

The Incredible Years: Parents, Teachers and Children
 Training Series
1411 8th Avenue West
Seattle, WA 98119
Fax: 206-285-7565
Web Site: www.incredibleyears.com
Email: incredibleyears@incredibleyears.com

REFERENCES

Brophy, J. E., & McCaslin, M. (1992). Teachers' reports of how they perceive and cope with problem students. *Elementary School Journal*, 93, 363-423.

Conroy, M., & Sutherland, K. (2008). Preventing and ameliorating young children's chronic problem behaviors: An ecological classroom-based approach. *Psychology in the Schools*, 46(1), 3-17.

Estrada, A. U., & Pinsof, W. M. (1995). The effectiveness of family therapies for selected behavioral disorders of childhood. *Journal of Marital and Family Therapy*, 21(4), 403-440.

Goleman, D. (1995). *Emotional Intelligence*. New York: Bantam.

Han, S., & Weiss, B. (2005). Sustainability of teacher implementation of school-based mental health programs. *Journal of Abnormal Child Psychology*, 33, 665-679.

Hindman, A. H., Skibbe, L. E., Miller, A., & Zimmerman, M. (2010). Ecological contexts and early learning: Contributions of child, family, and classroom factors during Head Start, to literacy and mathematics growth through first grade. *Early Childhood Research Quarterly*, 25, 235-250.

Ingersoll, R. M. (2002). *High turnover plagues schools*. USA Today.

Piaget, J. (1962). *Play, Dreams and Imitation in Childhood*. New York: Norton.

Piaget, J., & Inhelder, B. (1962). *The Psychology of the Child*. New York Basic Books.

Strain, P. S., Steele, P., Ellis, T., & Timm, M. A. (1982). Long-term effects of oppositional child treatment with mothers as therapists and therapist trainers. *Journal of Applied Behavior Analysis, 15,* 1163-1169.

Webster-Stratton, C. (1990). Dina dinosaur social skills, emotion and problem-solving curriculum. Seattle, WA: Incredible Years.

Webster-Stratton, C. (1994). The Incredible Years Teacher Training Series. Seattle, WA: Incredible Years.

Webster-Stratton, C. (1998). Preventing conduct problems in Head Start children: Strengthening parenting competencies. *Journal of Consulting and Clinical Psychology, 66*(5), 715-730.

Webster-Stratton, C., & Hammond, M. (1997). Treating children with early-onset conduct problems: A comparison of child and parent training interventions. *Journal of Consulting and Clinical Psychology, 65*(1), 93-109.

Webster-Stratton, C., & Herman, K. (2008). The impact of parent behavior-management training on child depressive symptoms. *Journal of Counseling Psychology, 55*(4), 473-484.

Webster-Stratton, C., & Reid, M.J. (2009). A school-family partnership:Addressing multiple risk factors to improve school readiness and prevent conduct problems in young children. In S. L. Christenson & A. L. Reschly (Eds.), *Handbook on school-family partnerships for promoting student competence* (pp. 204-227). Seattle Routledge/Taylor and Francis.

Webster-Stratton, C., & Reid, M. J. (2003). Treating conduct problems and strengthening social emotional competence in young children (ages 4-8 years): The Dina Dinosaur treatment program. *Journal of Emotional and Behavioral Disorders, 11*(3), 130-143.

Webster-Stratton, C., & Reid, M. J. (2007). Incredible Years Parents and Teachers Training Series: A Head Start partnership to promote social competence and prevent conduct problems In P.

Tolin, J. Szapocznick & S. Sambrano (Eds.), *Preventing Youth Substance Abuse* (pp. 67-88). Washington D. C.: American Psychological Association.

Webster-Stratton, C., & Reid, M. J. (2008a). Adapting the Incredible Years Child Dinosaur Social, Emotional and Problem Solving intervention to address co-morbid diagnoses. *Journal of Children's Services, 3*(3), 17-30.

Webster-Stratton, C., & Reid, M. J. (2008b). Strengthening social and emotional competence in socioeconomically disadvantaged young children: Preschool and kindergarten school-based curricula. In W. H. Brown, S. L. Odom & S. R. McConnell (Eds.), *Social competence of young children: Risk, disability, and intervention* (pp. 185-203). Baltimore: Paul H. Brookes Publishing Co.

Webster-Stratton, C., & Reid, M. J. (2010). The Incredible Years Parents, Teachers and Children Training Series: A multifaceted treatment approach for young children with conduct problems. In J. Weisz & A. Kazdin (Eds.), *Evidence-based psychotherapies for children and adolescents,* 2nd edition (pp. 194-210). New York: Guilford Publications.

Webster-Stratton, C., Reid, M. J., & Hammond, M. (2001a). Preventing conduct problems, promoting social competence: A parent and teacher training partnership in Head Start. *Journal of Clinical Child Psychology, 30*(3), 283-302.

Webster-Stratton, C., Reid, M. J., & Hammond, M. (2001b). Social skills and problem solving training for children with early-onset conduct problems: Who benefits? *Journal of Child Psychology and Psychiatry, 42*(7), 943-952.

Webster-Stratton, C., Reid, M. J., & Hammond, M. (2004). Treating children with early-onset conduct problems: Intervention outcomes for parent, child, and teacher training. *Journal of Clinical Child and Adolescent Psychology, 33*(1), 105-124.

Webster-Stratton, C., Reid, M. J., & Stoolmiller, M. (2008). Preventing conduct problems and improving school readiness: Evaluation of the Incredible Years Teacher and Child Training Programs in high-risk schools. *Journal of Child Psychology and Psychiatry 49*(5), 471-488.

CHAPTER 1

Children's Social and Emotional Competence ~ The Seeds of Academic Success: Research Evidence

Research indicates that nurturing children's emotional, social, and behavioral development is as important for their school learning and academic achievement as cognitive and academic preparedness (Raver & Zigler, 1997; Reinke, Stormont, Herman, Puri, & Goel, 2010; Zins & Elias, 2006). A school's ability to strengthen young children's emotional literacy and emotion regulation, to encourage meaningful friendships, and to form partnerships with parents is crucial. These tools provide the necessary foundation and scaffolding needed to support children's mental health, growth in learning, and eventual academic

Explicit, intentional, responsive teaching and nurturing of social and emotional skills can result in fewer aggressive responses and ultimate school achievement.

success. A key challenge for 21st century schools and teachers is educating culturally diverse students with varied family backgrounds, developmental abilities, and motivations for learning. Explicit, intentional, responsive teaching and nurturing of social and emotional skills, especially for young children who are at risk, can result in fewer aggressive responses, inclusion in prosocial peer groups, and ultimate school achievement (Bredekamp & Copple, 1997; Raver et al., 2008; Raver & Knitzer, 2002). The Report of the Surgeon General's Conference on Children's Mental Health proclaimed, "mental health is a critical component of children's learning and general health. Fostering social and emotional health as a part of healthy child development must therefore be a national priority." (U.S. Public Health Service, 2000, p. 3)

PREVALENCE OF SOCIAL, EMOTIONAL, AND BEHAVIORAL DIFFICULTIES IN YOUNG CHILDREN

Unfortunately many students entering elementary schools lack the social and emotional competencies necessary for school readiness. In fact, these difficulties impede their academic engagement and learning. Moreover, aggression in children is escalating, and it is evident among younger and younger children (Campbell, 1990, 1991; Webster-Stratton & Hammond, 1998; Webster-Stratton & Lindsay, 1999). The prevalence of disruptive behavior problems in preschool and early school-age children is about 10%, and may be as high as 35% for socioeconomically disadvantaged children (Rimm-Kaufman, Pianta, & Cox, 2000; Webster-Stratton & Hammond, 1998; Webster-Stratton, Reid, & Hammond, 2001).

These trends have disturbing implications for everyone, not just for the child and their families. Early onset conduct problems, marked by aggressive and oppositional behavior in young children, are key risk factors or "red flags" that signal the beginning of escalating academic problems, grade retention, and school drop out and are predictive of subsequent drug abuse, depression, juvenile delinquency, antisocial behavior, and violence in adolescence and adulthood (Guerra & Bradshaw, 2008; Kazdin, 1995; Keenan et al., 2011; Kupersmidt & Coie, 1990; Loeber & Farrington, 2000; Moffitt, 1993; White, Moffit, Earls, & Robins, 1990). Acts of murder, rape, robbery, arson, drunk driving, and abuse are carried out to a greater extent by persons with a history of chronic aggression stemming from childhood than by other persons (Hawkins et al., 1998; Loeber, 1990; Loeber & Farrington, 2001). Thus the problem of escalating aggression in young children is a concern for society as a whole, because of what it portends for the safety for ourselves and our children, regardless of our ethnicity, economic status, or community. Conduct disorder is one of the most costly mental disorders to society (Loeber & Farrington, 2001; Robins, 1981). A large proportion of antisocial children remain involved with mental health agencies throughout their lives and/or become involved with criminal justice systems. In other words, everyone pays in the long run, personally, financially, or both, when these children are left uncared for and their social, emotional, and academic behavior problems remain untreated (Campbell, Shaw, & Gilliom, 2000; Costello, Foley, & Angold, 2006; Eisenberg, 2006; Snyder, 2001; Tremblay et al., 1996).

Children who start school with difficulties controlling their negative emotions, paying attention, following teacher directions, and getting along with others do less well in school (Ladd, Kochenderfer, & Coleman, 1997; White et al., 1990). They are more likely to be rejected by classmates and to get less positive feedback from teachers, which, in turn, contributes to more off task behavior, less instruction time, and less learning (Asher, Parkhurst, Hymel, & Williams, 1990; Hanish & Guerra, 2002; Shores & Wehby, 1999). Disruptive behavior in the classroom takes time away from positive delivery of engaging lessons and activities and is stressful for teachers, for the disruptive child, and for other children in the classroom (Jones, Daley, Hutchings, Bywater, & Eames, 2007). Without successful intervention, disruptive behaviors continue to escalate and impede the academic and social growth of all

Without successful intervention, disruptive behaviors continue to escalate and impede the academic and social growth of all students.

students. Research suggests that by high school as many as 40% to 60% of students have become chronically disengaged from school (Klem & Connell, 2004), jeopardizing their potential for life success.

CHILD BIOLOGICAL AND DEVELOPMENTAL RISK FACTORS FOR SOCIAL AND EMOTIONAL DIFFICULTIES

Child biological risk factors are associated with increased social, emotional and behavioral difficulty in school; many children with early onset conduct problems also have social-cognitive, emotional regulation, language, and developmental delays that contribute to, or complicate their disruptive behaviors (Beauchaine, Neuhaus, Brenner, & Gatzke-Kopp, 2008; Coie & Dodge, 1998). Approximately 40% of young children with Oppositional Defiant Disorder (ODD) are comorbid for Attention Deficit Disorder (ADHD) (Hartman, Stage, & Webster-Stratton, 2003), and 50% of those with ADHD have ODD (Beauchaine, Hinshaw, & Pang, 2010; Hinshaw, 2002; Webster-Stratton, Reid, & Beauchaine, 2011). Many of these children also experience depression (Webster-Stratton & Herman, 2008) but their diagnosis is frequently masked as disruptive behavior due to their lack of emotional language skills (Garber & Horowitz, 2002). Children's emotional dysregulation has been associated with distinct patterns of responding on a variety

of psycho-physiological measures compared to typically developing children (Beauchaine, 2001; Beauchaine et al., 2008; McBurnett et al., 1993; Moffitt & Lynam, 1994). Children who enter school with poor school readiness skills, cognitive deficits, language and developmental delays, are more likely to have behavior problems, further exacerbating any preexisting learning problems (Malecki & Elliott, 2002; Menting, Van Lier, & Koot, 2011).

FAMILY RISK FACTORS

Children with social and emotional difficulties manifested as ODD, Conduct Disorder, ADHD, depression, anxiety, or social difficulties share a host of common family risk factors. Many come from families experiencing the stress of poverty, single parenthood, marital conflict, substance abuse, mental illness, or unemployment: stressors shown to

disrupt parents' ability to monitor their children; provide structured, predictable and safe environments; consistent, nurturing, and positive parenting interactions; and secure parent-child attachments (Belsky & Fearson, 2002; Domina, 2005; Evans, 2004; Lynam et al., 2000; Webster-Stratton, 1990b). Research on child and early brain development shows that responsive and nurturing parenting interactions play a pivotal role in the development of children's healthy cognitions and social and emotional brain architecture. Many empirical studies have also supported the cognitive social learning perspective on development of childhood aggression, depression, and poor social competence and self-regulation. Social learning theory posits that one contributor to early childhood internalizing and externalizing symptoms is negative or coercive encounters within a harsh social environment (Bandura, 1986), particularly critical responses from parents (Patterson, Reid, & Dishion, 1992). In these harsh interactions, children's depressive and aggressive behaviors may be selectively reinforced by parents' angry or critical responses, and, at the same time, these negative parental responses to conflict are directly modeled for children (Hawkins, Clarke, & Seeley, 1993). Parenting behaviors consistently associated with poor social and emotional competence include low levels of parenting competence (e.g., critical, hostile, unpredictable, inconsistent) (Deater-Deckard, Dodge, Bates, & Pettit, 1996; Ostrander & Herman, 2006), permissive, neglectful, and abusive discipline (Barth et al., 2005; Fantuzzo, DelGaudio, Atkins, Meyers, & Noone, 1998; Jaffee & Maikovich-Fong, 2011; Knutson, DeGarmo, Koeppl, & Reid, 2005) and lack of parental support and a nurturing relationship (Pettit, Bates, & Dodge, 1997). These parenting risk factors interact synergistically with the child's genetic, biological and developmental risk factors noted earlier. Emerging research indicates that parenting influences children's brain development and thereby behavioral development (Belsky & de Haan, 2011).

Emerging research indicates that parenting influences children's brain development and thereby behavioral development.

TEACHER AND SCHOOL RISK FACTORS

Quality of teacher-student-family relationships and use of evidence-based classroom management practices are also key teacher risk factors related to the development of children's academic underachievement, social and emotional difficulties, and conduct problems (Brophy, 1996; Conroy & Sutherland, 2008; Doll, Zucker, & Brehm, 2004; O'Connor, Dearning, & Collins, 2011; Walker, Colvin, & Ramsey, 1995). Low rates of praise, harsh discipline, negative teacher-student-parent relationships, failure to focus on social-emotional curriculum, and low emphasis on home-school collaboration are all linked to risk for poor academic performance, escalating aggression and rejection (Kellam, Ling, Merisca, Brown, & Ialongo, 1998; Simonsen & Fairbanks, 2008), and poor long-term adjustment for students (Hawkins, Smith, & Catalano, 2004; Reinke & Herman, 2002). Research has shown that teachers with students exhibiting disruptive behavior problems in their classroom find that these coercive behaviors tend to dominate their interactions, making teaching difficult and unpleasant (Shores et al., 1993). This results in teachers' providing these children with less instruction and easier tasks than to children who do not exhibit such difficult behaviors (Carr, Taylor, & Robinson, 1991). Moreover, teacher reinforcement for students' positive behavior is infrequent and reprimands are often non-contingent upon student behavior (Bierman et al., 1992; Stormont, Smith, & Lewis, 2007). As Patterson and colleagues (Patterson et al., 1992) have described, these patterns of negative or coercive interactions at school contribute to a cascade of negative outcomes for children with antisocial behaviors including peer rejection, negative school reputations, academic failure, and further escalation of their antisocial problems. Further, parent-teacher relationships are often strained due to the failure to develop supportive partnerships in order to promote home-school consistency and collaboration (Christenson & Sheridan, 2001).

On the other hand, considerable research has demonstrated that teachers' use of effective classroom management strategies can reduce disruptive

Research has demonstrated that teachers' use of effective classroom management strategies can reduce disruptive behavior and enhance academic achievement.

behavior (Conroy & Sutherland, 2008; Doll et al., 2004; Hawkins, Catalano, Kosterman, Abbott, & Hill, 1999; Kellam et al., 1998; Walker, 1995), enhance academic achievement (Brophy, 1996), and children's emotional and social competence and school readiness (Webster-Stratton, Reid, & Hammond, 2004; Webster-Stratton, Reid, & Stool- miller, 2008). Well-trained teachers can help children who  are aggressive, disruptive, and uncooperative to develop the appropriate social behavior and emotional self-regulation that is a prerequisite for their success in school (Walker, Schwartz, Nippold, Irvin, & Noell, 1994; Webster-Stratton et al., 2004; Webster-Stratton et al., 2008). Unfortunately, many teachers simply are not adequately supported to manage the escalating number of behavior problems in the classroom; some even enter the workforce without having taken a single course on behavior management, child development or cognitive social learning theory (Barrett & Davis, 1995; Evertson & Weinstein, 2006; Houston & Williamson, 1992); and very few have been trained to deliver evidence-based social and emotional literacy, social skills, and problem solving curricula. Surveys indicate that many schools do not use evidence-based social and emotional curriculum or use them with poor fidelity (Gottfredson & Gottfredson, 2002).

In a recent survey of elementary teachers, teachers reported that managing behavior in the classroom was their greatest challenge and the area in which they felt they needed additional training (Reinke et al., 2010). Teachers today are presented with more complex classrooms. Increasing numbers of students with English as a second language (National Clearinghouse for English Language Acquisition, 2009) and with emotional and behavioral problems are entering school (Walker et al., 1995). Further, increased classroom sizes and the inclusion of students receiving special education services in general education classrooms present challenges for teachers, who must provide instruction and manage classroom behaviors among diverse learners at different developmental stages. In fact, nearly half of new teachers leave the profession within five years, many citing student misbehavior as a primary reason (Ingersoll, 2002). Thus, to fully support teacher efforts in providing effective classroom management practices that nurture, encourage, and motivate students with varying developmental abilities and cultural backgrounds, additional training and consultation that is flexible and adaptive is required.

RESEARCH REGARDING SCHOOL-DELIVERY OF SOCIAL AND EMOTIONAL PROGRAMS

Social and emotional literacy programs (SEL) are likely to be most effective when offered early before students have developed the secondary risk factors of school failure, social rejection, formation of defiant peer groups, and a history of negative teacher and parent responses to their disruptive behaviors (Dishion & Piehler, 2007; Johnston & Mash, 2001). Findings from research syntheses and meta-analyses evaluating a variety of school-based social and emotional learning programs at all educational levels, but predominantly targeted at middle and high school age levels, has indicated significant positive improvements in a variety of target outcomes including reductions in aggressive behavior problems (Greenberg et al., 2003; Hahn et al., 2007; Wilson & Lipsey, 2007), depression (Horowitz & Garber, 2007), and increases in prosocial behavior (Durlak, Weissberg, & Pachan, 2010; Greenberg, Domitrovich, & Bumbarger, 2001). Moreover, there is growing evidence that the positive effects of these SEL programs may produce the additional benefits of enhancing students' cognitive development and academic performance (Durlak, Weissberg, Dymnick, Taylor, & Schellinger, 2011; Zins & Elias, 2006), whereas failure to achieve social and emotional competence may lead to later adjustment and academic difficulties (Guerra & Bradshaw, 2008). These researchers have also highlighted how contextual factors such as the quality of the school psychosocial environment, teachers' interpersonal skills and caring relationships with students, and proactive classroom management strategies and instructional approaches contribute to or moderate the impact of the SEL program on student outcomes (Smith, Schneider, Smith, & Ananiadou, 2004; Sologmon, Battistich, Watson, Schaps, & Lewis, 2000; Solomon, Battistich, Watson, Schaps, & Lewis, 2000). Other studies have shown that involving parents in these curriculum adds to the impact of the outcomes (Kumpfer, Alvarado, Tait, & Turner, 2002; Reid, Webster-Stratton, & Hammond, 2007b; Webster-Stratton et al., 2004).

INCREDIBLE YEARS (IY) UNIVERSAL TEACHER CLASSROOM MANAGEMENT PROGRAM ~ TIER 1

The IY Teacher Classroom Management Training (TCM) program, originally developed in 1994 by Dr. Webster-Stratton, is grounded in cognitive social learning and child development theories. It is a group format program for teachers, school counselors, and psychologists designed to promote teacher support networks and interrupt the negative cycle of disrupted teacher and peer social relationships and environments. To accomplish this the program trains

teachers in evidence-based behavior management practices, promoting committed and nurturing relationships and parent-teacher collaboration, development of behavior plans with appropriate developmental expectations for individual students, and ways to support students' learning problem solving, emotional regulation, self control and social skills.

The IY Teaching Pyramid™ serves as the landscape plan for delivering content (see Figure page 45) and is used to describe teacher program content structure. It helps teachers conceptualize effective teaching tools and how these tools will help them achieve their goals. A basic premise of the model is that a positive teacher-student-parent relationship and proactive teaching and coaching strategies precede discipline strategies, and that in effective classroom environments attention to positive behaviors occurs far more frequently than attention to negative behaviors. The bottom of the pyramid depicts teaching tools that should be used liberally, as they form the foundation to successfully nurture and scaffold students' learning growth. The base of the pyramid includes tools for connecting and building relationships with students such as coaching students' social, emotional, persistence and academic skills, providing encouragement, praise and special time with students, using family surveys to get to know students' interests, and building positive partnerships with parents as well as students. Tools for building relationships with parents include positive home communication, home visits,

Like the master gardener, the teacher must provide fertile soil, adequate sunshine, water and support for the seed to develop and begin to grow.

successful parent conferences, coordinated behavior plans and in-service information for parents about how to strengthen their children's learning at home as well as at school. Parents and teachers also work collaboratively to reinforce and motivate children who need more intensive interventions for targeted behaviors (e.g., incentive systems). Like the master gardener, the teacher must provide fertile soil, adequate sunshine, water and support for the seed to develop and begin to grow.

As teachers continue to move up the pyramid, other teaching tools are used such as predictable routines, schedules, rules, coaching, redirections and corrections which scaffold students' exploratory behaviors and

their drive for autonomy. Near the top of the pyramid are proactive discipline tools such as effective limit setting and planned pruning with consequences in order to eliminate the negative behaviors that are impeding the child's learning progress. Again the teacher, like the master gardener, carefully weeds and prunes, taking care not to prune too much of the plant for fear of destroying its growth. Finally, the top of the pyramid focuses on teachers helping students learn self-regulation, behavioral self-control, and problem-solving strategies so that they can be more independent in their learning. By the end of the program teachers have all the necessary tools to navigate some of the uncomfortable, but inevitable, aspects of nurturing their students' social, emotional and academic growth.

IY Teacher Classroom Management training (TCM) program is a group video-based modeling program designed to provide teachers with classroom management strategies to effectively manage challenging behaviors while also promoting optimal academic, social, and emotional learning for all students ages 3 to 8 years. The IY TCM program targets the key school risk factors (discussed above) that can lead to negative outcomes for students.

The training model is a 42-48 hour program delivered in groups by certified group leaders to teachers in six full-day workshops spread out monthly over the school year. The program utilizes self-reflective, experiential learning, group support, and specific training methods with a focus on teachers' own

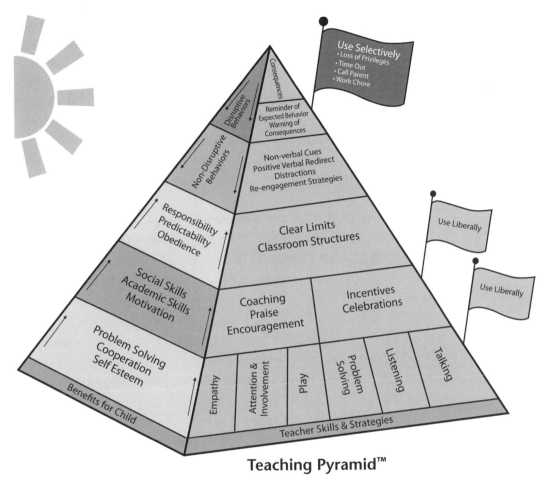

Teaching Pyramid™

self-monitoring and goal setting. Teachers are encouraged to be sensitive to individual student developmental differences (i.e., variation in attention span, activity levels, and developmental delays), cognitive stages (Piaget's preoperational or concrete operational thinking level), biological deficits (e.g., unresponsiveness to stimuli, heightened interest in novelty), family background experiences (i.e., abuse or neglect or poverty), cultural differences, and the relevance of these differences for teaching efforts that are positive, accepting, understanding, and consistent. The training attempts to build social support networks among teachers and reduce the isolation and stress that they commonly experience, especially those struggling with classroom management issues. The advantage of the group approach is that it allows teachers to capitalize on their collective knowledge and wisdom and support each other. More information on the methods and processes of delivering this training in schools can be found in the following articles (Webster-Stratton & Reid, 2007; Webster-Stratton, Reinke, Herman, & Newcomer, 2012).

IY UNIVERSAL CLASSROOM CHILD SOCIAL, EMOTIONAL, AND PROBLEM SOLVING CURRICULUM© (TIER 1) (DINOSAUR SCHOOL)

The classroom Dinosaur School curriculum is designed for children in preschool through 3rd grade (with different lesson plans for each age group). The content of the Dinosaur curriculum focuses on 7 units: learning school rules and how to be successful in school; emotional literacy, empathy, or perspective taking; interpersonal problem solving; anger management; and friendship and communication skills. Comprehensive manuals with lesson plans outline every lesson's content, objectives, DVD vignettes to be shown, and descriptions of small group activities. There are lesson plans for preschool (ages 3-5), kindergarten (ages 5-6), and grades 1 and 2 (ages 7-8) that gradually increase in complexity, building on the prior year's learning. There are

over 300 different small group practice activities that reinforce the content of the lessons and can be selected according to the developmental level of the child. These activities incorporate pre-reading and reading, pre-writing and writing skills, math and science concepts in conjunction with emotional and social learning. These content elements are widely acknowledged foundational instructional principles and social-emotional concepts believed to be a core component of transformational teaching in the early years. The curriculum lessons are delivered with the help of child-size puppets 2-3 times per week throughout the school year (60 lessons per year) in the format of a large group circle time lesson followed by a small group activity designed to practice the skills taught in the circle time. Teachers praise, coach, and reinforce curriculum skills taught during other times throughout the day. Please see the following articles for a more complete description of this curriculum (Webster-Stratton & Reid, 2003, 2004, 2008).

IY SMALL GROUP CHILD SOCIAL, EMOTIONAL AND PROBLEM SOLVING TREATMENT CURRICULUM© (TIER 2)

For children who need more intensive (Tier 2) intervention, there is a separate small group (4-6 children) Dinosaur treatment curriculum that is offered once a week for 2 hours, or twice a week as a school pull out program for an hour at a time. The program is offered over 18-22 sessions (36-44 hours) or longer as needed. The small group format gives the group leader or teacher opportunities to cover more content and engage in more practice activities than in the classroom curriculum, to set individual goals for each student's needs, and to use more intensive behavior management strategies for extreme behaviors (i.e., individualized token economy system).

The IY parenting programs promote positive partnerships with teachers to enhance children's learning across settings.

IY PARENTING PROGRAMS (TIER 2)

There are two separate BASIC parenting programs: preschool (3-5 years) and school age (6-12 years). Each of these video-based group discussion programs includes age- appropriate examples of culturally diverse families and children with varying temperaments. The BASIC programs are 14-20 weekly sessions (length depends on age of children and severity of problems). The foundation of the program is video vignettes of modeled parenting skills (over 300 vignettes, each lasting approximately 1–3 minutes) shown by a trained group leader to groups of 8–12 parents. The videos demonstrate social learning and child development principles and serve as the stimulus for focused discussions, self-reflection, problem solving, and collaborative learning. The preschool program is designed to help parents support their children's school readiness such as how to build their language and reading development, self-regulation and friendship skills as well as how to reduce behavior problems and to develop positive partnerships with teachers in order to enhance children's learning. The school age program is designed to promote positive parent-child relationships, to encourage responsible behavior, to set up predictable after school and homework study routines, to monitor children's whereabouts, to encourage children's confidence in their ideas and learning discoveries, and to collaborate successfully with teachers to achieve their goals.

RESEARCH REGARDING INCREDIBLE YEARS PARENT, TEACHER AND CHILD PROGRAMS

The IY Series have been the subject of extensive empirical evaluations and have been widely endorsed by various review groups including the Office for Juvenile Justice and Delinquency Prevention (OJJDP) as 1 of 11 "blueprint" model violence prevention evidence-based programs for treating and preventing disruptive behavior disorders and promoting social and emotional competence (Webster-Stratton et al., 2001; revised 2011). Further, all the parent, teacher, and child programs have been implemented as prevention programs with high risk populations and as well as treatment interventions with children with diagnoses such as ODD, ADHD and with developmental delays across a variety of settings and contexts with high fidelity.

IY TEACHER PROGRAM RESEARCH: EFFECTS OF TEACHER CLASSROOM MANAGEMENT (TCM) TRAINING PROGRAM

The 6-day teacher training program has been evaluated as an intervention program for classroom preschool and early school age teachers managing students, ages 3-8 years, with diagnosed Oppositional Defiant Disorder (ODD) (Webster-Stratton et al., 2004) and as a prevention program with Head Start and early primary grade classroom teachers working with multicultural students at high risk because of socioeconomic disadvantage (Webster-Stratton & Reid, 1999; Webster-Stratton et al., 2001). In both prevention and treatment contexts, intervention effects comparing teachers who received the TCM training to those who did not showed improvements in praise, nurturing, and positive classroom management strategies and decreases in harsh and critical teaching. Children in classrooms with teachers who received the training were significantly less aggressive with peers, more on-task, and more cooperative compared with control classrooms where teachers did not receive training (Webster-Stratton et al., 2001).

Two independent evaluations used the TCM program in combination with a mental health consultation approach (Raver et al., 2008; Williford & Shelton, 2008). Both provided support for the efficacy of this group training approach with preschool and elementary grade teachers and children. Findings indicated increases in teachers' use of praise and reductions in criticisms as well as increases in children's positive peer interactions and reductions in children's aggression in the classroom.

Children in classrooms with teachers who received the training were significantly less aggressive with peers, more on-task, and more cooperative compared with control classrooms.

The TCM has been evaluated in combination with the IY parent and child programs by the developer and as a stand alone program by independent researchers across diverse populations including in Jamaica (Baker-Henningham, Walker, Powell, & Meeks Gardner, 2009) and Wales (Hutchings, Daley, et al., 2007). The TCM has also been investigated as a stand-alone self-administered training program with preschool teachers (Shernoff & Kratochwill, 2007). A recent study evaluated the effects of breaking the training down from full day workshops held monthly to offering it weekly after school hours for 4 hours over an 8-week period. Results of this study indicated significant improvements from pre-post training in teachers' reports of use of positive classroom management strategies and sustained effects at follow up (Carlson, Tiret, Bender, & Benson, 2011).

IY CHILD PROGRAM RESEARCH: EFFECTS OF DINOSAUR CHILD TRAINING PROGRAM

Treatment Studies

The developer conducted three randomized studies (Webster-Stratton & Hammond, 1997; Webster-Stratton et al., 2011; Webster-Stratton et al., 2004) evaluating the effectiveness of the child training program for reducing conduct problems and promoting social and emotional competence and problem solving in children diagnosed with ODD/CD and ADHD. Results for these three studies found a consistent pattern of treatment effects with children who received the child training program showing significantly better problem solving and conflict management skills with peers than those who did not receive the child intervention. Results also indicated that children who received the combination of parent training plus child training showed more sustained effects at followup assessments than those who received either treatment alone.

Prevention Study

The classroom Dinosaur curriculum has been evaluated in Head Start and with primary schools serving high numbers of economically disadvantaged children. Results showed improvements in intervention students' conduct problems, self-regulation, and social competence compared with control students who participated in regular Head Start or elementary school education. Effect sizes comparing treatment versus control groups at post assessment showed the intervention had small to moderate effects on children whose baseline behavior was in the average range, but had large effects on children with high initial levels of conduct problems (Webster-Stratton et al., 2008).

IY PARENT PROGRAM: EFFECTS OF PARENT TRAINING PROGRAMS

Treatment Studies

The efficacy of the Incredible Years BASIC parent treatment program for children (ages 2–8 years) diagnosed with ODD/CD has been demonstrated in eight published randomized control group trials by the program developer and colleagues at the University of Washington Parenting Clinic (Reid, Webster-Stratton, & Hammond, 2007a; Webster-Stratton, 1981; Webster-Stratton, 1982, 1984, 1990a, 1992, 1994, 1998; Webster-Stratton & Hammond, 1997; Webster-Stratton,

Hollinsworth, & Kolpacoff, 1989; Webster-Stratton, Kolpacoff, & Hollinsworth, 1988; Webster-Stratton et al., 2011; Webster-Stratton et al., 2004). In all of these studies, the BASIC program has been shown to improve parental attitudes and parent–child interactions and reduce harsh discipline and child conduct problems compared to wait-list control groups. In addition, the BASIC program has been replicated in five different countries by independent investigators in mental health clinics with families of children diagnosed with conduct problems (Drugli & Larsson, 2006; Larsson et al., 2009; Lavigne et al., 2008; Scott, Spender, Doolan, Jacobs, & Aspland, 2001; Spaccarelli, Cotler, & Penman, 1992; Taylor, Schmidt, Pepler, & Hodgins, 1998) as well as in 6 studies with indicated populations (children with symptoms) and high risk populations (families in poverty) (Gardner, Burton, & Klimes, 2006; Gross et al., 2003; Hutchings, Gardner, et al., 2007; McGilloway, 2011; Miller Brotman et al., 2003; Posthumus, Raaijmakers, Maasser, England & Matthys, 2011). These replications were "effectiveness" trials done in applied mental health settings, not a university research clinic, and the therapists were typical therapists at the centers. Three of the above replications were conducted in the United States, two in United Kingdom, one in Norway and one in Holland. This illustrates the transportability of the BASIC parenting program to other cultures.

Prevention Studies in Schools

In the past decade, the parent programs were evaluated by the developer as a selective prevention program in schools with multiethnic, socio-economically disadvantaged families in three randomized studies with Head Start families and primary schools. Results of these studies suggest the program's effectiveness as a method of preventing the development of conduct problems and strengthening social and emotional competence in preschool and early school-aged children (Webster-Stratton, 1998; Webster-Stratton et al., 2001; Reid et al., 2007a). Similar results were reported by independent investigators with selective and indicated populations (Gardner et al., 2006; Gross et al., 2003; Hutchings & Gardner, 2006; Miller Brotman et

al., 2003). A recent study assessed the parent acceptability of an easily disseminated self-administered version of the IY school age parent program offered in schools to parents of children with externalizing problems. Results indicated the parents found this to be an acceptable delivery mechanism (Stewart & Carlson, 2010).

IMPLICATIONS FOR SCHOOLS

Research on school-based mental health and promoting children's social and emotional competencies has advanced greatly in the last decade. School administrators, policy makers, and teachers' willingness to envision, promote, and practice evidence-based social and emotional programming as a critical part of students' early academic learning standards is fundamental to schools' goals to successfully educate their students. Schools' success at partnering with parents in social, emotional, and academic curriculum, and in promoting evidence-based parenting programs makes a difference to children's eventual school success. Starting early by nurturing students to develop a strong foundation of emotional and social competence is the most effective way to achieve optimal academic growth and school achievement.

Starting early by nurturing students to develop a strong foundation of emotional and social competence is the most effective way to achieve optimal academic growth and school achievement.

REFERENCES

Asher, S. R., Parkhurst, J. T., Hymel, S., & Williams, G. A. (1990). Peer rejection and loneliness in childhood. In S. R. Asher & J. D. Coie (Eds.), *Peer rejection in childhood* (pp. 253-273). Cambridge: Cambridge University Press.

Baker-Henningham, H., Walker, S., Powell, C., & Meeks Gardner, J. (2009). A pilot study of the Incredible Years Teacher Training programme and a curriculum unit on social and emotional skills in community pre-schools in Jamaica. *Child: Care Health and Development*.

Bandura, A. (1986). *Social foundations of thought and action.* Englewood Cliffs, NJ: Prentice-Hall.

Barrett, E. R., & Davis, S. (1995). Perceptions of beginning teachers' needs in classroom management. *Teacher Education and Practice, 11*, 22-27.

Barth, R. P., Landsverk, J., Chamberlain, P., Reid, J. B., Rolls, J. A., Hurlburt, M. S., et al. (2005). Parent-training programs in child welfare services: Planning for a more evidence-based approach to serving biological parents. *Research on Social Work Practice, 15*(5), 353-371.

Beauchaine, T. P. (2001). Vagal tone, development, and Gray's motivational theory: Towards an integrated model of autonomic nervous system functioning in psychophysiology. *Development and Psychopathology, 13*, 1183-1214.

Beauchaine, T. P., Hinshaw, S. P., & Pang, K. C. (2010). Comorbidity of attention-deficit/hyperactivity disorder and conduct disorder: Biological, environmental, and developmental mechanisms. *Clinical Psychology: Science and Practice, 17*, 327-336.

Beauchaine, T. P., Neuhaus, E., Brenner, S. L., & Gatzke-Kopp, L. (2008). Ten good reasons to consider biological processes in prevention and intervention research. *Development and Psychopathology, 20*, 745-774.

Belsky, J., & de Haan, M. (2011). Annual research review: Parenting and children's brain development: the end of the beginning. *Journal of Child Psychology and Psychiatry, 52*(4), 409-428.

Belsky, J., & Fearson, R. M. (2002). Early attachment security, sub-sequent maternal sensitivity, and later child development: Does continuity in development depend upon continuity of caregiving? *Attachment & Human Development, 4*(3), 361-387.

Bierman, K. L., Coie, J. D., Dodge, K. A., Greenberg, M. T., Lochman, J. E., & McMahon, R. J. (1992). A developmental and clinical model for the prevention of conduct disorder: The FAST Track Program. *Development and Psychopathology, 4,* 509-527.

Bredekamp, S., & Copple, C. (1997). *Developmentally appropriate practice in early childhood programs.* Washington, DC: NAEYC.

Brophy, J. E. (1996). *Teaching problem students.* New York: Guilford.

Campbell, S. B. (1990). *Behavior problems in preschool children: Clinical and developmental issues.* New York: Guilford Press.

Campbell, S. B. (1991). Longtitudinal studies of active and aggressive preschoolers: Individual differences in early behavior and out-come. In D. Cicchetti & S. L. Toth (Eds.), *Rochester symposium on developmental psychopathology, Vol. 2: Internalizing and externalizing expressions of dysfunction* (pp. 57-90). Hillsdale, N.J.: Erlbaum.

Campbell, S. B., Shaw, D. S., & Gilliom, M. (2000). Early external-izing behavior problems: Toddlers and preschoolers at risk for later maladjustment. *Development and Psychopathology, 12,* 467-488.

Carlson, J. S., Tiret, H. B., Bender, S. L., & Benson, L. (2011). The influence of group training in the Incredible Years teacher class-room management program on preschool teachers' classroom management strategies. *Journal of Applied School Psychology, 27*(2), 134-154.

Carr, E. G., Taylor, J. G., & Robinson, S. (1991). The effects of severe behavior problems in children on the teaching behavior of adults. *Journal of Applied Behavior Analysis, 24,* 523-535.

Christenson, S. L., & Sheridan, S. M. (2001). *School and families: Creating essential connections for learning.* New York, NY: Guilford Press.

Coie, J. D., & Dodge, K. A. (1998). Aggression and antisocial behav-ior. In W. Damon & N. Eisenberg (Eds.), *Handbook of child psy-chology, Fifth Edition: Social, emotional and personality development* (Vol. 3, pp. 779-862). New York: Wiley.

Conroy, M., & Sutherland, K. (2008). Preventing and ameliorating young children's chronic problem behaviors: An ecological classroom-based approach. *Psychology in the Schools, 46*(1), 3-17.

Costello, E. J., Foley, D. L., & Angold, A. (2006). 10-year research update review: The epidemiology of child and adolescent psychiatric disorders: II. *Journal of American Academy of Child and Adolescent Psychiatry, 45*(1), 8-25.

Deater-Deckard, K., Dodge, K. A., Bates, J. E., & Pettit, G. S. (1996). Physical discipline among African-American and European-American mothers: Links to children's externalizing behaviors. *Developmental Psychology, 32*, 1065-1072.

Dishion, T. J., & Piehler, T. F. (2007). Peer dynamics in the development and change of child and adolescent problem behavior. In A. S. Masten (Ed.), *Multilevel dynamics in development psychopathology: Pathways to the future* (pp. 151-180). Mahwah,NJ: Erlbaum.

Doll, B., Zucker, S., & Brehm, K. (2004). *Resilient Classrooms: Creating Healthy Environments for Learning*. New York, NY: Guildford Press.

Domina, T. (2005). Leveling the home advantage: Assessing the effectiveness of parental involvement in elementary school. *Sociology of Education 88*(5), 233-249.

Drugli, M. B., & Larsson, B. (2006). Children aged 4-8 years treated with parent training and child therapy because of conduct problems: Generalisation effects to day-care and school settings. *European Child and Adolescent Psychiatry, 15*, 392-399.

Durlak, J. A., Weissberg, R. P., Dymnick, A., B., Taylor, R. D., & Schellinger, B. (2011). The Impact of Enhancing Students' Social and Emotional Learning: A Meta-Analysis of School-based Universal Interventions. *Child Development, 82*, 405-432.

Durlak, J. A., Weissberg, R. P., & Pachan, M. (2010). A meta-analysis of after-school programs that seek to promote personal and social skills in children and adolescence. *American Journal of Community Psychology, 45*, 294-309.

Eisenberg, N. (2006). Volume 3: Social, emotional and personality development. In W. Damon & R. M. Lerner (Eds.), *Handbook of child psychology, 6th ed*. New York: Wiley.

Evans, G. W. (2004). The environment of childhood poverty. *American Psychologist, 59*(2), 77-92.

Evertson, C. M., & Weinstein, C. S. (2006). Classroom Management as a Field of Inquiry. In C. M. Evertson & C. S. Weinstein (Eds.), *Handbook of classroom management: Research, practice, and contemporary issues* (pp. 3-15). Mahwah, NJ: Lawrence Erlbaum Associates Publishers.

Fantuzzo, J. W., DelGaudio, W. A., Atkins, M., Meyers, R., & Noone, M. (1998). A contextually relevant assessment of the impact of child maltreatment on the social competencies of low-income urban children. *Journal of American Academy of Child and Adolescent Psychiatry, 37,* 1201-1208.

Garber, J., & Horowitz, J. (2002). Depression in children. In I. H. Gotlib & C. L. Hammen (Eds.), *Handbook of Depression.* New York: Guildford Press.

Gardner, F., Burton, J., & Klimes, I. (2006). Randomized controlled trial of a parenting intervention in the voluntary sector for reducing conduct problems in children: Outcomes and mechanisms of change. *Journal of Child Psychology and Psychiatry, 47,* 1123-1132.

Gottfredson, D. C., & Gottfredson, G. D. (2002). Quality of school-based prevention programs: Results from a national survey. *Journal of Research in Crime and Delinquency, 39,* 3-35.

Greenberg, M. T., Domitrovich, C., & Bumbarger, B. (2001). The prevention of mental disorders in school-age chldren: Current state of the field. *Prevention and Treatment,* 1-62.

Greenberg, M. T., Weissberg, R. P., O'Brien, M. U., Zins, J. E., Fredericks, L., & Resnik, H. (2003). Enhancing school-based prevention and youth development through coordinated social, emotional and academic learning. *American Psychologist, 58,* 466-474.

Gross, D., Fogg, L., Webster-Stratton, C., Garvey, C., W., J., & Grady, J. (2003). Parent training with families of toddlers in day care in low-income urban communities. *Journal of Consulting and Clinical Psychology, 71*(2), 261-278.

Guerra, N. G., & Bradshaw, C. P. (2008). Linking the prevention of problem behaviors and positive youth development: Core competencies for positive youth development and risk prevention. *New Directions for Child and Adolescent Development, 122,* 1-17.

Hahn, R., Fuqua-Whitley, D., Wethington, H., Lowy, J., Crosby, A., & Fullilove, M. (2007). Effectiveness of universal school-based programs to prevent violent and aggressive behavior: A systematic review. *American Journal of Preventive Medicine, 33*(2), S114-S129.

Hanish, L. D., & Guerra, N. G. (2002). A longitudinal analysis of patterns of adjustment following peer victimization. *Development and Psychopathology, 14,* 68-89.

Hartman, R. R., Stage, S., & Webster-Stratton, C. (2003). A growth curve analysis of parent training outcomes: Examining the influence of child factors (inattention, impulsivity, and hyperactivity problems), parental and family risk factors. *The Child Psychology and Psychiatry Journal, 44*(3), 388-398.

Hawkins, J. D., Catalano, R. F., Kosterman, R., Abbott, R., & Hill, K. G. (1999). Preventing adolescent health-risk behaviors by strengthening protection during childhood. *Archives of Pediatrics and Adolescent Medicine, 153,* 226-234.

Hawkins, J. D., Herrenkoh., T., Farrington, D. P., Brewer, D., Catalano, R. F., & Harachi, T. W. (1998). A review of predictors of youth violence. In R. Loeber & D. P. Farrington (Eds.), *Serious and violent juvenile offenders: Risk factors and successful interventions* (pp. 106-146). Thousand Oaks: CA: Sage.

Hawkins, J. D., Smith, B. H., & Catalano, R. F. (2004). Social development and social and emotional learning. In J. E. Zins, R. P. Weissberg, M. C. Wang & H. J. Walberg (Eds.), *Building academic success on soical and emotional learning: What does the research say?* (pp. 135-150). New York: Teachers College Press.

Hawkins, W. E., Clarke, G. N., & Seeley, J. R. (1993). Application of social learning theory to the primary prevention of depression in adolescents. *Health Values: The Journal of Health Behavior, Education, and Promotion, 17,* 31-39.

Hinshaw, S. P. (2002). Preadolescent girls with attention-deficit/hyperactivity disorder: I. Background characteristics,comorbidity, cognitive and social functioning, and parenting practices. *Journal of Consulting and Clinical Psychology, 70*(5), 1086-1098.

Horowitz, J. L., & Garber, J. (2007). The prevention of depressive symptoms in children and adolescents: A meta-analytic review. *Journal of Consulting and Clinical Psychology, 74,* 401-415.

Houston, W. R., & Williamson, J. L. (1992). Perceptions of their preparation by 42 Texas elementary school teachers compared with their responses as student teachers. *Teacher Education and Practice, 8,* 27-42.

Hutchings, J., Daley, D., Jones, E. E., Martin, P., Bywater, T., & Gwyn, R. (2007). Early results from developing and researching the Webster-Stratton Incredible Years Teacher Classroom Management Training Programme in North West Wales. *Journal of Children's Services, 2(3),* 15-26.

Hutchings, J., Gardner, F., Bywater, T., Daley, D., Whitaker, C., Jones, K., et al. (2007). Parenting intervention in Sure Start services for children at risk of developing conduct disorder: Pragmatic randomized controlled trial. *British Medical Journal, 334(7595),* 1-7.

Ingersoll, R. M. (2002). High turnover plagues schools. *USA Today.*

Jaffee, S. R., & Maikovich-Fong, A. K. (2011). Effects of chronic maltreatment and maltreatment timing on children's behavior and cognitive abilities. *Journal of Child Psychology and Psychiatry, 52(2),* 184-194.

Johnston, C., & Mash, E. J. (2001). Families of children with attention-deficit/hyperactivity disorder: Review and recommendations for future research. *Clinical Child and Family Psychology Review, 4,* 183-207.

Jones, K., Daley, D., Hutchings, J., Bywater, T., & Eames, C. (2007). Efficacy of the Incredible Years Basic Parent Training Programme as an early intervention for children with conduct disorder and ADHD. *Child: Care, Health and Development, 33,* 749-756.

Kazdin, A. E. (1995). *Conduct disorders in childhood and adolescence.* Thousand Oaks, CA: Sage Publications.

Keenan, K., Boeldt, D., Chern, D., Coyne, C., Donald, R., Juax, J., et al. (2011). Predictive validity of DSM-IV oppositional defiant and conduct disorders in clinically referred preschoolers. *Journal of Child Psychology and Psychiatry, 52(1),* 47-55.

Kellam, S. G., Ling, X., Merisca, R., Brown, C. H., & Ialongo, N. (1998). The effect of the level of aggression in the first grade classroom on the course and malleability of aggressive behavior into middle school. *Development and Psychopathology, 10*, 165-185.

Klem, A. M., & Connell, J. P. (2004). Relationships matter: Linking teacher support to student engagement and achievement. *Journal of School Health, 74*, 262-273.

Knutson, J. F., DeGarmo, D., Koeppl, G., & Reid, J. B. (2005). Care neglect, supervisory neglect and harsh parenting in the development of children's aggression: A replication and extension. *Child Maltreatment, 10*, 92-107.

Kumpfer, K. L., Alvarado, R., Tait, C., & Turner, C. (2002). Effectiveness of school-based family and children's skills training for substance prevention among 6-8 year-old rural children. *Psychology of Addictive Behaviors, 16*, S65-S71.

Kupersmidt, J. B., & Coie, J. D. (1990). Preadolescent peer status, aggression, and school adjustment as predictors of externalizing problems in adolescence. *Child Development, 61*(5), 1350-1362.

Ladd, G. W., Kochenderfer, B. J., & Coleman, C. (1997). Classroom peer acceptance, friendship, and victimization: Distinct relational systems that contribute uniquely to children's school adjustment. *Child Development, 68*, 1181-1197.

Larsson, B., Fossum, B., Clifford, G., Drugli, M., Handegard, B., & Mørch, W. (2009). Treatment of oppositional defiant and conduct problems in young Norwegian children: Results of a randomized trial. *European Child Adolescent Psychiatry, 18*(1), 42-52.

Lavigne, J. V., LeBailly, S. A., Gouze, K. R., Cicchetti, C., Pochyly, J., Arend, R., et al. (2008). Treating Oppositional Defiant Disorder in primary care: A comparison of three models. *Journal of Pediatric Psychology, 33*(5), 449-461.

Loeber, R. (1990). Development and risk factors of juvenile antisocial behavior and delinquency. *Clinical Psychology Review, 10*, 1-41.

Loeber, R., & Farrington, D. P. (2000). Young children who commit crime: Epidemiology, developmental origins, risk factors, early interventions, and policy implications. *Developmental Psychopathology, 12*(4), 737-762.

Loeber, R., & Farrington, D. P. (2001). *Child Delinquents: Development, Intervention and Service Needs*. Thousand Oaks, CA: Sage Publications.

Lynam, D. R., Caspi, A., Moffitt, T. E., Wikstrom, P. H., Loeber, R., & Novak, S. (2000). The interaction between impulsivity and neighborhood context on offending: The effects of impulsivity are stronger in poorer neighborhoods. *Journal of Abnormal Child Psychology, 109*, 563-574.

Malecki, C. K., & Elliott, S. N. (2002). Children's social behaviors as predictors of academic achievement: A longitudinal analysis. *School Psychology Quarterly, 17*, 1-23.

McBurnett, K., Harris, S. M., Swanson, J. M., Pfiffner, L. J., Freedland, D., & Tamm, L. (1993). Neuropsychological and psychophysiological differentiation of inattentive/overactivity and aggression/defiance symptom groups. *Journal of Clinical Child Psychology, 22*, 165-171.

McGilloway, S. (2011). *Testing the benefits of the IY programme in Ireland: An Experimental study (RCT)*.

Menting, B., Van Ler, P. A. C., & Koot, H. M. (2011). Language skills, peer rejection, and the development of externalizing behavior from kindergarten to fourth grade. *Journal of Child Psychology and Psychiatry 52*(1), 72-79.

Miller Brotman, L., Klein, R. G., Kamboukos, D., Brown, E. J., Coard, S., & L., S.-S. (2003). Preventive intervention for urban, low-income preschoolers at familial risk for conduct problems: A randomized pilot study. *Journal of Child Psychology and Psychiatry, 32*(2), 246-257.

Moffitt, T. E. (1993). Adolescence-limited and life-course-persistent antisocial behavior: A developmental taxonomy. *Psychological Review, 100*, 674-701.

Moffitt, T. E., & Lynam, D. (1994). The neuropsychology of conduct disorder and delinquency: Implications for understanding antisocial behavior. In D. C. Fowles, P. Sutker & S. H. Goodman (Eds.), *Progress in experimental personality and psychopathology research* (pp. 233-262). New York: Springer.

O'Connor, E. E., Dearning, E., & Collins, B. A. (2011). Teacher-child relationship and behavior problem trajectories in elementary school. *American Educational Research Journal, 48*(1), 120-162.

Ostrander, R., & Herman, K. C. (2006). Potential developmental, cognitive, and parenting mediators of the relationship between ADHD and depression. *Journal of Consulting and Clinical Psychology, 74,* 89-98.

Patterson, G., Reid, J., & Dishion, T. (1992). *Antisocial boys: A social interactional approach* (Vol. 4). Eugene, OR: Castalia Publishing.

Pettit, G. S., Bates, J. E., & Dodge, K. A. (1997). Supportive parenting, ecological context, and children's adjustment: A seven-year longitudinal study. *Child Development, 68*(5), 908-923.

Posthumus, J. A., Raaijmakers, M. A. J., Maassen, G. H., Engeland, H., & Matthys, W. (2011). Sustained effects of Incredible Years as a preventive intervention in preschool children with conduct problems. *Journal of Abnormal Child Psychology.*

Raver, C. C., Jones, S. M., Li-Grining, C. P., Metzger, M., Champion, K. M., & Sardin, L. (2008). Improving preschool classroom processes: Preliminary findings from a randomized trial implemented in Head Start settings. *Early Childhood Research Quarterly, 23,* 10-26.

Raver, C. C., & Knitzer, J. (2002). *Ready to enter: What research tells policy makers about strategies to promote social and emotional school readiness among three and four year old children.* Mailman School of Public Health, Columbia University: National Center for Children in Poverty.

Raver, C. C., & Zigler, E. F. (1997). Social competence: An untapped dimension in evaluating Head Start's success. *Early Childhood Research Quarterly, 12,* 363-385.

Reid, M. J., Webster-Stratton, C., & Hammond, M. (2007a). Enhancing a classroom social competence and problem-solving curriculum by offering parent training to families of moderate-to-high-risk elementary school children. *Journal of Clinical Child and Adolescent Psychology, 36*(5), 605-620.

Reid, M. J., Webster-Stratton, C., & Hammond, M. (2007b). Preventing aggression and improving social, emotional competence: The Incredible Years Parent Training in high-risk elementary schools. *Journal of Clinical Child and Adolescent Psychology.*

Reinke, W. M., & Herman, K. C. (2002). Creating school environments that deter antisocial behaviors in youth. *Psychology in the Schools, 39*(549-559).

Reinke, W. M., Stormont, M., Herman, K. C., Puri, R., & Goel, N. (2010). Supporting children's mental health in schools: Teacher perceptions of needs, roles and barriers. *School Psychology Quarterly*.

Rimm-Kaufman, S. E., Pianta, R. C., & Cox, M. J. (2000). Teachers' judgments of problems in the transition to kindergarten. *Early Childhood Research Quarterly, 15*, 147-166.

Robins, L. N. (1981). Epidemiological approaches to natural history research: Antisocial disorders in children. *Journal of the American Academy of Child Psychiatry, 20*, 566-580.

Scott, S., Spender, Q., Doolan, M., Jacobs, B., & Aspland, H. (2001). Multicentre controlled trial of parenting groups for child antisocial behaviour in clinical practice. *British Medical Journal, 323*(28), 1-5.

Shernoff, E. S., & Kratochwill, T. R. (2007). Transporting an evidence-based classroom management program for preschoolers with disruptive behavior problems to a school: An analysis of implementation, outcomes, and contextual variables. *School Psychology Quarterly, 22*(3), 449-472.

Shores, R. E., Jack, S. L., Gunter, P. L., Ellis, D. N., DeGriere, T. J., & Wehby, J. H. (1993). Classroom interactions of children with behavioral problems. *Journal of Emotional and Behavioral Disorders, 1*(27-39).

Shores, R. E., & Wehby, J. H. (1999). Analyzing classroom social behavior of students with EBD. *Journal of Emotional and Behavioral Disorders, 7*, 194-199.

Simonsen, B., & Fairbanks, S. (2008). Evidence-based practices in classroom management: Considerations for research to practice. *Education & Treatment of Children, 31*(3), 351-380.

Smith, J. D., Schneider, H., B., Smith, P. K., & Ananiadou, K. (2004). The effectiveness of whole-school antibullying programs: A synthesis of evaluation research. *School Psychology Review, 33*, 547-560.

Snyder, H. (2001). Child delinquents. In R. Loeber & D. P. Farrington (Eds.), *Risk factors and successful interventions*. Thousand Oaks, CA: Sage.

Solomon, D., Battistich, V., Watson, M., Schaps, E., & Lewis, C. (2000). A six-study of educational change: Direct and mediated effects of the Child Development Project. *Social Psychology of Education, 4*, 3-51.

Spaccarelli, S., Cotler, S., & Penman, D. (1992). Problem-solving skills training as a supplement to behavioral parent training. *Cognitive Therapy and Research, 16,* 1-18.

Stewart, L. S., & Carlson, J. S. (2010). Investigating parental acceptability of the Incredible Years self-administered parent training program for children presenting externalizing behavior problems. *Journal of Applied School Psychology, 26*(2), 162-175.

Stormont, M., Smith, S. C., & Lewis, T. J. (2007). Teacher implementation of precorrection and praise statements in Head Start classrooms as a component of a program-wide system of positive behavioral support. *Journal of Behavioral Education, 16,* 280-290.

Taylor, T. K., Schmidt, F., Pepler, D., & Hodgins, H. (1998). A comparison of eclectic treatment with Webster-Stratton's Parents and Children Series in a children's mental health center: A randomized controlled trial. *Behavior Therapy, 29,* 221-240.

Tremblay, R. E., Vitaro, F., Bertrand, L., LeBlanc, M., Beauchesne, H., Boileau, H., et al. (1996). Parent and child training to prevent early onset of delinquency: The Montreal longitudinal-experimental study. In J. McCord & R. E. Tremblay (Eds.), *Preventing antisocial behavior: Interventions from birth through adolescence* (pp. 117-138). New York: Guilford.

Walker, H. M. (1995). *The acting-out child: Coping with classroom disruption.* Longmont, CO: Sopris West.

Walker, H. M., Colvin, G., & Ramsey, E. (1995). *Antisocial behavior in school: Strategies and best practices.* Pacific Grove, CA: Brooks/Cole.

Walker, H. M., Schwartz, I. E., Nippold, M. A., Irvin, L. K., & Noell, J. W. (1994). Social skills in school-age children and youth: Issues and best practices in assessment and intervention. *Topics in Language Disorders, 14*(3), 70-82.

Webster-Stratton, C. (1981). Modification of mothers' behaviors and attitudes through videotape modeling group discussion program. *Behavior Therapy, 12,* 634-642.

Webster-Stratton, C. (1982). Teaching mothers through videotape modeling to change their children's behaviors. *Journal of Pediatric Psychology, 7*(3), 279-294.

Webster-Stratton, C. (1984). Randomized trial of two parent-training programs for families with conduct-disordered children. *Journal of Consulting and Clinical Psychology, 52*(4), 666-678.

Webster-Stratton, C. (1990a). Enhancing the effectiveness of self-administered videotape parent training for families with conduct-problem children. *Journal of Abnormal Child Psychology, 18,* 479-492.

Webster-Stratton, C. (1990b). Stress: A potential disruptor of parent perceptions and family interactions. *Journal of Clinical Child Psychology, 19,* 302-312.

Webster-Stratton, C. (1992). Individually administered videotape parent training: "Who benefits?". *Cognitive Therapy and Research, 16*(1), 31-35.

Webster-Stratton, C. (1994). Advancing videotape parent training: A comparison study. *Journal of Consulting and Clinical Psychology, 62*(3), 583-593.

Webster-Stratton, C. (1998). Preventing conduct problems in Head Start children: Strengthening parenting competencies. *Journal of Consulting and Clinical Psychology, 66*(5), 715-730.

Webster-Stratton, C., & Hammond, M. (1997). Treating children with early-onset conduct problems: A comparison of child and parent training interventions. *Journal of Consulting and Clinical Psychology, 65*(1), 93-109.

Webster-Stratton, C., & Hammond, M. (1998). Conduct problems and level of social competence in Head Start children: Prevalence, pervasiveness and associated risk factors. *Clinical Child Psychology and Family Psychology Review, 1*(2), 101-124.

Webster-Stratton, C., & Herman, K. C. (2008). The impact of parent behavior-management training on child depressive symptoms. *Journal of Counseling Psychology, 55*(4), 473-484.

Webster-Stratton, C., Hollinsworth, T., & Kolpacoff, M. (1989). The long-term effectiveness and clinical significance of three cost-effective training programs for families with conduct-problem children. *Journal of Consulting and Clinical Psychology, 57*(4), 550-553.

Webster-Stratton, C., Kolpacoff, M., & Hollinsworth, T. (1988). Self-administered videotape therapy for families with conduct-problem children: Comparison with two cost-effective treatments and a control group. *Journal of Consulting and Clinical Psychology, 56*(4), 558-566.

Webster-Stratton, C., & Lindsay, D. W. (1999). Social Competence and early-onset conduct problems: Issues in assessment. *Journal of Child Clinical Psychology, 28,* 25-93.

Webster-Stratton, C., & Reid, M. J. (1999, November, 1999). *Treating children with early-onset conduct problems: The importance of teacher training.* Paper presented at the Association for the Advancement of Behavior Therapy, Toronto, Canada.

Webster-Stratton, C., & Reid, M. J. (2003). Treating conduct problems and strengthening social emotional competence in young children (ages 4-8 years): The Dina Dinosaur treatment program. *Journal of Emotional and Behavioral Disorders, 11*(3), 130-143.

Webster-Stratton, C., & Reid, M. J. (2004). Strengthening social and emotional competence in young children—The foundation for early school readiness and success: Incredible Years Classroom Social Skills and Problem-Solving Curriculum. *Journal of Infants and Young Children, 17*(2).

Webster-Stratton, C., & Reid, M. J. (2007). Incredible Years Parents and Teachers Training Series: A Head Start partnership to promote social competence and prevent conduct problems In P. Tolin, J. Szapocznick & S. Sambrano (Eds.), *Preventing Youth Substance Abuse* (pp. 67-88). Washington D. C.: American Psychological Association

Webster-Stratton, C., & Reid, M. J. (2008). Strengthening social and emotional competence in socioeconomically disadvantaged young children: Preschool and kindergarten school-based curricula. In W. H. Brown, S. L. Odom & S. R. McConnell (Eds.), *Social competence of young children: Risk, disability, and intervention* (pp. 185-203). Baltimore: Paul H. Brookes Publishing Co.

Webster-Stratton, C., Reid, M. J., & Beauchaine, T. P. (2011). Combining Parent and Child Training for Young Children with ADHD. *Journal of Clinical Child and Adolescent Psychology, 40*(2), 1-13.

Webster-Stratton, C., Reid, M. J., & Hammond, M. (2001). Preventing conduct problems, promoting social competence: A parent and teacher training partnership in Head Start. *Journal of Clinical Child Psychology, 30(3),* 283-302.

Webster-Stratton, C., Reid, M. J., & Hammond, M. (2004). Treating children with early-onset conduct problems: Intervention outcomes for parent, child, and teacher training. *Journal of Clinical Child and Adolescent Psychology, 33(1),* 105-124.

Webster-Stratton, C., Reid, M. J., & Stoolmiller, M. (2008). Preventing conduct problems and improving school readiness: Evaluation of the Incredible Years Teacher and Child Training Programs in high-risk schools. *Journal of Child Psychology and Psychiatry 49(5),* 471-488.

Webster-Stratton, C., Reinke, W. M., Herman, K. C., & Newcomer, L. (2012). The Incredible Years Teacher Classroom Management Training: The Methods and Principles that Support Fidelity of Training Delivery. *School Psychology.*

White, J., Moffit, T., Earls, F., & Robins, L. (1990). Preschool predictors of persistent conduct disorder and delinquency. *Criminology, 28,* 443-454.

Williford, A. P., & Shelton, T. L. (2008). Using mental health consultation to decrease disruptive behaviors in preschoolers: adapting an empirically-supported intervention. *Journal of Child Psychology and Psychiatry, 49(2),* 191-200.

Wilson, S. J., & Lipsey, M. W. (2007). School-based interventions for aggressive and disruptive behavior: Update of meta-analysis *American Journal of Preventive Medicine(33),* 130-143.

Zins, J. E., & Elias, M. J. (2006). Social and emotional learning. In G. G. Bear & K. M. Minke (Eds.), *Children's needs III: Development, prevention, and intervention* (pp. 1-13). Bethesda, MD: National Association of School Psychologists.

Nurturing Positive Relationships with Students

GETTING TO KNOW STUDENTS AND THEIR FAMILIES

Teachers working to promote positive growth in their relationships with their students is essential. Perhaps the most obvious reason to invest in this task is because a nurturing teacher-student relationship built on trust, understanding, and caring will foster students' cooperation and motivation, and promote their learning, social and emotional development, and academic achievement at school (Battistich, Schaps, & Wilson, 2004; Cawalti, 1995; Hamre & Pianta, 2006; Henricsson & Rydell, 2004; O'Connor, Dearing, & Collins, 2011). On the other hand, poor teacher-student relationships are associated with externalizing and internalizing behavior problems, school disengagement, drop out, and poor learning (Howes, 2000; Pianta & Stuhlman, 2004). Moreover, for disadvantaged students who come from abusive or neglectful homes, research indicates that even one caring, nurturing adult in that child's life can lead to resiliency and better long-term outcomes; often a special teacher is the person that can fill this mentor role for at-risk children. For high-risk primary grade children, a high-quality teacher-child relationship has been shown to be an important determinant of a child's ability to improve their behaviors (Baker, 2006; Buyse, Verschueren, Doumen, Van Damme, & Maes, 2008; Silver, Measelle, Armstrong, & Essex, 2005). Consequently, teachers can make a big difference to a child's future when they spend the extra effort developing positive relationships with students, particularly those who don't have a parent advocating for them (Rimm-Kaufman, Fan, Chiu, & You, 2007).

Teachers can make a big difference to a child's future when they spend the extra effort developing positive relationships with students.

Certainly teachers strive for positive relationships with all their students, but it is more difficult to build positive relationships with some children than with others. Why? Teachers have all had experience with difficult children who demand more attention than others; children who are disruptive, aggressive, unmotivated, or defiant, or who are frequently off-task and don't listen. These children can be particularly frustrating for teachers. It takes only one of these difficult children to bring an entire class to a halt. These are the children who can make teachers feel inadequate, causing them to get angry, yell, give excessive punishment, make harsh criticisms, actively avoid the child, or blame their parents. Although these responses to their misbehavior are natural, expressing them doesn't help promote good relationships in the classroom or reduce problems. How can teachers break the cycle of negative feelings towards some students and work productively with all students, especially the more difficult students and their families?

Let's think about why some children might be more difficult to manage in the first place. There are many possible reasons. Perhaps they have had negative school experiences in the past and, consequently, distrust teachers. Or, perhaps they have come from home situations where the adults are unresponsive, depressed, abusive, or too overwhelmed by their own stresses to meet their children's needs. Perhaps they have been in multiple foster homes. Children from home situations where there are insecure parental attachments do not perceive adults as caring; to them, adults are not a source of support and help. This history of nonsupportive relationships may have made them distrustful of adults, as well as defiant, aggressive and noncompliant (Ashman, Dawson, & Panagiotides, 2008; Belsky & Fearson, 2002; Dearning, McCartney, & Taylor, 2006; Dodge & Pettit, 2003). Some of these children may be starved for affection and act out because getting attention for misbehavior is better than no attention at all. Prior negative home life experiences may also lead to low self-esteem and low motivation, resulting in children's lack of belief in their own capacity for achievement. On the other hand, some children may be behaviorally difficult because of developmental, neurological, or biological issues such as attention problems, hyperactivity, impulsivity, or developmental or language delays. Thus they may be more easily distracted and find it difficult to listen and follow directions. Children with language delays often find it difficult to express their feelings and needs so they resort to grabbing or hitting to get what they want. Being tired or hungry can also contribute to distracted and off-task behavior.

The teacher must look past the disruptive behaviors and reach out to connect with the child.

Whatever the underlying reason for the misbehavior, it is important for teachers not to take children's misbehavior or negative attitudes personally or to blame the child (or parent) for not trying or not caring. Instead, the teacher must look past the disruptive behaviors and reach out to connect with the child. Developing positive relationships with these children is far from simple. As teachers know, it takes a commitment that must be renewed frequently. It takes consistent effort. It requires that teachers take a proactive stance, for if teachers simply react, they will usually respond out of frustration. This is easier said than done, but this chapter will discuss some concrete ways teachers can build positive relationships with all students.

GET TO KNOW THE STUDENT AS AN INDIVIDUAL

The first step in building positive relationships is getting to know students as individuals and showing an interest in what they are interested in. Teachers can start this process early, by sending out interest surveys to parents at the beginning of the year, asking for some personal information such as the child's special interests and hobbies, the nature of his or her temperament and personality, what helps the child calm down, what the parents see as their child's strengths and talents, and any particular concerns the parents have regarding their child.

One sure way of developing a meaningful relationship with a child involves getting to know the child's family and understanding any special circumstances. For example, it is important to know whether there has been a recent divorce, illness, or death in the family, what the current living arrangements are, what forms of discipline the parents use, what language is spoken in the home, and what the parents' cultural values and expectations are regarding school. This information can help teachers better understand the child's perspective and temperament so that they can tailor some of the classroom activities and discussions to include the child's special interests, personality, family situation and culture.

MAKE HOME VISITS

Home visits at the beginning of the year (even prior to school starting) are a powerful way to get to know students and their families and to gain a wealth of information about the child and family in a short period of time. While it may not be feasible to do home visits for all the students in a classroom, it could be invaluable for students who have some special social, emotional, and/or academic problems.

**Sample Interest Survey Letter
Regarding Student's Interests**

Dear Parents,

Welcome to First Grade! I am excited to get to know your child and looking forward to working with you over the next year to support your child's education. In order to get a "jump start" in developing a relationship with your child you can help me by filling out the following information and returning it to me as soon as possible. Knowing what activities and interests your child has helps me to develop curriculum that is exciting and meaningful for your child. Knowing areas you perceive as more difficult for your child helps me to stretch and encourage your child in new areas or places s/he might be tempted to avoid. Thanks for your help. Parents are the most important people in a child's life, and we need to work together for the benefit of your child. With home and school working together I know that each and every student can have the most successful year yet.

Child's Name:

Areas I see as strengths for my child: (academic or social)

Areas I see as more difficult for my child: (academic or social)

What I hope my child will learn this year:

My child's interests are: (include favorite magazines, toys, activities, outings, play acting, math, art, computer time, sports, etc.)

Things my child perceives as especially rewarding: (e.g., special privileges, leadership roles, special food, stickers, baseball cards, movies, etc.)

Things about my child that are special: (include pets, siblings, clubs, grandparents or other people involved closely with your child)

Looking forward to a great year!

Wouldn't a home visit from a teacher feel intrusive to parents?
How do teachers initiate these visits?

When planning a home visit, teachers need to explain to parents why the visit is beneficial (i.e., to get to know the child by seeing their bedroom, favorite animals, etc.). They can help parents understand that home visits help their child feel more comfortable with their teacher when school starts. Parents can be encouraged to let the child be the host or hostess for the visit, deciding what to show or share with the teacher. It is important to reassure parents that is not necessary for them to clean their house for a home visit, and to reassure them that the main reason for doing the home visit is to get to know the child and the family. A survey form sent out in the summer prior to school starting can ask parents to indicate whether they would be agreeable to having a teacher visit before school starts. By offering a home visit, the teacher is extending herself to build a bridge in an effort to promote stronger home-school bonds. This can be particularly important in the case of parents who may be reluctant to initiate communication with teachers either because of prior negative experiences with schools or teachers or because of cultural or language differences.

Some teachers find that home visits are more comfortable if they are structured. Having a form to fill out with parents can help "break the ice." This form can include questions about the child's interests, temperament, and special learning needs. Time with the child can also be structured by bringing a short activity to do with the child (crayons and paper, puzzle, puppet or game). Some teachers find it fun to bring along a special bag filled with different items from around the classroom (e.g., doll dress, marking pen, block, Lego, glue stick), and let the child pick out one thing to keep until the first day of school. On the first day of school, the student's task is to find out where this item belongs.

MAKE POSITIVE PHONE CALLS AND SEND NOTES HOME

Other strategies that foster supportive and collaborative relationships with students and their parents include teachers making positive phone calls to parents or sending emails or notes home to tell them about something special the child has accomplished that day. For example, a teacher might call parents to tell them about their child sharing something interesting or funny in class, or their child's willingness to try something new or their success at a particularly difficult task. In addition a teacher may call the student to give him or her a compliment about some aspect of their school behavior or work.

INVITE PARENTS TO PARTICIPATE

Teachers can also show their commitment to developing positive relationships with their students and their families by issuing invitations to parents to attend informal brown bag lunches or evening potlucks at school. These informal gatherings can be used as opportunities for teachers to share their classroom philosophy and discipline plan, to talk about the details of the curriculum, and to discuss ways the parents can support classroom learning through home activities. Parents can be encouraged to ask questions at these gatherings and invited to participate in the classroom by sharing something about themselves, their family and background (e.g., an interesting trip or special occupation or some aspect of their culture). They also can be invited to assist their child's teacher by reading to students in class or helping with

Parent-to-Teacher Communication Form

To:

Comments:

BICYCLE

MOTOCROSS

From: **Date:**

©*Incredible Years*®

some classroom activity, or going on a field trip. Parents who cannot get away from work to attend such meetings should not be left out but rather encouraged to participate in other ways such as recommending a special story they would like read in class or sending the teacher notes or emails with any concerns or questions.

SHOWING YOU CARE

Another way for teachers to get to know their students is to be involved outside of the classroom by eating lunch together, joining them at recess or attending an event in which they are participating (baseball or soccer games, dance or music recitals). This extra involvement is a lot to ask of a busy teacher who may need recess or lunch time to refuel after being with students all morning. These times of the day, as well as afternoons and evenings, may already be devoted to paperwork, planning, and parent communication. So teachers ask, "Are these home visits and play ground or lunch room visits really necessary? Don't I have a right to a personal life?"

While we would not expect teachers to give up all their lunches or after-school time to be with students, finding some time to be with individual students during the year is as essential to teaching as marking papers, preparing curriculum, and attending school administrative meetings. And this is especially true in the case of the difficult child or the child who is experiencing social, emotional or academic difficulties. Making this extra effort demonstrates a teacher's caring and commitment to developing relationships with their students. In the long-term this extra upfront investment of time will contribute to a more cooperative and caring classroom with fewer behavior problems and greater academic achievement (Wang, Haertel, & Walberg, 1994). Such efforts on the part of the teacher create a bank account of positive feelings and experiences between the teacher, student, and the family that can be drawn upon

In the long-term this extra upfront investment of time will contribute to a more cooperative and caring classroom with fewer behavior problems and greater academic achievement.

in times of conflict. In fact, research has shown that students, especially young children, will work for attention from teachers. When this attention is given for positive behaviors and is combined with a positive relationship, students have less need to devise inappropriate ways of forcing teachers to respond to them (Brophy, 1996). Teachers have told us that when they devoted extra time at the beginning of the year to building these relationships with children and with their families, they found they had more personal time because their classrooms were less stressful and they were not spending so much time managing behavior problems. Thus this initial investment of time paid off in the long run.

USE DIALOGUE JOURNALS AND DAILY GREETINGS

Another, less time consuming way of fostering closer relationships with students and their parents is to use "dialogue journals." When the children arrive in the morning, they spend 10 minutes writing (or drawing) anything they want in their "dialogue journals." Students are encouraged to share this writing with the teacher by putting their journals in his or her "in box" when they are ready for the teacher to read them. The students are given the choice of when or whether they want the teacher to read their dialogues. These journals are referred to as "dialogue" journals because the students often will ask the teacher questions to which she or he can respond with comments, questions, stickers, special notes or private chats. The dialogue journal approach allows teachers to have more personal discussions with each individual student as well as allowing for privacy. (Other children are not allowed to read dialogue journals without author's permission.)

While this dialogue journal approach requires that the student be able to read and write, it can be adapted for use with younger children. This could be accomplished by having the child draw a picture of something that happened at school or at home with a dictated caption or story. This journal might be sent back and forth between home and school as a way for parents, teachers, and the child to share their home and school worlds. Parents and teachers can both help with dictation, write comments about the stories, and read comments and discuss new pictures with the child. This approach fosters close communication between parent, teacher and child on a daily basis.

Another way teachers can promote positive relationships with their students is to greet each of them individually by name when they arrive at school. A high five, handshake or friendly personal word to each student as they arrive in the classroom is an easy and effective way to start the day with a positive contact. In fact, research has shown that daily teacher greetings at the door significantly increased on-task behaviors (Allday & Pakurar, 2007).

GIVE OUT "HAPPY GRAMS"

Giving out "happy grams" is another way to build positive relationships with students. A "happy gram" is a brief written statement announcing a child's success or accomplishment or something the teacher has enjoyed about the student's participation in class. These are read in school with the teacher and then are sent home to the parents. These happy grams may say things like, *"Today I enjoyed hearing about Anna's pet rabbits at home. She is good at sharing with others in class"* or, *"Patrick was very friendly today. I noticed that he helped when Robby fell down on the side walk"* or, *"Gregory controlled his anger and was able to talk about his feelings. He is building good self-control skills."* See Incredible Years web site for other examples teachers may down load for personal use.

 www.incredibleyears.com/Teacher Resources/index.asp

Being listened to by teachers enables children to feel valued and special and fosters a supportive and trusting relationship out of which academic performance will flourish.

LISTEN TO STUDENTS

Finding the time in a hectic day for a teacher to listen to students' understandings, perspectives, and feelings about their learning is probably one of the most powerful ways a teacher can foster a positive relationship with students. Carl Rogers originally developed the concept of 'student centered' learning, which is based on the belief that both emotional and cognitive domains of our personalities need to be developed if effective learning is to take place (Rogers, 1983). He offered a daring challenge to teachers to teach

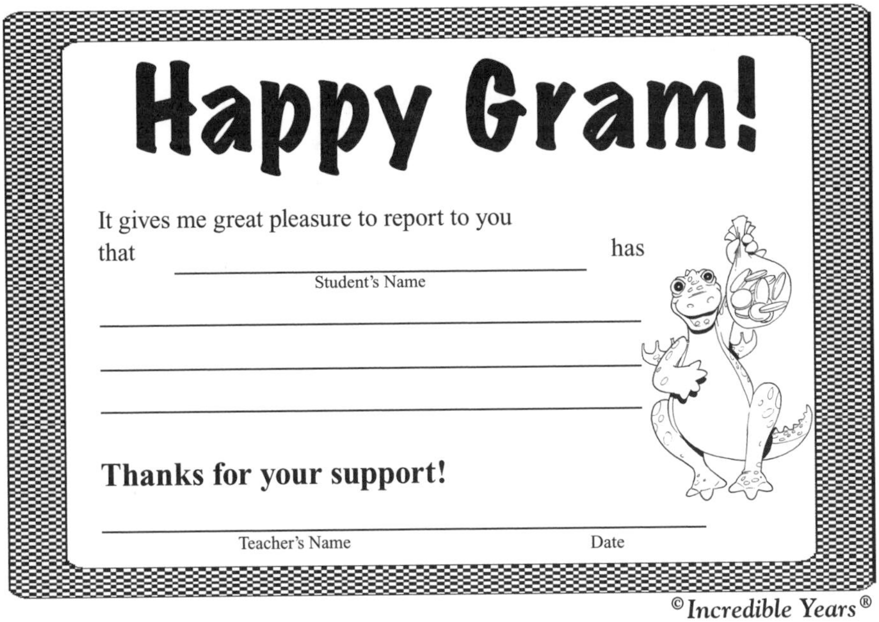

Happy Gram!

It gives me great pleasure to report to you
that _____ has
                Student's Name

_____

_____

_____

Thanks for your support!

_____   _____
        Teacher's Name   Date

©Incredible Years®

less and listen more. Given the demands for meeting particular curriculum goals, it is unlikely all learning will be handed over to students. However, if there is not some attempt on the part of teachers to listen to students' feelings, perceptions, and concerns, then there may be a fundamental mismatch between the teacher's goals and the students' motivation to accomplish them. A child may feel significantly relieved and unburdened just by being able to talk to someone about her experiences and worries. Moreover, children's self-esteem and self-confidence can be raised by a teacher who takes an interest and respects them for their expertise and interests. Being listened to by teachers enables children to feel valued and special and fosters a supportive and trusting relationship out of which academic performance will flourish.

SET UP LISTENING AND SHARING CIRCLE TIMES TO PROMOTE RELATIONSHIPS

Providing regularly scheduled listening and sharing circle times (at least once a week) lasting 15 to 30 minutes (length of time depends on the age of the students) is an ideal way of assuring that teacher time is committed to listening to students and to giving them opportunities to get to know each other. The "listening bear" game discussed below can be used during circle time as one way of getting to know more about students' interests and feelings. For young children it is helpful if the person speaking or sharing an idea holds a special hand-held object (e.g. stuffed animal or toy microphone) so that everyone in the group knows who is speaking and who is listening. When finished sharing ideas, the speaker passes the microphone to the next child to speak. Older children may not need this kind of prop, but will still look forward to these regularly scheduled sharing times that are non-competitive, honest, and fair. (See Chapter 12 for more information on how to use Circle Time to help students solve problems and Chapter 13 for information about learning friendship skills and compliment Circle Time.)

CIRCLE TIME
Games and Activities

GETTING TO KNOW EACH OTHER

Use a "Listening Bear"

One fun strategy for getting to know your students is a "Listening Bear." "Listening Bear" (an actual teddy bear) goes home each day with a student who has demonstrated exceptional listening in class that day. When Listening Bear is at a student's home, he is listening, watching and participating in all that goes on in the family (he may go to restaurants, baseball games, etc.). The family members are asked to write in the journal about the bear's visit to the family—that is, what the bear saw and did while he was there. If the child cannot write, she or he may dictate to the parents. The next day the student brings Listening Bear back to school with his or her journal that is read aloud in circle time to the class. This is a very effective way to get to know students and their families, and it reduces some of the pressure on the child because the story is told from Listening Bear's perspective. It also fosters a home experience between the parents and child that can be shared at school. While it is fun, it also reminds everyone of the importance of listening. *(Teachers should be sure that all the students get to take Listening Bear home at some point.)* This idea can be modified to address children's specific needs (e.g., using a "Sharing Bear" for a shy child).

Peaches and Popsicles

To make sure students sit beside different students at circle time, alternatively label them a 'peach' or 'popsicle.' Then the teacher or a chosen child calls out one of the categories (e.g., peaches) and all peaches change seats with someone else.

Finding Out Similarities

Start the circle time discussion by asking about why it is important to learn more about others. Then pair up each of the students (peaches with popsicles) and give them 2 minutes to find out two things they both enjoy doing outside school. They both must agree to the activities. Now send around the toy microphone and each child has to say, "we both like...." If other children agree with this they may say, "yes" or show a "thumbs up." This same game can be played by asking children to find out their favorite food, sport, TV program, or color.

The same game can be played by asking students to find out two ways they might be different—for example, hobbies, food preferences and interests. This game honors the similarities as well as differences among children in the class.

I Know Your Name

Ask the students to stand up in their circle. Ask a child to call out the name of another student (not a best friend) and throw a beanbag to that person. The person who catches the beanbag must call out another child's name and throw it to them. The game continues until all the children have been named.

Who has gone?

The children sit in the circle wearing blindfolds. A chosen child who is not wearing a blindfold touches someone from the circle. The other children have to ask the chooser questions to try to guess the identity of the child touched. Each child is allowed one question and one guess. The child who makes the correct identification then becomes the next chooser.

Birthday game

The children are all sitting in a circle. The teacher calls out any month of the year and all the students who have birthdays that month run round the outside of the circle until they reach their spots and sit down again. The game continues until all the months have been called.

SHOW STUDENTS YOU TRUST THEM

Any positive relationship must be built on a foundation of trust. Trust is established gradually, as children discover that teachers are there for them and will do everything in their power to help them. Difficult children will need massive amounts of support, attention and caring before they will fully trust a teacher—for difficult children have probably received considerable negative feedback in the past. Difficult children are accustomed to teachers giving up on them, expressed in behavior such as criticism, put-downs, ridicule, and even ignoring them. To build a positive relationship with difficult students, teachers need to take every opportunity to demonstrate they have confidence in these students' abilities and that they have high expectations for them. For example, teachers can show their confidence in a difficult child by giving him or her special responsibilities such as passing out the assignments or snack, taking attendance, helping the teacher organize some materials, or helping a peer. Usually the well-behaved students are chosen for these responsibilities, leaving the more difficult child with the impression that he is not capable. Another way to help students feel trusted is to encourage them to help each other. Teachers can channel children's natural preoccupation with each other into positive interactions by giving them opportunities to collaborate on assignments, working in pairs or in small groups. While teachers can simply allow students to ask for help from another student when they feel a need, this will often leave out the less popular students. The teacher will be wise to pair up students strategically. For example, the child who is somewhat behaviorally difficult may be particularly good in an area such as reading, math, or sports. This child should be encouraged to help a child who is less skilled in this area. When students help each other, their self-esteem rises, and they feel valued and trusted. Moreover, cooperative learning has been shown to enhance academic achievement (Wang, Haertel, & Walberg, 1994).

ALLOW STUDENTS TO MAKE CHOICES

Another way to promote meaningful relationships with students is to allow them to make choices. So often in the classroom children do not have a choice; their only option is to comply or not comply. But if teachers can give them more substantial choices as often as possible, they increase the likelihood that students will feel responsible and committed to what goes on in the classroom. Giving choices also gives students the freedom to say no in appropriate ways and shows them teachers respect their right to say no. This respect is essential to developing a trusting relationship. Choices can be given to children about such things as what book they would like to read, what activity they choose for free play, and what work chore they do.

PROMOTE POSITIVE SELF-TALK IN STUDENTS WHO LACK CONFIDENCE IN THEIR ABILITY TO ESTABLISH RELATIONSHIPS

Some children lack confidence in their ability to establish meaningful relationships. They often have considerable negative self-talk based on their prior school experiences and on how others have responded to them. When faced with a teacher who is sincerely trying to get to know them, they repeatedly think, "She doesn't really like me, I'm a trouble maker" or, "Teachers don't care about me, it's just a job." These self-statements decrease their motivation to learn and to develop trusting relationships. It is important for teachers to identify this self-talk, not to take it personally, and to help such children replace these self-defeating statements with more positive self-talk. Teachers can give them statements to repeat to themselves such as, "I can ask for help. My teacher wants to help me." "My teacher says I'm good at math. I'll keep trying," "I can do it." "If I think I can, I can." "With some work I can do it." Have a rule that for every negative statement children make about themselves, they must counter with two positive statements. This practice helps them develop a more positive self-image.

Students who lack confidence in themselves will be more difficult to get to know because they may be defensive, nonresponsive, and will probably reject the efforts teachers make to reach out to them. This is to be anticipated and expected when working with a student who has experienced parental rejection, abuse, and deprivation. These are the students who need a teacher who refuses to be rejected by them and who consistently, patiently, and repeatedly offers caring, encouragement and hope. These are the students whose teacher can make a critical difference to their future.

SHARE SOMETHING PERSONAL ABOUT YOURSELF

One teacher shared with us an experience she had with several students who were reluctant to volunteer any personal information about themselves either individually or in class. The teacher approached the problem by sharing with them some personal information about herself and telling them some funny experiences that happened to her when she was growing up. She said the children became engaged in asking her questions about these events, which eventually led to their disclosing more about themselves. In this teacher's example, she is modeling self-disclosure and a willingness to be known to her students. The result can be a child's greater feeling of comfort with the teacher as well as greater intimacy among classmates.

THE IMPORTANCE OF CHILD-DIRECTED PLAY
WITH YOUR STUDENTS

One of the most powerful ways for promoting positive relationships is through teacher play times with students. Why? When teachers are playful with students and engage in play activities with them, the relationship between teachers and students is temporarily made more equal. That is, instead of the usual hierarchical relationship where the teacher dominates or is in charge of what the child must do in the classroom, in the play situation the teacher and student are having fun together as equals. In fact, the teacher may be following the students' directions. This opportunity for reciprocity in any relationship serves to build intimacy and trust. It also can promote cooperation, for the teacher can model compliance to the students' suggestions. Teacher-student play fosters children's positive feelings towards the teacher and contributes to a student's motivation to learn and please his or her teacher. Teachers, too, will find that this play makes their job more fun.

This opportunity for reciprocity in any relationship serves to build intimacy and trust and can promote cooperation.

It is important to remember that children learn through play. Play is a time when children can try out ideas, take risks, try on different roles, share feelings and thoughts, and be intimate. It provides a safe context for children to learn.

Is there such a thing as too much play in the classroom?

Some teachers have expressed fear that if they are playful in the classroom, they will lose control of their students; that is, the students will become too silly and wild. While being playful can be a very effective way of promoting close relationships with students, it is still important for the teacher to be able to set limits when needed and provide structure. Even if play does get a little out of hand in a classroom and a teacher needs to reign it in, this, in itself, is a helpful learning process for students. Since young children are emotionally labile and can have difficulty regulating their emotions, it is helpful for them to learn how to make the transition from silly fun time to calmer activities. The teacher models this regulatory process for them, and students learn how to regulate their emotions by being led through a process of being silly and excited to calming down to do some discussion.

Another fear is that students will not respect a teacher who is playful. Some teachers are reluctant to sing or "be goofy" or use puppets because they feel embarrassed and worry that their students will laugh at them. For these teachers, frequent practice being playful with students will soon dispel the embarrassment and replace the fear of being laughed at with the students' delight. Certainly being playful does not mean allowing disrespect in interactions. The paradox is that we often find that the playful teachers actually have created an environment where there is more respect because teachers show students the respect of giving them opportunities to take the lead and students reflect that respect back to teachers. Moreover when these playful teachers need to be assertive and impose consequences for some infraction, the contrast in their demeanor from the playful teacher to the serious teacher gets the students' immediate attention and compliance.

A related concern for some teachers is that their colleagues or the students' parents will perceive their playfulness as unprofessional or as not taking their job or the schoolwork seriously. This fear of disapproval from others can dampen a teacher's efforts to be creative and experiment with playful approaches to teaching. We urge teachers to remember it is this very creativity and willingness to take risks and to approach students at their developmental level that is the "art of teaching." It is important for parents to see teachers modeling this developmentally appropriate teaching style.

Finally, some teachers argue that there is so much curricula and "work" to cover that there is no time for play. This reflects the widespread belief in our society that the time adults and children spend playing together is frivolous and unproductive. Being playful with children should not be perceived as separate from curriculum; it is, rather, an integral part of curriculum, a process that enhances a child's learning or work and in fact, motivates them to learn. Remember if teachers are serious all of the time, if school is no fun, students will come to dislike school. The ultimate goal of schooling in the first years is to help students perceive school as enjoyable, a place where students and teachers value and trust each other, a place where individual differences and learning styles are appreciated and respected, a place of sharing and growth.

Creativity and willingness to take risks and to approach students at their developmental level is the "art of teaching."

Sometimes it is difficult for teachers to be playful with certain students, particularly those who are impulsive, noncompliant, aggressive, or disrespectful with teachers. It can be difficult to let go of the negative feelings about these problem children and be playful with them. These are the very students who probably have had very few child-directed joyful play opportunities or other positive experiences in their lives either with peers or with adults; they are the ones who need it most. While it may seem counterintuitive, investing time in play with these children (and building a relationship with them) will lead eventually to increased respect and cooperation.

TIPS FOR MAKING PLAY MORE EFFECTIVE

Be Playful Yourself

One idea to foster playfulness is for teachers to keep a special box that contains items such as a wig, glasses with springing eyeballs, a microphone, funny t-shirts, a magic wand, or a noise maker. The teacher can surprise students when they arrive by wearing something funny from this box, or can turn to it when students' attention is wavering. For example, the teacher might put on the wig and pull out the microphone to announce a special instruction or transition to a new activity. Or, the teacher may wave the musical magic wand over a student who is listening and following directions. This playfulness serves to keep children engaged and motivated so that they continue to learn.

Follow Your Students' Lead in Play Interactions

Some teachers try to structure play by giving lessons on what to do; how to build the castle the right way, to make the perfect valentine, or complete the puzzle correctly. Possibly they believe that in this way they are making the play a worthwhile activity. Unfortunately, the result of this undue emphasis on the product of play is a string of commands and corrections that usually make the experience unrewarding for both students and teachers.

The first step for these play times with students is to follow their lead, ideas, and imagination, rather than imposing your own ideas. Don't structure or organize activities for them by giving commands or instructions. Don't try to teach them anything. Instead, imitate their actions and do what they ask you to do. Teachers will soon discover that when they sit back and give students a chance to exercise their imagination, their students become more involved and interested in playing, as well as more creative. This approach fosters students' ability to play and think independently. Moreover, when teachers follow students' lead, they show respect for their ideas and demonstrate compliance with their requests. This modeling of compliance to appropriate requests from students helps students become more compliant with teachers' requests in other situations. Moreover, it contributes to reciprocity in the relationship—a power balance, so to speak. Such reciprocity leads to closer and more meaningful relationships.

Be an Appreciative Audience ~
Provide plenty of sunshine

It is important to be a good audience when you play with your students. Some teachers become so involved in giving instructions or playing themselves that they ignore the child or take over what he or she is doing. When playing with students it is important to focus the teacher's sunshine on them. These playtimes may be one of the few times in their interactions with and adult where they can be in control (as long as they are not misbehaving). It is also one of the few times when they can have applause for what they are doing without a lot of rules and restrictions getting in the way. Think of the teacher as an appreciative audience with a job to sit back and watch and provide sunshine to whatever students create with enthusiastic coaching and praise for their efforts.

CONCLUSION

Teachers can make a big difference to a child's future when they spend the extra effort and time nurturing positive relationships with all their students. This is not always an easy task and requires a teacher's consistent commitment to this process and a willingness to become intimate with students and their families. However, when a teacher does this she becomes a powerful model, because by demonstrating her caring she is modeling important social relationships skills for her students to learn and is contributing to students' self-esteem and emotional development and perspective regarding learning. This emotional security in young children's relationships with their teachers is the necessary foundation for them to be able to feel confident to try out their imaginations, test new ideas, make mistakes, solve problems, communicate their hopes as well as their frustrations, and gradually grow and gain academic skills.

To continue the gardening metaphor, teachers who nurture relationships with students are carefully planting seeds in well-prepared soil, adding a protective layer of compost, watering, and allowing sun to shine as the new seedlings begin to grow.

TO SUM UP...

Nurturing Positive Relationships with Students

☀ **Show students you care by:**
- giving them a personal greeting each day when they arrive.
- asking about their feelings e.g., dialogue journals.
- asking about their life outside of school e.g., listening bear.
- listening to them.
- occasionally eating in the cafeteria with students.
- recognizing birthdays in some way.
- sending cards and positive messages home e.g., happy grams.
- finding out about their hobbies and special talents e.g., interest surveys.
- making home visits.
- sharing something personal about yourself.
- spending time playing with them—at recess or during free classroom time.
- establishing positive relationships with every child regardless of their academic or social abilities.
- getting to know their parents through home visits and classroom meetings.
- calling parents periodically to report their child's success or accomplishments.

☀ Show students you believe in them by:

- identifying negative self-talk.
- promoting positive self-talk.
- communicating your belief they can succeed.
- making "I can" cans out of empty juice cans and drop strips of paper in them on which students have written skills they have learned—e.g., math facts, spelling words, sharing with others, helping (This is also useful to show parents the child's progress).
- making phone calls to students to applaud their special efforts or accomplishments.
- helping every child in the classroom to appreciate others' special talents and needs.
- following their lead, listening carefully to their ideas and being an "appreciative audience" at times.

☀ Show students you trust them by:

- inviting students to help with daily tasks and classroom responsibilities.
- offering curriculum choices.
- encouraging collaboration among students.
- encouraging students to help each other.
- sharing your thoughts and feelings with them.

The Incredible Years®
Teacher Classroom Management Self-Reflection Inventory
Teachers Nurturing Positive Relationships with Students

Date: _____ Teacher Name: _____

Teachers learn extensively from self-reflection regarding their classroom management and the teaching strategies they are using that are working or not working. From these reflections teachers determine personal goals for making changes in their approaches to bring about the most positive learning climate they can. Use this Inventory to think about your strengths and limitations and determine your goals.

Building Positive Relationships with Children	1 = NEVER 3 = OCCASIONALLY 5 = CONSISTENTLY
1. I greet my students upon arrival with personal and positive greeting (e.g., using child's name).	1 2 3 4 5
2. I interact with my students with warmth, caring and respect.	1 2 3 4 5
3. I speak calmly and patiently to my students.	1 2 3 4 5
4. I listen to my students and avoid judgmental or critical responses.	1 2 3 4 5
5. I provide sincere, enthusiastic, and positive feedback to my students about their ideas.	1 2 3 4 5
6. I personalize my communications with individual students (e.g., ask about life outside of school, their special interests, hobbies or favorite books; share something personal about self to children; acknowledge birthdays).	1 2 3 4 5
7. I spend special time with each of my students (e.g., on playground, during meals, unstructured play time).	1 2 3 4 5

8. I send home positive message cards to parents to tell them about their children's' successes or accomplishments (e.g., happy grams).	1 2 3 4 5
9. I make positive calls to parents to tell them about their children's successes or positive behavior.	1 2 3 4 5
10. I communicate belief to my students that they can succeed and promote their positive self-talk.	1 2 3 4 5
11. I individualize each student's needs, interests and abilities (e.g., planning activities or stories based on special interests of children).	1 2 3 4 5
12. I help children in the classroom to appreciate each other's special talents and needs and their cultural background.	1 2 3 4 5
13. I am child-directed in my approach and behave as an "appreciative audience" to their play. I avoid question-asking, directions and corrections when possible.	1 2 3 4 5
14. I share my positive feelings when interacting with my students.	1 2 3 4 5
15. I invite my students to help with classroom jobs and responsibilities.	1 2 3 4 5
16. I adjust activities to be developmentally appropriate for each child.	1 2 3 4 5
17. I play with children in ways that provide teacher modeling, prompting and guided practice.	1 2 3 4 5
18. I work to convey acceptance of individual differences (culture, gender, sensory needs) through diverse planning, material and book selections, and discussion topics.	1 2 3 4 5
19. I participate in pretend and imaginary play with my students.	1 2 3 4 5

Future Goals Regarding Ways I will Work to Build Relationships with Identified Students:	Total

REFERENCES

Allday, A., & Pakurar, K. (2007). Effects of teacher greeting on students on-task behavior. *Journal of Applied Behavior Analyses, 40,* 317-320.

Ashman, S. B., Dawson, G., & Panagiotides, H. (2008). Trajectories of maternal depression over 7 years: Relations with child psychophysiology and behavior and role of contextual risks. *Development and Psychopathology,* 20(1), 55-77.

Baker, J. A. (2006). Contributions of teacher-child relationship to positive school adjustment during elementary school. *Journal of School Psychology,* 44(3), 211-229.

Battistich, V., Schaps, E., & Wilson, N. (2004). Effects of an elementary school intervention in students "connectiveness" to school and social adjustment during middle school. *The Journal of Primary Prevention* 24, 243-262.

Belsky, J., & Fearon, R. M. (2002). Early attachment security, subsequent maternal sensitivity, and later child development: Does continuity in development depend upon continuity of caregiving? *Attachment & Human Development,* 4(3), 361-387.

Brophy, J. E. (1996). *Teaching problem students.* New York: Guilford.

Buyse, E., Verschueren, K., Doumen, S., Van Damme, J., & Maes, F. (2008). Classroom problem behavior and teacher-child relationship in kindergarten: The moderating role of classroom climate. *Journal of School Psychology,* 46(4), 367-391.

Cawelti, G. (1995). Handbook of research on improving academic achievement. Arlington, VA: *Educational Research Service.*

Dearing, E., McCartney, K., & Taylor, B. A. (2006). Within-child association between family income and externalizing and internalizing problems. *Developmental Psychology,* 42(2), 237-252.

Dodge, K. A., & Pettit, G. S. (2003). A biopsychosocial model of the development of chronic problems in adolescence. *Developmental Psychology,* 39, 349-371.

Hamre, B. K., & Pianta, R. C. (2006). Student-teacher relationships. In G. G. Bear & K. M. Minke (Eds.), *Children's needs III: Development, prevention and intervention* (pp. 59-71). Bethesda, MD: National Association of School Psychologists.

Henricsson, L., & Rydell, A. M. (2004). Elementary school children with behavior problems: Teacher-child relations and self-perception. A prospective study. *Merrill Palmer Quarterly Journal of Developmental Psychology, 50*(2), 111-138.

Howes, C. (2000). Social-emotional classroom climate in child care, child-teacher relationships and children's second grade peer relations. *Social Development, 9*(2), 291-204.

O'Connor, E. E., Dearing, E., & Collins, B. A. (2011). Teacher-child relationship and behavior problem trajectories in elementary school. *American Educatinal Research Journal, 48*(1), 120-162.

Pianta, R. C., & Stuhlman, M. W. (2004). Teacher-child relationships and children's success in the first years of school. *School Psychology Review, 33*(3), 444-458.

Rimm-Kaufman, S. E., Fan, X., Chiu, Y. J., & You, W. (2007). The contribution of a Responsive Classroom Approach on children's academic achievement: Results from a three year longitudinal study. *Journal of School Psychology, 45*, 401-421.

Rogers, C. (1983). *Freedom to learn for the 80's.* Columbus, Ohio: Merrill.

Silver, R. B., Measelle, J. R., Armstrong, J. M., & Essex, M. J. (2005). Trajectories of classroom exernalizing behavior: Cotnributions of child characteristics, family characteristics, and the teacher-child relationship during the school transition. *Journal of School Psychology, 43*(1), 39-60.

Wang, M., Haertel, G., & Walberg, H. (1994). What helps students learn. *Educational Leadership*, December/January, 74-79.

The Proactive Teacher~
Scaffolding the Environment

When students are disruptive or behave in ways that are coun-terproductive to students' learning, it's all too easy for teachers to automatically react emotionally. The understandable impatience, frustration and distress teachers feel towards negative behavior in the classroom undermines their ability to think strategically about how best to respond in order to modify the child's behavior. Rather than reacting to problem behaviors when they arise, teachers can anticipate the kinds of classroom conditions that are likely to produce disrup-tive or disengaged behaviors and take *proactive* steps to prevent them. Research has shown that proactive teachers structure and scaffold the classroom environment and the school day in ways that make problem behaviors less likely to occur (Burden, 2006; Conroy & Sutherland,

2008; Doll, Zucker, & Brehm, 2004; Doyle, 1990; Good & Brophy, 1994; Jones & Jones, 2007; Simonsen & Fairbanks, 2008; Ysseldyke & Christenson, 1994). They establish predictable schedules, consistent routines, clear limit setting and norms of behavior that help students feel calm, safe, and successful. Classrooms that have few clearly communicated standards or rules are more likely to have students who test and misbehave to see what rules are in effect. This chapter covers some of the proactive strategies used by teachers to help create a safe and reliable environment for their students to learn and a place where problem behaviors are less likely to occur.

PROVIDE A PREDICTABLE AND SAFE LEARNING ENVIRONMENT

Classroom structure provides the basic scaffolding framework that supports the child's ability to learn. A proactive approach includes predictable classroom routines and schedules, how transitions are handled, and clear guidelines for the expected behaviors. When expectations are unclear or inconsistent, students are more likely to unwittingly misbehave. This is often met with a punitive teacher response which, in turn, leads to a cycle of further misbehavior and negative interactions (Reinke & Herman, 2002).

Classroom Rules Should be Stated in terms of Observable Behaviors

The first step to setting clear expectations is to have classroom rules that are clearly spelled out, posted in a visible location in the classroom, and reinforced when students follow them (Grossman, 2004). There should be no more than 5-7 rules that are stated in positive behavioral terms. For example, a rule such as "sit on your carpet square" is clear, whereas "no fooling around" is vague and focuses on something negative. The rules should be stated in terms of observable behaviors; that is, behaviors you can see. For example, "keep your hands to yourself" is preferable to "show respect" or "be nice" because a child will have a clear mental image of what specific behavior is expected. Similarly, "complete all homework and put it on my desk the next morning" is preferable to "be responsible about your homework" because the required behavior is clear and unambiguous.

Rules such as "be a good citizen" or "be responsible" are less effective, especially for early school age children because they are ambiguous, and it is unclear what specific behaviors are being asked for. Effective rules are developmentally age-appropriate, specific, stated positively, easy to understand and enforceable (Scheuermann & Hall, 2008). For young children who don't read, posted rules should include pictures of a child following the particular rule.

Effective rules are developmentally age-appropriate, specific, and stated positively.

Involve Students in Discussion About Rules

Teachers can involve students, even those as young as age four, in developing the classroom rules and discussing why they are important. For example, on the first day of class the teacher should have a discussion with her students to derive the important classroom rules. The teacher can start by asking, "What do you think our classroom rules should be?" As the students generate ideas for the rules, the teacher can ask them why each rule is particularly important. For example, the teacher could explain, "Rules help students feel safe and they make our classroom a friendly place where all of us can learn." Often teachers will need to help students state the rules in terms of positive behaviors. For example when a student suggests the rule of "No kicking, no biting, no hitting," the teacher can say, "Yes, keeping our bodies to ourselves is a very important rule. Let's add it to our list." When teachers collaborate with students about the rules, students will feel more ownership in them and be more committed to adhering to them. Usually students

will generate all the important rules, but if they don't, teachers can always add the missing ones and then lead a discussion about why they are important.

In addition to establishing rules it is essential to discuss the consequences for breaking the rules. Students need to know exactly which behaviors will result in a loss of privilege, Time Out, or cool-off time away from the class. Teachers and students can have a discussion about making good choices in the classroom and about the consequences for following rules versus not following the rules. (See Chapters Seven, Eight and Nine for consequences for breaking rules.)

Teach and Role Play the Rules One at a Time

Once the rules have been discussed on the first day of class, then the teacher should make sure that all students understand what each rule means and what it looks like to follow each rule. For older children this may be done over two–three days and reviewed, as needed, throughout the year. Younger children or children who have difficulty with impulse

Eyes on Teacher

control will take much longer to be able to consistently remember to follow the rules. At the preschool level teachers spend several days or even a week on one rule as children learn how to follow these new expectations for a classroom setting. Most preschool and kindergarten teachers will spend some time reviewing or reminding students about rules each day throughout the school year. Some of the most common rules for preschool and elementary school children are as follows:

- keep your hands and feet to your own body (safety rule)
- listen to the teacher and follow directions
- put up a quiet hand to ask a question (talking rule)
- talk about arguments and problems (problem-solving rule)

- speak quietly and politely to each other (use inside voice)
- listen with eyes on teacher
- use walking feet inside school

For young children, the rules will initially need to be stated, described, and modeled very specifically. Let us say the first rule the teacher focuses on is raising a quiet hand to talk. The teacher asks one of the students to give a demonstration of what a quiet hand looks like. Once the student has demonstrated this, several other students may also take a turn, each receiving teacher praise and approval for doing it correctly. The teacher may set up a practice in which she asks the whole group a question and students are prompted to raise their quiet hands in order to answer. The role plays and practice ensure that the students understand exactly what behaviors are required in order to follow the rule. After the rule is taught, the teacher will prompt the behavior multiple times throughout the day. For example, "Raise your quiet hand if you can tell me…."

Quiet hands up in class

Pictures of each rule should be put on the posted rules list. For older children, several smaller rules may eventually be categorized into a more general rule. For example, keeping hands to self, entering the classroom quietly, staying in seat, and walking in the hallway may be called the "safe or quiet movement rule." Or, speaking politely, sharing, and washing hands might be called the "manners rule."

Planning Positive Consequences for Following Rules

When a rule is first being taught, the teacher needs to respond with praise and encouragement every time s/he notices the students following the rule. The teacher may even set up an incentive program (e.g. tickets, stickers, hand stamps) to help students who have particular difficulties remembering to follow the rules. For example, the teacher may say, "That is fantastic, you remembered the rule about using your walking feet when you come in from outside. Thanks. You can pass out the markers!" One study found several factors influenced whether students complied with teacher rules in the classroom. These included training students on the rules and expectations at the beginning of the year, teacher monitoring and immediate praise for following the rules, and follow through with consequences when rules were violated (Evertson & Weinstein, 2006; Witt & VanDerHeyden, 2004).

Carefully Consider Physical Placement of Particular Students

Another important aspect of classroom structure is consideration of where each student is sitting in relationship to the teacher. All children benefit from being close to the teacher, but this is especially true for inattentive, disruptive children who are easily distracted. Sitting them close to the teacher makes it easier to signal or redirect them to a task without disrupting the rest of the group. In addition, the physical arrangement of a classroom should be set up to maximize teacher-student interactions while minimizing distractions. Teachers should be able to visually scan every student and easily move about the classroom to monitor students' work and behavior.

Seating in relation to peers is another important factor. Children who have more difficulty focusing will often benefit from being placed near peer models who are capable of ignoring distractions and who can set a good example for their less attentive peers. Seating arrangements should be rotated, however, so that the peer role models do not become resentful of children who have a harder time working quietly. Occasionally seating choice can be used as an incentive for a student who has difficulty focusing, but would like to sit in a particular spot. For example, a teacher might say, "If you can work quietly and stay focused in that spot, then you may work there today."

Establish Predictable Routines and Planning for Transitions

Making a transition from an interesting activity to another activity (perhaps one that is less interesting) can be difficult for all young children, but especially for those who are inattentive, impulsive, distractible, or have finally got themselves focused on the task. Teachers can help make a smoother transition by preparing children

DINOSAUR SCHOOL SCHEDULE

  ARRIVAL

  HOMEWORK

  LEARN NEW THINGS

  BATHROOM BREAK

  LEARN NEW THINGS

  SNACK

  ACTIVITY

  COUNT DINOSAUR CHIPS

  GOODBYE

ahead of time and by having predictable and smooth routines surrounding the transitions. Uncertainty about routines leads to behavior problems, while predictable routines help avert problems.

One way to make the routine predictable and clear is for teachers to post the daily classroom schedule on the wall so that children can see, predict, and check the order and times of daily activities. For nonreaders, it is important to include visual pictures of each activity. Some anxious or inattentive children may benefit from a small personal schedule posted on their desks so that they can track each transition as it occurs or even put a check mark on it when it is completed. Well-established routines reduce stress for both students and teachers and prevent disruptions caused by student confusion (Peterson, 1992).

One way to help with transitions between activities is to prepare students for the end of an activity by saying, "In five minutes we will be finished with art time and will go to recess," or "When the bell goes off in 3 minutes, we will need to put away our books." For young children who don't have a concept of time, these time warnings may be tied to the completion of a particular activity. For example saying, "You have time to put three more blocks on your tower, and then it is clean up time," or "There is time for one more turn on the slide, and then we will line up to go in." When it is time for the actual transition, an attention-getting strategy such as music, switching the lights off and on, or a standard clapping rhythm will help signal the change from one activity to another. Teachers should also announce changes in the usual schedule, taking special care to make sure that students who have difficulty with transitions understand the changes. It may even be helpful to have this student physically change the order or placement of the events on the daily schedule posted or be the one to make the announcement about the change to the whole class. For example, the student could replace the agenda item that depicts small group activity with the new activity, such as a field trip and could then explain this change to his peers.

In addition to having a familiar, predictable routine for transitions, it is also helpful for the students to practice and rehearse exactly what will happen during these transitions. A teacher can say, "Before we go to music, what should you do with your reading books?" or "After we get into the cafeteria, what will you do?" or, "When you go in, remember to hang your coats, hats, and lunch boxes in your cubicles." Very young children and children with attention problems will need multiple rehearsals to be able to remember these steps. Frequent practice, step-by-step reminders, assigned peer buddies, and visual cues are all helpful ways to support children during transitions. Positive practice helps these routines to eventually become automatic.

Frequent practice, step-by-step reminders, assigned peer buddies, and visual cues are all helpful ways to support children during transitions.

Greetings and Farewells

Beginning and ending the day are important transitions that should have predictable rituals. It is important to give a welcoming personal greeting and a positive farewell to each student, every day. All students appreciate this extra teacher attention, and this can be a crucial way to build a bond with more challenging students. A personal morning greeting can provide a connection between the teacher and student, start the day on a positive note, and give the teacher a chance to assess the student's mood and state of mind as the school day starts. The end-of-day goodbye is a chance to praise the student for accomplishments during the day, repair the relationship if there were challenges, and predict a fresh positive start for the next day. A recent study found that greeting middle school students at the door as they entered the classroom increased student on task behavior significantly (Allday & Pakurar, 2007).

Give Hyperactive and Inattentive Students Opportunities to Move in Appropriate Ways

While all children need opportunities for movement during the school day, this is especially important for younger students and those who are hyperactive, impulsive, or inattentive. Ideally, teachers can build

legitimate opportunities for movement into the day, some for all students (e.g., dancing to a math song, or moving between work stations) and some specifically for a student that needs more movement (e.g., passing out papers or taking a message to the office). Another way to accommodate a particular student who needs more movement is to provide a "wiggle space" in the classroom: a place to go when the student needs a break from sitting. This place may be a quiet area of the room or particular place marked with adhesive tape on the floor. Particular students can be excused to use the wiggle space when the teacher sees the need, or may be taught to use the space responsibly on their own. The expectation is that the wiggle space is used quietly, that students are still attending to the lesson, and they may even bring work with them. Thus using the space should not disrupt classroom activities or learning. As with any new classroom routine, teachers will need to devote some time and training so that students understand the appropriate use of the wiggle space. Wiggle space rules may include: only one student in the wiggle space at a time, quiet voices in the wiggle space, a limit on the number of times a student may go each day, rules for attending to the lesson during wiggle-space use, and how long a student can spend in the wiggle space. The teacher may even decide to reserve the wiggle space for only one or two children who have particular difficulty staying seated. These students may be given a certain number of wiggle space tickets each day so that they can choose when they want to trade in a ticket for a chance to go to the wiggle space. At first, when the wiggle space is new, all students will be interested and will want to try it. As the novelty wears off, students who do not need to use the space will likely lose interest and move on, leaving it available for students who really need it.

Use Creative Ways of Getting and Holding Children's Attention

Most young children have difficulty shifting their attention to listen to teachers, especially if they are absorbed in an activity and making a discovery. Consequently, it is important for teachers to use innovative strategies to catch and hold their students' attention. If a child's attention is wandering, he or she will not hear the instructions and, consequently, will be further removed from the task at hand. Teachers need multiple ways of engaging children and ensuring they are listening to the instructions. Strategies such as using jokes, praising students who are paying attention, varying tone or volume of voice (e.g. whispering often gets children's attention), doing something funny such as wearing weird goggles or a hat to give a particular instruction, asking students to read the teacher's mind, making a game of playing Simon Says, or asking the children to mimic a clapping pattern all serve to get the students' attention. Novelty and playfulness are always good ways to keep children engaged. For example, a teacher may say, "I'm going to ask my next question to someone wearing green," or, "If you can hear my voice, put your hand on your nose." These simple instructions will engage children's attention so that they are prepared to hear the next important information that the teacher wants to share.

Another strategy to get students' immediate attention is to use the "show me five" freeze signal. This signal is a short hand way of asking for students to be ready to listen while showing five behaviors (one for each finger on a hand): hands to self, feet on floor, eyes on teacher, mouth closed, and ears listening. When young children are learning all the behaviors in "show me five," they may have a picture of a hand placed on their desk. As they show each of the five behaviors, the teacher might put a sticker on one finger to represent the

Dina's School Rules "Show Me Five"

specific behavior that was demonstrated. After students have learned how to show all the behaviors at once, "show me five" becomes a short hand signal that the teachers can use to gain students attention. At this point, she may use a hand signal, whisper the command, use a bell to trigger the behaviors, or have a special "show me five" challenge paired with a special treat for children who are able to follow the rules for a certain period of time. Indeed, this is the challenge of teaching young children, coming up with new and interesting ways of engaging children in the learning process.

A *talking meter* is another way that teachers can signal to students the amount of noise permitted in the classroom. When the arrow points to the green light, students follow choice time rules of using inside voices to freely talk with each other, pointing to the yellow light means quiet talking and moving about is permitted with the focus on a school assignment or project, and the red light means the students must stay in their seats to work independently and put up their hands quietly to ask a question. This meter can also be explained and practices with students in the beginning will help this learning.

Working the Room—Monitoring and Scanning

Research has shown that the more time a teacher spends behind her desk, the more the disruptive and off-task students will be. Walking around the classroom and providing vigilant monitoring and visual and auditory scanning is key to effective classroom management. Several things happen when the teacher walks around. First, the teacher can provide coaching and praise to the group and individual children for work in progress. Second, the teacher can catch problems early and can stop and help redirect students as necessary. This leads to less frustration on the part of students and more support for their learning efforts.

© *Incredible Years*®

Walking around the room also permits the teacher to monitor noise levels and off-task behaviors. The teacher can point to the visual rules cues of quiet hand up, working hard, or the noise meter to unobtrusively signal children of the need to quiet down or attend to their work. Actually, simply walking over to the area of the room where the noise is occurring will often stop the noise without any verbal or nonverbal reminder.

Remember it is also important that the teacher has arranged her classroom furniture and desks in such a way that she can visually scan the room at any time and have every child in her view.

GIVING EFFECTIVE COMMANDS AND INSTRUCTIONS

While proactive plans for teaching rules, managing transitions, and monitoring the room will help to increase students' cooperation, remember that all students will test their teachers' rules and commands. This is especially true if teachers have been inconsistent in the past and not enforced their rules. Be prepared for such testing, as it is only by breaking a rule that children come to learn that it is really in

Children's protests are driven by their developmental drive to explore and discover the limits of their environment.

effect. Consistent consequences for misbehavior will teach students that good behavior is expected. Research shows that typical children fail to comply with their teachers' requests about one-third of the time while children with the diagnoses of Oppositional Defiant Disorder or Conduct Disorder will non-comply 2/3 of the time or even more (Forehand & McMahon, 1981). Most young toddlers and preschoolers will argue, scream, or throw temper tantrums when a desired activity is prohibited. This is normal testing of the limits and driven by their developmental drive to explore and discover and their distress when this is prohibited. School-age children, too, may argue, swear or protest when an activity or object is denied (Tremblay et al., 2000). This is also normal behavior, and a healthy expression of a school-age child's need for independence and autonomy. When such protests happen, don't take them as a personal attack. Remember, students are simply testing classroom rules to see if their teacher is going to be consistent. If teachers are inconsistent, students will probably test even harder the next time. Try to think about students' protests as learning experiences, ways that they can explore the limits of their environment and learn what behaviors are appropriate and inappropriate.

Chapters Eight and Nine will cover ways to handle disruptive behaviors when they do occur. However, it is also possible that part of the reason for noncompliance may be the result of the way the rules or instructions are phrased. Instructions that are vague, such as, "Settle down" or, "Show me you're ready" are difficult for a child to follow, for they don't tell the child what behavior is expected. Commands that are expressed as criticisms, such as, "Seven-year-olds don't do that!" or, "Why can't you follow the directions?" or, "You never listen" are more likely to lead to resentment and opposition than to desired behavior. Negative commands that say what behavior you want stopped but not what positive behavior you want to see, for example, "Cut that out" or "Stop running," leave it up to the child to decide what to do instead. Commands expressed as questions, such as, "Do you want to put your name on your paper?" confuse children, because they can't tell whether they are being given a command or a choice. Teachers should strive for clear, short, specific commands and instructions expressed in positive terms. Here are some ways which research has shown will maximize the effectiveness of your commands (e.g., Van Houten, Nau, Mackenzie-Keating, Sameoto, & Calavecchia, 1982).

Teachers should strive for clear, short, specific commands and instructions expressed in positive terms.

Allow for Lead Time

Some teachers give commands abruptly, without any warning. Picture the scene: Jenny is totally absorbed, painting at the easel. Suddenly the teacher walks over and tells her to put away her paints. What happens next? Likely there is much unhappiness, protesting and resistance from Jenny. As discussed above, a proactive teacher gives warnings and reminders regarding upcoming transitions. Whenever feasible, it is helpful for a teacher to give a warning prior to a command. If Jenny's teacher had noticed that she was engrossed in painting and said, "In two more minutes, it will be time to put your paints away," Jenny would probably not have made a fuss because she was given time to prepare for the change.

Students' requests and preferences should be considered, as well. For instance, if your students are busy reading books, you might say, "When you finish the page you are now reading, I want you to put your books away." If a student makes a polite and reasonable request to finish three more pages because she is almost at the end of the chapter, it may be reasonable to grant her request, if possible. If you are sometimes responsive to your students' wishes, you are more likely to obtain compliance than if you always expect immediate obedience.

Settle your class first—use descriptive comments

Before teachers give instructions about a transition, teach a new idea, or give a reminder of a rule, it is necessary for the class to be quietly settled. All too often teachers yell out instructions to students when the classroom is noisy and unsettled. In this case many students will not hear the instructions, and students will learn that this noise level is the expected classroom behavior. Instead teachers should use an attention-getting strategy, and then wait for the class to quiet before proceeding. For example, the teacher might say, "I'm looking for quiet mouths and listening ears. I see Jon and Seth are ready to hear my instructions. I see Kyla and Mary's voices are turned off. I'm going to wait for a few more quiet voices so that everyone can hear me. Oh, now Seth is ready." This type of descriptive comment is not intrusive and often makes it unnecessary to give a direct command or positive correction regarding the noisy students.

Use Student's Name and Gain Eye Contact

The average teacher gives a general command from 20 feet away, "You need to put away…." This causes problems because the child may not realize the command was directed at her and the teacher is so far away that she cannot easily ensure follow through with the command. Therefore it is recommended that commands be given when the teacher is within 3 feet of the student. Research has also shown that gaining eye contact with the student will improve compliance significantly. However, forcing eye contact with statements such as, "Look at me when I'm talking to you" is unhelpful. It is better to ask for eye contact, and if it isn't given, to speak to the ears. Extended eye contact can be confrontational. Moreover, in some cultures, eye contact with a person of authority is considered disrespectful. An effective use of these strategies would be to walk over to the student, put a hand on her shoulder and say, "Marie, please look at me." If Marie looks, the teacher might say, "Thank you! I know you are listening to me when I see your beautiful eyes. Please get out your reading folder." If Marie had not looked up, the teacher might keep her hand on Marie's shoulder, bend down and say in a quiet voice, "Marie, please get out your reading folder."

Give Clear Positive Commands

Once teachers have students' attention, giving a clear positive command will increase the chances of student compliance. Sometimes teachers give commands that are vague or nonspecific, such as: "Watch out," "Be careful," "Be nice," "Be good," "Knock it off," "Settle down," or, "Show me you are ready." These statements are confusing because they do not tell the student specifically what behavior is expected. Another type of unclear command is that which is stated as a descriptive comment. For instance, the teacher says to a student at lunch time, "Oh Denise, your milk is spilling all over the table!" or "Billy, your math book is not open and ready!" There are two problems with these kinds of statements. First they contain an implied criticism, pointing out something that the teacher is clearly unhappy with. This is likely to breed resentment in the student, which does not lead to cooperative behavior. Second, while a command may be implied in these statements, the teacher never says what it is she would like the student to do, "Denise, please hold the milk pitcher with two hands and pour into the glass" or "Billy, please open your math book to page 10."

A third type of unclear direction is the "Let's" command such as, "Let's finish drawing," or "Let's clean up the art table." This can be confusing for young children, especially if the teachers have no intention of becoming involved. For instance, a teacher who has been doing a play dough sculpture project with the students now wants them to put away the clay. She says, "Let's put the play dough away." If the teacher intends to work with the students to clean up the project, then this is an effective way to communicate her intention. If she enthusiastically begins cleaning, it is likely that her students will work with her to clean up. If on the other hand, her intention is that the students clean up the project by themselves, then using "let's" direction sends a confusing and unfair message to the children. In this case, a clear command would have been, "Now it's time to clean up. Please put your play dough in this bag."

Question commands can be particularly confusing for children. For example, the teacher who says to a student who is wandering around the room, "Are you supposed to be over there? I didn't think so," or, "Are you supposed to be sharpening your pencil now? Where are you supposed to be?" At issue here is the subtle distinction between a request and command. A request implies that the student has the option of choosing whether or not to do what is requested. Teachers who expect students to comply but phrase commands as a question are providing a confusing message. Another problem with question commands is that teachers may find themselves backed into a corner. If teachers say, "Would you like to put the books away now?" or, "Do

The more specific teachers can be about the positive behavior they want to see, the more chance there is that students will understand and comply.

you want to put your name on your paper?" the student may legitimately answer "no!" The student can't tell whether he or she is being given a command or a choice.

In summary, the more specific teachers can be about the positive behavior they want to see, the more chance there is that students will understand and comply. "Do" commands, with the action verb at the beginning of the sentence, are most effective. For example, "Please come and sit in your seat," "Write your name on the top of your papers," "Put the books away under your desk," "Walk slowly," "Speak with your inside voice," "Face this way." Here the action verb is the first word in the command and students cannot miss it. Nor can they miss the message that a command is being given, and that the teacher's intention is that the command is followed!

Reduce the Number of Commands

Few teachers are aware of the actual number of direct commands they give their students. Would it surprise you to hear that our research indicates that the average teacher gives approximately 35 commands in half an hour? In classrooms where children have more behavior problems, the number rises to more than 60 commands in half an hour. Moreover, research has shown that as the number of teacher commands increases (particularly critical or negative commands) so do the number of behavior problems (Brophy, 1996). Frequent repeated commands do not improve a child's behavior. Therefore, it is essential for teachers to evaluate both the number and type of commands given, only use those that are necessary, and be prepared to follow through.

Often when a few students misbehave and refuse to follow directions, teachers respond by repeating and escalating direct commands, even when some students are already doing as requested. For example, the teacher says, "Please put away your reading books now," and some students begin to put away their books while others continue reading. The teacher, focusing on those who are not following the instructions,

becomes irritated and repeats the command a second and third time. She says, "I said put those books away now! Haven't you put those books away yet? Norah, your books aren't put away. Yari, why isn't your book away?" However, if the teacher had praised the students who were following her directions, the repeated commands might not have been necessary. Certainly her escalating negativism and confrontational manner is not likely to induce cooperation in difficult children.

Sometimes teachers give commands about issues that are not important. They might say, "Color that frog green, not yellow," "Quit wiggling," or, "Stop fiddling with your hair." These orders are unnecessary. Students should be allowed to decide such matters for themselves rather than become involved in a battle of will with teachers. It's important to remember that if teachers are constantly giving commands, it is impossible for students to obey or for teachers to follow through on all of them. The result is that confusing messages are given to students about the importance of commands. Moreover, difficult students often respond to excessively authoritarian approaches by "digging in their heels" in defiance.

Before giving a command, teachers should think about whether or not the issue is important and worth following through with a consequence if the student doesn't comply. One exercise that can be helpful is for teachers to write down the important rules for the classroom. There will probably be 5-7 that are "unbreakable." These are the ones that are posted where the entire classroom can see them. In this way, everyone, including temporary teachers and aides, will know what the rules are. Such a list might include:

- Helmets must be worn when riding tricycles on the playground
- Keep hands, feet, and mouths to self (no hitting or hurting others)
- Talk with an inside polite voice in class
- Walk in the classroom
- Follow teacher's directions

Once the important rules are clarified, it will be easier for teachers to set priorities on commands to give and follow through with and to reduce other, unnecessary commands. The result is that students will learn that the teacher's commands are important and compliance is expected.

One Command at a Time

Sometimes teachers string commands together in a chain, without giving the student time to comply with the first command before going on to several more. For young children, this can result in information overload. For example, the teacher says to her preschool classroom, "It's time for recess. I want you to put your markers away, pick up your papers, go in the hall and get your coats on, and wear your boots because it's raining." A series of commands such as this is difficult for youngsters to remember. Most children can retain only one or two things at a time. Another problem with rapid commands is that the teacher is not able to praise the students for complying with any of the individual commands. This string of commands usually results in noncompliance partly because the student simply can't comply with everything, and partly because there is no reinforcement for compliance.

Another type of chain command involves the teacher saying the same thing over and over again as if the child has not heard it. Many teachers repeat the same instruction four or five times, and their students quickly learn that there is no real need to comply until the fifth time. Moreover, chain commands reinforce noncompliant behavior by the amount of attention constant repetition provides.

Instead of repeating commands as if expecting students to ignore them, teachers should state the command once, slowly and clearly, focused on the expected positive behavior. Teachers should then wait to see if the students will comply (counting silently to five may help give students the time they need). The beauty of giving a command to a room of students is that it is likely that at least a few students will begin to follow directions right away, this provides the teacher with a chance to praise their compliance while waiting for slower students to catch up.

After giving a command, teachers should pause and wait about 5 seconds for compliance.

Allow Time to Comply

In addition to chain commands, teachers sometimes give "no-opportunity" commands that do not allow students a chance to comply with requests. For instance, Ninya's teacher says, "Put away the books," and then he starts putting them away himself before she complies. Or Rino's teacher says, "Get down from that swing" and removes him from the swing before waiting to see if he will comply. While immediate compliance is sometimes necessary, especially around safety issues, for the most part children deserve an opportunity to succeed at complying.

After giving a command, teachers should pause and wait about 5 seconds for compliance (counting silently can help). Waiting after the command forces teachers to pay attention to whether the student has complied or not. Often, when given the chance, students do comply (and the teacher should remember to praise)! If the student has not complied after about 5 seconds, then the teacher can consider that he is noncompliant and can follow through with a consequence.

Give Realistic Commands

Occasionally teachers give commands that are unrealistic or not appropriate for the age of their students. For instance, a preschool teacher asks Lisa, a four-year-old girl, to share her favorite stuffed animal with another child in the classroom or, a second grade teacher expects Carl, an inattentive, impulsive and uncoordinated child to do a sewing activity that involves threading a needle. These requests will fail because they're not realistic for Lisa's age or Carl's developmental ability. Other examples of unrealistic or inappropriate commands include expecting an seven-year-old to work quietly on independent seatwork for 30 minutes with no teacher or peer contact, a three-year-old to be quiet while adults have a long discussion, or children of any age to eat everything on their plate all the time.

Teachers should strive to give commands that they believe their students are capable of carrying out successfully. This will avoid setting up students for failure and teachers for frustration. It is especially important to give clear and realistic instructions to students who are inattentive, hyperactive, and impulsive. These children are not likely to have the ability to work independently for very long or to complete an activity that requires concentration without help and scaffolding.

Avoid Criticisms and Negative Labels

If teachers are too angry when they give a command, they may inadvertently encourage noncompliance by yelling or including a criticism with their command. For example, a teacher might say, "Billy, why don't you sit still for once in your life!" Or he might say in a sarcastic voice "Billy, sit still. Do you think you could manage that?" He might say, "Seven-year-olds don't do that!" Or, "Why can't you follow directions? When will you ever learn? How many times do I have to tell you?" Sometimes a frustrated teacher might use a negative global label about an entire class such as, "This class is full of trouble makers," or, "These students always..." or, "These students never..." Labeling and put-downs are included with a command as a way of venting frustration because a student or a classroom has not done something that the teacher has asked them to do many times before. While the frustration may be merited, and all teachers feel this way at times, expressing these feelings to students in this way is counter-productive. The student who senses the teacher's frustration and discouragement may choose not to comply as a way of retaliating for the criticism.

Maintaining a positive or encouraging tone is especially important in the case of students with behavior problems. All students will "shut down" or become upset and defensive when they hear negative comments or an angry tone, but challenging students are usually hyper-sensitive to negativity from adults. When they hear negative comments or a critical tone of voice from an adult, they may dysregulate emotionally, that is, become disengaged, anxious, frustrated, and disorganized. As a result they will not be able to process the learning or hear instructions. When teachers find themselves becoming negative with a particular student or class, this is a signal that something needs to change. The teacher needs help or support from peers, a chance to calm down, and a regrouping to come back with a firm and positive message to children about the expectations. At times, a teacher may be able to change the tone of the interaction with the class or a particular student by using humor or by modeling the use of a calm down strategy, "Whoa, you know, I need to take a couple of deep breaths here. I'm losing my cool and that's not going to help any of us. Okay, let's all rewind and start again!"

Maintaining a positive or encouraging tone is especially important in the case of students with behavior problems.

Use Start Commands

A stop command is also a type of negative statement because it tells a student what not to do. "Stop shouting," "Don't do that," "Quit it," "Shut up," "Cut it out," "Enough of that," " No you can't because you've left a mess," are all stop commands. Not only are these critical of the student, but they focus on the misbehavior instead of telling the child how to behave correctly. Research has indicated that harsh or critical commands and comments on the part of teachers can actually increase disruptive behaviors in the classroom (Van Acker & Grant, 1996).

Sports psychologists have found that if the coach tells the pitcher, "Don't throw a fast ball," a fast ball is just what the pitcher is most likely to throw; not out of orneriness but simply because that is what the coach's words have made him visualize. It's worth making every effort, therefore, to give 'do' commands that detail the positive behavior you want from your child, rather than 'don't' commands. Instead of saying, "Don't call out when I'm teaching," "Stop wandering around" or "Don't yell out" say, "Please speak quietly," "Stay in your seat please" or " Quiet hands up please." Whenever a student does something the teacher doesn't like it's important for him to think of the desired alternative behavior and then phrase the command to focus on that positive opposite behavior.

Use commands that focus on "positive opposite" behaviors.

"When—Then" Commands

Occasionally teachers give commands that sound like threats, "You keep getting out of that seat and you're asking for trouble!" or "You're going to be sorry that you did that." While the intention may be to warn or signal children that they are getting in trouble, these kinds of threats and their vaguely implied consequences tend to cause children to be defiant and negative rather than compliant.

Use "when—then" commands that tell students in advance the exact positive consequences of their actions. In the examples above, the teacher could say, "When you're sitting down, then I'll help you with your math problem," or "When you finish putting your paints away, then you can go outside to recess." First you get the appropriate behavior that you want, and then you provide some positive consequence. This type of command gives your students the choice to comply or not to comply, and knowledge of the consequences of each choice. Once a teacher has given the "when—then" command, it is important to ignore all protests and arguments, and to follow through with the consequences. When the student puts the paints away, he can go outside, but not before. If the student doesn't put the paints away, then the teacher must calmly enforce the consequence of staying inside during recess. Obviously, this kind of command should only be used if teachers can allow the students to decide whether or not to comply.

Give Students Options and Choices

Most of the time, teachers give commands that students are expected to follow—for example, putting up a quiet hand, waiting one's turn, doing the math lesson. But there are other times when a teacher gives a student a choice between two different options or even a choice about whether or not to comply. At these times a student has real options and sometimes may legitimately refuse a teacher's request. Such moments of real choice create a temporary shift in the balance of power between teachers and students. This is an important developmental experience for children because for so much of their lives they are expected to conform to adult expectations and rules. In order to develop a trusting relationship with a student, it also means that the teacher must respect a child's decision not to share some aspect of their lives. Teachers must become conscious of when a situation requires compliance and when a "no" response or an alternative choice from a student is acceptable. If students can see their teachers respecting their decision at these times, they are more likely to comply with the teacher's commands at other times.

There are times when teachers need to prohibit their students from doing something they really want to do. At these times it is important to provide the student with a suggestion of what to do instead or an alternative choice. For example, "You cannot work on the computer now, but if you finish your seatwork, you may have computer time after lunch" or "Right now your toy from home needs to sit on my desk, but you may take it outside at recess." Such an approach can help reduce power struggles because, instead of fighting about what your student cannot do, you're giving the child another positive option.

Give Short Commands and Instructions

Smothered commands are shrouded in explanations, questions or a flurry of words. For instance, the teacher says to the students, "Put away these toys," followed by many questions about why all the toys and paints are out and what they are drawing. The result is that the original command is forgotten. A related problem is that teachers sometimes give too many explanations with a command. They probably believe that giving a long explanation will increase the likelihood that their students will cooperate, but this cognitive, highly verbal approach usually has the opposite effect. Most children will argue with the rationale and try to distract their teachers from the original command.

Keep teacher commands clear, short and to the point. If a teacher needs to give some rationale for the command, it should be brief and either precede the command or follow the student's compliance. Suppose a teacher asks his students to tidy up the classroom. As they proceed he might add, "Thanks, you're doing a great job. I really needed this room cleaned up because we're having a parent meeting here tonight." Remember to ignore arguments and protests about teacher commands as giving attention to them will actually reinforce noncompliance.

Follow Through with Praise or Consequences

Sometimes teachers do not notice whether or not their students comply with their commands. If there is no follow-through and students are neither reinforced for their compliance nor held accountable for their noncompliance, then teachers must expect that their commands will be ignored.

Praising compliance encourages students to be more cooperative and to value teacher requests. If students don't do as they're told, then teachers must give a warning statement. This should be an "if—then" statement: "If you don't put your books away Kevin, then you'll lose a minute of recess." Teachers should wait five seconds to see whether or not the child does as requested. If the child complies, he should be praised and if he still doesn't comply, he should be given one warning that a privilege will be removed. (Please see Chapter Nine for more information on compliance training.)

Below are examples of unclear, vague or negative commands as well as possible positive alternative commands.

Ineffective Command	Effective Positive Command
"Let's put away the toys." "Why don't we...?"	"Please put the toys in the bin."
"Don't yell." "You over there, Shut up."	"Use an inside voice."
"Stop running." "Let's don't do that anymore."	"Walk in the hall."
"Why don't you put your name on your paper?" "Be nice, be good, be careful" "Watch it."	"Please put your name at the top."
"Quit whining."	"Use a friendly voice."
"Didn't I tell you to pick that up?"	"Pick up the crayon and put it on the desk."
"Can't you stay in your seat? I've told you before."	"Sit down please."
"You made a mess! Can't you be careful? Go wash up you are not doing that now."	"Take this sponge and wipe the paint off the table."
"Are you supposed to be doing that?"	"Write only on the paper please."
"You, I mean you, get over here-now! Listen I don't care how you speak at home but in my class..."	"Come here. You need to use polite language."
"Do you want to run the lesson, eh?"	"Please raise a quiet hand if you want to talk."
"I've shown you how to do that a hundred times, here I'll show you again."	"Take the needle and poke it through the hole. I know this is hard."
"I'm fed up, get over here, don't argue with me, go."	"Sit down here. We both need to calm down. Let's take a deep breath together and start again."
"Why haven't you started to work?"	"Read this first sentence out loud."
"Why can't you be better behaved?"	"Please keep your hands to yourself."
"How many times do I have to tell you not to kick the ball out of the playground."	"The ball needs to stay in the playground. If it goes over the fence again, I will keep it for the rest of recess."
"You are never ready on time."	"When you have all your materials in your desk, I will call you to line up for recess."

CONCLUSION

Having a clear classroom structure and rules, a predictable schedule and giving specific commands does not require a teacher to be authoritarian and rigid or to expect 100 percent compliance from students. Rather, the emphasis is on being proactive (not reactive) and thinking carefully about the set up of the classroom, scaffolding the schedule and transitions and how commands and requests of students are being made by teachers. It's important to strike a balance between a student's choices and adult rules.

Proactive teaching and giving commands is harder than one might first expect. In some situations, teacher commands should be given clearly, as absolutes. In situations involving seat belts, hitting, not running into the street, and limitations on computer use, for instance, teachers need to have control over their students and must state their rules and commands in a positive, polite, respectful, and firm manner. There are other situations where direct commands are not needed and it is preferable to use physical redirection, reminders, nonverbal cues, proximity praise, working together, or humor to engage the distracted child. There are other situations where teachers can give up control and avoid unnecessary commands or unrealistic expectations and give students choices. Students may legitimately have control over decisions such as what activity to choose at free time, what work to complete first, whether or not to eat all the food on their plates, what stories to read, and what colors to use on their pictures. Under some circumstances teachers and students can problem-solve and learn to share control.

What is key to effective limit setting is striving for balance in the use of control with students.

Introducing negotiation and discussion with children as young as four or five can provide excellent early training for learning conflict management skills. What is key to effective limit setting on the part of teachers is striving for *balance* in the use of control with students, that is, balancing the use of direct and indirect control approaches as well as offering students legitimate opportunities at times for problem-solving and sharing control. And as always it is important to strive for a higher ratio of positive to negative methods.

The proactive teacher-gardener carefully plants seeds so that there is space for them to grow, thinks about which plants will grow well together, sets up a trellis to support new vines to cling to, gently trains stray branches with twine, and accepts that even with this careful planning, the seeds will sometimes take on a life of their own and grow in unexpected directions.

TO SUM UP...

The Proactive Teacher ~ Scaffolding the Environment

- Develop clear classroom rules (stated positively) and discuss them with children ahead of time.
- Limit the number of rules to 4-7 rules. Have fewer rules for younger children.
- Post rules in the classroom for everyone to see. Young children will need pictures to remind them of the rules.
- Make sure all students understand the meaning of the rules. Model and practice what each rule looks like.
- Have predictable schedules and routines for handling transitions, and also use pictures.
- Be sure to get children's attention before giving instructions.
- Place inattentive or easily distractible children close to the teacher's desk or near the teacher.
- Strive for clear, specific commands expressed in positive terms.
- Redirect disengaged children by calling out their name in a question, standing next to them, making up interesting games, and nonverbal signals.
- Use positive warning reminders about the behavior expected rather than negative statements when children are exceeding the limits.
- Give frequent teacher attention, coaching, praise and encouragement to children who are engaged and following directions.
- Be creative in your use of redirecting strategies—avoid repeated commands. Instead, use nonverbal cues and engaging activities.

The Incredible Years ®
Teacher Classroom Management Self-Reflection Inventory
Proactive Teacher Strategies

Date: _____ Teacher Name: _____

Teachers learn extensively from self-reflection regarding their classroom management and the teaching strategies they are using that are working or not working. From these reflections teachers determine personal goals for making changes in their approaches to bring about the most positive learning climate they can. Use this Inventory to think about your strengths and limitations and determine your goals.

Proactive Teacher – Rules and Commands	1 = NEVER 3 = OCCASIONALLY 5 = CONSISTENTLY
1. I state rules positively and clearly and they are posted on the wall. They are reviewed and practiced as needed.	1 2 3 4 5
2. I use nonverbal cues and signals to communicate rules as well as words (e.g., pictures of rules such as raise quiet hands, quiet voice, five on the floor, ears open).	1 2 3 4 5
3. I have taught children the "show me five" signal and use it.	1 2 3 4 5
4. I state requests or give directions respectfully using brief descriptions of positive behaviors desired (e.g., "please keep your hands to your own body").	1 2 3 4 5
5. I use "when-then" commands.	1 2 3 4 5
6. I give students choices and redirections when possible.	1 2 3 4 5
7. I avoid negative commands, corrections, demands, and yelling at children.	1 2 3 4 5
8. I get children's attention before giving instructions.	1 2 3 4 5

9. I redirect disengaged children by calling out their name with a question, standing next to them, making up interesting games, and nonverbal signals.	1 2 3 4 5
10. I give frequent attention, praise and encouragement to children who are engaged and following directions.	1 2 3 4 5

Proactive Teacher - Schedules

1. My classroom routines and schedules are consistent, predictable and allow for flexibility.	1 2 3 4 5
2. I post classroom schedules on the wall in a visible place for children, parents and visitors.	1 2 3 4 5
3. Visual pictures/cues are used to indicate different activities on schedule (e.g., small group circle time, unstructured play time, teeth brushing or hand washing, outside play, lunch).	1 2 3 4 5
4. My classroom schedule alternates active and vigorous activities (outside activities or free choice) with less active activities (story time).	1 2 3 4 5
5. I provide a balance between teacher-directed and child-directed activities.	1 2 3 4 5
6. I have a system in place for students to choose between play areas or activities during unstructured times (center cards for activity areas such as block center, dress up and kitchen pretend play area, book area).	1 2 3 4 5
7. The length of structured learning times are tailored to children's developmental levels (10-20 minute blocks for preschool and kindergarten, 20-30 minutes for 1st-3rd grades).	1 2 3 4 5
8. My structured learning time includes many active responses from children (e.g., singing and movement, stretch breaks, holding cue cards, acting out responses, answering verbally as group, puppet play) to encourage high rates of engagement.	1 2 3 4 5

9. I have times during the day schedules for free play where children are allowed to choose materials, participate in imaginary play, and interact freely with peers. (For preschool classrooms free play makes up 1/3-1/2 half of school time; for elementary classrooms, a substantial block of time is available each day).	1 2 3 4 5

Proactive Teacher - Transitions

1. I avoid unnecessary transitions and keep waiting time minimal.	1 2 3 4 5
2. I systematically teach students the expectations for transitions and practice them.	1 2 3 4 5
3. I warn students before a transition begins and transitions are not rushed.	1 2 3 4 5
4. I use a consistent cue to signal a transition (e.g., bells, song, clap, lights turned on and off).	1 2 3 4 5
5. I use visual pictures/cues and auditory sounds to note schedule, transition cards, tape on floor for line up, quiet area, pictures for daily jobs).	1 2 3 4 5
6. I start circle time activity when a few children are ready to begin and do not wait for everyone.	1 2 3 4 5

Proactive Teacher - Classroom Environment and Organization

1. My classroom is well equipped with a variety of toys and materials so that children of all skill levels have something to play with.	1 2 3 4 5
2. My classroom is organized by learning centers and number of children allowed in a center is limited with visual reminders of how many children are allowed (e.g., hooks with names, clothespins etc.).	1 2 3 4 5

3. I have put picture labels are on low shelves to help children find and return materials.	1 2 3 4 5
4. I have provided toys that promote social interaction in all learning centers (e.g., puppets, wagons, large floor puzzles, turn-taking games etc.).	1 2 3 4 5
5. I have a systematic rotation plan in effect to increase novelty and curiosity (e.g., sand or bubble table open at certain times).	1 2 3 4 5
6. My classroom provides visual cues to children to signal whether an area or activity is open or closed (e.g., stop sign, sheet covering sand table or computer).	1 2 3 4 5
7. Materials are enlarged in my classroom for children with visible motor impairments (e.g., larger crayons, paper, etc.) and stabilized for better manipulation (taped to table, Velcro board, trays).	1 2 3 4 5
8. I provide visual cues throughout classroom to remind child of target skill (e.g., sharing, helping, teamwork).	1 2 3 4 5
9. A large physical structure is provided in my classroom for circle time and children sit on carpet squares or mats.	1 2 3 4 5
10. I prepare materials for small group activities so they are ready to go before children arrive for the day.	1 2 3 4 5
11. I plan cooperative activities are planned on a daily basis (e.g., large collages, class books, cooking activities etc.).	1 2 3 4 5
12. Children are visible at all times. Shelving is no higher than 4 feet tall.	1 2 3 4 5
13. I place inattentive or easily distractible children close by me.	1 2 3 4 5

Future Goals for Proactive Strategies–Rules, Schedules, Transitions, Environmental Structure and Planning:	Total

REFERENCES

Allday, A., & Pakurar, K. (2007). Effects of teacher greeting on students on-task behavior. *Journal of Applied Behavior Analysis, 40,* 317-320.

Brophy, J. E. (1996). *Teaching problem students.* New York: Guilford.

Burden, P. (2006). *Classroom management: creating a succcessful K-12 learning community.* Hoboken, NJ: Wiley.

Conroy, M., & Sutherland, K. (2008). Preventing and ameliorating young children's chronic problem behaviors: An ecological classroom-based approach. *Psychology in the Schools, 46*(1), 3-17.

Doll, B., Zucker, S., & Brehm, K. (2004). *Resilient Classrooms: Creating Healthy Environments for Learning.* New York, NY: Guilford Press.

Doyle, W. (1990). Classroom management techniques. In O. C. Moles (Ed.), *Student discipline strategies: Research and practice.* Albany, NY: State University of New York Press.

Evertson, C. M., & Weinstein, C. S. (2006). Classroom Management as a Field of Inquiry. In C. M. Evertson & C. S. Weinstein (Eds.), *Handbook of classroom management: Research, practice, and contemporary issues* (pp. 3-15). Mahwah, NJ: Lawrence Erlbaum Associates Publishers.

Forehand, R. L., & McMahon, R. J. (1981). *Helping the noncompliant child: A clinician's guide to parent training.* New York: Guilford Press.

Good, T. L., & Brophy, J. E. (1994). *Looking in classrooms.* New York: Harper Collins.

Grossman, H. (2004). *Classroom behavior management for diverse and inclusive schools.* New York: Rowman & Littlefield Publishers, Inc.

Jones, V. F., & Jones, L. S. (2007). *Comprehensive classroom management: Creating positive learning environments.* Boston: Allyn & Bacon.

Peterson, R. (1992). *Life in a crowded place: making a learning community.* Portsmouth, NH: Heinemann.

Reinke, W. M., & Herman, K. C. (2002). Creating school environments that deter antisocial behaviors in youth. *Psychology in the Schools, 39*(549-559).

Scheuermann, B. K., & Hall, J. A. (2008). *Positive behavioral supports for the classroom*. Upper Saddle River, NJ: Pearson/Merrill Prentice Hall.

Simonsen, B., & Fairbanks, S. (2008). Evidence-based practices in classroom management: Considerations for research to practice. *Education & Treatment of Children, 31*(3), 351-380.

Tremblay, R. E., Japel, C., Perusse, D., Boivin, M., Zoccolillo, M., Montplaisir, J., et al. (2000). The search for the age of "onset" of physical aggression: Rousseau and Bandura revisited. *Criminal Behavior and Mental Health, 24*(2), 129-141.

Van Acker, R., & Grant, S. H. (1996). Teacher and student behavior as a function of risk for aggression. *Education & Treatment of Children, 19*(3), 316-334.

Van Houten, R., Nau, P. Mackenzie-Keating, D., Sameoto, D. & Calavecchia, B. (1982). An analysis of some variables, influencing the effectiveness of reprimands. *Journal of Applied Behavior Analysis, 15*, 65-83.

Witt, J. C., & VanDerHeyden, A. M. (2004). Troubleshooting Behavioral Interventions: A Systematic Process for Finding and Eliminating Problems. *School Psychology Review, 33*(3), 363-383.

Ysseldyke, J. E., & Christenson, S. L. (1994). *The instructional environment system-II*. Longmont, CO: SORRIS West.

CHAPTER 4

Promoting Children's School-Readiness Growth with Academic, Persistence, Social and Emotion Coaching

In the first chapters we have talked about the importance of teachers nurturing their students' social and emotional growth by promoting positive relationships with their students and their families and by scaffolding a safe classroom learning environment by setting up predictable routines, clear rules, and effective limit setting. These are core teaching strategies that provide the foundation of the teaching pyramid described in Chapter One that supports early school age children's learning growth and eventual academic achievement.

In this chapter we will discuss another foundational teaching tool; that is, scaffolding children's learning interactions with peers and teachers with coaching methods that support their school readiness growth, academic success, and social emotional development. This coaching involves using descriptive comments to highlight specific learning skills such as persistence with learning something new, focused activity, cooperation, emotion regulation, and patience. This approach addresses the social, cognitive, emotional, behavioral, and academic elements of children's school readiness. School readiness implies that students have made significant progress toward developmental milestones including a strong bond or attachment with their teachers, peers, and schools; a sense of self, autonomy and desire to explore; and the language and behaviors needed for social and emotional expression and self-regulation. This chapter begins by covering specific ways of teachers interacting with students using different types of coaching and then explores how this type of descriptive language can help to foster specific academic, behavioral, social, and emotional development.

All types of coaching described in this chapter recommend the use of *descriptive commenting,* a form of commentary where the teacher enters a student's internal and imaginary world, narrates his ideas, thoughts, feelings and interests, helps him feel confident by being an "appreciative audience" and providing focused attention on his learning process. This language does not include questions, unnecessary commands, or corrections and often sounds like a sports announcer's play-by-play description of a game. These expanded descriptions of a student's activity promote a student's cognitive awareness of what she is seeing, doing, thinking or feeling, building her self-confidence, and supporting her creativity, independence, and struggle to discover and learn something new. For many teachers, this is a novel way of communicating and, at first, may feel uncomfortable and artificial. The discomfort will diminish as teachers practice in a variety of situations and see their students' emotional and behavioral responses. Teachers who use these descriptive coaching methods consistently find that their students come to love this kind of attention, feel more strongly attached to their teachers, persist at the activity despite feeling frustrated and show gains in academic, social, and emotional competency (Webster-Stratton, Reid, & Stool-miller, 2008). Teachers can tailor this type of descriptive coaching to focus on many different aspects of children's development and their specific social, emotional or academic needs. This chapter will focus first on teacher coaching of academic skills and concepts (colors, numbers, letters, vocabulary, patterns) and academic behaviors (sustained attention, focus, thinking, listening), both of which promote children's language development, persistence with learning and a positive teacher-student relationship. Next the chapter will cover teacher social and emotion coaching, which promotes cooperative and shared learning in the classroom, friendships, emotional literacy, and self-regulation. As noted in Chapter One the quality of teacher attention and coaching and the prosocial foundation emerges as one of the most important factors in helping students become school ready, motivated and successful learners (Caprara, Barbaranelli, Pastorelli, Bandura, & Zimbardo, 2000; Duncan, et al., 2007; Reinke & Lewis-Palmer, 2008).

The quality of teacher attention and coaching and the prosocial foundation emerges as one of the most important factors in helping students become school ready, motivated and successful learners.

ACADEMIC COACHING ~ ENHANCING VOCABULARY

Studies have shown that teachers can help young children expand their language vocabulary and development by modeling words for them and naming objects and actions in their world (Whitehurst, et al., 1999). The beauty of this kind of commenting is that it can be tailored to each child's interests and developmental level. Students with delayed language and few words will benefit from repeated pairing of language and vocabulary with the objects they are exploring and the actions they are using. Children with typically developing vocabularies will be especially tuned in to new words that help to explain their actions in more detail, or that provide them with more information about their activities. Teachers of preschool children can start this language coaching by simply naming objects, actions, or positions (on, under, inside, beside, next to) of things children are doing in the classroom such playing with blocks, working on a drawing, math, or science project, eating lunch, or playing on the playground. Teachers describe the things that students are interested in at the time that the student is exploring the object. For example the teacher of a three-year-old with delayed language might watch his play and say, "Marcus has the yellow giraffe. It's walking along. It bumped into a big hippo. Oh, it jumped over that hippo's stomach. Now it's eating the cow." This repeated pairing of the animal names with actions and positions will gradually help the child learn the vocabulary and concepts. A teacher of a four-year-old with more advanced language skills might say, "I see you have the tall giraffe who is reaching high to eat the Acacia leaves. I think I see his long tongue! In real life his tongue is 18 inches. That's about as long as your arm, and his tail is longer than I am!" As the boy picks up another animal the teacher says, "And here comes a strong leopard with a spotted coat, slinking through the grass." This commenting indicates how interested a teacher is in what the child is doing and is an invaluable teaching tool because it bathes children in rich language while providing important information about the size and movements of the objects they are touching.

So far our examples have been one-sided, with the teacher talking while the child plays. Many times children will be absorbed in their play and may let the teacher's language wash over their heads. This is just fine. Children don't need to respond to teacher's language to benefit from hearing these descriptive comments. Other times students will actively engage the teacher with comments of their own, questions, or responses to something a teacher said. In this case, the most important thing is to follow the student's lead. A primary grade teacher might say, "I see you are interested in reading that story about trains. That picture looks like the locomotive is powered by a steam engine. I wonder what is boiling the water?" The teacher waits for a response from the child who says, "Coal is doing that" and she builds on the child's knowledge by saying, "You are right. Steam engines were powered by coal or wood. You know a lot about trains. It looks like this page also has diesel engines." Remember it is important for teachers to be child-directed in communication; that is, describe what the student is already doing or showing interest in. Don't be too directive or "teachy" with this commenting as this may interfere with the child's curiosity, exploration and sense of self-discovery and independence. Pause after a description and wait to see what the student will share about his knowledge of the subject and then respond by listening attentively and building on that knowledge with enthusiasm.

Coaching Specific Academic Skills and Concepts

In addition to basic vocabulary, teachers can use coaching to tailor their interactions to many different academic skills. At the preschool level this might include numbers, colors, patterns, prepositions, letters, shapes, textures, categories, and sizes. Think about this next example where a teacher describes her preschool student's work on an alphabet puzzle.

> Jolie brings over an alphabet puzzle to work on with the teacher. Jolie holds up the letter T–and the teacher says T several times and then says, "You are holding the green letter T." Jolie repeats the name "T." Then Jolie looks for where it goes on the puzzle and puts it into the space for the T. The teacher says, "You are smart for remembering that Teddy Bear starts with a T." Jolie replies, "T is for Teddy bear." The teacher replies enthusiastically, "Yes you are right. You are listening to beginning sounds!" Next Jolie finds the place for the letter "N" and the teacher praises her by saying, "Good for finding the right place for that yellow letter N. It comes earlier in the alphabet than T." Jolie finds the spot for L and says, "L–lemon." The teacher repeats enthusiastically, "Good job, L is for lemon! La, La, Lemon."

This preschooler is able to match most of her letters to their places in the puzzle and she is beginning to recognize and be able to label some beginning letters and sounds. Children learn these skills at widely different rates and some preschoolers won't have the persistence to sit still to do a complex letter puzzle for very long. The important thing is that the teacher is making this learning process fun and following the child's interests and readiness for learning. This teacher pays attention to the things that the student is interested in and uses her descriptive language to encourage her play. This approach is likely to lead to more learning than if the teacher had handed the student the pieces one-by-one and asked her "Where does this go?" "What is this letter?" "What starts with the letter L?"

As children enter elementary school, academic concepts become more complicated, but the idea of descriptive coaching still applies. At this level teachers may coach students on skills such as more complicated math concepts of addition and subtraction, pattern recognition, reading and sounding out words, writing words, writing sentences or even paragraphs. See the example below of a teacher coaching a table group of students who are doing math problems using manipulatives.

"I see that John is using a grouping strategy. He's putting his blocks into groups of 10 so that it will be easier to count them. That is a smart addition trick. Oh, I see that Layla is using different colored blocks to represent different parts of the word problem. Your yellow blocks are the oranges and your blue blocks are the apples. You've both figured out different ways to help yourself solve this problem. Mary, I appreciate how neatly you are writing your numbers—you are really taking the time to get the numbers lined up as you write them—that will help you when you are ready to add them up and it will help me when I look at your work."

This teacher's commenting is focusing on the academic strategies that the students are using as well as their problem-solving skills. Her comments let each child know that she notices his or her efforts and is also helping the group see that there are different ways of working on the problems.

Avoid Too Much Question-Asking

Many teachers have a tendency to ask a string of questions while interacting with children, "What color is that?" "Where does it go?" "How many cars are there?" "What are you making?" "Is that the right way to put it together?" "How does it go on?" "Count all the blue ones." "What are you going to do with that?" Through such questions, teachers are intending to help the student learn, but all too often it has the reverse effect.

Asking too many questions or giving too many directives when interacting with a student can be intimidating to him and make him feel he has to perform for the teacher, particularly if the teacher knows the answers to her questions! Too many questions from teachers can cause children to feel tested, to refuse to speak and retreat into silence, particularly if they fear they might make a mistake and aren't sure of the answer. So it is important to balance question asking with about ten times more descriptive comments and coaching statements than questions.

Balance question asking with about ten times more descriptive comments and coaching statements than questions.

Think about a teacher of a three and a half-year-old girl who still doesn't know all her colors and shapes. This teacher is concerned and has a goal to help this child learn these important school readiness concepts.

> *Teacher asks, "Lily, what color is this?" Child shrugs and Teacher says, "It's red. Can you say red?" Child repeats, "red." Teacher says, "Now what about this one? What color is it?" Child says, "red" and Teacher says, "Yes! What shape is it?" Child says, "square." Teacher says, "No it's a triangle. Can you say triangle?" Lily refuses to answer.*

While it is easy to identify with this teacher's wish to teach this child, think about the impact of this interaction on the child's comfort level with her teacher, her creativity, and her feelings about herself. This kind of rapid-fire question-asking has made the play activity into a test, one in which the child often isn't successful, and which may seem never-ending. In contrast, think about applying the descriptive commenting principles from above to the same girl with the same goals of teaching colors and shapes.

> *"Lily, you've got a yellow block in each hand. Those two blocks are rectangles. The rectangle blocks are going on top of each other. You're stacking them. Two yellow blocks. They're getting high! Now you're adding a red triangle to a make a pointy top. One red triangle on top.*

There are lots of colors and shapes. I wonder what color you'll choose next." Lily replies, *"I've got orange."* The teacher replies, *"Oh, yes I see! You know your colors. That is an orange circle!"*

In this scenario, the teacher has repeatedly labeled the word yellow, as well as two other colors. She has also given the shape names and has talked about position. In contrast to the first example, think about how Lily might feel in this scene. Perhaps she feels supported by her teacher, interested in the tower she is building, and proud of her efforts. This is likely to make her open to receiving new information about the colors and shapes that her teacher labels. It is very likely that she might turn to her teacher and hold up another yellow block saying, "I have a yellow one?" Or, she may start to ask her teacher for information, "What color is this one?" This second example is much more likely to actually result in Lily learning and retaining the important information that her teacher wants her to learn.

Two types of questions are worth thinking about. The first type is asking children to produce a correct response to factual information. For example, "What color is that?" "How do you spell…?" This type of question is really a type of command or a test since it requires children to perform. Usually these are questions that the adult knows the answer to, and the child knows that a correct answer is important. Another kind of question asks children to define what they are doing or why they are doing it a particular way. For example, "What are you going to build?" "What is that picture?" "What are you writing about?" Often, these questions are asked out of a genuine desire to understand what a child is thinking or making, and usually the adult is trying to connect with the child. The issue here is that even these open-ended questions often occur before the child has even thought about the final product or had a chance to explore his ideas. Perhaps the child doesn't know what he wants to build, or draw, or write about. Or perhaps he doesn't want to build at all. Maybe he'd rather feel the texture of the blocks or run them around like cars. Through the question, the teacher puts the emphasis on the product rather than the process of play. Question-asking may break children's concentration and distract their focus from the creative exploration process. Instead, teachers can use descriptive commenting and academic coaching as a nonthreatening way of bonding and communicating with students and teaching an academic concept without demanding performance. Although this chapter encourages teachers not to ask many questions, the occasional question is not a problem, and it can show that a teacher is genuinely interested in her student's thoughts, feelings or ideas. For example, questions such as, "How can I help?" or statements such as "I am curious to see what you will do next" are non-testing questions because the teacher doesn't know the answer in advance, they don't focus on the product, and they allow the child to take the lead on the response. When teachers ask this type of question, it is important they pause to listen for an answer and then respond with interest. If teachers do not receive an answer, it is best to go back to descriptive commenting.

Academic coaching is a nonthreatening way of bonding and communicating with students and teaching an academic concept without demanding performance.

Promoting Reading Readiness—Modeling, Repetition, and Praise

Reading with children is an important way of building their language and reading readiness or reading skill. The descriptive commenting ideas discussed above can also be adapted and applied to reading. Teachers can let students pick out books on topics they are interested in and designate a quiet reading section in the classroom where there are no distractions. Preschoolers will benefit from information about the pragmatics of reading a book (looking at the cover, noticing the author and illustrator, seeing which side of the book opens). For example, "This book is called *Goodnight Moon* by Margaret Wise Brown. She wrote this story. Clement Hurd is the illustrator. He drew the pictures." As the teacher reads, she keeps her pace slow and notices the children's reactions as they look at and talk about the pictures. Teachers can have fun labeling or asking students to find objects in the pictures as well as reading the real story words.

Teachers can extend the ideas in the pictures to the students' own experiences. For example, if there is a picture of a dog or cat, ask the students about a particular dog or cat that they know, "The cat in this story is an orange striped cat. I know Jimmy has a cat at home. I wonder what color your cat is, Jimmy?" Or talk about a time one of your students did something that is pictured in the book, "That swing looks like the one you all play with on our playground. Do you remember how high you were swinging and how well you shared the swing with each other by taking turns?" Don't put pressure on students to name the pictures, but if they copy your words, praise their efforts and repeat the word. Teachers can also extend students' vocabulary by adding to their words. For example if a child points and says fire engine, the teacher can repeat, "Yes, a big, red fire engine. They look like they are in a hurry." If there are sentences, teachers can run their finger under the words as they read them. If there are large letters on the page, teachers can name them and make the letter sound. Teachers and students can take turns sharing what they are seeing on the page.

Teachers of older students who are already reading may let students take a turn reading or read to each other. Older students will also have fun predicting what is going to happen next in the story, thinking about the feelings of the characters in the story, making up an alternative ending, and talking about what character they most identify with. At any age students love to be read to! One of the precursors to creating good readers is to create a love for books. So one primary goal is to make reading fun. Children's natural reading ability and attention span will vary. Some children may be able to sit and read or listen for long periods of time; others will lose interest after a few minutes. Some children are beginning to read at four years old, while others don't master reading until they are seven or eight years old. While it is important to be aware of children who have significant learning problems, much of the variation in reading attention and aptitude is developmentally normal and pushing too hard may make a child dislike the process of reading because they feel inept.

Building Blocks for Reading With CARE

The following are some key points to remember about reading with students:

Comment, use descriptive commenting to describe pictures, actions and stories.

- Take turns interacting and reading.
- Pause teacher reading to let students respond.
- Describe the pictures or read the words putting your finger under the words (modeling).
- Let children who are readers take turns reading with you or with each other.
- Make a game of reading with expression—thinking about how characters would say different lines.
- Let the children be the storyteller by encouraging them to talk about the pictures and stories and praising their ideas (practice).

Ask open-ended questions.

- "What is your favorite picture on this page?" (observing and reporting)
- "Do you remember a time you did that?" (connecting story to something in child's life)
- "I wonder what's happening here?" (storytelling, encouraging being curious and exploration)
- "What is that a picture of?" (promoting academic skills)
- "How might she be feeling now?" (exploring feelings)
- "What is going to happen next?" (predicting)
- "I wonder if you can think of a different ending to the story? (creative thinking)
- "Why do you think the author made that choice?" (analyzing the author's intentions)
- "What do you think is the main idea of this part of the story?" (recognizing key points)
- "Can you retell what happened so far?" (summarizing)

Respond with praise and encouragement to children's thinking and responses.

- "That's right! That train has a lot of cars."
- "You are really thinking about that."
- "Wow, you know a lot about animals."
- "I love hearing you talk about these pictures. You are really learning to read."
- "I think your story is really creative. You are a good story teller."
- "You are getting so good at expressing the feelings of the characters when you read."
- "You are paying attention to the punctuation when you read."

Expand on what children talk about.

- "Yes, I think he's feeling excited, too, and he might be a little scared as well."
- "Yes, it is a horse; it's also called a mare."
- "Yes, that boy is going to the park. Do you remember going to a park?"
- "Wow I really like your ending to the story. Can we act that out with puppets?"
- "Your prediction of what would happen was a great idea. Can we write your story down in your journal to read another time?"

Pre-writing and Writing Readiness

Coloring and writing with children is a lot of fun and is another opportunity for teachers to use descriptive and academic commenting. This is also a strategic way to model and encourage students' writing skills? Give the preschool child some crayons on a large piece of paper. Let the child draw on the page and use academic coaching to talk about the colors, designs and images he is drawing. Teachers can record with a crayon or marker the student's stories or descriptions next to his drawings. Teachers can experiment with many different ways to encourage preschooler's writing: try drawing or writing together in the sand with a stick, make designs with a finger in shaving cream or whip cream on a tray, use bath crayons in the water table or write words with paint brushes or finger paints. As each student creates his own art, use academic coaching to give words to their actions and ideas. For example, "Your blue line is going across the bottom of the page. Now your red line is on top of the page." Describe the kinds of lines the child is making, "That's a straight line going up the side of the wall. It looks like the letter I. Now there's a curvy line going across. That part is going around in circles like the letter O." If the student talks about what he is drawing or tells a story about it, write it down on the bottom of the page and show delight in his story and the book he is making. These are all beginning reading and pre-writing skills.

This kind of descriptive commenting can also be used with school-age children who are capable of writing words and sentences. As the child is writing a teacher can comment, "You have written four sentences now with some great, complex words. Can we read your story together?" Or, "I see that your first paragraph is finished! It has a main idea sentence and then three sentences that add information and details to your idea." Or, "You have written about the feelings of your character in that story, I am really getting to know about him and am thinking about what he will do next." Or, "You are really carefully paying attention to where your letters are on the line. That makes it easy to read your writing." "You have a capital letter at the beginning of each sentence and a punctuation mark at the end! You remember all of the writing rules that we have been learning." "Looks like you are writing nonfiction. You have many true details in your essay!"

PERSISTENCE COACHING

Persistence coaching is a method of talking to children that will help them begin to learn to persist with difficult tasks and continue to try hard despite frustrations, obstacles and difficulties. With this type of coaching, the teacher helps the child to recognize when he is concentrating, working hard, staying focused, paying attention and being calm or patient. The child will begin to learn that it is normal to struggle to learn something new, but with patience, persistence, practice and teacher support, he can eventually accomplish the task and feel proud of it. This is an important life message.

*Persistence coaching
is when the teacher names
the child's internal cognitive
state when she is being
patient, trying again,
staying calm, concentrating,
focusing or persisting
and working hard with
a difficult task.*

Children vary in their temperament and learning styles. Some are calm, quiet, slow to warm up, patient, focused, or attentive whereas others may be active, energetic, impulsive, inattentive, angry, or easily frustrated. Many children display more than one of these different traits at different times of day or in different situations. Despite these temperament variations, most young children will need teacher support to be able to persist and stay patient with a difficult task without getting overly frustrated or giving up. Some children will need more support to stick with it than others. *Persistence coaching* is when the teacher names the child's internal cognitive state when she is being patient, trying again, staying calm, concentrating, focusing or persisting and working hard with a difficult task. This type of coaching is beneficial for all children but is particularly important for inattentive, impulsive, and hyperactive children as well as children who are anxious and depressed. It helps them recognize times when they are focused, on-task and attentive, and working hard or confidently and what it feels like to be in that state. This coaching provides the brain scaffolding that a child needs to be able to stay calm and persistent for longer at learning something new than he would be able to do on his own.

In the next example a teacher is walking around in a large 2nd grade classroom while the students are working on a project to write sentences. Notice what coaching strategies this teacher uses.

"Diana is really working hard on her fine and detailed printing, and she is being very meticulous," and "Holly is printing slowly and carefully. She is really focusing." "Michael is really concentrating on his work and trying again to redo some of this letters." "Sidney is sticking with this project." "I am seeing some nice printing in this classroom. Our classroom will be an incredible classroom of great writers and authors ~ I can tell that! " Her tone of voice is sincere, warm and enthusiastic. The warm affect in her tone of voice and positive prediction is very encouraging, reinforcing and keeps the students working hard.

Here we see the teacher is focusing on the process of writing and working on this activity, rather than waiting to see the outcome. This approach has the positive side effect of reminding the whole classroom what they should be doing and providing an image of their eventual success. The next example, Soleil, an early school-age child is doing an art drawing activity that involves cutting some big sticky packing tape. Soleil is frustrated with her ability to cut and the teacher uses persistence coaching (and emotion coaching) to give her enough support so that she continues to persist with the activity.

> *Soleil asks the teacher for help cutting the sticky tape. The teacher says, "I will hold the tape while you cut. It is hard to cut, but I think you can do it." Soleil cuts the tape and the teacher enthusiastically says, "You cut the tape yourself!" Soleil responds, "I cut it" and the teacher asks, "Are you proud of yourself for cutting?" Soleil nods "Yes." The teacher replies, "You seem very proud of your work, and you are working really hard. You keep trying." When Soleil cuts again, the teacher says enthusiastically, "You did it" and then comments, "You seem happy that you were able to do that by yourself." As Soleil continues to work at cutting the teacher comments, "You are working hard and being very patient with the cutting process. It seems to be getting easier and easier for you."*

This teacher's persistence coaching helps Soleil to stay involved and persist with a difficult task. She readily acknowledges that Soleil is attempting to do something that is very difficult, which adds to the sense of accomplishment for Soleil. This is a new kind of language for many teachers. Statements such as, "You are working hard," "You are really focused," "That is frustrating and hard to do but you are staying patient with it," "You are really thinking, waiting and planning what to do next," "You figured it out yourself," or "You really concentrated and you solved the problem" are all examples of persistence coaching. This type of coaching can help your students modulate their feelings of frustration and desire to give up and stick with a difficult task without getting too dysregulated. The essence of learning is becoming able to continue to keep trying, to struggle with some discomfort or anxiety and at times failure in order to become more independent and resilient.

Scripts for Academic and Persistence Coaching

As we have seen academic and persistence coaching is a powerful way to strengthen students' language skills and academic concepts and to help them continue to try hard to learn something even when it is difficult and frustrating. Use this coaching checklist to reflect on your use of particular coaching skills.

TEACHER ACADEMIC COACHING CHECKLIST

Check which kinds of cognitive and academic behaviors you typically coach. Identify any you want to strengthen.

Academic Coaching: Objects, Actions, Shapes, Positions	Examples
❒ Colors, letters	"You have the red car and the yellow truck."
❒ Number counting	"There are one, two, three dinosaurs in a row."
❒ Shapes	"Now the square Lego is stuck to the round Lego."
❒ Names of objects	"That train is longer than the track."
❒ Sizes (long, short, tall, smaller than, bigger than, etc.)	"You are putting the tiny bolt in the right circle."
❒ Positions (up, down, beside, next to, on top, behind, etc.)	"The blue block is next to the yellow square, and the purple triangle is on top of the long red rectangle."
❒ Patterns, categories	"You are putting all six four-legged animals in one category, the four birds in another category and three insects in a third category. That is good sorting."
	"You're circling all the pictures that start with the 'tr' blend sound!"

Persistence Coaching: Cognitions & State of Mind	Examples
❒ Working hard	"You are working so hard on writing those words and thinking about where the next letter will go."
❒ Concentrating, focusing	"You are so patient and keep trying different ways to make that piece fit together."
❒ Staying calm, patient	"You are staying calm and trying again."
❒ Trying again	"You are thinking hard about how to solve the problem and coming up with another great solution to make a ship."
❒ Problem solving	"That math problem is difficult and you are working out how to add all those numbers together by thinking hard."
❒ Thinking skills	"You are thinking about your friend and helping him read that book."
❒ Reading	"You are really focused on your reading and taking your time."
❒ Going to do it	
❒ Being aware of another child's work activity	"Your friend is really concentrating too. You are both good learners."
Coaching School Readiness Behaviors	**Examples**
❒ Following teacher's directions ❒ Listening to teachers	"You followed directions exactly like I asked you. You really listened."
❒ Independence while working	"You have figured that out all by yourself."
❒ Exploring and trying out ideas ❒ Being curious about how things work	"You are really curious and exploring what makes that work in many different ways."
❒ Cooperating with other students on projects	"You are working as a team to figure out the plot of that story."

Children's brain neurological self-control, self-regulation, and persistence ability can be strengthened by teachers' coaching responses.

Keeping Developmental Expectations Appropriate—Laying the Brain Foundation for the Future

Developing concentration, persistence, and patience depends a lot on the student's particular temperament style and neurological, language, or stage of brain development. These cognitive skills develop at different times and there is a wide range of normal developmental variation across children. Remember children have immature brain development and acquire skills in stages. In the three- to eight-year-old age range the ability to pay attention and follow directions, persist at something even though frustrated, and control aggressive responses are developing skills. A few remarkable three-year-olds will already show some degree of self control while some eight-year-olds may still struggle with waiting, sitting still and staying regulated. During this stage of development children's brain neurological self-control, self-regulation, and persistence ability can be strengthened by teachers' coaching responses. In other words, a teacher might say to a student, "You are really waiting for a turn on the computer. I see you want it, but you are really being patient and waiting for your turn." This persistence coaching may help the child to wait and prevent him from pushing the child away in order to use the computer. With repeated persistence coaching, exposure to the concepts of being patient, calm, and persistent with a new learning activity, children will begin to internalize these words. By the early school age years children will be able to control more of their behavioral responses and attention span, but there will still be many children who don't develop control of their self-regulation skills, impulsivity, aggression, and ability to sustain their attention with a difficult task until six or seven years. So it is important for teachers to have realistic developmental expectations for each student and to vary the scaffolding given so that each child is supported according to their individual needs. Teachers' academic and persistence coaching will help to lay a firm brain foundation to support all students' learning in later years.

SOCIAL COACHING

Now that we have talked about how academic and persistence coaching helps strengthen children's language acquisition and school readiness concepts, we will discuss how to use *social coaching* to help students develop important friendship skills.  Strengthening children's social skills is important because classrooms where there is cooperative learning have been shown to predict improved academic achievement (Brown & Palincsar, 1989; Cawelti, 1995; Wang, Haertel, & Walberg, 1994). Social coaching and descriptive commenting can support children's friendship and communication skills, and their sense of self and independence. Children learn social skills through modeling, prompting, coaching, practicing, and receiving positive feedback. Social interactions involve complicated steps that must be repeated many times, and supported, encouraged and coached by teachers.

Children's social development progresses in much the same way that physical development does. Just as babies progress from holding up their heads, to sitting up, to pushing up, to crawling, to creeping, to walking, a parallel step-by-step process also occurs for children as they learn to become socially and emotionally mature. Toddlers under the age of three are egocentric, engage in parallel play, make very few initiations to peers and have very few prosocial skills. As children enter preschool and begin to interact with others, their first attempts are usually selfish! Preschoolers rarely share, wait, or take-turns! This is the age of "mine–mine–mine," and "I want what I want when I want it!" and curious exploration. Moreover, preschoolers are moving from the age of parallel play to increasing interactions with peers, but many do not have the prosocial skills to initiate or sustain positive, cooperative play for very long. One of the major developmental tasks for children of this age is to learn to interact in socially appropriate ways. These skills are invaluable to almost every interaction that a child will

Social skills, a prerequisite for academic learning, involve self-regulation, how to give and get help from others, work together, listen to others, communicate with others, and problem-solve.

have in the school environment for years to come. Social skills are also a prerequisite for academic learning since they involve self-regulation, how to give and get help from others, how to work together, how to listen to others, how to communicate with others, and how to problem-solve (Durlak, Weissberg, Dymnicki, Taylor, & Schellinger, 2011). Children who lack these skills suffer socially, but also are likely to exhibit behavioral difficulties in the classroom that impair their academic learning (Brown & Palincsar, 1989; Durlak, Weissberg, & Pachan, 2010).

Modeling Social Skills and Empathy During Teacher-Student Interactions

The first aspect of social coaching involves teachers modeling appropriate social skills themselves during teacher-student interactions. Remember that children learn by imitating or modeling what teachers do and say and even mirror the feelings shown on the teacher's face! When teachers interact with their students in ways that are respectful of their ideas or share their positive feelings, smile, offer friendly suggestions, compliment them, help them with a difficult activity, comply with their requests, or cooperate with them, they are modeling all these important social and relationship skills. Students will learn just by watching teachers demonstrate each skill. These are all behaviors that are harder for a preschooler or early school age student to learn in a play interaction with a same age peer because many times the other child doesn't have the developmental ability to engage in or model these positive interactive behaviors himself. When, a teacher or another adult plays with or responds to a child in this prosocial way, this modeling can take place. In the next example, think about what social skills the teacher is modeling as she plays with a group of four-year-old children using play dough, cookie cutters, a rolling pin, and some other wooden kitchen utensils.

> *The teacher says to Kyla, who has cut out a play dough butterfly with her cookie cutter, "You made a pretty butterfly,"* (models giving a compliment) *and Kyla replies, "Now I am making a monster." The teacher responds with eagerness, "That's a creative idea. I would like to see your monster."* (shows interest in her idea) *Next the teacher*

notices that Sam needs more play dough and she offers, "I can see you need more play dough, I will be your friend and share my play dough with you. Would you like my green play dough?" (models understanding of his perspective and sharing and being helpful) *Sam takes the play dough from the teacher's outreached hand and says,* "Thank you." *The teacher replies,* "You are very welcome. That was polite of you to say 'thank you.'" (models and praises his social skill) *Riley says,* "I need some blue play dough." *The teacher says,* "Riley, what a great way to ask for what you need. I think Annie was listening to you. I wonder if she will share some blue with you?" (praises appropriate social skill and gently prompts positive response). *Annie says,* "Here is some of mine." *The teacher responds,* "Annie you are a good friend to Riley. I'm having so much fun watching you friends sharing this play dough. You look like you're having fun being together. You are a real team." (models emotion sharing)

In this example the teacher is modeling and labeling the social skills of praise, agreement to another's idea, understanding of another's needs, sharing, offering to help, and polite behavior. Notice that the teacher described her own social behavior when she said, "I will be your friend and share my play dough with you" so that the children can learn what it looks like when one shares and that this behavior is something friends do with each other. The teacher also shares that she understands Sam's needs when she said, "I can see

Teachers modeling empathy helps children learn how to think about someone else's feelings and point of veiw.

you need more play dough." Thus she is modeling thinking about someone else's point of view or desires, a concept that is called by some developing *"theory of mind."* First, the teacher models an awareness of another's needs (empathy) and then labels this friendly behavior as sharing. Later the teacher extends this concept to the children's awareness of their peer's needs. As the teacher plays with this group, actively reinforcing and modeling these social skills, as she sees them use the skills with each other, she extends her descriptive comments to help them see how this is making each other feel.

Prompting Social Skills and Empathy During Teacher-Student Interactions

As we have seen in the prior example, modeling is when teachers model or demonstrate the social behaviors that they would like to encourage in their student's behavior, such as when the teacher modeled saying, "You are welcome" which showed the appropriate language response to someone saying "thank you." *Prompting*, on the other hand, is when teachers subtly prompt the student to use a particular social behavior. For example, a teacher can "prompt" a child's social behavior during play by asking for help with something, offering an idea, or asking for a turn with something her student is using. If the student responds to the teacher's prompt by accepting the teacher's request for help using her idea, or giving the teacher a turn, then the teacher can coach the student's friendly response by clearly and positively describing their social skill. For example, first the teacher prompts, "Could I have a turn with play dough?" The child says yes and gives her some play dough. The teacher replies, "That was so friendly. I wanted to play with the play dough and you shared it with me." This teacher prompt and her response is encouraging the child to understand someone else's perspective – a beginning step towards empathy or a theory of mind. However, if the child does not agree to share or help when a teacher uses a prompt, the teacher should model waiting and respect by saying, "I can see you are not ready to share yet, and I can wait for a turn. I'll play with the paint while I wait." Again, this teacher response indicates the teacher is modeling her understanding of the child's perspective as well as how to wait for a turn.

It is best not to force a child to share, for this will defeat the teacher's purpose. However, teachers can begin to teach a young child how to share or help others by modeling these behaviors herself, occasionally prompting, and coaching and praising the behavior whenever it does occur. It will often be easier for a student to share with a teacher or another adult than it will be to share with a peer, so teacher-child sharing is a good place to start. See if you can identify the "modeling" and "prompts" by this teacher as the group continues to play.

Kyla asks her teacher to make a worm for her out of play dough and the teacher agrees and starts making it. Kyla says, "Thank you" spontaneously and the teacher responds with a smile, "You are welcome." Then she asks Kyla, "Can I have some more of your blue play dough? I don't have enough to make a big worm." Kyla responds by handing her some more blue play dough and the teacher replies, "Thank you for sharing with me. That was friendly." A few minutes later, the teacher says, "It is getting so long and big I think I need some help. Sam you are a good roller, could you help?" Sam starts working with her on the worm and the teacher replies, "Wow, thank you Sam. You are such a helper, we are a team and are making this together, this is fun."

It is important to model and prompt social behaviors and enthusiastically describe them through coaching language whenever they occur. Remember that excessive prompting can be overwhelming for a child and can lead to resistance. Try to use 10 times more descriptive comments or coaching statements than prompts.

ADJUST COACHING FOR CHILD'S DEVELOPMENTAL LEVEL

The various coaching methods can be delivered strategically and tailored to meet a number of academic, social, and other behavioral goals according to children's needs and developmental levels. See below for examples of modeling and coaching statements for teacher-student interactions. Level 1 represents children who are developmentally still engaged in parallel play.

Teacher-Student Social Coaching: Child Developmental Play Level 1

The following table provides some examples of the script for Level 1 teacher social coaching. You can think of this as learning a new language to speak with your students. You might want to write some of these statements down to have handy to practice while you are interacting with your students. It may feel awkward at first but like learning any new language with practice it gets easier.

TEACHER SOCIAL COACHING SCRIPTS CHECKLIST (LEVEL 1)

Check which kinds of social behaviors you typically model, prompt, coach or praise. Identify any you want to strengthen.

Social/Friendship Skills	Examples
Teacher Models	
❒ Sharing	"I'm going to be your friend and share my marker with you."
❒ Offering to Help	"If you want, I can help you by holding the bottom while you put another on top."
❒ Waiting	"I can use my waiting muscles and wait until you're finished using that."
❒ Suggesting	"Could we build something together?"
❒ Complimenting	"You are so smart in figuring out how to put that together."
❒ Behavior-to-Feelings	"You shared with me. You knew I wanted to play with that too. That is so friendly and makes me feel happy."
	"You helped me figure out how to do that. I feel proud that you could show me that."
Teacher Prompts	
❒ Self-Talk	"Hmm, I really wish I could find another piece to fit here."
	"Hmm, I'm not sure I know how to put this together."
❒ Asking for help	"Can you help me find another round piece?"
	"Can you share one of your cars with me?"
	"This is hard, I might need some help."

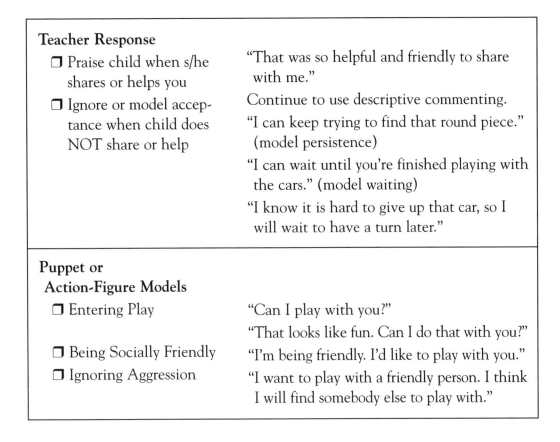

Teacher Response

- ❑ Praise child when s/he shares or helps you
- ❑ Ignore or model acceptance when child does NOT share or help

"That was so helpful and friendly to share with me."

Continue to use descriptive commenting.

"I can keep trying to find that round piece." (model persistence)

"I can wait until you're finished playing with the cars." (model waiting)

"I know it is hard to give up that car, so I will wait to have a turn later."

Puppet or Action-Figure Models

- ❑ Entering Play

- ❑ Being Socially Friendly
- ❑ Ignoring Aggression

"Can I play with you?"

"That looks like fun. Can I do that with you?"

"I'm being friendly. I'd like to play with you."

"I want to play with a friendly person. I think I will find somebody else to play with."

Teacher Peer Group Social Coaching

Teacher social coaching while students are playing with peers is immensely valuable for modeling and promoting social skills and strengthening friendships among classmates. Peer social coaching is somewhat different than individual teacher-child coaching because now teachers are facilitating the social interactions and relationships between students, rather than with the teacher. For example, a teacher can comment on times when she notices children are initiating friendly verbal interactions with each other, helping a friend, sharing with others, waiting and taking turns, or using words to ask for what they want. This social coaching will strengthen children's ability to learn social skills and to develop friendships. Teachers will adjust this type of coaching to the developmental level of their students. In preschool many children are just beginning to learn these friendship skills and some children are developmentally more impulsive, inattentive, distracted and energetic than others while others are more fearful and withdrawn so learning particular social skills can be more difficult for them. Young children are still in the age of curiosity, individual exploration and discovering their sense of self and autonomy. As children enter grade school, most children will begin to be able to apply more and more of the friendship skills with others that they have learned in preschool. This is when social coaching efforts will truly start to show some payoff. However it is important to remember that children still show great developmental variability in their ability to consistently apply their knowledge about social skills. In every 2nd and 3rd grade classroom there are likely to be several children who still struggle to regulate their emotions during social situations, and these children will need more intensive social and emotion coaching.

The following example shows a primary grade teacher using this social coaching language while he is teaching a group reading lesson using the blackboard. The students are participating from their desks. Think about what social skills these children are learning.

> *The teacher asks Lisa to read a word and when she has difficulty he says, "Can you ask Susie to help you with that word?" Susie helps Lisa by whispering the word in her ear, and Lisa says the word. The teacher responds, "Lisa, I love the way you accepted help and how you worked well with Susie." As the teacher continues to point to words, he asks the whole classroom to say the next word together. When they do so, he looks at the class and says, "I appreciate all those who have been listening, thinking and working together. This classroom is like a team. You are friends helping each other to learn. Thank you. You are all learning to read."*

Here we see that the teacher is helping his students learn how to help each other, how to ask for help, and what the benefits are for everyone. He is creating a feeling that the classroom is a family helping each other to succeed.

The following is another example of how teacher social coaching might occur in a 1st or 2nd grade classroom when students are working on a cooperative project.

The teacher walks over to a table where four boys are making a papier maché volcano. They are arguing over what shape it should be. The teacher says, "Sounds like you are trying to figure out what your volcano is going to look like. I can hear that you are all describing different ideas. It's good that you are talking together." Marcus replies, "They're not listening to my idea. I want it to be a really tall and skinny volcano with a deep pit on top." The teacher responds, "You described your idea really well, and I noticed just then that the others were listening. Now that they heard your idea, could you ask John what his idea is?" Marcus says, "John, what do you want to do?" John replies, "I want a really wide volcano like Mount St. Helen's." The teacher responds, "Marcus, it was really friendly of you to ask John, and all of you listened to him." (Teacher repeats this process until all ideas are heard.) *The teacher says, "Wow, you all have really good ideas and you were respecting each other as you shared your ideas. This is what good friends do. I wonder what should happen next? Can anyone think of a way to compromise and be a team together so that you can build this volcano?"* (If children are able to continue problem solving on their own, teacher might reinforce this process and move on. If children need more structure, she might introduce a possible solution and ask the children how they could make that solution work.)

In the next example in a preschool classroom, Kyla is seated on the floor next to her friend Jolie. They are each working on building a rather complex Lego structure and are having some trouble sharing and working together. See if you can pick out the prompts and peer coaching skills the teacher uses to try to facilitate some interactions and use of social skills.

Kyla begins to grab a Lego from Jolie's pile of blocks. The teacher notices this and says to her, " I can see you want that block, you can ask Jolie for that green rectangle Lego by saying, 'Can I have one of your green Legos please?'" Kyla repeats the words, but in a quiet voice, looking away from Jolie. The teacher says, "Kyla, I don't think Jolie heard you. Can you use a louder voice and say her name,

'Jolie, can I please have the green Lego.'" Kyla repeats the request in a louder voice. Teacher praises saying, "Wow! What a polite way to ask." Jolie continues playing, seemingly unaware of the request so the teacher says, "Jolie, I heard Kyla ask you for a green Lego. Can you let her know if she can use it?" Jolie says, "No, I'm not done with it." Teacher says, "Jolie, thank you for answering your friend. Kyla, I think that Jolie will let you have a turn when she is done. I see you waiting for a turn. I wonder what you can build while you wait?" As Kyla works with the blue Legos the teacher says, "You are very patient and doing some good waiting, and I think you have strong waiting muscles." Kyla responds by giving the teacher a blue Lego and the teacher thanks her and praises her for nice sharing, "You are good at sharing and that makes me feel happy." Then the teacher describes Jolie's structure by saying, "Jolie, you are working hard building that big fort. You are really concentrating." Jolie responds by handing some of her green Legos to Kyla who seems not to notice. The teacher responds, "Thank you Jolie. That is very friendly sharing" and she points out to Kyla, "Your friend Jolie is sharing her green Legos with you now. You can say, 'Thank you.'" Kyla says, "Thank you" and the teacher replies, "You're welcome" and Jolie repeats this. The teacher prompts Kyla, "Can you share some of your blue Legos with your friend, Jolie? That would be called trading ~ a green one for a blue one."

Without this teacher's social coaching, these two children would likely have had few positive interactions with each other. It's probable that they would have worked on independent parts of their Lego project until one of them grabbed what she wanted from the other and created some crying or unhappiness. This coaching was necessary for them to have this opportunity to learn what words to use to ask for what they want, to be able to wait, and even to be aware of each other's requests, needs or helping behaviors. These children are moving from Level 1 where they are completely in parallel play to Level 2 where they are beginning to interact with peers, but need much support to do so. At this stage, the teacher serves to provide the script for the interaction, giving the children the words to say to help navigate the social interactions. Try to avoid vague phrases like, "Use your words" because very often young children don't know what words to use to get what they want. Instead model or gently suggest to them the words they can use. If they copy your words, praise them and if they ignore you, let it go.

Teacher Peer Group Social Coaching: Child Developmental Play Level 2

The following table provides some examples of the script for teacher social coaching with multiple children. Remember that without teacher coaching, young children are unlikely to initiate much sharing or helping behaviors and will likely have conflicts over things that each other wants. With this type of peer group social coaching, teachers can prompt the children to notice each other's moods, needs and activities and help support their social interactions. Teachers can still use themselves as a prosocial model remembering all the teacher-student coaching tips from the Level 1 table shown earlier.

Social Skills Training with Children of Different Ages and Developmental Stages

The practicalities of classroom activities means that most of the time the teacher will be facilitating interactions between students who are at very different developmental levels or different temperament styles. All of the ideas for coaching level 2 peer play will be useful when coaching students of differing developmental abilities. However, primary grade teachers in particular will also need to take into account that there are additional challenges to accommodate the differing developmental levels of children (ages 5-8 years). Even children who are at the same chronological age can be at very different stages socially, emotionally and developmentally. Some children in this age range are still in Piaget's "preoperational level" of cognitive development and are intermixing fantasy and reality and unable to understand the rules of games, or temperamentally cannot wait and take turns, whereas others are in the "concrete operational level" and are obsessed by the rules (Piaget & Inhelder, 1962). Without teacher support and social coaching, interactions between early school age children can lead to anger and bullying on the one hand, or withdrawal

TEACHER SOCIAL COACHING SCRIPTS CHECKLIST (LEVEL 2)

Check which kinds of social behaviors you typically model, prompt, coach or praise. Identify any you want to strengthen.

Social/Friendship Skills	Examples
Teacher Coaches	
❐ Asking for What They Want	"You can ask your friend for what you want by saying, 'Please can I have a turn on the computer?'"
❐ Asking for Help	"You can ask your friend for help by saying 'Can you help me?'"
❐ Asking a Friend to Wait	"You can tell your friend you are not ready to share yet."
	If your student responds to your prompt by using his or her words to repeat what you said, praise this polite asking or friendly helping.
Teacher Prompting	
❐ A Child to Notice Another Child	"Wow, look what a big tower your friend is building."
	"You are both using green markers."
	"I think Tim wants to tell you something."
❐ Initiate Interaction With or Helping Noticing Another Child	"Your friend is looking for small green pieces. Can you find some for him?"
	"Your friend has no cars and you have 8 cars. He looks unhappy. Can you share one of your cars with your friend?"

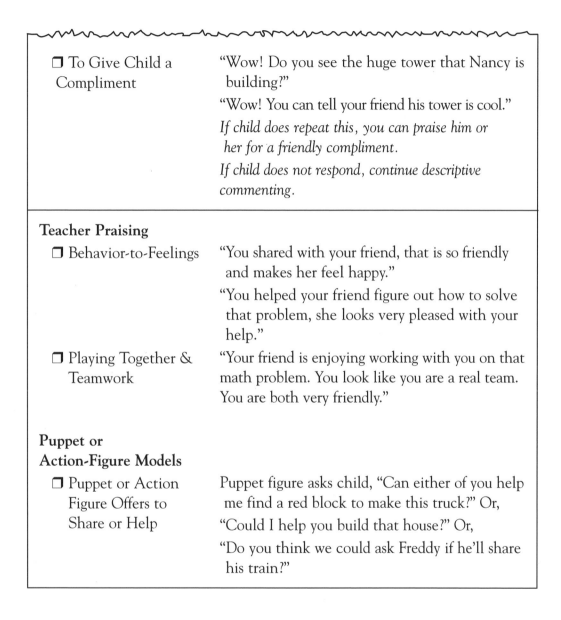

❒ To Give Child a Compliment	"Wow! Do you see the huge tower that Nancy is building?"
	"Wow! You can tell your friend his tower is cool."
	If child does repeat this, you can praise him or her for a friendly compliment.
	If child does not respond, continue descriptive commenting.

Teacher Praising

❒ Behavior-to-Feelings	"You shared with your friend, that is so friendly and makes her feel happy."
	"You helped your friend figure out how to solve that problem, she looks very pleased with your help."
❒ Playing Together & Teamwork	"Your friend is enjoying working with you on that math problem. You look like you are a real team. You are both very friendly."

Puppet or Action-Figure Models

❒ Puppet or Action Figure Offers to Share or Help	Puppet figure asks child, "Can either of you help me find a red block to make this truck?" Or,
	"Could I help you build that house?" Or,
	"Do you think we could ask Freddy if he'll share his train?"

and anxiety on the other hand. It is important that children not be criticized by teachers for their inability to understand the rules of a game because it is part of normal developmental variation in the 3-8 year age range and something they can't help. It is also important to help protect more advanced children's games and possessions from the destructiveness of hyperactive, disruptive students who can easily ruin a complicated Lego model or art project that a child has spent hours building. Thus, when coaching children, teachers need to be sensitive to protecting developmentally delayed children from being bullied or isolated, while at the same time protecting the more developmentally advanced child from the impatience and tantrums of a more impulsive child. With patience, teachers can coach children in such a way that children learn the skills of being empathic and forgiving of each other. If teachers enlist their more empathic and developmentally advanced or articulate children in the process, they can actually be great models of positive social skills for children who are less skilled at this. See if you can identify the strategies the primary grade teacher is using in the next example to promote social skills between two children who are at two different developmental levels.

> *The teacher suggests that Liz, an anxious, fearful girl, use her words to ask her friend, Matias, to use the computer. The teacher models the words for her to use by saying, "Tell Matias, 'please can I have a turn on the computer?'" When Matias shares the computer, the teacher prompts the girl to say, 'Thank you' and shows appreciation to Matias for sharing with her by saying, "Thank you for thinking of your friend's feelings. That was very kind. Can you help her learn how to do that matching game on the computer? I saw you were good at that." The teacher thanks Matias for his help, "Wow you have taught your friend how to match those pictures. You are a team, I'm proud of how you helped Liz, you both are like a team and had a good time." Matias responds, "She did a good job." The teacher responds, "Wow you are really good at giving compliments, see how happy Liz is now."*

In this interaction the two children are learning social skills as a result of this teacher's social coaching. Other children in the classroom listening to this exchange will also learn about what behavior gets the teacher's attention and approval. Liz is learning to be brave enough to use her words to ask for what she wants and to be polite when she gets what she wants. She is learning from the modeling and prompting by the teacher as well as from Matias' helping behaviors. In turn, Matias is learning to be patient and caring for a friend. He receives praise from the teacher and then passes this praise on to his friend. Without this teacher's coaching, none of this learning would have likely happened. Instead Matias would have continued on the computer and the girl would have stood by helplessly watching.

Here is another example of a preschool teacher coaching four children playing in the kitchen area of the classroom.

Daniel asks his friend Lia to put the crackers in the bowl and not in the cupcake tin. The teacher repeats Daniel's request to Lia and models what to do by putting her own crackers in the bowl. Lia copies her by putting her crackers in the bowl as well. The teacher praises and hugs Lia for listening and following her friend's suggestions. She says, "Lia that was very friendly." Another child, Seth, watches this and decides to put his crackers in the bowl too. The teacher then prompts Daniel, "Daniel did you see that Lia and Seth both did what you asked them to do? They are good friends. You can say, thank you." Daniel ignores this response and stirs the crackers in the bowl with a spoon and then suggests, "We need some liquid." The teacher hands him a pan of pretend warm milk saying, "I will share my milk with you." (modeling cooperation) *Lia and Seth ask for milk too and the teacher lets Daniel know that his friends want more milk. A fourth child, Julie, joins in the group and wants to cook as well. Daniel says, "I need more crackers." Lia says, "These are mine" and points to her crackers. Seth says, "These are mine" as well. The teacher confirms that Seth and Lia have crackers but Julie doesn't have any crackers. The teacher suggests, "I wonder if anyone could be a good friend and share crackers with Julie. She doesn't have any." The teacher asks Daniel for some ideas for what they will do to help Julie. Daniel then notices that Lia has given Julie some of her crackers. He says to the teacher, "Look Lia gave Julie some of her crackers."* (He is now noticing Lia's social skill) *The teacher replies, "Lia you are really friendly and generous, you have made Julie feel happy because you shared your crackers with her."* (The teacher reinforces Lia's social behavior and ignores the fact that Daniel is not sharing.) *Daniel notices the teacher's praise to Lia and says,*

"Julie you can have some of mine too" and Seth watching this also gives her some of his crackers. The teacher responds, "Wow you are building a real team helping each other, that is what friends do for each other."

This teacher does a combination of prompting behaviors and descriptive commenting of social behaviors to get the children to notice what each other needs and how they are helping each other. She models social skills, and praises their sharing efforts. She does not give attention at times when the children ignore her suggestions or when they are selfish, so that these interactions will not turn into power struggles. This back and forth prompting and coaching is teaching the children appropriate social interactions and helping them develop positive relationships.

Coaching of children's social interactions is probably one of the most exhausting and important tasks for teachers. It often involves a juggling act, with the teachers trying to alternate their attention, coaching, prompting and encouragement between many students who are each wanting their teacher's undivided attention. It involves meeting the developmental needs of children at different stages of language, social and emotional development and being able to see the interaction from the different points of view of each child. In the long run, this social coaching will pay off and will result in a happier classroom with children who will learn to help each other, cooperate and are able to appreciate each other's differences and strengths. In turn, this will lead to greater academic learning as well.

EMOTION COACHING TO ENCOURAGE BEHAVIORAL SELF-REGULATION

The fourth kind of foundational building block for the teaching pyramid that is helpful for nurturing students' learning is called *"emotion coaching."* This communication approach helps children begin to develop feelings literacy; that is, a vocabulary for expressing their emotions to teachers and others. Teachers start this coaching by naming the students' emotions whenever they see a child is experiencing an emotion such as being happy, confident, calm, surprised, excited, curious, proud, brave, frustrated, sad, lonely, worried, disappointed, tense, or angry. Labeling the feeling at the time that the child is experiencing it allows the child to associate the feeling word with an internal emotional state. Once children have developed

Emotion coaching eventually leads to children's development of empathy for others' feelings and viewpoints.

an emotion vocabulary, then they can recognize their own feelings and verbally share their feelings with others. This results in their ability to more easily regulate their emotional and behavioral responses. Did you know that most preschoolers only know 2.5 words for feelings —mad and sad and sometimes happy? Even then, they often cannot correctly distinguish between mad and sad. The goal is to help children to have a richer vocabulary to express their feelings, hopefully to recognize more happy feelings than negative or distressful ones, and to learn how they can cope with their negative feelings. Using emotion coaching when children are feeling unpleasant or uncomfortable emotions will help to build their self-confidence and scaffold their ability to self-regulate when upset. Commenting on their happy, joyful, proud, calm, curious, brave and excited emotions will increase their self-awareness of these pleasant moods. Children who can understand, verbalize, and regulate their own feelings will ultimately be able to recognize feelings in others and sensitively respond to them. Thus, emotion coaching eventually leads to children's development of empathy for others' feelings and viewpoints.

Scripts for Emotion Coaching

The following is a list of emotions and scripts that can be commented upon when interacting with your students during the day. Use this checklist to reflect on the type of emotion words you focus on with your students and practice using some different emotional vocabulary than you normally use. Think about the needs for individual students' behavior plans for target emotion vocabulary you will try to coach them.

TEACHER EMOTION COACHING CHECKLIST

Check which kinds of emotions you typically model, prompt or coach. Identify any you want to strengthen for specific children.

Emotions	Examples
❏ Happy	"You look like you are having fun playing with your friend, and he looks like he is happy and excited doing this with you."
❏ Frustrated	"That is frustrating and hard to do but you are staying calm and patient and keep trying again to figure out how to it. I think you are going to get it."
❏ Proud/Pleased	"You look proud of that drawing, I know that you worked for a long time to get the details just the way you wanted them!"
❏ Confident	"You seem confident and calm when reading that story. You seem like you feel very sure about your reading!"
❏ Patient	"You are so patient. Even though it fell down twice, you just keep trying to see how you can make it taller. You must feel pleased with yourself for being so patient."
❏ Disappointed	"I can see you are disappointed that he wouldn't share with you. But you stayed so calm and were just so brave by going to ask someone else to play. That is a very strong thing to do."
❏ Worried/Fearful	"You look afraid to do that. Sometimes that can be scary. I think you have the courage to try that out."
❏ Jealous	"I can see you are a bit jealous and wish you had one of those. I wish I had one too. Maybe we can ask him to show us how it works. You are getting braver every day."

❏ Forgiving	"You are forgiving of your friend because you know he made a mistake. Everyone makes mistakes sometimes. I am proud of you for still being his friend."
❏ Curious	"You are so curious. You are trying out and discovering every way that can work."
❏ Embarrassed	"It is embarrassing to spill that everywhere. Sometimes I drop things too and get paint all over my clothes, and then I am a bit embarrassed too."
❏ Caring	"You are so caring and thoughtful. You are thinking about your friend's feelings and are really helpful and kind. Your friend looks like she feels calmer now because you helped her."
❏ Mad	"I can see you are really mad that he grabbed that away from you. I am really proud that you kept your body calm and used your words."
❏ Nervous	"I can see you are nervous the whole thing will fall down. You are being careful and patient and staying calm."

Coaching Positive Emotions

Coaching positive or pleasant emotions is straightforward. Practice noticing and labeling each emotion that you see, along with the reason a child may be feeling that way. For example, "You look like you are really excited about finishing that project! Your whole body is bouncing!" or, "Your face looks so proud right now. It was hard to finish that problem together but you did it!" or, "You've got the biggest smile on your face. Your wrote that word neatly and carefully," or, "You read that book to your friend and that made her feel happy." "It looks like your hard work paid off. You seem really satisfied with the way that

Teachers should notice five times more positive than negative feelings in children.

this project turned out. I know it took careful and patient planning." If teachers provide the name for the emotion and some information about what behavior led to the emotion, they are helping the student link the feeling with the cause. Teachers can also include information about the clues they used to guess the emotion (smile, bouncing body). This will help the teacher tune the child into physical cues about feelings. Try to coach as many positive feeling states as you can. If teachers pay attention to a range of positive feelings, children will actually start to be in a positive feeling state more often. In other words, teacher attention to these feelings can make children feel happier, more joyful, and more proud of themselves. A good rule of thumb is to try to notice five times more positive than negative feelings in children.

Pair Negative Emotion Coaching with Coping Responses

Coaching children's negative or unpleasant emotions is a little trickier because excessive teacher attention to negative emotions can make children feel more frustrated, angry, or sad. However, if done skillfully, coaching of unpleasant emotions can help children feel validated and understood, as well as help them regulate their mood and calm down and learn that these unpleasant feelings are normal reactions and change with time. To do this it is important to pair teacher comments about children's negative feelings with positive coping statements. For example, a child is having trouble learning to add two-digit numbers together and the teacher says, "That is frustrating, but you are staying so patient. I see you working hard. You keep trying and I think you are going to get it right!"

Teachers validate the unpleasant feeling, avoid giving it too much attention, and focus on a coping response.

Or, a child is disappointed because he wanted to finish a project, but it is time to move on to another activity. The teacher says, "That must be very disappointing for you. I'm really sorry. Even though you are unhappy about having to stop, you are staying calm and starting to put things away. Let's make a plan to give you some time to work on this project later. " Note that the goal is not for children to immediately change unpleasant feelings into happy ones, but rather to suggest that the child has the ability to cope with the unhappy feelings. In this way, teachers validate the unpleasant feeling, avoid giving it too much attention, focus on a coping response to the negative feelings, and predict an eventual positive change in the negative feeling. This may even pre-empt a negative response, such as a temper tantrum.

However, it is also possible that a child may be too dysregulated to listen to a teacher's emotion coaching. If a teacher has labeled the unpleasant emotion once and provided the coping strategy, and the child continues to cry hard or to tantrum, then it is a good idea for the teacher to back off, ignore it, and give the child some space to calm down himself before talking again. Additional attention or talking during the tantrum will likely prolong the fussing. When the child has finally calmed down, then the teacher can label that emotion. "Your body is looking much calmer now. You really tried hard to calm yourself down. You are getting strong at learning to do that. Come and join us at the reading table." When one student is out of control, unhappy, tantruming, or whining excessively, teachers can help the other students by labeling his feeling and then coaching them to give the student privacy. For example, "John is frustrated right now. The best way to help him is to give him some privacy to calm down and then we'll be able to help him feel better. You can help him by ignoring."

When one student is out of control, teachers can help the other students by labeling his feeling and then coaching them to give the student privacy.

Sensitive teachers will be tuned in to the difference between tantrums or crying because things are not going a student's way and true unhappiness, hurt, or grief. A typical tantrum is best ignored, while a student who is truly heart-broken will need more teacher support and understanding. In these situations, a teacher can still label emotions and provide coping thoughts, but may also provide more support through the emotional reactions. For example the teacher may say, "Billy, I am so, so sorry to hear that your dog died. I know how much you loved him, and I see that you are so sad and maybe a little mad. Sometimes it's hard to keep our bodies safe when we're feeling so awful, and it can take a long while to feel better. Let's find a place where we can sit together, where your body can be safe."

Tailoring Emotion Coaching to Your Student's Temperament

Once teachers have learned how to generally coach children's emotions, the next task will be to tailor emotion coaching to the particular temperament or emotional needs of each individual student. Remember we talked about how every child is different temperamentally and developmentally. For example, a withdrawn, anxious, isolated, or fearful child will benefit from focused coaching when he takes risks and tries something new. The teacher can say, "You are so brave, you put up your hand and shared something interesting" or, "That was really courageous to invite him to help you" or, "I could see it was scary to talk to that girl, but you did it and now you are enjoying playing together!" On the other hand, children who are angry and defiant should receive extra emotion coaching at times when they are calm, relaxed, patient, joyful and agreeable. For example, the teacher can say, "You seem happy and peaceful now. You went along with your friend's suggestion and it worked out well for you both." Children who are impulsive and inattentive need to be coached especially when they are staying calm, patient, and are able to wait and are thoughtful in their responses. The next example shows a teacher working with a preschool child who is often impulsive, inattentive, and quick to throw a tantrum when he doesn't get what he wants.

> *The child is sitting at the lunch table waiting for the other children to come. The teacher says, "Gregory, you are waiting so patiently. Your body is calm and still! I can see from your face that you are excited that it is lunch time, but I appreciate that your hands are to your own body! Would you help me pass out these cups. As Gregory passes out cups, the teacher comments, "You are passing carefully and slowly, and each cup that you put down is staying right side up. I bet you are proud of being able to help your friends. I'm grateful to have such a calm, patient helper!"*

This teacher recognizes that it takes a great deal of self-control for Gregory to sit still, control his body, and pass out cups. She wants to highlight his calm body so that he associates the regulated feeling with the word, and with her approval for his self-control. She also gives him a special job to further reinforce her pride in his ability to stay regulated.

In the next example, think about the emotion coaching used by a 2nd grade teacher who is working with a girl who has a reading delay.

Anna is trying to read the book out loud to her teacher. She is strug-gling with the words. The rest of the class are reading silently on their own. She tries to read a word and can't say the word, and her teacher responds, "This is frustrating and hard work but you are staying calm and keep trying. I think you are going get it, it starts with the letter bb.. bee" and Anna repeats the letter, "b..eev..er." The teacher repeats the word and says, "Wow, that's not easy but you were patient and you did it, you look proud. Each day you learn more words. Let's try the next word."

As demonstrated in this example, the teacher supports Anna's insecure and frustrated feelings by pointing out her persistence and predicting her eventual success. She gives Anna a bit of scaffolding to help her be successful and to build her self-confidence and ability to stay focused on this difficult learning process.

Combine Emotion and Persistence Coaching

Remember the persistence coaching we discussed earlier? Emotion coaching can often be combined with persistence coaching because tasks that require persistence can often be frustrating and difficult at first. However if a child persists, then proud feelings of accomplish-ment and self-confidence may result. Notice how the teacher in this next example combines persistence and emotion coaching to help Soleil with the frustrating task of cutting and using large, sticky packing tape. The task is beyond the girl's developmental ability and could be quite frustrating. Most children would give up. Let's see how this teacher encourages the girl's need for independence as she continues to try to do this difficult task herself.

Soleil is working hard on cutting some big sticky tape and the teacher comments, "You are being very patient with the tape and now you have cut three pieces of tape." Soleil starts to cut again and asks the teacher to hold the tape. The teacher holds the tape for her and

Soleil successfully cuts another piece of tape. The teacher smiles at her and appreciates her accomplishment by saying, "You look proud of your cutting." As Soleil puts the tape on her picture, the teacher comments, "You have been so focused on this work. Do you like this picture?" And when Soleil says yes, the teacher says, "I am glad you like your picture, you have worked hard on it." Soleil cuts another piece of tape but seems to be getting upset. The teacher asks, "Are you getting frustrated with the tape?" Soleil says "No" but looks more frustrated and asks her teacher for help. The teacher acknowledges her feelings by saying, "It is frustrating when the tape gets stuck together. You're doing a great job of keeping your body calm even though you are frustrated. You keep working at it and are patient." The teacher continues by saying, " You are working so diligently with the tape and you are feeling so..." The teacher leaves a pause here so that Soleil has a chance to identify her own feeling.

Here is an example of how a teacher is combining the persistence coaching discussed earlier with the emotion coaching strategies. The teacher effectively helps her student keep working on this frustrating task by acknowledging the frustrated feelings but then moving on to her persistence at working hard, staying focused, and staying calm. The teacher gives her just enough support to keep her student going without taking over the activity and doing it for her. Soleil ends up feeling very proud of her accomplishment.

Using Pretend Play to Promote Social and Emotional Skills

Pretend or imaginary play is a good way for teachers to help their students practice social and emotional skills by using all the coaching skills mentioned above: prompting, modeling, descriptive comments, and encouragement. Using a puppet, doll, or action figure can be a fun way to enter into children's imaginary worlds. For example, through the use of a puppet teachers can ask a child, "Will you play with me?" These are the friendly words a young child needs to learn to initiate an interaction with a peer. If the student ignores the puppet's overture, the puppet can ask again, modeling how one can keep trying. Or, if this still doesn't work, the puppet can say, "I'm disappointed but I'll be patient and wait until you have finished with that and then maybe you will play with me." On the other hand, if the student

Imaginary play with teachers helps students learn empathy skills.

agrees to let the puppet play with him the puppet can reply, "Thank you. That makes me happy. You are a friend. What shall we do?" Teachers can also engage in imaginary play by pretending to be a hungry horse or happy cow or grumpy pig, or by making the noise of a tired airplane or train. For example, if some students are making play dough cookies, the teacher can pretend they are real and say, "I'm hungry, can I have a taste of your green cookie?" If one of the students offers the teacher a bite, the teacher pretends to eat some and then comments on how good they taste. "I'm so happy to enjoy your delicious cookies! Thank you for being such a kind cook." With pretend phones teachers can make up imaginary calls. Using doll houses or Legos with figures (e.g., doctor, policeman) a teacher can have a character pretend to be sick or model coming to the rescue when a house is burning down. By taking on the role of a character or action figure in pretend play, the teacher is helping her students practice social skills, express feelings with emotion language, and understand the emotions of another. It can be a powerful way to promote children's imaginary worlds as well as to help them experience the perspective and feelings of another character. This is the beginning of empathy development.

After kindergarten, there seems to be less time in school schedules for imaginary play. Teachers in these classrooms can try to foster students' fantasy world by asking them to write or tell stories about certain situations. For example, the teacher can present some typical classroom scenarios such as, a child wants to read a book someone else is reading and that person won't share the book with her, or a child who is accused by other children of cheating at a game.

Then the teacher can ask the children to write or transcribe stories about the children's feelings or what things they can do to be friendly or feel better. Afterwards groups of children could work together to act out their plays taking on the various parts. Many children's books are written around social problems (sharing, bullying, friendship problems). These can be used as jumping off points for children to brainstorm, role play, or write about solutions.

Extending Coaching Skills to Other Times than Play

Social, emotion, academic, and persistence coaching is a way of communicating and interacting that teachers can use most any time during the day – such as during lunch times, during work time, in the school hallway, or on the play ground. By using this coaching throughout the day teachers will be contributing to their students' optimal language, social and emotional development as well as strengthening their relationship with them. In the next example two teachers are using child-centered social coaching during breakfast with the children at their table. Think about what these children are learning.

> *The teacher praises Rebecca for good eating. She is eating yogurt, and the teacher says, "That is very healthy food." Can you pass the bowl of yogurt to your friends to see if they want any more?"* (Prompting a share.) *She says, "Okay" and the teacher thanks her, "You are a good yogurt sharer."* (Praise for sharing.) *Another child observes this sharing and imitates it by passing the cookie plate and the teacher responds, "Malcolm, thank you for passing those, you are really helping your friends and they look pleased."* (Modeling a polite response.) *Another child says, "Anyone want some carrots?" The teacher responds, "Wow sharing points all around. You can dip your carrots in the yogurt."* (Descriptive praise.) *The teacher says, "Food tastes better when you share it, don't you think?"*

Coaching can be used during work time in older students' classrooms, perhaps as the teacher circulates around the room to monitor students' progress. See how this next teacher combines all the different types of coaching.

"John, thank you for taking your time to check your work." (persistence) *"Maya, I'm so proud of you for figuring that out. I can see it was hard, but you stuck with it. You must be feeling really good about your accomplishment."* (persistence and emotion coaching) *"Let's see Andrew. It looks like you're stuck on that part. You've got the first part of the word right. I'm going to let you work with your buddy to get that next part."* When he gets some help, the teacher says: *"Thank you two for working together on that—it's important to be able to get help from a friend."* (social coaching) *"Simon, I see you are using alliteration in that sentence—so many words that start with 'l'. That sentence is fun to say!"* (academic coaching) *"Sally, I appreciate the way you are sitting quietly and calmly in your seat while you work."*

We can see that this teacher is tailoring her comments to the needs of each student. She is also able to fit in this coaching as part of her regular teaching routine.

Teach and Encourage Parents to Use Descriptive Commenting and Coaching Strategies at Home with their Children

Encourage your students' parents to do this child-directed descriptive commenting and coaching during their play and reading times at home with their children. Teachers can offer workshops to parents to train them in these coaching skills at monthly parent night meetings or by sending home regular newsletters. Incredible Years has a specific 4- to 6-session School Readiness Parent Program that teachers can use for showing preschool and kindergarten parents video examples of coaching methods. If English is not the parents' first language, encourage them to speak in the language that they know best because when they do so their rhythm, cadence and tone of voice will be more natural and fluent. This commenting has the same effect regardless of what language it is done in. Encourage parents to find books in their own language or tell them stories about their culture and help them feel proud of their language. For children in a

Teachers can offer workshops to parents to train them in these coaching skills or send home regular newsletters.

bilingual environment, the number of words the child can speak will be split between the two languages s/he is learning. Also help parents understand that sometimes children who are exposed to more than one language are initially a little slower to use either language because they are sorting out the different sounds and meanings. Tell them not to worry because these initial delays will go away eventually and their child will be able to distinguish between different syllables and use the two languages with ease after a while.

CONCLUSION

When teachers interact with their students using a child-directed approach coupled with academic and persistence coaching they are showing students they are interested in what they are thinking and doing and that they appreciate their curiosity, discoveries and exploration of ideas. This approach strengthens the teacher-student learning relationship as well as supporting students' cognitive and language development and process for learning academic skills. By doing this teachers are scaffolding children's attention and beginning to help them learn how to stay focused, calm and to persist with their work despite many classroom distractions and feelings of frustration as they try to learn something new or explore an idea. As teachers support this learning and cognitive brain development, they are still allowing for children's developmental need for autonomy and independent exploration, which further enhances their motivation to learn.

When teachers use social and emotion coaching with students, they are modeling empathy and understanding and helping their students develop specific social skills and emotional literacy. This approach enhances teachers' emotional connections with their students as well as setting the stage for promoting supportive friendships with their classmates. In so doing, teachers are strengthening their students' social and emotional brain development because understanding and expressing feelings is the first step toward self-regulation and eventual development of empathy for others' point of view. Understanding and using specific social skills such as asking, waiting, cooperating, sharing, complimenting and forgiving are core to successful friendships, increased sense of security and self-confidence and better cooperative learning processes among children. By scaffolding students' negative feelings with emphasis on their coping responses (waiting patiently and trying again in contrast to whining or giving up) teachers are giving more focused attention to students' positive feelings and coping strategies, and are helping them learn how to stay calm despite feelings of frustration as they try to learn something new. Academic, persistence, social and emotion coaching are tools at the bottom of the teaching pyramid that help to build a stable classroom foundation that optimizes children's ability to learn.

To continue the gardening metaphor, by carefully selecting coaching tools according to students' individual developmental needs, teachers are training and gently supporting weaker branches of the plant until they have the strength to flourish amidst a variety of other types of plants.

TO SUM UP...

Teacher Academic and Persistence Coaching Skills

Academic and Language Coaching
- Use many more descriptive comments than questions.
- Describe children's actions, objects, positions (inside, beside, next to), colors, numbers, shapes.
- Notice and talk about what students are interested in.
- Prompt children with language difficulties to communicate by modeling words and suggesting sentences to repeat.
- Praise and give positive feedback to students for expressing their ideas (that is a great suggestion you gave!).
- Use new and more complex words to expand children's vocabulary.
- Listen to, imitate, or mirror student's words and sentences.
- Describe your own actions to your students (e.g., "I'm putting my folder in my desk now).
- Share your feelings of joy with your students.
- Avoid correcting or criticizing a child's exploration process; praise self-discovery and creativity.

Persistence Coaching
- Describe when students are working hard, concentrating, being calm, staying patient when doing an activity, being curious or engaged in the discovery process.
- Describe students' persistence with a frustrating activity by trying again, sticking with it, thinking of a new way to do it, and staying focused.

- Listen carefully to your students and try to understand what they are telling you about their thoughts, ideas and discoveries.
- Comment and praise your students for listening to their peers or to you.
- Use puppets to make up stories and model persistence coaching using the puppets words.
- Use make-believe games such as toy telephones or hand puppets or dramas to encourage communication.
- Encourage students to discover, explore, experiment and provide support when mistakes are made.
- Curb your desire to give too much help—give just enough support to avoid frustration but not so much you take over the exploration —encourage students' problem solving thinking process.
- Inform parents about academic and persistence coaching methods which they can use at home in their play interactions; tailor coaching to students' particular learning needs.

TO SUM UP...

Teacher Social Coaching

Teacher-Child Interactions
- During play interactions, model social skills for children such as offering to share, waiting, giving a compliment, taking turns, asking for help.
- Prompt children to ask for help, take a turn, share something, or give a compliment and then praise them if it occurs; let it go if the child does not respond to your prompt.
- Praise children any time they offer to share with friends or help them.
- Participate in pretend and make-believe play with children by using a doll, action figure, or puppet to model skills such as asking to play, offering to help, taking a turn, giving a compliment, calming down with a deep breath and waiting, and apologizing.

- Model and prompt children with a suggestion of the appropriate friendly words to ask for what they want or to make a suggestion.
- Try to give enough help so children are successful, but not so much help that you take over.

Peer Group Teacher Social Coaching

- Occasionally prompt students to notice what their peers are doing or to help another student in some way.
- Help children understand that when they have shared, that the other person felt happy; this helps them see the connection between their behavior and another's feelings.
- Praise and encourage children's teamwork and cooperation.
- Use descriptive comments instead of asking questions.
- Prompt, coach, and praise children's friendly behaviors whenever you see them (e.g., sharing, helping, taking turns, being polite).
- Laugh and have fun with your students.
- Help parents know about specific social skills you are working on in the classroom throughout the year.
- Help parents know about good friendship matches in the classroom so they can set up play dates.

TO SUM UP...

Teacher Emotion Coaching Skills

- Try to understand what the students are feeling and wanting.
- Describe children's feelings when teachers see them ~ avoid asking a child what they are feeling or why they are feeling that way because they may not have the words to tell you.
- Label children's positive feelings more often than their negative feelings.
- When naming negative feelings such as frustration or anger, point out the coping strategy the child is using: "You look frustrated, but you are staying calm and trying again."

- Praise children's self-regulation skills such as staying calm, being patient, trying again when frustrated, waiting a turn, and using words.
- Support children when they are frustrated, but recognize when a child is too upset to listen and just needs space and privacy to calm down.
- Model the words and encourage children to use words to use to express their feelings and needs.
- Help students learn ways to self-regulate such as taking deep breaths, saying "I can calm down" or, "I can wait" or, "I can solve the problem" when getting frustrated.
- Praise and encourage children when they stay calm in a frustrating situation.
- Cuddle and soothe younger children when they are hurt or frightened.
- Model as a teacher staying calm and patient when responding in frustrating situations.
- Help parents know about emotion words teachers are promoting in the classroom and specific ones targeted for their children (e.g., being brave for anxious student; or being patient for impulsive student; or being happy for sad student).

**The Incredible Years®
Teacher Classroom Management Self-Reflection Inventory
Teacher Coaching Strategies**

Date: _____ Teacher Name: _____

Teachers learn extensively from self-reflection regarding their classroom management and the teaching strategies they are using that are working or not working. From these reflections teachers determine personal goals for making changes in their approaches to bring about the most positive learning climate they can. Use this Inventory to think about your strengths and limitations and determine your goals for teaching your students.

Academic, Persistence, Social and Emotion Coaching	1 = NEVER 3 = OCCASIONALLY 5 = CONSISTENTLY
1. I give more attention to positive social behaviors and emotions than to inappropriate behaviors and negative emotions. (5:1)	1 2 3 4 5
2. I have identified positive social behaviors, emotions, and academic behaviors I want to coach in particular students on their behavior plans.	1 2 3 4 5
3. I model positive self-talk, positive emotions and social behaviors in my interactions with my students and with other teachers or adults in the classroom.	1 2 3 4 5
4. I make positive calls to parents to compliment them about their children's successes or positive behavior.	1 2 3 4 5
5. I communicate my belief to students that they can succeed and promote their positive self-talk.	1 2 3 4 5

6. I help children learn how to compliment each other and have compliment circle times.	1 2 3 4 5
7. I prompt children in the classroom to notice another child's friendly behaviors or persistence with a difficult task.	1 2 3 4 5
8. When students are frustrated, I focus on their persistence and patience working hard to solve a difficult problem.	1 2 3 4 5
9. I share my positive feelings (proud, happiness, joy, courage) when interacting with children.	1 2 3 4 5
10. I use descriptive and academic commenting during my interactions with my students (e.g., describing objects, positions, colors). I target language delayed students for additional descriptive coaching.	1 2 3 4 5
11. I use persistence coaching with all my students – and I especially target students with attention difficulties for this coaching.	1 2 3 4 5
12. I use social coaching with all my students when they are playing with peers and I target socially inappropriate or withdrawn children especially for this coaching.	1 2 3 4 5
13. I use emotion coaching with all my students – and I use more positive emotion words than negative. I target positive emotion coaching for aggressive children.	1 2 3 4 5
14. When I use negative emotion coaching I qualify the negative emotion with recognition of positive coping or calming behavior the student is using to continue to problem solve.	1 2 3 4 5

15. I avoid use of questions, corrections, criticisms and demands when coaching children.	1 2 3 4 5
16. I focus on children's efforts and learning– not just end result.	1 2 3 4 5
17. I make efforts to teach and encourage parents to use coaching strategies with their children and communicate with them about targeted social, emotional or academic skills.	1 2 3 4 5
Future Goals Regarding Attention, Praise and Coaching Strategies:	Total

REFERENCES

Brown, A. L., & Palincsar, A. S. (1989). Guided cooperative learning and individual knowledge acquisition. In L. B. Resnick (Ed.), *Knowing, learning and intruction: Essays in honor of Robert Glaser* (pp. 393-451). Hillsdale, NJ: Lawrence Erlbaum Associates.

Caprara, G. V., Barbaranelli, C., Pastorelli, C., Bandura, A., & Zimbardo, P. G. (2000). Prosocial foundations of children's academic achievement. *Psychological Science, 302-306.*

Cawelti, G. (1995). *Handbook of research on improving academic achievement.* Arlington, VA: Educational Research Service.

Duncan, G. J., Dowsett, C. J., Claessens, A., Magnuson, K., Huston, A. C., & Klebanov, P. (2007). School readiness and later achievment. *Developmental Psychology, 43,* 1428-1446.

Durlak, J. A., Weissberg, R. P., Dymnick, A., B., Taylor, R. D., & Schellinger, B. (2011). The Impact of Enhancing Students' Social and Emotional Learning: A Meta-Analysis of School-based Universal Interventions. *Child Development, 82,* 405-432.

Durlak, J. A., Weissberg, R. P., & Pachan, M. (2010). A meta-analysis of after-school programs that seek to promote personal and social skills in children and adolescence. *American Journal of Community Psychology, 45,* 294-309.

Piaget, J., & Inhelder, B. (1962). *The Psychology of the Child.* New York Basic Books.

Reinke, W. M., & Lewis-Palmer, T. (2008). The classsroom check-up: A class wide teacher consultation model for increasing praise and decreasing disruptive behavior. *School Psychology Review, 37*(3), 315-332.

Wang, M., Haertel, G., & Walberg, H. (1994). What helps children learn? *Educational Leadership, December/January,* 74-79.

Webster-Stratton, C., Reid, M. J., & Stoolmiller, M. (2008). Preventing conduct problems and improving school readiness: Evaluation of the Incredible Years Teacher and Child Training Programs in high-risk schools. *Journal of Child Psychology and Psychiatry 49*(5), 471-488.

Whitehurst, G. J., Zevenbergen, A. A., Crone, D. A., Schultz, M. D., Velting, O. N., & Fischel, J. E. (1999). Outcomes of an emergent literacy intervention from Head Start through second grade. *Journal of Educational Psychology, 91*, 261-272.

Spotlight Sunshine on Positive Behavior Growth: Importance of Teacher Attention, Encouragement and Praise

Children who need love the most ask for it in the most unloving ways; the same can be said of children most in need of positive attention, coaching, praise, and encouragement.

The Importance of Teacher Attention, Encouragement, and Praise

When we look at the classroom environment to see what factors help students become motivated and successful learners, the quality of the teacher's attention emerges as one of the most important. Consistent and meaningful encouragement and praise from a teacher build children's self-confidence and contributes to trusting and supportive relationships. This, in turn, increases students' academic commitment and performance and reduces disruptive behavior (Sutherland, Wehby, & Copeland, 2000). A host of research indicates that the simple use of contingent behavior-specific praise and attention to positive student behavior reinforces and nurtures children's growing emotional, social, and academic competence (Reinke & Lewis-Palmer, 2008). Moreover, teachers who deliver high amounts of praise typically experience lower rates of off-task or disruptive behaviors, leaving more time for academic teaching (Reinke & Lewis-Palmer, 2007). Contingent praise increases the intrinsic motivation of students, their feeling of competence (Cameron & Pierce, 1994), and their on-task behavior. In one study praise resulted in an increase of on-task classroom behavior from 49% to 86% (Sutherland et al., 2000).

Unfortunately, research has shown that teachers give three to fifteen times as much attention to student misbehavior (e.g., talking out, fiddling, out of seat behavior) than to positive behavior in their classrooms (Brophy, 1996; Martens & Meller, 1990; Walker & Buckley, 1973; Wyatt & Hawkins, 1987). Not surprisingly, this attention reinforces the misbehavior, leading to increased classroom behavior problems, particularly for children who are starved for adult attention. When teachers begin to shift their attention away from inappropriate behaviors, while increasing coaching, encouragement and praise for positive behaviors, there is usually a dramatic effect on the behavior of targeted individual students, and also on the overall classroom atmosphere. In this chapter we will look at research-validated ways of giving appropriate attention, praise, and encouragement (Brophy, 1996; Cameron & Pierce, 1994; Walker, Colvin, & Ramsey, 1995) and examine some of the practical issues and concerns that typically accompany this topic.

QUESTIONS TEACHERS ASK

Won't praising some children create insecurity in others who don't get praised?

"Doesn't praise given to one child make the other children who didn't get praised feel bad?"

Sometimes teachers are reluctant to praise or to give positive attention to one child because of their fears that there will be possible negative ramifications for other children. For example, some teachers worry that if they praise one child, the children seated nearby will feel inadequate because they were not praised. It is true that all children in a classroom need to receive positive attention and praise from their teachers. However, this does not mean that every child must receive the same praise at the same time.

It is important that the praise be genuine and matched to each child's individual efforts.

As long as the teacher gives consistent, positive, and contingent attention to every student at some time for positive behavior, children will not feel they are being treated unfairly. In fact, it is important that the praise be genuine and matched to each child's individual efforts, so different children will receive praise for different behaviors at different times. Over time, with periodic doses of positive attention from their teacher on a regular basis, children will feel secure enough in their relationship with their teacher to avoid jealousy when others receive praise. In fact, with time they will even learn to celebrate each others' successes in meeting their own personal goals.

Isn't it more important for children to judge their own work for themselves than to depend on teachers' praise?

"How early can you encourage children to judge their work for themselves?"

Indeed, it is also important for children to eventually learn to self-reflect and self-evaluate; that is, to pass judgment on their own work and feel pride in their accomplishments without relying on external sources of approval. This is an important long-term goal, yet the teacher needs to be aware of the particular world view of each individual child. For example, children who come from a family environment characterized by positive feedback, a commitment of support, and a relationship with parents that centers on building the child's self-esteem, may have the self-confidence to begin to evaluate their own work. Self-evaluation and self-praise is a developmental process and even children from positive family environments vary in the age at which they develop this kind of internal motivation and positive self-regard. Most young children, who are still developing emotionally and socially, need some external validation for their learning efforts. In fact, adults need this too, regardless of their age or how self-confident they may be.

Unfortunately, some children do not come from supportive family circumstances that provide this positive nurturing. Some children have experienced a great deal of negative feedback, criticism, and even abuse from their parents for their misbehaviors. Other children have parents who are so overwhelmed or depressed with their own problems that they have been unable to focus on their children's needs or interests. Consequently these neglected children may feel their parents don't care about them. Other children may be struggling with biological issues that make it extremely hard for them to self-regulate, follow directions, and function successfully in structured environments. For these children, their biology gets in the way of performing in ways that lead to success, positive teacher attention, and praise. Many of these children described above may have been expelled from previous schools and experienced rejection from teachers and peers. Children come to their teachers with very different experiences of what relationships with adults are all about and varying degrees of self-esteem. The child with behavior problems is likely to have a very negative view of what it means to have relationships with adults. Likewise, such a child may have a negative self-evaluation and low self-worth. If such a child is left to do his own self-evaluation of his work, he will likely pronounce it worthless.

External positive scaffolding is necessary to support high risk children's emotional, social and academic growth.

For these children, teachers will need to supply extra amounts of positive and consistent *external coaching, praise and scaffolding* that the child has not experienced in the crucial early years. Teachers can think of this added support as providing a kind of "environmental scaffolding" for the child; necessary to support his emotional regulation and academic and social growth. This positive teacher encouragement may be needed for several years before the messages internalize and the child develops a positive self-image and is capable of realistic self-evaluation without this external scaffolding.

As mentioned above, biological or genetic factors also play a role in a child's ability to self-evaluate. A child who is inattentive, impulsive, and/or hyperactive will be delayed in learning to self-evaluate, as this requires the ability to reflect on one's actions and anticipate outcomes. Hyperactive and inattentive young children live "in the moment" and do not easily learn from past experiences or anticipate future events. These children need much more external positive scaffolding from the teachers than children who are by temperament more reflective.

Doesn't teacher praise lead to students' reliance on external approval?

"Doesn't praise create a student who will only be motivated by external approval rather than internal motivation?"

Sometimes teachers worry that too much praise may be bad for children. Perhaps they feel that students who are praised too often may become conceited, narcissistic, overly confident, or have an inflated or unrealistic view of their actual abilities. Perhaps they fear that children may become dependent on praise—a form of external reinforcement. Research provides evidence to the contrary: children who are appropriately encouraged, coached, and praised by parents and teachers internalize the positive approval and develop positive self-esteem (Cameron & Pierce, 1994). They typically feel self-confident in their ability to learn and to manage failures and grow up to need less praise in the long run because they have developed more confidence in their own unique abilities and ability to self-evaluate and work out problems (Brophy, 1981). This effect is especially likely if children are praised for their persistent process and sustained efforts at working towards goals, rather than for finished products or final achievements.

This question concerning internal motivation is somewhat related to the question about self-evaluation noted above: the concern on the part of some teachers that praise (or positive attention, or any social reward) from adults will create a child who is dependent upon external adult approval and who will not develop an internal sense of worth. Sometimes teachers fear that over time, children will need greater and greater amounts of praise in order to achieve the same effect and will fail to develop intrinsic motivation to learn. A research article reviewing 96 experimental studies comparing rewarded students to non-rewarded students did not support this theory but rather just the opposite. Children who received lots of positive feedback from parents and teachers had an increase in intrinsic motivation (Cameron & Pierce, 1994). Children who are praised are self-confident, have high self-esteem, and seem to internalize these early messages so as not to need them in the future (Gable, Hester, Rock, & Hughes, 2009). Moreover, children who have received a lot of praise are popular with other children and give other children and adults positive feedback; that is, they have modeled this positive communication and use it in their interactions with others. On the other hand, the children who demand praise and are dependent on others' evaluations are those insecure children who have received very little positive feedback and have low-esteem. Unfortunately, the children who most need the positive attention and praise rarely get it. The reality of most classrooms is that the problem children receive far more criticisms and negative attention than praise statements or positive attention.

Can teacher praise to one student stifle creativity in others?

"If you praise a student's answer, isn't there a danger that all the other students will copy that answer or tell you their answer is the same? Might they be afraid to give a different answer for fear the teacher's response won't be as enthusiastic?"

Some teachers worry that if they respond to one student's answer with labeled praise (such as praising a child's choice of a particular subject to discuss), every other student will imitate that student, so that suddenly that student's answer becomes the "correct" answer. It is true that children will watch to see what behaviors teachers give attention to and then will repeat those behaviors in order to get the attention as well. This is an expected part of the learning process; and using one child's answer as a model to motivate other children is a good teaching strategy. Once teachers have children working for their positive attention (and not the negative attention), the next step is for teachers to use this technique to broaden the range of students' responses; that is, to reinforce diverse, creative and unique ideas. So the teacher might say to the students, "That was an interesting and thoughtful answer. Does anyone else have a different experience they would like to share?" As students realize they will not receive the same kind of positive attention for repeating another student's answer, eventually they will become less likely to copy someone else's responses to get attention and more motivated to generate their own ideas.

How often should you praise a child?

"If a child is spelling a word, should you praise each letter or wait until the spelling of the word is completed?"

Whether the praise is given for each correctly spelled letter or saved until the spelling of the word is correctly accomplished will depend on the child's particular abilities and motivation. For children who are reluctant to take risks, frustrated with their spelling ability, or insecure about their relationship with the teacher or peers, praising frequently during the process (after each letter), will be important, for it will give the child confidence to keep trying. The principle here is shaping the desired behavior; that is, breaking the behavior down into small components and praising each small component. For the child who is a good speller and confident in the class-room, praising the end result may be sufficient. Or perhaps praise might even be given for a different goal, rather than focusing on spelling at all.

In general teachers should make sure they have at least four positives for every criticism or corrective statement.

It is also important for children to learn that it is okay to make mistakes. If they feel that positive attention will be withdrawn if they make a mistake, then they will be unwilling to take the risk in the first place. Thus, if a child gets one or two letters wrong, the teacher should praise the child's efforts and focus on the five letters that were correct rather than focusing on the mistakes. For example, "that was a very good effort and you thought about the spelling care-fully, you got all but one letter absolutely correct!"

In general teachers should make sure they have at least four positives for every criticism or corrective statement they make to a child. Teachers may need to set up self-monitoring and colleague feedback methods to record the amount of praise they give their students, particularly students who are difficult to praise (Mesa, Lewis-Palmer, & Reinke, 2005).

Some children don't seem to respond to praise—why?

Some children, usually those who have experienced excessive criticism and other negative feedback, are uncomfortable with praise and may show no response or even reject teachers' efforts to praise. Such children are well-defended, in psychological armor. They act as if they don't care about praise. One reason for a lack of response may be that they don't have the social skills; they don't know how to respond to teachers when they get positive feedback, so they shut down instead. Another possible reason is that the quality of the teacher-student relationship is fragile. When faced with these responses, it is easy to think the praise is not working or the child is unmotivated or doesn't care to please the teacher. Teachers must work extra hard to continue giving positive attention, coaching, and praise to these children who are not reinforcing them for their efforts (Kalis, Vannest, & Parker, 2007).

Children who are inattentive, impulsive, and distracted will miss praise that is vague or delivered in a neutral tone of voice. Such children will have trouble interpreting a neutral facial expression and may even interpret it as negative when teachers mean to be positive. For these children the praise needs to be underscored with an enthusiastic tone of voice, clear descriptions ("labeling") of the positive behaviors, and clearly positive facial expressions. Think of this as a need to use a megaphone when praising this type of child.

Developmental age can also influence children's responses to praise. While younger children usually respond best to praise given enthusiastically in front of the whole classroom and overheard by others, sometimes secondary students find the praise given in front of their peers embarrassing and fear they will be teased as a "suck up" or "teacher's pet." The embarrassment factor can be reduced by being more private and personal and less obvious.

Extra effort must be made
for children who reject praise.

How can you praise a child for work that doesn't meet your expectations?

How can you use praise when the child's work is not adequate and you want to direct the child toward something better?

Perhaps the teacher's goal is to encourage the students to use more detail in their drawings, but one child has submitted a completed drawing with very few details. Wouldn't it be counterproductive to praise this student's drawing? Actually it would be better to praise what the child has done well in that particular picture and avoid being critical of its simplicity. Praise and positive attention will add to the child's pleasure in drawing and that pleasure will lead to her wanting to continue to draw. Then the teacher might turn to another child's drawing and talk about its use of detail, thus conveying to the first child how she might expand on her picture. Later, when the children are working independently, the teacher could talk privately with this particular child about her drawing, expressing interest in the picture, and encouraging her to add more details. Praising students doesn't mean teachers are protecting children from getting appropriate feedback and further encouragement to try out new ideas.

Skillful and thoughtful recognition of unique aspects of children's work in front of peers can encourage students to value differences and discourage comparison.

Doesn't it set up competition and resentment for teachers to compare children to other children?

Illustrating a few children's work as excellent models to stimulate other children's work can be effective as long as the teacher demonstrates examples from all children from time to time and illustrates a variety of creative ways to approach the work. Since there is such variability in children's developmental abilities, it is important to recognize and communicate the value of each child's work. For example, the teacher might highlight the unique aspects of an art project (even though that child couldn't write) or the hard work a particular child used in completing a project. The teacher might make a single comment about each child's work or highlight several students on one day and others on a subsequent day. Skillful and thoughtful recognition of unique aspects of children's work in front of peers can encourage students to value differences and discourage comparison of students with each other.

Why should difficult students get more praise than other students? It's not fair to the other students!

Children with challenging behaviors often need higher doses of praise and attention than other students. The reason for this is that typically they have been the brunt of adult criticism and peer ridicule, and as a result their self-esteem is low. Such children want attention so badly that they would rather have negative attention for misbehavior than no attention at all. Consequently, teachers need to develop skills that prompt them to notice the positive behaviors in difficult children: to "catch them being good." This cannot be left to chance; it must be planned, for there may be relatively few episodes of good behavior. In the case of difficult children, it can be hard to remember to praise and give positive recognition. Teachers need a concrete plan for what particular behaviors they want to promote in individual children with problems and how they will reinforce those behaviors.

Teachers may also be concerned that it is *not fair* to praise some children more than others. The question of fairness in the classroom is an interesting one to ponder. Most teachers probably wouldn't argue that the child who has a language or reading delay is entitled to extra tutoring, or the child with a physical handicap will need physical therapy, or the child with pneumonia needs an antibiotic. It would seem then that the same rights hold for the child with attention difficulties, social and peer relationship problems, and environmental disadvantages. Moreover, this extra attention to the problem child in the form of labeled praise, encouragement, and incentives for improvements will in the long run be beneficial for all the students in the classroom because these labeled descriptions of the expected academic and social behaviors act as a reminder for everyone. In addition, the teacher is modeling empathy and acceptance of individual differences in children's abilities to learn social, emotional and academic skills.

One final point in regard to the issue of fairness. It isn't fair that some children come from homes where they are loved and provided with predictability whereas others do not, but that is the reality. It is therefore even more important that we set up classroom interventions that adjust for these individual differences in relationship abilities and family environments.

MAKING PRAISE AND ENCOURAGEMENT MORE EFFECTIVE

As with any other classroom strategy, praise can be given in ways that lead to multiple positive outcomes for children or can be given in less effective ways that may confirm some of the negative outcomes mentioned above. Thus the issue is not whether praise is good or bad, but what constitutes effective praise and encouragement. The remainder of this chapter will explore ways that teachers can make their praise effective for all students in the classroom.

Be Specific
Vague praise is often given quickly in a chain, with one comment following another. For example, the teacher might say, "Good job...

good...fine..." Unfortunately while these statements do convey some degree of positive attention, they are nonspecific and unlabeled. It is unclear what aspect of the student's behavior that the teacher is praising with these words.

It is more effective to give praises that are labeled and behavior-specific. Labeled praise describes the particular behavior that you like. Instead of saying "Good job," you would say, "You have worked so hard and have figured out that entire puzzle all by yourself," or "Wow, what a wonderful job you've done of picking up all those blocks when I asked. You really listened well and followed my directions." By pinpointing exactly what you like about a child's behavior (independent work, compliance to teacher's request), the praise statement conveys much more to the student and informs him what specifically was praiseworthy about his behavior so that he can do it again. Specific praise provides a stronger motivator of future behavior.

A few examples of ways to praise...
"You do a super job of..."
"Good idea for..."
"What a wonderful job you've done of..."
"That's correct. That's a cool way to..."
"You are a real problem-solver for..."
"Great thinking..."
"My! That...was great teamwork."
"You are being a good friend by..."
"Pat yourself on the back for..."
"Give me five for..."
"Thanks for being so patient and waiting while I was..."
"I like the way you remembered to walk quietly to your desk."
"I knew you'd remember to get ready for the next activity without any reminders."
"Keep at it, you are working really hard and getting it!"
"Thank you _____, for making a quiet choice during work time. Your neighbors appreciate your thoughtfulness."
"You are really good at sharing your ideas with the class, that is really helping us all learn."

Show Enthusiasm

Some praise is ineffective because it is boring, offered in dull tones, with no smiles or eye contact. The same words may be repeated over and over again in a flat, unenthusiastic voice. Such praise is not reinforcing or encouraging to children.

The impact of a praise statement can be increased by using nonverbal methods of conveying enthusiasm. Smile at the child, greeting her with warmth in your eyes or giving a pat on the back. The praise should be stated with energy, variety, care and sincerity. Words thrown over the shoulder in a careless fashion will be lost on the child. Children easily pick up on praise that is insincere, and bask in praise that is genuine.

Remember children who are inattentive, impulsive, and distracted will be likely to miss praise that is delivered in a neutral tone of voice or is vague. These children in particular need praise that is underscored by means of an enthusiastic tone of voice, clear descriptions ("labeling") of the positive behaviors, clearly positive facial expressions and positive touch.

Praise and Encourage the Child's Efforts and Progress

In addition to praising specific observable behaviors such as sharing, helping, or correct answers to questions, it is important to praise a child's efforts, improvement, and willingness to try something that is not easy for them. For example, to the child who has had a difficult time reading, the teacher could say, "You have really worked hard at trying to read. See how many pages you have finished all by yourself! Look at the progress you have made!" or, "See how you have improved in your reading. You recognize most of the words now." This approach places the emphasis on the child's persistent effort, feelings of success, and progress rather than the teacher's evaluation of the child's reading ability, per se, or the teacher's feelings of pleasure. When teachers give children social rewards for improvement, they are

Place the emphasis on the child's persistent effort, feelings of success, and progress rather than the teacher's evaluation.

Focusing on the process of learning, rather than the product strengthens self-esteem.

measuring them against themselves, not against others in the classroom or against some other external standard. Teachers can also do this by showing them their earlier work in the year and noting how it has changed.

Another way to encourage students is to use a strategy we call, "tailgating." This is when the teacher repeats something the child has said and then builds on it with a comment that expands the idea. For example, a student says, "I am drawing a rocket to fly in the air" and the teacher replies, "Yes you are drawing a rocket and you've drawn some powerful engines to propel it very far. That is awesome!" This tailgating serves to encourage the child because it validates the child's ideas and lets the child know that the teacher is really attending to the detail in his drawing.

Focusing on the process of learning, rather than the product strengthens self-esteem because it helps students remain invested in their work and their learning process, instead of measuring themselves by the outcome of their efforts. If the outcome is less than perfect, they can still take pride in their work because their teacher has rewarded their efforts to learn with her attention.

Remember to Build Up Your Bank
Account with Your Students

A few more examples of phrases

"You must feel proud of yourself for..."
"See how you have improved in..."

"You have worked so hard..."

"That's a creative way of..."

"You are a real problem-solver for..."

"Hey, you are really thinking, you..."

"Wow, you have learned how to..."

"It helps us when you..."

"You put a lot of thought into that..."

"You took the time to clean up the art materials, that's very thoughtful."

"You really know how to tidy up. You put all the lids on the felt pens!"

"It's a pleasure to have a class like this because..."

"You went out of your way to help this morning by..."

"You are making a good choice."

"You figured it out...Way to go!"

"I'd love to call on you now, but I need to give someone else a chance."

"What a good way to be a friend by helping him with that."

Promote Child Self-Praise

In addition to praising effort and progress, teachers can help the child learn how to recognize his or her own feelings of accomplishment by the way they phrase the praise. For example, a statement such as, "you must feel proud of yourself for reading that entire chapter all by yourself" focuses on the child's own positive recognition of his work.

Teaching children to recognize their own achievements is vital. Otherwise they may wait for others to notice, which can be an endless wait. The goal is for students to eventually be able to look inside themselves for self-approval. For example, when a teacher addresses a question to the class it is likely that many children want to answer and the children who don't get called on may feel left out or devalued. One way to encourage children to self-regulate and self-praise is to say, "All those who had the same answer, pat yourself on the back for your answer." Thus each child gets to reinforce herself with a pat on the back and be noticed for her ideas, rather than feeling disappointed because she didn't get called on.

Avoid Combining Praise with Put-Downs

Sometimes, teachers give praise and, without realizing it, they contradict it by being sarcastic or combining it with a criticism. This is one of the most disruptive things a teacher can do in the reinforcement process. For example, the teacher says to a student, "You finally finished your homework, but why couldn't you complete it on time?" or, "You picked up the toys like I asked. That's great. But next time how about doing it before I have to ask?" or "You didn't hit today." The criticism or correction on the part of the teacher negates the effect of the praise; children, particularly those who are insecure, are more likely to remember the negative comment than the positive praise. Praises mixed with criticisms are very confusing for young children to interpret. Consequently try to keep praise "pure," uncontaminated by qualifiers. If a teacher wants his students to learn something else such as completing homework on time, then he will be more effective if he sets this up as a specific goal to be discussed on a separate occasion.

Try to keep praise "pure," uncontaminated by qualifiers.

Praise and Encourage Social and Academic Behaviors

When teachers track the kinds of praises they usually give, they often find that they are most likely to notice and praise a particular type of behavior. For example, some teachers find they praise academic excellence and cognitive competence but rarely praise social competence and emotional regulation or vice versa. Some teachers find they praise only outstanding work relative to the whole class, rather than accomplishments relative to the individual child's growing abilities. It is important for teachers to be aware of these predispositions and try to praise a variety of cognitive, behavioral, social and self-regulation behaviors. In fact, for young children, we would expect that social skills such as listening, waiting, thinking, cooperation, sharing, paying attention and appropriate question-asking would be praised liberally, for these are the foundation for developing academic skills. Even for older school age children, teachers should use a balance of praise and encouragement directed at both academic and social and emotional behaviors. In order to get a perspective on what aspects of students' behaviors are praised, a teacher might ask a colleague to spend an hour in recording what behavior and how often she praises.

In addition to praising how students behave and perform socially, emotionally and academically, teachers should encourage other aspects of the child's unique personality, such as a child's patience, thoughtfulness towards others, persistence, creativity, enthusiasm, friendliness and willingness to try something new. Even a student's grooming, hair cut or clothing may be commented on by teachers, for this teaches students that these are important social aspects to be aware of when developing friendships.

Praise Difficult Students More Often

As we noted earlier, children who most need our praise and other social rewards are often the most difficult to praise and reward with our attention. Because of their inattentiveness, disengagement, and oppositional behavior, they are not reinforcing to teachers and often elicit the teacher's criticisms rather than praise. How can teachers avoid this trap? By understanding that these difficult children can extinguish teaching efforts, teachers can make conscientious efforts to be sure they extend extra encouragement and praise to these children. All children will eventually respond to the same behavioral principles, but children with developmental delays, attention, or behavioral problems will need the praise or attention more often. They require more learning trials, with behaviors broken down into small component parts followed by repeated praise and encouragement from teachers, before they will learn the new behavior.

Some simple reminder strategies may help remind teachers to praise. For example, a teacher might put a sticker on the clock; each time she looks at the clock and sees the sticker, she can prompt herself to praise. A teacher might put a number of beans or coins in one pocket; the challenge is to move the coins to the other pocket by the end of the day, giving a praise each time one is moved. A teacher might select three target students each day with the goal to give each of these students five praises during the day.

Remember the Shy Student

Just as teachers must work hard at finding behaviors to praise in the obstreperous child with behavior problems, they must remember to praise the non-demanding, shy student who is normally cooperative. Such children are sometimes invisible in the classroom and need to be noticed for their kindness, generosity, helpful participation, and for working hard to complete an assignment.

Target Specific Behaviors to Encourage According to Individual Students' Needs

It can be very effective for a teacher to target the particular behaviors she wants to strengthen in each individual student. For example, s/he may plan to praise the quiet, withdrawn student every time he ventures an answer or participates in a discussion. On the other hand, s/he may plan to praise the overbearing, controlling child for being able to wait his turn or for letting someone else go first to answer a question. The same approach goes for strengthening academic skills. For the child who has difficulty writing and spelling, the teacher can plan to praise the child's efforts in order to keep up the child's interest in writing. For the child who writes well, the teacher might focus on his expansion of ideas or organizational skills.

For the oppositional and highly distractible child, the single most important behavior to target for praise is the child's compliance to teacher directions. This is key because a teacher must have student compliance in order to be able to socialize or teach anything. Thus for these students, the teacher's first efforts must be to notice any time they follow the teacher's directions and listen carefully to their instructions.

A few examples of behaviors to encourage and praise

Sharing
Talking politely
Quiet hand up
Helping a classmate
Giving a compliment to another classmate
Complying to teacher requests, listening and following directions
Solving a difficult problem

Achieving something that was hard for a particular student
Cooperating on the playground
Persisting with a difficult academic task (working hard)
Thinking before answering
Putting classroom materials away
Completing homework assignments on time
Being thoughtful
Being patient
Staying calm and cool and in control in a conflict situation
Walking in the hallway
Trying something difficult for the first time
Following one of the classroom rules

In order to plan systematically for strengthening certain behaviors teachers can complete a written behavior plan such as that shown below (See Chapter Ten). By identifying the negative or inappropriate behaviors teachers would like to see less of and when they are most likely to occur, teachers can then identify the appropriate positive opposite prosocial behavior they would like to replace them with. This will help teachers be more specific with their praise statements and more consistent in paying attention to the behaviors when they do occur. This plan can also be shared with co-teachers or playground supervisors as necessary. Start this process by picking one behavior to work on at a time. The other advantage to teachers identifying which target behaviors they want to reinforce ahead of time is that they can double the impact when they tell other teacher aides or parent volunteers in the classroom to praise them as well.

Teachers can double the impact when they tell other teachers or parents which behaviors to praise.

Use Proximity Praise

At times, the strategy of proximity praise can seem like magic! Instead of focusing on the student who is disengaged and daydreaming, the teacher praises other students who are attending to the task and completing

Behavior Plan: Jenny Grade 1

Negative Classroom Behaviors to Reduce	Occasion	Desired Positive Opposite Behaviors to Increase	Specific Praise
poking, touching other students	in line	keep hands to own body	responds well to praise–"you are doing a good job keeping your hands to yourself?"
speaks without raising hand	small group discussion	raise a quiet hand	does not like to be hugged–"wow you remembered to raise a quiet hand"
talks while directions are given	large classroom	listen quietly when directions given	give attention to and praise listening behavior–"you are listening carefully and doing just what I asked you to do"
off-task, daydreaming	independent work time	pay attention and concentrate	"you are working hard on that picture, I can tell you have really been concentrating"

their work. This use of proximity praise serves as a means of reminding and redirecting the disengaged student as to what behavior is expected without drawing attention to him or her. For example, the teacher says, "I like the way Frederick is getting his books put away so we can go to recess," or, " I will ask Anna to answer since she has a quiet hand up." Often this prompt results in 20 other students scrambling to put away their books or raise their quiet hands.

Use Noncontingent Praise

In addition to contingent behavior-specific praise (praise given contingent in a particular positive behavior occurring) it is also important for teachers to give noncontingent praise. Noncontingent praise or encouragement is general praise that is contingent on nothing that the child has to do to earn the approval. Examples of this include, "It is nice to see you this morning," or "It is fun working with you," Or, "I am so glad to have you in our class." These encouraging words build a climate of unconditional positive regard of the teacher for the students.

Have Positive Expectation for All Students

Positive expectations are a powerful motivator. If a teacher believes a child can learn and communicates that belief, verbally or nonverbally, he or she is likely to keep trying. On the other hand, if teachers are convinced that a child is likely to have trouble, they will probably communicate that message, and the child probably won't keep trying. Teachers can show faith in their students by encouraging comments such as, "See you are able to do this, I knew you could," or, "I know this is hard, but with practice I know you will learn to do it."

Use General Praise to Groups of Students

So far, we have been looking at the use of teacher praise and encouragement used with individual children. Praise can also be an effective tool for a group of children because of the potential power of peer pressure to motivate students. For example teachers may divide their classroom into teams. When a teacher notices a team following her directions or a class rule she might say, "I am very pleased with Team 6 because Team 6's listening has improved immensely today," or, "I see everybody at the Dinosaur table is ready for recess with their books away, and their chairs put in quietly. That is fantastic." The teacher may also combine this verbal praise for teams with an incentive system such as earning points which can be collected and turned in for a prize. This is described in more detail in Chapter Six.

Acknowledge the Difficulties of Learning Something New

The teacher says to the students after teaching them subtraction for the first time, "I know this is hard stuff to learn, and it was a lot of concentrated work today. But each day it will get a little bit easier and by the end of the year you will be very good at this." The recognition that something is hard from the point of view of the teacher reduces distance between teachers and students. Having a closer relationship with the teacher (while maintaining appropriate boundaries) heightens the "reward" value of the teacher's attention. This closer relationship will contribute to a child sharing more of his or her accomplishments as well as being more open about his or her areas of difficulty.

Encouragement is also needed when students make mistakes or feel they have failed. The teacher might say, "Okay, you made a mistake. That's okay. It is easy to make mistakes, we all do. What can you learn from that mistake? What will you do differently next time?" Here the teacher acknowledges that making mistakes is part of the learning process and then encourages the student to think about what was learned from the experience. It also helps for teachers to model this themselves. For example, the teacher says, "Oops I goofed. I made a mistake. It's messed up. What I need to do is to fix it."

Encourage Children to Praise Themselves and Others

Giving children positive recognition in the form of praise and encouragement has another value as well. Ultimately we want children to learn to praise others, for this is a skill that will help them build positive relationships with other children. To reinforce this, a teacher a might point out a group of children who are doing something special together with a particular project. For example, saying, "Look class, I want you to see how our friends Mark, Jennifer, and Shayla are doing quiet, focused, teamwork!"

Teachers can ask students to nominate a student (never a close friend) for an award that week. For example, the teacher might say, "Today I want you to nominate a student who has shown a recent improvement in work or behavior," or, "I want you to nominate someone who is always kind or hardworking." If the teacher tries this approach, it is important that she devise categories that cover all the positive qualities of all the children and that she have a system to make the selection fair. Be sure to keep records of who is chosen from week to week so that all the children eventually get a turn. The names of the nominator and nominee and positive behavior can be posted on the board. During the rest of the day the class and teachers watch out for the positive behavior that has been nominated.

A teacher can also watch for and encourage students to praise another student's work. A compliment circle (described in detail in Chapter 13) is one way of encouraging children to compliment or praise others. When children share in the teacher's role of identifying other children who are engaged in positive behaviors, such as sitting quietly or cooperating, it also serves to reinforce the desired behavior for themselves. It is very reinforcing for children to be identified by their peers as behaving well. For some children this form of social reward is even more reinforcing than a teacher's attention.

Self Praise

We also want students to learn to praise themselves, for this will help them attempt and stay with difficult tasks. A teacher might say, "I'm impressed with this project. What do you like about your work here?" Students can also be encouraged to share something they feel proud about. For example, the teacher might say, "Jamila tell the group about your reading today." Jamila may respond, "I feel proud because I worked hard and finished reading my book." This ability to reflect on one's own performance is an important aspect to the development of self-evaluation.

Nonverbal Encouragement

Nonverbal signals of encouragement are very helpful so teachers can give students recognition without disrupting the entire class. For example, the teacher can use signals such as a thumbs up sign, a "high five" or positive wink to acknowledge a child who deserves to be specially noticed for some achievement.

Another way to increase the impact of positive approval is to combine it with nonverbal support in the form of a hug, or a pat on the shoulder. Don't be hesitant to show your affection. Just think how much more powerful a hug coupled with lots of verbal praise must be.

Behavior Doesn't Have to Be Perfect to Deserve Recognition

Behavior doesn't have to be perfect to deserve teacher praise or positive attention. In fact, when children are first attempting a new behavior, they need to be reinforced for each small step toward the goal. If required to wait for reinforcement until they have mastered the new behavior, they will have to wait too long, and may give up altogether. Praising a child at every step along the way reinforces the child for her efforts and learning. This process, known as "shaping," sets the child up for success.

Working the Room

One of the ways to increase teachers' use of positive recognition is to "work the room" looking for positive behaviors; that is, while the students are working independently, a teacher circulates throughout the room and responds with attention and praise whenever she sees the desired behavior occurring. Teachers can use independent work time as an opportunity for actively reinforcing individual behavior. Circulating around the room also makes teachers more accessible to students who want to ask for help.

Shine a praise light on the positive behavior as often as possible.

When a teacher is working with a small group of students or an individual, she should look up every 3 or 4 minutes and monitor the students who are working independently. Then take a moment to notice and reinforce their positive behavior.

Use Classroom Compliment Circle Times to Promote Peer Praise

Classroom circle times can be used as compliment times to teach students how to give and receive positive feedback or compliments from each other. It is important that students not always look to adults to receive positive feedback; they need to receive it from their peers as well. During a compliment circle, each student is encouraged to say one nice thing about what one of their classmates did that day or week. For example, "Lisa was helpful when she helped me with my math." Young preschool and kindergarten children may find it helpful to pass a stuffed animal to the person who is going to receive the compliment. Thus children who have difficulty verbally expressing a compliment can still give a nonverbal compliment to another child by giving them the animal to hold. Also songs can be a fun way to introduce compliments. One song we use for compliment time is: "Hello Peter, how are you? Compliment a friend and we'll clap for you." Then as soon as the child gives a compliment to someone, the class claps for him.

Involve Parents in Your Praise Campaign

Once a teacher has defined the target behaviors she will increase her praise and attention for, it can be helpful to share this plan with the students' parents. Teachers can tell parents which behaviors they are praising and ask for support in praising the same behaviors at home. Teachers and parents can share stories about home-praise through notes, e-mails, charts, journals, diaries, or phone calls. This positive home-school communication can reinforce a particularly challenging behavior for a student. Teachers can also find out if there are specific target behaviors that the parent is working on at home and offer to increase their praise for these behaviors at school. See the Teacher-To-Parent Communication Letters on the web site about home compliment times that teachers can send to their students' parents.

 **www.incredibleyears.com/TeacherResources/index.asp**

CONCLUSION—DOUBLING THE IMPACT

The task of teaching a child a new behavior is a long and laborious one. For the fastest progress, teachers would shine a praise light on the positive behavior every time it occurs, but that is an impossibility given the realities of the classroom. Still, it should be the goal to spotlight desired behavior as often as possible in the beginning. If there is more than one adult in the classroom, all teachers should discuss behavioral goals for each student and work together to praise and encourage these consistently. This kind of strategic planning and teamwork dramatically increases the speed with which students will progress toward those goals. In addition, teachers can double the impact by building on each other's praise and by encouraging parents to celebrate their children's successes. Remember the impact of praise hinges on the quality of the teacher-student relationship because if a supportive relationship is not in place, praise will not be reinforcing.

In other words, it is necessary to both water the relationship as well as to provide sunshine to encourage student growth.

TO SUM UP...

Teacher Attention, Encouragement & Praise

- Pinpoint what it is you like about the behavior and be specific labeling the positive behaviors in your praise.
- Praise with sincerity and enthusiasm, and in a variety of ways. Make a big deal out of it.
- Don't wait for behavior to be perfect before praising.
- Praise individual children as well as the whole class or small groups.
- Use praise consistently and frequently, especially when a child is first learning a new behavior. Remember, it is the most powerful form of positive recognition you can give a child.
- Children who are inattentive, highly distractible, and oppositional need frequent attention and praise whenever they are behaving appropriately.
- Praise children according to your individual behavioral goals for them—including both academic, emotional self-regulation skills and social behaviors.
- Don't stay behind your desk during independent work time; rather, circulate around the room giving recognition for positive behaviors.
- When you give a direction, look for at least two students who are following the direction—say their names and restate direction as you praise the fact that they are following it.

- Develop a concrete plan for how you will remember to provide consistent praise such as a sticker on the clock or your watch, coins in your pocket, timer, etc.
- Focus on students' efforts and learning, not just the end result.
- Focus on students' strengths and areas of improvement.
- Express your belief in your students' abilities.
- Do not compare one student with another student (or sibling).
- Praise yourself for your persistent efforts!

The Incredible Years®
Teacher Classroom Management Self-Reflection Inventory
Teacher Attention, Encouragement and Praise

Date: _____ Teacher Name: _____

Teachers learn extensively from self-reflection regarding their classroom management and the teaching strategies they are using that are working or not working. From these reflections teachers determine personal goals for making changes in their approaches to bring about the most positive learning climate they can. Use this Inventory to think about your strengths and limitations and determine your goals.

Attention, praise, & encouragement	1 = NEVER 3 = OCCASIONALLY 5 = CONSISTENTLY
1. I use labeled praise statements with positive affect and combine praise with coaching methods – I get close to child, smile and gain eye contact. I give praise immediately when behavior occurs.	1 2 3 4 5
2. I give more attention to positive social behaviors than to inappropriate behaviors. (5 praises:1correction)	1 2 3 4 5
3. My praise is sincere and enthusiastic.	1 2 3 4 5
4. I have identified positive behaviors I want to praise immediately and give attention to with all students.	1 2 3 4 5
5. I have identified "positive opposite" behaviors I want to praise in targeted children with behavioral difficulties. I work hard to notice when these students are behaving appropriately.	1 2 3 4 5

6. I use proximal praise strategically (e.g., praise nearby child for behavior I want from another child).	1 2 3 4 5
7. I work hard to give special time to children who are withdrawn or isolated to promote more peer interactions.	1 2 3 4 5
8. I model positive self-talk as well as praise to other teachers or adults in the classroom.	1 2 3 4 5
9. I make positive calls to parents to compliment them about their children's successes or positive behavior.	1 2 3 4 5
10. I communicate my belief to students that they can succeed and promote their positive self-talk.	1 2 3 4 5
11. I help children learn how to compliment each other and have compliment circle times.	1 2 3 4 5
12. I prompt children to notice another child's special talent or accomplishment.	1 2 3 4 5
13. I use "positive forecasting" statements to predict a child's success when s/he is frustrated with a learning activity.	1 2 3 4 5
14. I share my positive feelings (proud, happiness, joy, courage) when interacting with children.	1 2 3 4 5
15. I use self-encouragement bubbles for my students so they can learn how to self-praise.	1 2 3 4 5
16. I provide physical affection with verbal affection and praise with my students.	1 2 3 4 5
17. I praise individual children as well as whole class or small groups.	1 2 3 4 5

18. I focus on children's efforts and learning– not just end result.	
19. I talk with parents (via telephone or email or Teacher-to-Parent Communication Home Activity letters) about targeted behaviors in their children that they can praise.	1 2 3 4 5
Future Goals Regarding Attention, Encouragement and Praise Strategies:	Total

REFERENCES

Brophy, J. E. (1981). On praising effectively. *The Elementary School Journal, 81,* 269-275.

Brophy, J. E. (1996). *Teaching problem students.* New York: Guilford.

Cameron, J., & Pierce, W. D. (1994). Reinforcement, reward, and intrinsic motivation: A meta-analysis. *Review of Educational Research, 64,* 363-423.

Gable, R. A., Hester, P. H., Rock, M. L., & Hughes, K. G. (2009). Back to basics: Rules, praise, ignoring and reprimands revisited. *Intervention in School and Clinic, 44,* 195-205.

Kalis, T. M., Vannest, K. J., & Parker, R.I. (2007). Praise Counts: Using self-monitoring to increase effective teaching practices. *Preventing School Failure, 51*(3), 20-27.

Mesa, J., Lewis-Palmer, T., & Reinke, W. M. (2005). Providing teachers with performance feedback on praise to reduce student problem behavior. *Beyond Behavior,* 45-55.

Reinke, W. M., & Lewis-Palmer, T. (2007). The effect of visual performance feedback on teacher use of behavior-specific praise. *Behavior Modification, 31*(3), 247-263.

Reinke, W. M., & Lewis-Palmer, T. (2008). The classroom check-up: A class wide teacher consultation model for increasing praise and decreasing disruptive behavior. *School Psychology Review, 37*(3), 315-332.

Sutherland, K., Wehby, J., & Copeland, S. (2000). Effect on varying rates of behavior-specific praise on the on-task behavior of stutents with EBD. *Journal of Emotional and Behavioral Disorders, 8,* 2-8.

Walker, H. M., Colvin, G., & Ramsey, E. (1995). *Antisocial behavior in school: Strategies and best practices.* Pacific Grove, CA: Brooks/Cole.

CHAPTER
6

Strengthening Positive Behavior: Using Incentives to Motivate Students

In the previous chapters we discussed the importance of teacher attention, specific coaching methods, encouragement, praise, and positive teacher-student relationships as tools for building the foundation of the teaching pyramid in order to nurture and promote all students' successful learning growth in the classroom. However, when students have difficulty with a particular behavior or area of learning, teacher attention, coaching, and praise may not be strong enough reinforcers to motivate them. Indeed, learning to read, to write, knowing how to engage in socially appropriate behavior, and use of self-regulation skills are slow and arduous developmental learning processes and sometimes children feel they are not making any headway. Students may be aware that some of their peers are successfully learning to read and write and do math problems but believe they are not making any progress and feel discouraged by their perceived failure. They may not be able to see the small steps they are making to learn to identify letters and eventually to read words or to recognize numbers and how to add or subtract them. Some students may feel lonely, unsuccessful socially, even rejected and left out at times, while feeling other children do have friends. Still others may struggle or feel incapable of listening and following a teacher's instructions while seeing that their peers seem to easily know what to do.

© *Incredible Years*®

Making Learning Tangible

One way of assisting this learning process is to use tangible markers such as stickers, hand stamps, points, special rewards, or celebrations to give students concrete evidence of their progress. Tangible rewards provide extra incentives for children to tackle a difficult learning area and can sustain a child's motivation until a positive relationship has been developed with the teacher that will make praise and attention more motivating. Research has indicated a multitude of positive results from using incentive programs, such as: increased classroom participation, on task work, and attention (Jones & Jones, 2007), cooperative behaviors, improving spelling and math accuracy (Nevin, Johnson & Johnson, 1982), decreasing transition time (Yarbrough & Skinner, 2004), reducing talking-out and out of seat behavior (Barrish & Saunders, 1969; Embry, 2002), and decreasing more serious behavior problems (e.g., Rhode, Jenson, & Reavis, 1992). When using incentive programs to motivate students to learn something new, it is, of course, important to continue providing social approval, coaching methods, and encouragement as well. The impact is greater when both types of social and tangible rewards are combined.

Incentive programs involve planning in advance, which specific behaviors will result in a reward for a particular student. This type of program, which is like a behavioral contract, is recommended when teachers wish to increase a rare behavior or a behavior that is particularly difficult for a student to learn. Let's look at a concrete example.

Transition Tickets

A teacher was having difficulty with her second grade class whenever they came in from recess. As students came into the classroom they poked, pushed and teased each other, and took a great deal of time getting settled down to their classroom work. She found she was yelling at them constantly and that it took about 30 minutes before the class was finally engaged in their work. In fact, she noticed that any transition, be it from recess, lunch, or gym, was difficult for her students to manage without conflict. Her goal was help her students transition more smoothly to their work without a lot of classroom disruption. To achieve this, she planned a "transition ticket system" with her students. First, she wrote the work assignment on the board so that when the students entered the class they would know exactly what to do. For example, she might write on the board, "start writing in your dialogue books," or, "get out your reading books and read the first page of chapter 3" and so forth. Whenever she noticed students settling into their desks and following the directions on the blackboard she gave them a transition ticket which was color-coded for the week. These tickets were kept in a special box inside the students' desks.

Transition tickets were given out every time the students entered the class during the day, so they had an opportunity to earn up to 4 tickets a day. On Fridays each student counted his or her tickets and traded them in for prizes. The teacher discussed with the students the kind of treats or prizes they would like to earn. The prize box

had a variety of tangible rewards (pencils, erasers, sugarless gum, marbles, baseball cards, small plastic dinosaurs, fake tattoos, and bubbles) as well as nontangible rewards (lunch with the teacher, line leader at recess, choosing an activity for gym, choice of classroom snack, opportunity to bring special item from home to share with class). In addition to counting each student's individual tickets, the students counted the total number of tickets the entire class earned each week and posted these on a large thermometer on the wall. When the entire class had earned 2000 tickets (top of thermometer), they would have a celebration. The teacher found that when she focused her attention on those students who were settling into work with her coaching, praise, and attention coupled with giving out a ticket, the class soon settled down quickly without her yelling. Moreover, everyone enjoyed the game and planning their classroom celebration.

In this example, it is noteworthy that this teacher was specific about the problem behaviors and the positive ones with which she wanted to replace them. She chose specified periods of the day to focus on these behaviors and offered her students several opportunities a day to be successful and earn a ticket. Another significant aspect of this example is that it is developmentally appropriate for 7- to 8-year-olds, who love to collect and trade in things. Moreover most children this age have the developmental capacity to wait a week before trading in their tickets. Also the fact students received a coupon at each successful transition gave them an immediate reward as a marker of their achievements. This immediate feedback is particularly important for more impulsive children, who might otherwise have difficulty waiting until the end of the week. Later when transitions were going smoothly, this teacher modified her ticket system to achieve other goals (based on individual student needs and goals). Each student collected tickets which were akin to money vouchers, which could then be used to buy items at a school market day (children bring things they want to sell on market day). Another time when her budget for prizes was small, she set up a system whereby students put their tickets in a special raffle jar. At the end of the week there was a raffle and tickets were drawn for a prize. This teacher was successful because she tried to make the program fun for her students by involving them in the planning of their rewards and celebrations.

For younger preschool children, a successful incentive program will need to be simpler, with the opportunity for children to earn something immediately. For example, the teacher may give a stamp on a card, wristband, or hand, or give stickers for specified target behaviors (helping, sharing, following directions) as soon as she sees the desired behavior. At the end of the day each child can see how many stamps s/he has earned for being a helper and feel proud as s/he shares the successes with parents.

While incentive programs may seem simple, there are in fact many pitfalls to be avoided if they are to be effective. In the first part of this chapter, we will discuss some of the erroneous objections that have sometimes been raised to using incentives with students, and in the second part we will discuss some common problems teachers encounter when trying to set up these programs. Based on research regarding incentive systems, we will describe the most effective and practical approaches to making them work (Cameron & Pierce, 1994; Elliott & Gresham, 1992; Emmer, Evertson, Clements, Sanford, & Worsham, 1994; Stage & Quiroz, 1997; Walker, Colvin, & Ramsey, 1995; Walker, 2002; Yarbrough & Skinner, 2004). We will discuss a variety of ways in which teachers provide extra incentives to motivate children to learn social and academic skills.

SOME QUESTIONS TEACHERS ASK

Don't incentive programs set children up for failure in the future because they become hooked on external rewards and fail to develop their internal motivation?

Sometimes teachers worry that incentives such as hand stamps, tickets, stars, and pizza parties will lead to students becoming "hooked" on external rewards and will not serve them well in the long run. They believe that if they use incentives, children will not develop internal motivation and will not be able to function in future classes where teachers may not use incentive programs. They worry that students will learn to manipulate the system and learn to respond to simple requests from teachers by saying, "What am I going to get for it?"

Actually there is no research evidence that this happens if incentive programs are implemented appropriately (Cameron & Pierce, 1994). It is important to emphasize that incentive programs are not a substitute for other means of motivating students: building meaningful relationships with students, reinforcing them with attention, coaching and praise, stimulating their interests in certain areas, and setting individual goals. Incentive programs are merely an adjunct strategy for the student who has some particular emotional, social, or academic difficulty, who is resisting or avoiding trying a particular task, or who is unresponsive to other reinforcers. Because tangible rewards are immediate, they are also useful for getting a whole class quickly under control so that they will attend to what is being taught. The idea behind these incentive programs is to gradually phase them out as children gain the confidence and skills that will strengthen their internal motivation to persist. Incentives might be thought of as a kind of *external scaffolding* to help children until they can do it on their own.

Incentives might be thought of as a kind of external scaffolding to help children until they can do it on their own.

How can you set up incentive programs for some children in the classroom and not for others? It's not fair. Won't this cause other well-behaved children to misbehave in order to get the rewards?
Teachers may be concerned that it is unfair to give rewards to some children and not to others. Actually, the issue here is that it is really more fair to individualize teaching strategies according to what individual students need because every child has different abilities. Just as a doctor prescribes according to what medicine is most appropriate for a given illness, so the teacher must determine the specific learning needs of each of her students as well as what motivates them. Rather than thinking that it is unfair to use individualized reward systems or to worry that students might misbehave in other to participate in an

incentive system, it is important for teachers to think about the message that accompanies the use of incentives.

Teachers should think carefully about how to explain incentive programs to the class about the message that students are given about the reason for these programs. For example, the teacher might say, "Everyone in our class has different goals. Jessie's goal is to stay in her seat. She and I have worked out a program to help her remember to sit. And we are going to give her a special cheer if she can make her goal." Here the teacher elicits student support for the program and explains its purpose to the students thus reducing competition or jealousy or ridicule from other students. In fact, the teacher might even set up a classroom celebration when Jessie achieves her goal. Most children in a classroom will accept this explanation, particularly if they are self-confident and successful. Students who seem particularly jealous of the special incentive that Jessie is receiving might be given a different individualized goal. "John, it seems like you would really like to earn some stickers too. Let's think of a good goal for you. What is something that you need to work on?"

Often there are ways to provide some kind of low-intensity system for all students in the class so that no one feels excluded, and then provide more frequent incentives for students with particular needs. In other words, all students have a chance to earn the reward sometimes.

Should you let parents know about good and bad days?

A common strategy used by teachers is to send home daily behavior charts with stickers of happy faces for good behaviors and frowning faces for misbehaviors. In general, we recommend teachers do not mix their reinforcement and punishment systems (in this case, combining both kinds of stickers on the same chart), as the negative feedback (frowning face) will negate the positive feedback (happy face). In fact, the attention given (either by the teacher or the parent) for a frowning face may end up being greater and therefore more reinforcing than the attention given for a happy face. This is especially

Teachers should not mix their reinforcement and punishment systems.

true for children with behavior problems who tend to focus more on criticism than on praise or approval.

Another possible side effect of sending negative feedback home is an unpredictable negative response from parents. Some parents may become angry and resentful towards the teacher for sending home a negative report and may even blame teachers for the problem. Sending home negative feedback might also result in parents punishing the child for what happened at school. Parents may punish out of frustration with their child or a feeling they are "supposed to do something" about the teacher's note about the misbehaviors. This results in the child receiving a double punishment from home and school. Punishment at home for school behavior is unlikely to be effective since the disciplinary action happens at least several hours after the misbehavior occurred. Moreover, such a reaction from parents will only damage the parent-child relationship. Teachers should emphasize that when sticker behavior charts are sent home, it is the job of the parents to be supportive and encouraging of their children's successes and to refrain from commenting on the blank spaces where no stickers were earned (sometimes parents may punish a child for earning only 5 or 6 out of 7 happy faces). Parents can be instructed to predict success for the next day and to review important rules, "I know you're going to have a good day tomorrow. I bet you are able to meet your goal of listening to the teacher." Thus parents will give their children the consistent message that they believe they can succeed and that they want them to try their very best at school. Teachers can assure parents that they will handle any misbehavior as soon as it occurs at school and will quickly move on to a new learning experience so that the child can be successful.

When do you begin to involve the child in evaluating his or day?
While incentive programs do give students concrete feedback about their successes, teachers should still encourage children to reflect about how they did that day. For example a teacher might have a thermometer showing the range from calm (blue for cool) to overexcited (red hot) and the child might point to how he thought he did during the day. This would give the teacher an opportunity to give realistic and

specific feedback on times when the child successfully calmed down. Similar thermometers might be used for level of involvement in classroom activities. (See Chapter Nine for an example of a Calm Down thermometer.) Often children with behavior problems will focus on their mistakes during the day; by reviewing the positive efforts made by the child (for example, times when the child successfully earned a sticker for being calm) the teacher can help the child learn to make more positive attributions about his day. By reviewing the times of the day it was hard to be patient, they can make a plan for how they

By reviewing the positive efforts made by the child, the teacher can help the child learn to make more positive attributions about his day.

will handle it next time they find themselves in a similar situation. Another self-reflective approach is to have children complete a form called a *self-encouragement bubble* for various things that occurred during the day regarding such things as friends, school work and frustrations. This can be completed verbally and transcriptions taken down by the teacher, or alternatively the teacher can ask the student to do drawings or writing for each category.

ESTABLISHING OBJECTIVES

Be Specific about Appropriate Behaviors

Teachers sometimes set up tangible reward programs that are vague about which appropriate behaviors will result in a reward. For instance, Billy is disruptive in class, he can't sit still in circle time, pokes the other children next to him, and constantly interrupts the teacher's discussions with the students. Billy's teacher says to him, "When you are good in school, you can pick a reward," and "if you behave well at circle time, you can have a treat." The teacher refers to a vague trait, "goodness," but is unclear about what specific behavior will earn Billy a reward. If teachers aren't clear about the behaviors they want, students are unlikely to be successful. Billy may even, in all innocence, demand a treat because he thinks he was good at school while the teacher felt

My Self-Encouragement Bubble

I'm a good problem-solver.
I'm good at math.
I can face up to the problem and solve it.
I'm not a quitter.
I can cope with this.
I can calm my body down.
I'm good at sharing.
I can wait.
I am very helpful.
I am a friendly person.
I am good with words.
I ignore noises around me.
I can go to my seat without being asked.
I do what's best for myself.
I am incredibly brave.
I love to share my things.
I'm a good leader.

his behavior was disruptive. He might argue, "But I was good. I want a treat!" Indeed, he thought he was good because he shared once with another child and tried to behave. Unfortunately, his teacher's view of "good" is more rigorous.

The first step in setting up an incentive program is to think clearly about which misbehaviors are bothersome. How often do they occur, and what is the alternative positive behavior? If, like Billy's teacher, the teacher wants a preschooler to be less disruptive at circle time, he might say, "If you sit quietly by my side and keep your hands in your lap while we have circle time, then you can earn a special sticker." Or, "every time you put up a quiet hand and wait to be called on, you will earn a hand stamp." Here the positive behaviors are described clearly for the child. Being specific also makes it easier for a teacher to know whether or not she should follow through with a reward.

Make Steps Small

One reason many incentive programs fail is that teachers make the steps or behavioral expectations so big that their students feel that earning a reward is impossible and give up trying—or don't even try in the first place. In the "circle time" example above, if Billy was four years old, very active, in the habit of jumping out of seat constantly and interrupting every two minutes, it would be unrealistic to expect him to stay by the teacher's side quietly for very long. Thus, a program that involved earning a sticker for staying seated quietly for a 20-minute circle time discussion would be doomed to failure.

A good reward program incorporates the small steps required to achieve the goal. First, observe how often the misbehaviors occur for several days. This baseline will be key to establishing the right steps for planning an incentive program. Then the teacher chooses the specific behavior he wants to work on first. For example, if the teacher notices that Billy can sit for five minutes, then this would be the first step to reinforce. The program would involve giving Billy a sticker every five minutes he sits still and keeps

Remember, the idea is to progress with shaping the small steps needed to eventually achieve the desired goal.

his hands in his lap. In this example, the teacher starts with physical sitting as her first priority, and after she has gained success with the child sitting, she will move on to other goals such as teaching him how to put up a quiet hand instead of constantly verbally interrupting. With this approach, Billy has a good chance of being successful and earning some stickers. Once he can sit still for five minutes without a problem, the teacher can make the reward contingent on sitting for a little longer. Remember, the idea is to progress with shaping the small steps needed to eventually achieve the desired goal.

A note of caution here, if Billy is, by temperament, very hyperactive, the teacher will progress slowly and will need to adjust her expectations for how long she can expect him to sit still at this age. Ten minutes may be the most he can realistically be expected to achieve at this developmental stage. Consequently, if circle time in her classroom is usually 15 to 20 minutes, she will want to give a child such as Billy, an appropriate way he can move around without causing disruptions. For example, after he has achieved his five or ten minute goal for sitting, he is permitted to get up and go to a special place in the room called, "Billy's Wiggle Space," where he can move around quietly. Then, when he is ready he can come back to the circle and sit down and have an opportunity to earn another sticker for sitting still.

Pace Steps Correctly

The opposite problem occurs when teachers make the steps too easy. In this situation, the students are not motivated to work for the reward or they undervalue it because they get it so easily and often. This is rarely a problem in the beginning since most teachers make the steps too big. However, it can become a problem as the program continues. For instance, after a few weeks, let's say Billy is consistently getting a sticker for every 5 minutes sitting at circle time. Unless the teacher makes the program more challenging by asking him to both sit still and put up a quiet hand before receiving a sticker, the stickers may lose their reinforcing value.

A good rule of thumb is to make it fairly easy to earn a reward when children are first learning a new behavior. Initially, children need repeated successes to appreciate the rewards and the teacher approval, and to understand they are capable of the desired behavior. Then teachers can make it a little harder. Gradually, the rewards are spaced further and further apart (intermittently) until they are not needed at all. Ultimately, teacher approval can maintain the behaviors. Be careful, however, sometimes teachers who are feeling successful with their program step it up too quickly, and students then regress in frustration at their inability to succeed. Constant monitoring of the correct pacing of the steps is one of the keys to successful incentive programs for changing behavior.

Choose the Number of Behaviors Carefully

Programs sometimes fail because too many negative and difficult behaviors are tackled at once. We have seen highly motivated teachers start reward programs involving stickers given throughout the school day for compliance to teacher directions, not teasing peers, quiet hands up, staying seated, not poking, and working hard. Such programs are too complex. The pressure to succeed in many different areas of life may seem so over-whelming that children give up before starting. Another drawback of this approach is that it requires constant monitoring by the teachers all day long. Simply observing a student's compliance to teacher requests throughout a day will require a tremendous amount of effort because these situations occur frequently. Remember, if a teacher cannot real-istically monitor the student's behavior and follow through with con-sequences, even the best-designed program is bound to fail.

There are three main things to consider when deciding how many target behaviors to help children learn at one time: the frequency with which each behavior occurs; the student's developmental stage; and what is realistic for the teacher to carry out. With regard to fre-quency, remember that behaviors such as noncompliance, interrupting, touching others, or jumping out of seat may occur often and therefore will require much teacher supervision. This means that realistically a teacher will not be able to focus on more than one such behavior at a time. The second important point to consider is the developmental ability of the student. Young children require easily understandable programs that focus on one or two simple behaviors at a time. Learning to be compliant to teacher requests or to share with another child are major developmental tasks for a young child. Each will require many repeated learning trials, time, and much patience on the part of the teachers. However, as children mature (school age and adolescence), tangible reward programs can become more complex because older children understand and remember them better. In addition, problem behaviors at this stage usually occur less frequently and are easier to monitor. For a school age child, therefore, it would be possible to estab-lish a successful program that included points for remembering to bring in homework, helping put away sports equipment at gym, and settling down quietly to work when returning from recess.

Evaluation of how much monitoring a teacher can realistically expect to be able to do is the third factor in deciding which child behaviors to focus on. Even if a teacher has a co-teacher or assistant, it is difficult to monitor a behavior such as following teacher directions, throughout the day. This will be true, particularly if a teacher has a class of 30 children including three or four children who are on incentive programs for particular problems. Therefore, a teacher will want to choose the time of the day when she can focus on the behaviors she wants to increase. For instance, many children have difficulties during the unstructured or free play times or transitions and this may be the time a teacher wants to really focus on coaching, praise and incentives for cooperative and sharing behavior. Some teachers like to focus their incentive programs on difficult times such as transition times or recess or unstructured play times. Nonetheless, the key aspect is that teachers set up a program that is realistic and that the teacher can find the time to follow through consistently with the coaching, praise and rewards.

Set up a program that is realistic and that the teacher can find the time to follow through consistently with the coaching, praise and rewards.

For example, for a high frequency behavior such as interrupting all day long, a teacher might decide that she will put the incentive system into place for her morning and afternoon circles (or in some cases for just one circle time). During these targeted times, she will try to be as consistent as possible with providing a tangible incentive for the student's quiet hand. At other times of day, she will try to ignore interrupting and when possible, praise the student for raising his quiet hand. Once the circle time interrupting has decreased, the teacher may be ready to tackle another time of day. It is also possible that the hand raising may generalize to other times of day and an incentive system may no longer be needed for those other times.

Focus on Positive Opposite Behaviors

Another problem occurs when teachers focus exclusively on negative behaviors. Teachers can clearly identify the negative behaviors they want to eliminate, such as fighting, interrupting, poking, running, disobeying, loud voices, and disturbing others during work time in class. Their incentive program outlines the rewards that children will receive for going an hour without fighting, poking, or interrupting. So far, so good; but the program hasn't gone far enough. While it tells students clearly what they should not do, it neither describes clearly the positive opposite behavior

Behavior Plan: Jenny Grade 1

Negative Classroom Behaviors to Ignore	Occasion	Desired Positive Opposite Behaviors	Specific Reinforcers
poking, touching other students	in line	keep hands to own body	responds well to praise–does not like to be hugged "wow you remembered to raise a quiet hand"
speaks without raising hand	small group discussion	raise a quiet hand	20 coupons for quiet hand equals choosing book for story time
talks while directions are given	large classroom	listen quietly when directions given	use listening self monitoring sheet–10 pts per day=choosing special activity at free time
off-task, daydreaming	independent work time	pay attention and concentrate	happy grams for on-task work

the teacher expects nor rewards the appropriate replacement behavior. Rather it is rewarding the absence of negative behavior. Thus, inappropriate behavior receives more teacher attention and behavioral description than description of the desired appropriate behavior.

It is important to identify the positive opposite behaviors that are to replace the negative behaviors and to include them in the incentive program. For example, programs should include rewards for the presence of cooperative behaviors such as sharing, taking turns, playing quietly with a peer, keeping one's hands to oneself, talking with a quiet voice in class, putting up a quiet hand, waiting a turn, working attentively on a project, coming in to class and sitting down quietly, using words when angry, or following teacher directions. It is critical that the positive behaviors be spelled out as clearly as the behaviors that are to be eliminated. In the behavior plan for Jenny which we discussed in Chapter Five, the teacher now adds some incentives to her praise planning. Although the plan below focuses on four different behaviors, keep in mind that these behaviors would be targeted one at a time. New behavioral goals would be added as the student had success with earlier goals, and incentives would be faded out for goals that were met with success for a period of time.

When to Individualize Programs

In the "Transition ticket" example, it was appropriate to set up an incentive program that involved the entire class since many of the students needed help with this problem. However, sometimes it is not helpful to do an incentive program with everyone in the class, in fact, it might even decrease some students' motivation. For example, a teacher was concerned because some of her students were not reading books. Therefore she set up an incentive program that involved giving a reward to every student who finished reading two books per month. The danger with this type of reward is that it is not individualized. For those students who were already reading and motivated by their own enjoyment of reading, setting a limit on two books may actually decrease the number of books they would try to read. Other students with extreme difficulty reading might perceive the goal as unattainable and, therefore, not motivating. A teacher who wanted to use a group incentive system for reading might still give rewards for reading, but have different students read different numbers of books or books with different levels of reading complexity to obtain that reward.

At times incentive programs may need even more tailoring according to the needs and abilities of the particular student who is having difficulty completing the assignment. For example, if a student has reading or learning difficulties, the teacher might want to provide incentives for that student for trying to read each day for 15 minutes, not necessarily for finishing a book or chapter. Moreover, the teacher will want to be sure that this child is given books that are not too advanced for his level of reading and that address some of his special interests (dinosaurs, trains, airplanes, horses, fairies). The goal for such a child will not be completing a certain number of books per month, but rather providing the encouragement so that s/he continually is engaged in the process of trying to read. On the other hand, if a teacher has a student who is capable of independent reading but simply does not organize himself sufficiently to get any reading done, then the incentive program might be set up for completing a certain number of pages during a set period of time each day. It is essential that teachers understand the nature of the child's behavioral difficulties because only then can they design effective incentive programs.

CHOOSING THE MOST EFFECTIVE INCENTIVES

Once teachers have chosen target behaviors, the next task is to choose appropriate rewards or incentives. Tangible rewards can include stickers, stars, points, stamps pencils, books, bookmarks, or decals. Often non-tangible rewards are even more highly valued by students. These might include special privileges such as lunch with the teacher or a preferred peer, the chance to show a special talent to the class, extra time with a preferred activity, a few extra minutes of recess or free time, the opportunity to visit another class, sit in a special chair, pick a song for the class, or be a teacher's helper.

It is important to remember that what is motivating for one student may not be for another; some children crave praise and adult attention, others are wary of adult approval and would rather work for stickers, gum, or wrist band stamps, others like to earn special privileges. For many young children (ages 4-6 years), hand stamps or stickers on a page are rewarding in themselves, making it unnecessary to provide additional material rewards. As children get older, saving up coupons or stickers and trading them in for something desirable adds to the effectiveness of the incentive program. Children are reinforced twice; once when they earn the point or sticker and again when achieve their longer term goal. These kind of trade-in or point systems also begin to develop children's ability to remain motivated in the face of delayed gratification. One way to get to know what might be particularly reinforcing for a particular child is to send home an interest survey to parents to get some information about the child's interests, hobbies, and what things are especially reinforcing for the child. Parents can be very helpful to teachers in determining what incentives will motivate their child.

Some ideas for making learning tangible

- Putting "I can" notes in a box on student's desk
- Having students make accomplishment albums
- Filling in one statement on student's self-encouragement bubble each day (e.g., "I can go to my seat without being asked")
- Encouraging students to applaud each other's accomplishments
- Using positive time out (visit to principal for special accomplishment)
- Teaching self-approval (pat oneself on back)
- Phone call to parents to tell of student's accomplishments
- Compliment cards and charts
- Playground raffle tickets for cooperative behavior
- Phone call to student to congratulate on accomplishment
- Providing materials for students to make each other "play ground power" awards for positive behaviors at recess

Inexpensive Tangible Items

- Points, marbles, stickers (which can be traded in for prizes)
- Stickers or pin-on badges with messages (e.g., Well done for being a good listener, I was helpful today, I keep the playground rules, I join in well with others)
- Tickets that are traded in for a prize
- Special prize boxes

  - Pencils, erasers, markers, scissors
  - Small note pads
  - "Cool" stickers (e.g., scratch and sniff stickers)
  - Baseball or soccer cards
  - Bubbles
  - Pretzels, crackers, sugarless gum
- Surprise notes
- Bubble bath, small soap
- Art supplies—sequins, glue stick
- Post card
- Puzzle, maze, "brain teaser," joke
- Stamp
- Play dough
- Beads, shells, polished rocks
- Posters
- Mystery prize (a prize put in a decorated envelope or box)
- Spin the Wheel of Fortune for a prize
- Fake Tattoo

Special Privileges (Non-tangible Rewards)

- Lunch with teacher
- Read student's favorite book to class
- Work on favorite activity
- Choose special video for class to watch
- Field trip
- Invite special visitor to class

- Share a talent or hobby with class
- Choose which seat to sit in that day
- Chance to eat lunch with another class
- Being teacher's helper for the day
- Line leader
- Homework pass (10 compliment cards = homework pass for one night)
- Listen to 5 minutes of favorite music with class
- Extra computer time
- Extra 10 minutes of recess on Friday
- Play board game
- Five minutes of conversation time where students can sit anywhere they wish and chat at the opening or closing of the day (as long as no one is left out)
- Disco time
- Visit to another classroom (where child has relationship with that teacher)
- Opportunity to help a younger child in another class or work with a secretary
- Face painting
- Stuffed animal friend to sit on desk for day

Be Sure Student Incentives are Age Appropriate

For preschool children incentive programs should be clear, simple, and playful. Preschoolers love to collect different stamps and stickers or perhaps even earn a little prize from a surprise grab bag. There is no need to complicate the system for young children with reward menus or trading things in for bigger prizes. Just receiving the sticker coupled with teacher encouragement and seeing their sticker chart fill up is all the reward they need.

Once children have learned the concept of numbers and understand the notion of days in a week and of time passing (around 6 years and up), they like to participate in programs where they collect things and trade in things. This is the age when "collections" start. Remember all those collections of baseball cards, rocks, coins, and stamps? At this age children can be offered the chance to collect stickers and trade them in later for a bigger prize.

Choose Inexpensive Incentives

Believe it or not, we have seen reward programs that have bankrupted their teachers' classroom budgets for the year. Even when schools can afford more expensive incentives, use of these is not necessary and teaches children to expect big rewards for their successes. It is counterproductive if the emphasis is placed on the magnitude of the reward, rather than on the satisfaction and pride felt by both the teacher and child at the child's success.

In general inexpensive or no-cost privileges are more powerful reinforcers. Young children often like to earn special privileges such as those listed in the reward suggestion boxes. Small food items such as raisins, pretzels, a pizza party, or choosing a favorite snack can also be appealing. While it is our belief that small, and mostly healthy, food incentives are not harmful to children, some teachers prefer not to use food incentives at all. The beauty of reward systems is that there is an almost endless menu of ideas, so each teacher (and student) can pick favorite rewards.

Special Recognitions and Celebrations

One powerful and inexpensive motivator for many students is to have "special recognition" awards. These may be given to a student who has shown dramatic improvement in some area, who has shown improvement in a particularly difficult area, or who has completed some special achievement. While we often think of awards as being for academic achievement, special recognition can be awarded for social behavior too. When students receive positive recognition from others, especially teachers and classmates, they begin to feel capable and believe they can successfully contribute. When possible, these awards should be recognized by the principal. For example, the student may go to the principal's office to shake his or her hand or be given the award in front of an assembly of students. Notice of these awards should be sent home to parents so they can be informed of their child's successes.

SPECIAL RECOGNITIONS AND CELEBRATIONS

EXAMPLES

Top Dog Award

One example of this is the "Top Dog" award—"top dog" can be a stuffed animal who sits on the desk of the student who has been the best citizen for that week. When children get to be "top dog" they get to be first in line and go to lunch first because they have shown they are responsible. The goal of being "responsible" or "best citizen" may be defined differently for each child, in line with their individual goals.

Feather in Your Cap

Another example of special recognition is to earn "a feather in your cap." Children can earn a "feather" from the teacher for saying something nice to someone or doing something nice for someone else without being asked. The feather is a picture of a feather which says, *"This is a feather in Johnny's hat earned because he helped in math."* The teacher sticks these feathers on the wall in a vertical column starting at the floor level; when the feathers for the class reach the ceiling, the whole class earns a celebration. This system rewards cooperation and the social skill of praise. It might also be used for academic achievements as well.

Golden Acorn Award

A variation on the feather method of encouraging students is the growing tree. At the beginning of the year the class creates a huge barren oak tree. Then every time a student improves or reaches a particular target goal, s/he would receive a blooming leaf with the words, " I have learned to . . ." and would put this leaf on the tree (also a note is sent home to tell parents of the achievement). Five leaves on the tree lead to a student earning a Golden Acorn Award. The child places a golden acorn on the tree and if she chooses, she can sit on the golden chair and receive questions about her hobbies, interests and life experience (or some other celebration). Three acorns lead to a golden squirrel which leads to an even bigger celebration. This system can be individualized for students to focus on their own particular targeted goals based on their learning needs.

Compliment Chart

A fourth example of a way to recognize students is called the compliment chart. Here the teacher has a chart posted in the classroom and records whenever the class receives a compliment from a teacher or parent or student. Once the students achieve a certain number of compliments they also earn a celebration. Another version of this is to give out compliment cards to individual children. The teacher might set up a contract with students, for example, when the class gets 10 compliment cards they earn a homework free night.

Other Special Recognition and Celebrations

- Win special "Award Bear" to take home
- Wear special button, ribbon or tie acknowledging the child's achievement
- "Top Dog" Award—stuffed dog given to child who wins
- "Feather in Your Cap" Award—feathers which are mounted on walls around the room
- Citizen of the Week Award
- Popcorn or ice-cream party
- Compliment Chart—teacher keeps track of compliments given to students
- Mystery Super Hero Student
- Get to become Wizard Happy—that is to wear the wizard hat and cloak and make a special wish.
- Giant of the Week—a quality such as helpfulness or patience is selected for the week. The teacher and other children watch for this quality in others and nominate this student.

Involve Students in the Incentive Program

Occasionally teachers choose tangible rewards that are more rein-forcing for themselves than for their students. A related problem is teachers who take too much control over the program. We have seen elaborate charts with pictures pasted on them and fancy stickers cho-sen by the teachers, not the children. Unless children are given some control, the program is likely to fail. The goal of a tangible reward pro-gram should be to teach students to take more responsibility for their own behavior. If students sense that teachers are unwilling to delegate some control, they may dig in their heels for a fight, in which case their focus is shifted from the pleasure of cooperation and good behavior to the satisfaction of winning a power struggle by escalating their bids for negative attention.

Find out what is most rewarding for each of your students. Teachers can do this by priming themselves with lots of ideas for rewards, just in case students don't have any to start with. However, try hard to get students to come up with their own suggestions. A teacher might say to a reluctant child, "You like playing with the computer. How about putting an extra 15 minutes of computer time on your list?" And remember that a reinforcement menu does not need to be completed in one discussion but can be added to as students think of other things to work for. If teachers use stickers, it is more effective to ask students what kind of stickers they like (e.g., dinosaur, sports, animals) and involve them in drawing up charts and deciding how many stickers particular items are worth. Older students love the possibility of earn-ing a homework free night or the chance to bring something to share with their classmates. Get students involved in the fun of the game and excited about how to earn the items.

Calculate Daily and Weekly Rewards

Sometimes teachers not only make the rewards too big and expensive, but they also make the time interval until their students can earn them too long. Suppose Billy's teacher says, "When you get 100 stickers for sitting still during circle time, we will have a class party." Depending on how many stickers can be earned in a given day, it may take Billy a month or longer to earn the reward. Very young children (ages 3-4)

*Older children
who are inattentive,
hyperactive, and impulsive
by temperament
may still need
a daily reward.*

will need an immediate reward (sticker or stamp on hand as soon as the behavior occurs). Kindergarten children, ages 5-6 will begin to be able to delay gratification a little longer, but most will give up if they don't receive a reward on a daily basis. By 7-9 years of age, most children are able to wait a week to earn a prize, particularly if they have an interim marker of their accomplishments (visual chart, jar of marbles, box of coupons). However, it is always important to pay attention to individual children's developmental ability. Older children who are inattentive, hyperactive, and impulsive by temperament may still need a daily reward. These hyperactive children live "in the moment" and part of their developmental difficulty is an inability to anticipate consequences and see ahead to a future goal (Barkley et al., 2000). They need far more immediate reinforcement to learn from their experiences.

To set a realistic value on rewards, first the teacher determines how many stickers, points or stamps could be earned in a day if the student was 100 percent compliant with the program. For instance, Tom, a seven-year-old, is a shy, withdrawn and anxious child. He is usually alone in the class, rarely says anything in class discussions and appears to have no friends. Let us say the teacher's goal is to help him participate more in class and to foster some positive peer friendships. Thus the teacher sets up a program where Tom can earn stamps for putting up his hand and suggesting an idea in class, asking the teacher a question, and helping another child with something. Based on the teacher's baseline observations she calculates that probably the most Tom will earn in one day is six stamps. Tom's reinforcement menu should therefore include small items worth four stickers, so that when he is on target with two-thirds of the positive behaviors in one day, he can choose something from the list. It would also be a good idea to have other items ranging in value from 8 to 15 points so that he could choose to wait two to three days before cashing in his stamps to receive a larger reward (e.g., time on the computer). Waiting for Tom to get 100 stamps to earn a prize would take 17 days if he were perfect every day. If he was successful two-thirds of the time, 100 points would take 25 days. Almost no child will stay motivated with a system that requires this much delayed gratification. The key to setting up effective reinforcement menus is not only a creative list of incentives for students to earn, but also a realistic price for each item, based on the child's usual daily salary of points or stamps. For higher frequency behaviors the price of items would be higher than for lower frequency behaviors.

Note that for an isolated child such as Tom, it would important also for the teacher to be prepared to praise and encourage other children in the classroom when they play with Tom so that he gets more opportunities for social interaction. The teacher might also share with the students that when Tom earns a certain number of points there will be a classroom celebration, thus all the children will become invested in Tom's success with the program.

Appropriate Behavior, Then the Reward

What is the difference between a bribe and a reward? Consider a teacher who says to the screaming student, "Eliza, you can have this book if you'll stop screaming." Or a teacher whose student refuses to do what she asks, who says, "Sunjay, I'll give you this snack if you put those toys away afterwards." In these examples, the book and snack are bribes because their offer is prompted by inappropriate behavior, and the snack was even given *before* the desired behavior occurs. The teachers are teaching their students that if they behave badly, they will be rewarded.

Rewards should be given for positive behaviors after they have occurred. It is helpful to remember the "first—then" principle. That is, first you get the behavior you want and then your student gets a reward. In the example, Eliza's teacher could set up a program to help her with her screaming and she might say, "Eliza when you go a whole circle time speaking politely (without screaming), I will let you choose the book we read at story time." First the teacher gets the desired behaviors and then gives the reward. In the second example, Sunjay's teacher might have said, "When you put your toys away this morning, you can eat your snack." In these examples the children learn that it pays to make positive choices, but that there is no reward for inappropriate behavior.

Use Tangible Rewards for Everyday Achievements

Some teachers save tangible rewards for their students' special achievements such as getting "A's" on a report card, or doing an outstanding drawing, reading a particularly difficult book, going the whole day without interrupting, or having a week with no temper tantrums. This is actually an instance of making the steps towards the final goal too big. Not only do the teachers wait too long to give the rewards, but they save the rewards for perfection. This gives their students the message that everyday behaviors, such as trying out a new color combination in a drawing, or trying to read a book out loud to the class even when the student is a poor reader, or a child stopping himself from interrupting too much, don't really count.

Student Name				

Think about giving small, frequent rewards. Certainly teachers can plan rewards for special achievements, but they also should be used for smaller steps along the way, such as rewards for the student who has shown the most improvement in reading, who has risked trying something new, or has worked hard to stay calm in class. Only by rewarding the effort and small steps can the larger goals of good grades, consistent compliance, or good relationships with friends be accomplished.

Replace Tangible Incentives with Social Approval

Teachers often worry about using too many tangible incentives. They are concerned that their students will learn to behave correctly only for a payoff instead of developing internal controls. This is a legitimate concern, and it could possibly happen in two kinds of situations. The first involves the teacher who is "sticker dependent," giving stickers or points for everything the child does but forgetting to provide social approval and praise. In essence, this teacher is teaching the child to perform for payoffs rather than for the pleasure both teacher and child feel about the accomplishments. The second situation arises when the teacher does not plan to phase out the tangible incentive program and maintain the behaviors with coaching and social approval. In other words, the students are not given the message that the teacher expects they will eventually be able to accomplish the task or perform the behavior on their own without rewards.

The use of tangible rewards should be seen as a temporary measure to help students learn new behaviors that are particularly difficult. They must be accompanied by social rewards. Once students have learned the new behaviors, the teacher can gradually phase out the tangible rewards and maintain them with social reinforcers. For instance, Sonja was put on a sticker program because she threw tantrums when her mother tried to leave her at preschool. Sonja enjoyed earning stickers for calmly saying goodbye to her mother, and her tantrumming occurred less and less often over the subsequent weeks. Next Sonja's teacher might say, "Now that you are coming to school and saying goodbye like a big girl, and earning lots of stickers, let's make the game more fun. Your challenge will be to say goodbye for two days and then you will earn your sticker." Once Sonja is successful on a regular basis for two days, the interval can be extended to four days, and so forth, until stickers are no longer necessary. At that point, her teachers may want to stop using stickers or save their use if necessary to help her with a different problem behavior. The teacher could say, "You remember how well you did several months ago learning to go to school like a big girl with the sticker game we played? Well, let's help you learn to share with your friends by using stickers." Thus, reward programs can be phased out and begun again later for different behaviors when necessary. It is often the case that as the child masters the challenging behavior, it begins to become a habit that the child no longer thinks about. At this point, the child will often stop asking for the reward because he or she is no longer focused on the behavioral challenge. At this point the behavior has often moved from being conscious to automatic and from extrinsically to intrinsically motivated. When this happens the system can be faded out with little fanfare.

An important aspect of a reward program is the message that accompanies the reward. Teachers must clearly communicate that not only do they approve of their student's success, but they also recognize that the child's effort—not the payoff, per se—is responsible for the success. In this way, teachers help the child to internalize successes and take credit for them. For example, Sonja's teacher says to Sonja as she gives her the sticker, "I'm proud of you for coming into school like such a big girl. You've worked hard and you must feel good about it. You are certainly growing up." Here Sonja's teacher gives the student (not the sticker) the credit for her accomplishments. Moreover this example points out that this teacher is relying more on her social relationship with Sonja than the sticker system.

Have Clear and Specific Reward Menus

Another common difficulty in reward programs is that the rewards are too vague. A teacher says to a student, "When you do what I ask you to do and earn lots of points, you can get a prize." The child asks, "What is the prize?" and the teacher responds, "Well, we'll see, there will be something, if you get lots of points." In this example, the teacher is vague about the reward and about how many points it will take to earn it. The result is that the student will not be very motivated to earn points.

Effective reward programs are clear and precise. Teachers and their students should write down the rewards they have agreed upon and the value of each item. This menu should be posted in a place where everyone can see it. Younger children who do not read do best with charts that contain pictures of target behaviors and rewards. The child can help by drawing the pictures him or herself or by cutting out pictures from magazines.

Coming into Class Calmly without Disruptions

The following plan could be used for several students who had difficulty with transitions or could be used for all students in the class. These cards could be taped to students' desks and the teacher could quietly go around the room and give a stamp to students who were following directions.

	M	T	W	Th	F
Morning Arrival					
After Morning Recess					
After Lunch					
After Afternoon Recess					
After P.E.					
Daily Total					

A stamp means coming into class and sitting down at your desk and starting your work right away without teasing or poking.

On Fridays we will count everyone's individual stamps:

12 stamps = prize from grab bag
16 stamps = two prizes
1500 stamps for whole classroom = celebration ice cream party

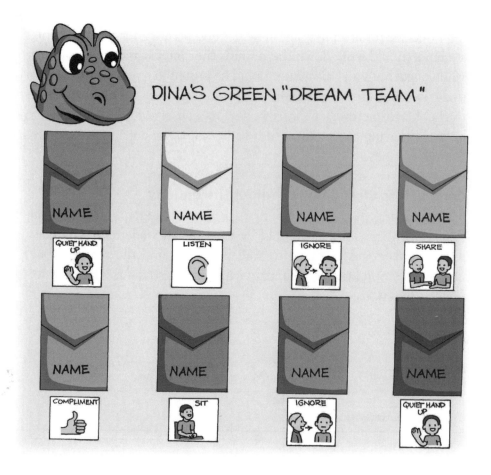

Use Team and Group Incentives as well as Individual Incentives

We often lament the power of peer pressure, yet peer pressure can be a powerful tool in the hands of teachers, a tool for motivating students. As was seen in the example above, in addition to the individual incentives, there is a classroom incentive (ice cream party) for the collective work of the entire classroom. This incentive has the effect of promoting class cooperation. Sometimes children can be motivated by group competition—the teacher divides the class up into small groups or teams of 4-6 students, and the teams compete to earn an agreed-upon reward for a particular behavior. For example, the team who earned the most points for a particular accomplishment (e.g., coming up with the most solutions to a problem, getting ready first to go to lunch, being on task, following classroom rules, etc) may win a prize. Or teams of children may save up points to earn the privilege of being the first team to decide where they will sit the next week. This approach works well for school age children who enjoy the fun of a competition as long as the teacher helps every team to be successful over time. Moreover, the teacher can set up the game so that it is possible for several teams to win, that is by rewarding all teams who achieve a certain goal such as a particular number of points.

For preschoolers the teacher can still reinforce cooperative team-work behavior by various means such as putting a teddy bear on the table for the team of children who gets ready to leave school first. Actually this has been used with fifth graders as well as kindergartners!

Team Games: Small group games can be used to focus on positives and to celebrate group and individual efforts in learning and behavior. For example, one teacher set up the following team approach to help her first grade classroom become calmer, quieter and more task focused. She began by setting up classroom teams consisting of five students per team who were seated together at a table. Each of the teams had a badge with their group motif (e.g., animals, plant name). Once her class had settled into its new groupings she explained that points could be gained by the groups for the following behaviors:

- lining up without pushing
- settling in their group quickly and quietly after recess
- cooperating in their group
- leaving their table clean and tidy
- staying at low levels on the noise meter
- staying on task doing their work in their chairs

She explained that as the group points added up they could be trad-ed for a range of rewards. If all the groups achieved a common target (e.g., 500 points) then the whole class could have a treat. Sometimes teachers can enhance points gained by having an audible timer go off at random times during the day. The group most on task at the point the timer goes off gains extra points. Note that it is important in these systems that the teacher clearly establishes that s/he is the umpire and the only one who can decide if a group has earned a point.

One novel way of implementing this approach is to give each team a board game or poster that has drawing of a maze or road or team sport on it. In our dinosaur school, we have developed Wally's baseball game (see picture). Every time the small group (or team) gets a point students color in one foot space on the baseball board game. When the group moves 10 spaces (1st base), each group member earns a piece of gum. When they move 20 spaces (2nd base), each group member gets a sticker or stamp. At 30 spaces (3rd base), they can have five minutes extra recess. At 40 spaces (home base), they can play a board game or do a quiet activity of their choice. It is important that each group gets to first base relatively quickly so that they experience some success. When every team gets back to home base, then the class plans a party.

Be Positive

What happens if a teacher puts a lot of effort into setting up a reward program for a particular child, but the student fails to earn points? A teacher may be tempted to respond by criticizing or lecturing the student on why s/he should try harder. Unfortunately, not only would this give the child a discouraging message about his or her ability (which could become a self-fulfilling prophesy), but the negative attention and ensuing power struggle could inadvertently reinforce misbehavior or noncompliance with the program. In other words, the student would get more payoff for not doing the program than for doing it.

If the student fails to earn points or stickers, it is best for the teacher to calmly say, "You didn't get one this morning but I'm sure you'll earn one this afternoon. I'll be watching. I'm sure you can do it." If a teacher is going to predict the future, it is helpful to convey a positive expectation. However, if the student continues to have difficulties earning points, the teacher should re-evaluate and make sure that the steps and behaviors were not too unrealistic.

School-Wide Incentives

In addition to using these programs for individuals, teams, and whole classrooms, it is even possible to set up a school-wide incentive plan.

WALLY'S BASEBALL TEAM

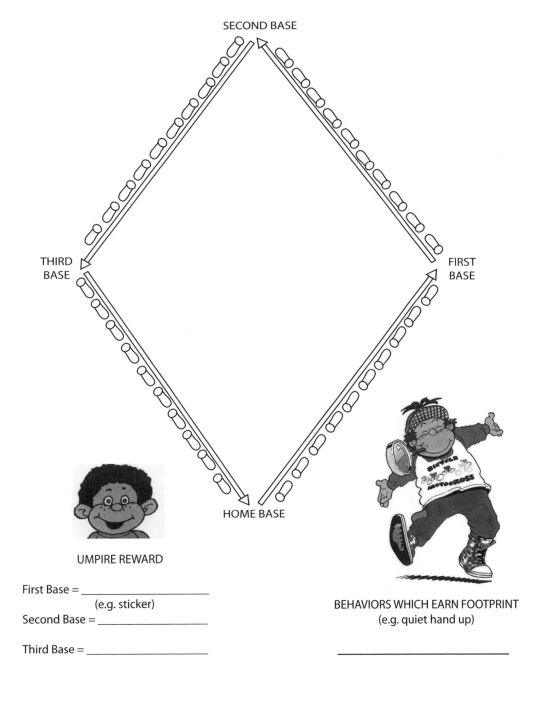

SECOND BASE

THIRD BASE

FIRST BASE

HOME BASE

UMPIRE REWARD

First Base = _____
(e.g. sticker)

Second Base = _____

Third Base = _____

BEHAVIORS WHICH EARN FOOTPRINT
(e.g. quiet hand up)

_____

This can be accomplished by developing a chart that can be posted on the school office door next to a list of the school rules. The principal announces over the intercom that there will be a mystery motivator for the first class to achieve a particular goal. In addition a whole-school award can be earned when a larger collective goal is reached. All school staff are given coupons that they can award to students for following particular school rules. In this way, the program can include school-wide goals for improving cooperative behavior across settings: classrooms, hallways, cafeteria, gym, playground, and school buses. Students who earn coupons bring them to the office and receive help recording their coupons on the school chart. The impact of this for the individual student can be increased by having the secretary call the student's parents or send home a card letting the parents know about the child's success as a member of the *Principal's School Rules Club!* Each Friday the principal announces the class who wins the mystery motivator prize for the week and shares the group progress towards the school reward.

OTHER PRINCIPLES OF EFFECTIVE INCENTIVE PROGRAMS

Use Rehearsal to Explain Expected Behaviors

Once a teacher has clearly identified the positive behaviors that she will put on her incentive program, it is important that these behaviors be explained clearly. With young children it is not enough just to talk through the expected behaviors, but rather they need to be modeled and practiced or rehearsed. Practice enables recall and short-term memory. For example, a teacher can have the students practice putting up a quiet hand or move to their seats without talking or touching others before the timer goes off. As these expected behaviors are practiced the teacher can be supportive and give positive feedback.

Make Your Incentive Programs Fun and Playful

There are all sorts of ways to make incentive programs fun for children. Here are some examples:

GAMES AND ACTIVITIES

Tic-Tac-Toe

A teacher plays a tic-tac-toe game with her class. First she specifies the behaviors she expects such as everyone sitting quietly in circle, cleaning up toys, or putting away snack by the time the buzzer goes off. Each time the class achieves the agreed upon goal, she gives the class an X on the tic-tac-toe game. When the class gets a straight line, they earn 10 minutes of free play or some special activity that they have chosen. This type of tic-tac-toe game could also be used individually on a student's desk or for a small group of students on their table as an incentive program. Note that there are no "O's" in this game—when the goal is not achieved, the teacher predicts that children will be able to earn an X next time.

Name_____ Date: _____
Dina's Behavior Chart
My goal is to get _____ green and blue balloons for _____
_____

©The Incredible Years®

Color-in Pictures

For young children, their successes might be colored in on a picture at various times during the day. For example, children are given a picture showing a dinosaur with some thought balloons which represent different times during the day (circle time, recess, small group activities, snack etc.). If the child (or classroom) achieves the agreed upon behaviors then they can color in the balloon—green for outstanding and blue for good. At the end of the day they see if they have been able to get five green colored balloons, which earns them a special sticker, a maze or a prize of some sort.

Use Cartoons of Expected Behaviors

Cartoon pictures of the expected behaviors (e.g., quiet hand up, working quietly at seat, friendly talk, giving compliments to others, or listening to teacher) placed on the students' desks can be a concrete cue to remind children of the expected behavior and aid short-term memory. Teachers can even add an incentive chart to the bottom of these pictures for the teacher or child to fill

in whenever they are successful at demonstrating the target behavior. We also like to add the positive self-talk statement that accompanies the behavior for those students who are able to read.

Surprise Rewards

Children love surprises! For example, a teacher gets out her toy microphone and says, "Announcing the greatest class in the universe! For cleaning up the playground so stupendously, you are awarded an ice-cream party!" Or, a teacher takes out her magical and musical wand and passes it over the head of students who have transitioned quickly to circle time and announces their magic skills. Unlike many of the systems described above, these rewards can be things that a teacher gives out spontaneously using the "catch them being good" principle. Children are delighted by the novelty and excitement of surprises. Interspersing surprise rewards with rewards that are set up in advance can also combat the issue of children who only seem to want to work for a reward. With surprise rewards, the child never knows when s/he might earn one!

Another incentive program that has a surprise element built in is the "mystery super hero" game. Here the teacher picks three students' names out of a hat and tells her class she has three names but she isn't going to say who they are. Then she explains that she will be counting every time she notices these particular students helping someone, putting up a quiet hand, or working hard on an assignment. If by the end of the day these mystery students have each earned 10 points, they will be the mystery super heroes and can choose a special activity for the class to do. The advantage of this system is that every child in the classroom thinks s/he might be one of the names picked so it encourages everyone to work hard. It is important that the mystery students are only identified if they have achieved the goal. If one of the three doesn't achieve the goal of 10, the teacher should not identify that person.

Dot-to-Dot Game

Another fun incentive game is for the teacher to play dot-to-dot with the whole class or with groups of students or an individual student. In this game, each time the student, small group, or classroom accomplishes a specified target behavior, a student fills in one dot-to-dot number. When the drawing is completed, the class or student earn a celebration such as extra computer or recess time on Friday.

Dina Dinosaur's
Wheel of Fortune

© *Incredible Years®*

Spinner Wheel of Fortune Game

One playful way to determine the reward a child will receive for achieving a behavioral goal is to allow him or her to spin the wheel of fortune. The spinner has the possibility of landing on a number of possible rewards. Each of these may be given more or less space on the pie diagram (i.e., more expensive items being smallest wedge in pie). Some rewards listed on the pie might be 10 minutes of extra recess, 5 minutes of extra computer time, choosing the book for the class to read, treat from the magic grab bag, choice of music to listen to during quiet time, popcorn party, and homework pass. It is a good idea to laminate these spinners and use washable marker so teachers can change the rewards throughout the year. (See example of Dina's Wheel of Fortune)

Mystery Motivators

Perhaps because of the surprise element, we have found that children of all ages love the idea of working for a mystery motivator (Moore, Waguespack, Wickstrom, Witt, & Gaydos, 1994; Rhode et al., 1992). The teacher writes down on a piece of paper what the mystery motivator is and puts the paper in a large, decorated envelope. Next this envelope is put in some very visible place in the front of the classroom (e.g., taped on blackboard). The teacher then tells the students that if they earn a certain number of stickers or points, they can open the mystery motivator. The teacher can redirect children when they are on the verge of misbehaving by saying, "Remember the mystery motivator."

For example, the mystery motivator could be used for teaching the classroom rules. The teacher does this by preparing a pile of happy faces on cards that have been laminated. Whenever she notices a student following one of the classroom rules (e.g., quiet hand up, going seat quietly, helping someone), she puts a happy face on her desk. She says to the student, "You went straight to your seat, you earned a happy yes face for everybody." Students who earn happy faces put them in a jar on the teacher's desk or tape them to a chart on the board. Then at a certain point in the day, when an agreed upon number of happy faces have been collected, she permits the mystery motivator to be opened. Mystery motivators can include any of the things outlined above. A teacher can add to the fun of this by writing or drawing the mystery motivator with an invisible pen which can only be revealed when a special marking pen is scribbled on top of it.

Programs such as the one described here can be used with whole classes, teams, or with individuals for clearly defined behaviors.

Keep Incentive Programs and Discipline Programs Separate

Some teachers create tangible reward programs and then mix in punishment. For instance, a student may receive stickers for sharing and have them taken away for fighting. The stickers then take on negative rather than positive associations. This approach can be even more problematic if the child is left with a negative balance. If the only prospect is to earn stickers to get out of debt, all the positive incentive for good behavior is gone. The natural outcome is for the child to become discouraged and abandon all efforts to change.

Keep a reward program separate from the discipline program. Removing earned points or rewards as punishment will defeat the purpose of the program, which is to give attention to appropriate behaviors. If a teacher wants to use privilege removal as a discipline technique, keep any privileges you foresee withdrawing (time off recess, computer time) off your reward menu. (Please see Chapter Eight for information on privilege removal.)

Keep Control of your Program

There are several ways a teacher can lose control of their reward program. The first is by paying for "almost" performance; that is giving rewards to students when they haven't earned the required points or stickers. This usually happens because students argue for them, claiming they've done everything required. Unfortunately, it undermines the rules of the contract as well as the teacher's authority. It is also likely to result in the students escalating their begging and debating with the teacher over the attainment of points. Instead of a behavior problem being solved, a new one is created. Lack of follow-through can be a second problem. This happens when students have behaved according to the program but the teacher fails to notice the behaviors or forgets to give them the stickers or to allow them to trade them in at the agreed upon time. If the rewards are given very late or in an inconsistent manner, their reinforcing value is minimal.

In order for these programs to work, teachers must be consistent limit-setters. All children will test the limits and try to see if they can get rewards for less work. That's natural, but it means that teachers must be prepared for this testing, stay committed to the program, and ignore arguments, debates or pleading when students have not earned enough points. Finally, teachers need to keep control of the rewards. Prizes and stickers should be hidden and awarding points and stickers determined by the teacher, not the children. (See Chapter Seven for more information on how to set limits and ignore misbehaviors.)

Use "I can" cans on children's desks to teach positive self-talk

Teachers can put an empty can on each child's desk and label it the "I can" can. Whenever the teacher notices the child sharing, cooperating, helping, being friendly she writes these behaviors out as "I can" state-ments and put them in the can for the child to take home. For example, "I can help others," "I can listen to the teacher well," "I can cope with this conflict," " I can sit in my seat without rocking," "I can move quickly to my seat without disturbing others," "I can stay in my seat until the egg timer goes off," and so forth. Doing this helps the child challenge negative self-talk and rehearse positive self-statements and positive behavior at school. If these notes are re-read at home with parents, the impact is doubled.

Sharing Successes with Parents – Happy Grams and Awards

When a child's success at school is shared with that child's parents, another reinforcer comes into play—namely, parental attention and approval—and the child gets a "double dose" of reinforcement. Teachers can send home notes, special awards or "Happy Grams" (or make phone calls) throughout the year announcing a child's special accomplishment or sharing a particularly good day. See Incredible Years web site for award certificates to download.

http://www.incredibleyears.com/TeacherResources/index.asp

Not only does this kind of gesture work wonders for a teacher's relationship with the student and parents, it also is a form of teaching, for it shows parents that teachers want them to recognize what their child has accomplished. It also helps strengthen parents' involvement in their child's school experience. Moreover, teachers are building up what might be seen as a "positive bank account" with that student and parents, which creates a trusting relationship between teacher and par-ents. If it becomes necessary to discuss a behavior problem concerning their child, parents who have a positive relationship with the teacher will be more open and more able to collaborate with her in addressing the problem.

An additional benefit of sending home awards or compliment notes to parents about some positive aspect of the child's behavior or attitude is that it helps the parents focus the child on his or her successes, thus preparing the child to behave in similar ways the next day.

Attention: _____
Parent's Name

I'm very proud to announce that

_____
Student's Name

**has made an AWESOME IMPROVEMENT
in our classroom because**

_____

_____

_____

_____

_____   _____
Signed   Date

COOL DUDE AWARD
Presented to

_____
for

____ being strong enough to control anger

____ staying "cool" when faced with a problem

____ finding problem-solving solutions

____ helping and supporting another child

____ teamwork in the classroom

_____
Signed   Date

Super Star Award

presented to

_____

because

_____

_____

_____

_____   _____
Signed   Date

CONCLUSION

Teachers can both support and motivate students' learning progress with the creative use of a variety of incentives such as stickers, hand stamps, points, special rewards, or celebrations. These tangible markers also give students concrete evidence of their progress, particularly when struggling with a difficult developmental tasks such as learning to read, or staying calm when frustrated, or persisting with a difficult problem. Teachers must lavish this same type of intensive attention, coaching and reinforcement on students who are learning new and difficult behaviors, and will gradually be able to use less intense interventions as students internalize the learning.

In gardening, newly planted and weaker plants need fertilizer, frequent watering, and lots of care. As plants grow deeper roots and become more established, they are able to grow more independently and require less constant gardener attention.

TO SUM UP...

Using Incentives to Motivate Students

- Identify one to two positive behaviors you want to increase first. These may be contracted with the whole class or set up as individual goals according to children's particular needs.
- Explain to the class or individual child which behaviors will result in a reward.
- Select the incentives. Stars and stickers can be good motivators for young preschool children. School-age children like to earn points, tickets, or chips and trade them in for something they have chosen on a reinforcement menu.
- The reinforcement menu should be planned in advance with children—it should be specific.
- Allow young children to earn rewards daily. Older school-age children should earn something every few days.
- Don't reward "almost" performances.
- Be sure to fulfill your end of the agreements.
- Always combine tangible rewards with social rewards, such as labeled praise, coaching and encouragement.
- Remember, what is a meaningful reinforcer for one student may not be reinforcing for another. Individualize the incentives as much as possible. Involve parents in suggesting ideas for what is reinforcing for their children.

- If you use charts to keep track of progress, review the charts every day with your class.
- Set a goal to increase the number of positive notes and phone calls you make home to parents and children each week.
- Write on the board the names of children who make a special achievement—either academic or social. This reinforces good behavior and is a reminder to all the class of the expected behavior.

Some Do's and Don'ts

Do:

- Clearly define the desired academic and social behaviors.
- Identify small steps towards the goals.
- Gradually increase the criteria for the reward (make it challenging).
- Begin by choosing only one or two behaviors to work on.
- Focus on positive behaviors.
- Choose inexpensive rewards.
- Offer rewards that can be earned on a daily basis.
- Involve students in choosing the rewards.
- Give the reward after the behavior occurs (first/then).
- Reward everyday achievements and successes.

Don't:

- Be vague about the desired behaviors.
- Make the steps too big for the child.
- Make the steps too easy for the child.
- Create complex programs involving too many behaviors.
- Focus on negative behaviors.
- Offer expensive rewards, or rewards that cannot be furnished immediately.
- Use rewards that take too long to earn.
- Choose rewards that are not motivating to the child.
- Offer rewards as bribes.
- Be stingy with social rewards.
- Take away rewards that were earned previously.

The Incredible Years®
Teacher Classroom Management Self-Reflection Inventory
Using Incentives to Motivate Students

Date: _____ Teacher Name: _____

Teachers learn extensively from self-reflection regarding their class-room management and the teaching strategies they are using that are working or not working. From these reflections teachers determine personal goals for making changes in their approaches to bring about the most positive learning climate they can. Use this Inventory to think about your strengths and limitations and determine your goals.

Positive attention, praise, & incentives	1 = NEVER 3 = OCCASIONALLY 5 = CONSISTENTLY
1. I combine enthusiastic and labeled praise along with rewards given to students for targeted behaviors.	1 2 3 4 5
2. I give more attention to positive social behaviors than to inappropriate behaviors. (5:1)	1 2 3 4 5
3. I use spontaneous or surprise rewards or incentives to celebrate students' progress.	1 2 3 4 5
4. I have identified positive social and emotional as well as academic behaviors and thoughts I want to reward according to individual students' needs and goals.	1 2 3 4 5
5. I have identified positive opposite behaviors I want to reward with tangible rewards in targeted children with behavioral difficulties. This has been developed on my behavior plans.	1 2 3 4 5
6. I have a variety menu of different kinds of incentives (e.g., special privileges, prize box, extra time with teacher, mystery motivator, treat, raffle tickets).	1 2 3 4 5

7. I use group incentives to promote teamwork (e.g., when the jar is full of chips the whole class can have a pizza party).	1 2 3 4 5
8. I have talked with parents about what incentives they think are reinforcing for their children that can be used in the classroom (e.g., baseball cards, train books).	1 2 3 4 5
9. I have talked to parents about combining my incentive system at school with an incentive system at home for similar goals and I let parents know about their children's successes.	1 2 3 4 5
10. I communicate my belief to children that they can succeed in achieving their goal and promote their positive self-talk.	1 2 3 4 5
11. I continue to teach children how to compliment each other and have compliments circle times.	1 2 3 4 5
12. I prompt other children in the classroom to reward another child's special accomplishment (e.g., gets to give out the friendship cape or bear).	1 2 3 4 5
13. I use "positive forecasting" statements to predict a child's success in earning a prize.	1 2 3 4 5
14. I set up incentive programs for individual children as well as team and whole class rewards.	1 2 3 4 5
15. I have talked openly with the class about issues of fairness. We communicate as a class about individual differences and have created an atmosphere where all children know they are working on different goals. I help each child understand his or her own individual goals.	1 2 3 4 5
16. The behavior plans for incentive systems that I have developed are developmentally appropriate and individualized for each student.	1 2 3 4 5

17. I send home positive report cards, happy grams, and special awards with children (super star award, awesome improvement, self-control award, feelings award, helping award, etc.).	1 2 3 4 5
18. I have identified special privileges that students might work toward earning.	1 2 3 4 5
19. I encourage my students to applaud and reward each other's accomplishments.	1 2 3 4 5
20. I combine academic, persistence, social and emotion coaching alongside my use of incentives systems.	1 2 3 4 5
Future Goals Regarding Incentive Strategies:	Total

REFERENCES

Barkley, R. A., Shelton, T. L., Crosswait, C., Moorehouse, M., Fletcher, K., Barrett, S., et al. (2000). Multi-method psycho-educational intervention for preschool children with disruptive behavior: Preliminary results at post-treatment. *Journal of Child Psychology and Psychiatry, 41*(3), 319-332.

Barrish, H. H., & Saunders, M. (1969). Good behavior game: Effects of individual contingencies for group consequences on disruptive behavior in a classroom. *Journal of Applied Behavior Analysis, 2*(2), 119-124.

Cameron, J., & Pierce, W. D. (1994). Reinforcement, reward, and intrinsic motivation: A meta-analysis. *Review of Educational Research, 64,* 363-423.

Elliott, S. N., & Gresham, F. M. (1992). *Social skills intervention guide.* Circle Pines, MN: American Guidance Service.

Embry, D. D. (2002). The Good Behavior Game: A best practice candidate as a universal behvioral vaccine. *Clinical Child and Family Psychologoy Review, 5*(4), 273-297.

Emmer, E. T., Evertson, C. M., Clements, B. S., Sanford, J. P., & Worsham, M. E. (1994). *Classroom management for secondary teachers.* Boston: Allyn & Bacon.

Jones, V. F., & Jones, L. S. (2007). *Comprehensive classroom management: Creating positive learning environments.* Boston: Allyn & Bacon.

Moore, L. A., Waguespack, A. M., Wickstrom, K. F., Witt, J. C., & Gaydos, G. R. (1994). Mystery motivator: An effective and time efficient intervention. *School Psychology Review.*

Nevin, A., Johnson, D. W., & Johnson, R. (1982). Effects of group and individual contingencies on academic performance and social relations of special needs students. *The Journal of Social Psychology, 116*(1), 41-59.

Rhode, G., Jenson, W. R., & Reavis, H. K. (1992). *The tough kid book.* Longmont, CO: Sopriswest, Inc.

Stage, S. A., & Quiroz, D. R. (1997). A meta-analysis of interventions to decrease disruptive classroom behavior in public education settings. *School Psychology Review, 26,* 333-368.

Walker, H. M. (2002). The First Step to Success program: Preventing destructive social outcomes at the point of school entry. *Report on Emotional and Behavioral Disorders in Youth, 3*(1), 3-6, 22-23.

Walker, H. M., Colvin, G., & Ramsey, E. (1995). *Antisocial behavior in school: Strategies and best practices.* Pacific Grove, CA: Brooks/Cole.

Yarbrough, J. L., & Skinner, C. H. (2004). Decreasing transition times in a second grade classroom:Scientific support for the Timely Transitions game. *Journal of Applied School Psychology, 20*(2), 85-107.

CHAPTER 7

Managing Misbehavior: Ignoring and Redirecting

In the first six chapters we have focused on proactive and positive teaching tools from the bottom of the teaching pyramid. These strategies are meant to be used liberally, as they form the foundation for supporting children's emotional, social, and academic learning and will prevent many classroom behavior problems from occurring. However, despite of the best proactive classroom management on the part of teachers, misbehavior will still occur. To manage these challenging behaviors, a classroom discipline plan is fundamental to proactive classroom management. Without a clear discipline plan, student misbehaviors are often met with teacher responses that are scattered, inconsistent, and reactive.

Proactive discipline plans are associated with increases in student academic achievement as well as social behavior.

The next layer of the teaching pyramid introduces the use of the least intrusive discipline teaching tools, which are used to reduce specific targeted behaviors. These include rules and expectations for positive behaviors that are clearly delineated, predictable schedules, distractions and redirection, clear limit setting and prompting students to use self-regulation strategies which they have been taught. Moreover, teacher reprimands are brief and used infrequently with a higher ratio of positive than negative interactions (Kalis & Vannest, 2007). Research indicates that classrooms with such proactive discipline plans are associated with increases in student academic achievement as well as social behavior (Gable, Hester, Rock, & Hughes, 2009).

However, research has shown that teachers are more likely to rely on more intrusive or punitive and inconsistent consequences in the classroom than positive techniques when responding to discipline problems (for review see Bear, 1998; Brophy, 1996; Hyman, 1997; Martens & Meller, 1990). This is true despite the widespread recognition of the limitations and negative effects of punishment, especially when used as the primary and first strategy of response. In this chapter we cover the first steps of a progressive discipline plan hierarchy in which less intrusive and less severe consequences are always tried first. This is called the *"law of least disruptive intervention."* Chapters Eight and Nine introduce steps in the discipline hierarchy higher up the pyramid and guide teachers through the development of a full discipline plan with progressively more intensive interventions. Chapter Ten puts all the elements together in a comprehensive discipline hierarchy behavior plan.

IGNORING MISBEHAVIOR

Research has shown that planned ignoring, in combination with differential reinforcement, is extremely effective for reducing inappropriate behavior in students (Didden & De Moor, 1997; Gable et al., 2009; Hall & Lund, 1968; Madsen & Becker, 1968). Planned ignoring

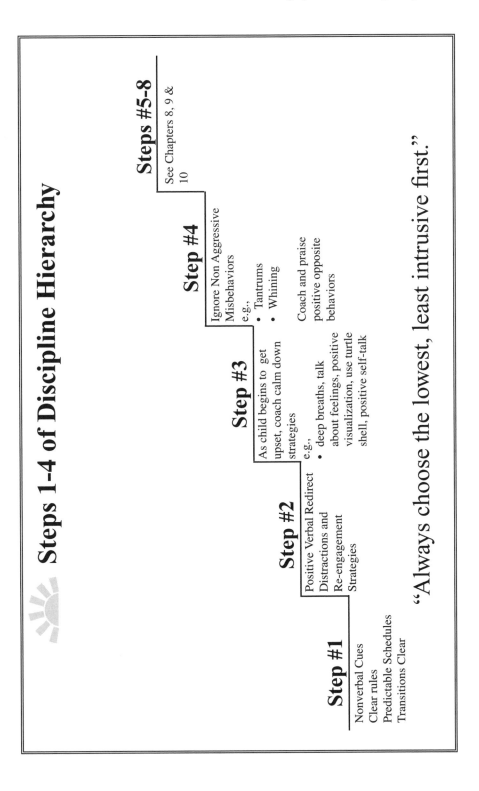

Steps 1-4 of Discipline Hierarchy

Step #1

Nonverbal Cues
Clear rules
Predictable Schedules
Transitions Clear

Step #2

Positive Verbal Redirect
Distractions and
Re-engagement
Strategies

Step #3

As child begins to get
upset, coach calm down
strategies

e.g.,
• deep breaths, talk
  about feelings, positive
  visualization, use turtle
  shell, positive self-talk

Step #4

Ignore Non Aggressive
Misbehaviors
e.g.,
• Tantrums
• Whining

Coach and praise
positive opposite
behaviors

Steps #5-8

See Chapters 8, 9 &
10

"Always choose the lowest, least intrusive first."

occurs when the teacher systematically withholds attention or ignores the targeted negative behavior until it stops, and quickly returns her attention when the student is behaving appropriately. In one sense ignoring misbehavior is unnatural, for there is a natural tendency for teachers to attend to students who are out of their seat or being disruptive or argumentative. However, teacher attention only reinforces that behavior. Ignoring can be a powerful tool for modifying behavior, since it deprives the child of the attention all children want. While ignoring is highly effective, it is also probably the hardest teaching tool for teachers to actually use. The following discussion will help teachers deal with some of the problems that they encounter when trying to use the ignore strategy to manage their students' minor misbehaviors.

Choosing Behaviors to Ignore

Minor inappropriate or low-level attention seeking behaviors such as whining, teasing, arguing, eye rolling, pouting, calling out, and tantrums (i.e., behaviors that are not dangerous or hurtful to other children or adults) can often be eliminated if they are systematically ignored. Sometimes teachers feel ignoring is not discipline. In fact, it is one of the most effective teaching tools that can be used with students. Teachers who ignore their students when they behave inappropriately give no payoff (or power) to the student for continuing the misbehavior. By not giving the misbehavior attention, the teachers are also not engaging in a power struggle with the student. When ignoring is consistently maintained, students will eventually stop what they are doing because it doesn't achieve their goal to get teacher attention. Moreover, if students receive teacher coaching, encouragement and praise for the opposite prosocial behaviors (e.g., speaking politely, sharing, cooperating, and controlling their temper), they will learn it is more beneficial to behave appropriately than inappropriately.

There are also some child behaviors that are irritating to teachers but cannot actually be controlled by children. For example, the hyperactive child may not be able to stop wiggling and fidgeting in his seat, the impulsive child may not realize that he is talking aloud, and a child with language delays may stutter and pause involuntarily. These behaviors certainly should not be disciplined and need to be ignored or redirected by teachers. Attending to them will only make these behaviors worse and will cause other children to attend to them as well.

Avoid Discussion and Eye Contact

Sometimes teachers think they're ignoring their students' misbehavior when they are actually giving it considerable attention. They may have stopped talking to a student but continued glaring, grimacing, or in other ways letting the student know that the misbehavior is affecting them. Some teachers ignore by avoiding eye contact with the student but continue to make critical or sarcastic comments. In both instances, the misbehaving student is successful in receiving teacher attention and, perhaps, a powerful negative emotional response as well.

Effective ignoring occurs when teachers are able to neutralize their reactions to what the student is doing. The teacher's facial expression should be neutral, eye contact is avoided, and discussions are stopped. Ignoring also involves moving away from the student, especially if the teacher has been in close contact. Just as the most powerful form of positive attention includes moving closer with a smile, eye contact, verbal praise, and physical touching, the most powerful form of ignoring is a neutral expression, involving no eye contact, no communication, and a turning away of the body.

Use Consistent Ignoring—Be Prepared for the Misbehavior to Get Worse at First

Sometimes well-intentioned teachers start to ignore misbehavior such as tantrums or arguments without being prepared for the students' possible response. Most children will initially react to ignoring with an increase in negative behaviors to see if they can get their teacher to back down. For instance, five-year-old Hanook wants to play with a pointed bubble wand but his teacher removes it because it is dangerous. He cries about this for

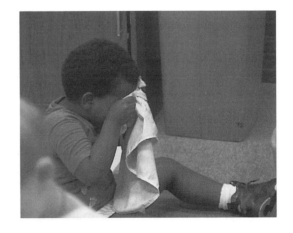

Remember, when teachers first start ignoring a misbehavior it will usually get worse.

several minutes and insists on grabbing it from her. Finally the teacher takes the bubble wand away and puts it on a high shelf, all the while ignoring his protests. Hanook escalates his demands, throws himself on the floor, and tantrums to see if he can get the bubble maker back. This tantruming goes on for ten more minutes until the teacher, exasperated and worn down by his crying, says, "All right, you can have it!" By giving in to gain the short-term benefit of making life more peaceful, the teacher has created a long-term problem: Hanook has learned that if he tantrums long and hard enough, he will get what he wants. Thus, he has been reinforced for his inappropriate behaviors.

Remember, when teachers first start ignoring a misbehavior it will usually get worse. In fact, if the student's behavior gets worse when a teacher begins to ignore, that is a signal that the strategy is working! Teachers must be prepared to wait out this testing period if the behavior is to improve. If the teacher gives in, her students will learn that behaving inappropriately is an effective way to get what they want. The example of Hanook and his teacher is not unlike an experience you may have had with a vending machine. You put your change in for a soft drink, but don't get one, nor can you get your money back. You press the return button several times and when this doesn't work you try the drink button again. Depending on how thirsty or cross you are, you may persist in pressing the buttons and even try banging on the machine. Finally, if no soft drink appears, you give up and move on to something else because there has been no payoff for your banging. You are also likely to avoid this particular machine in the future, since it did not produce the drink you wanted. However, if by some stroke of luck a soft drink pops out during your banging, then you know that the next time you can't get a soft drink, the trick is to bang hard and long enough.

Children can learn to be persistent. This is one of the reasons that ignoring is so difficult for teachers to carry out. Most children will test their teacher's ignoring skills by escalating their misbehaviors. If a teacher decides to use this teaching tool she must be prepared to wait out this period by remaining firm and being equally persistent in her resolution to ignore.

Ignore and Distract

Choosing to ignore misbehavior doesn't mean that there is nothing positive you can do to improve the situation. In fact, failure to provide distractions or suggestions for alternative, more appropriate behavior can lock teachers and children into a power struggle and cause the children to prolong the misbehaviors. Consider this scenario: Johnny asks his teacher if he can use the paints. When his teacher refuses permission, Johnny starts yelling and screaming. His teacher effectively ignores this tantrum by walking away and in a couple of minutes the screaming subsides. At this point, Johnny's teacher fails to notice his quiet behavior or to distract him by redirecting him to play with something else. Johnny, feeling ignored, begins to scream again, in an attempt to gain his teacher's attention. The teacher's ignoring efforts have been wasted because Johnny did not experience the benefit of getting attention back when his tantrum stopped. From his point of view, his teacher has not heard him and he needs to scream louder!

Use distractions or redirections to reduce your student's reaction to being ignored or being denied something. Distractions are particularly useful with three- and four-year-olds, but they also work with older children. For example, once Johnny stopped screaming, his teacher could have prevented further outbursts by giving him attention and suggesting some other interesting activity he might like to try. In another example, a student starts whining when told she can't use the computer. The teacher ignores her until she stops whining, and then asks her if she wants to help clean the fish tank. The idea is to ignore her secondary misbehavior in response to being told she can't have something, and then distract her as soon as she starts behaving more appropriately. Of course, if she misbehaves again in response to the redirection or distraction, the teacher will need to resume ignoring.

*Use distractions
or redirections
immediately following
your use of the
ignore strategy.*

Another way to combine distraction with ignoring is to distract yourself from your student's inappropriate behaviors. Teachers can do this by talking to another student, or involving themselves in something else. If a teacher is ignoring a student who is having a tantrum, s/he may want to go over to other children who are playing quietly and comment on their activity or their ability to cooperate. If the student thinks the teacher has been distracted, he or she will quickly stop misbehaving. Then the teacher can turn her attention back to the student and coach or praise his or her first cooperative behaviors.

Move Away from the Student but Stay Nearby

It may seem reasonable to ignore a student's misbehaviors by walking to the other side of the room. This can be an effective technique if the child is clinging and physically demanding attention. However, the difficulty with going too far away is that the teacher won't be able to pay attention to and reinforce the appropriate behavior as soon as it returns. When ignoring, it is best to physically move away by standing up and walking to a part of the room nearby. This way the teacher can monitor her student's behavior and reinforce him as soon as he stops misbehaving. For example, as the teacher is going around the room assisting students, Freddie, calls out from across the room, "Miss, hey Miss!" The teacher realizes that if she goes over to Freddie or asks him to wait, she will be giving attention to his calling out, so she decides to tactically ignore it. She doesn't look at him or comment on his behavior and continues to work with several students. She does comment to the class in general, "Anyone who needs help can raise a hand, and I will come over." Freddie calls out again, "Miss, come on, I need your help, please! I only want to ask a question." The teacher continues ignoring and moves on to help another student. Freddie sulks for a while and then begins to do some writing. At this moment she goes up to him and casually asks, "Can I see your work?" and reaches for his book. She simply and quietly reminds him, "Remember to put up a quiet hand and wait, then I will happily come over."

IGNORING TEACHES SELF-CONTROL

Some teachers do not use ignoring because they feel it is disrespectful to their students and harmful to their self-esteem. They are concerned that this approach will damage their relationship with their students. Other teachers do not ignore because they feel it does not punish their student enough for the misbehavior. They say, "How can you ignore behaviors like swearing or yelling? These behaviors need punishment."

Research indicates that ignoring is an effective discipline approach because it maintains a positive teacher-student relationship based on respect rather than fear. If teachers can ignore screaming or swearing instead of responding with yelling or criticizing the student, they show students that they can maintain self-control in the face of conflict and anger. When teachers remain calm in the face of negative student behaviors, these behaviors lose their power or ability to control others and students soon realize that there is little effect or payoff in continuing to use them.

Teach Other Students to Ignore

Sometimes ignoring backfires because even though the teacher ignores the student's misbehavior, the other students give it attention by laughing at and teasing the child. If this is happening, teacher ignoring will not work because the student is still managing to get attention for his misbehavior from his peer group. If other students are responding and giving attention to a particular child's misbehaviors, they need to be taught the skill of ignoring their friend's tantrums and arguments when they occur. Teachers can say to the tantruming student's classmates, "We can best help Jeremy right now if we ignore him and give him privacy until he has calmed down." It is important for teachers to teach students how and when to ignore. This helps them to understand what it means to ignore and provides them with a prosocial solution to handle conflicts they may have in the classroom or playground. During circle time lessons teachers can teach, model, and practice how to ignore certain behaviors. For example, students can be taught how to ignore distractions or tantrums in the classroom and how to ignore teasing or hurtful behavior. The following is an example of a circle time lesson script wherein the teacher uses a puppet to teach students the ignoring skills.

CIRCLE TIME SCRIPT
Freddy Learns to Ignore

Teacher: *(holding a puppet)* Well, my friend Freddy (puppet) has a bit of a problem he wants to share with you today. Freddy, can you tell us what happened?

Freddy: Well, I was sitting in circle time in my classroom and one of my friends kept talking and whispering and I couldn't hear the teacher. I asked him to stop but he kept on talking.

Teacher: Freddy, that sounds hard. How were you feeling when that happened?

Freddy: I was really frustrated.

Teacher: You know Freddy, I do have an idea for this problem. When someone is distracting me and bothering me I do something called ignoring. *(turns to students)* Can you all say the word ignore?

Students: Ignore

Teacher: Yes, Freddy ignoring is when you pretend you can't hear or see someone. You can even turn your body away and focus on the teacher. Try it. Pretend I am the boy in circle time who is bothering you, and you are ignoring me. Pretend Kendra over there is your teacher. You can even look at her while you ignore me. Ready?

Teacher: *(in role as boy, starts to whisper in Freddy's ear)*

Freddy: *(turns his body away and looks away at his friend)*

Teacher: Wow, I see Freddy turning his whole body away. His eyes are focused on his teacher, and he isn't listening to anything I am saying. Freddy is really strong, he has big ignore muscles! Who else thinks they can try this too?

Teacher: *(Calls another child to come up and act out the same scenario.)*

NOTE: *Teacher or puppet are always the ones teasing or distracting the child—do not put a child in this role. It is important that the children only act out the positive behaviors.*

Teacher: (*After several children have practiced ignoring*) You know Freddy, ignoring is a great way to help a friend who is making a bad choice in school. When friends are whispering, talking, poking, or making a lot of distracting noise, they need privacy to calm down and remember to make a good choice. What do you think we could do when your friend starts to pay attention again?

Freddy: Well, I think we could give him a friendly signal. How about a silent thumbs up?

Teacher: I think that's a great idea. It's a helpful thing to ignore a friend who is bothering you or making noise, but it's not friendly to ignore someone who is paying attention and wants to be your friend!

After teaching students the concept of ignoring, teachers will need to work hard to reinforce and encourage the skill at first. Teachers can prompt ignoring behavior whenever needed. For instance if a child is poking or whispering during circle time, the teacher might say to the children next to him, "Jeremy and Sam, I think you can use your really strong ignoring muscles right now! See if you can look right at me! Wow! You are so good at ignoring." At first, the teacher will need to put a lot of effort into this coaching. Teachers can also prompt ignoring by letting the class know of their plan to ignore. If a student begins to tantrum or whine, the teacher might say: "I'm choosing to ignore right now. I think you'll be able to ignore too!" Students will feel reassured that the teacher is aware of the misbehavior and has a plan. Eventually, students will learn to ignore and may even be able to prompt each other to ignore.

It is important to know the limits of your students' capacity to ignore. Most students can learn to ignore minor disruptions for a long time. However behaviors that are very loud and disruptive will be harder to ignore. In addition, easily distracted students will find it harder to ignore distractions. Sometimes teachers may need to provide other strategies to help students continue to ignore. This may mean allowing a student or group of students to move away from the disruptive child: "Billy, Shandra, and Maya, you may bring your books to the carpet and read quietly here. I see how hard you are working to ignore." Or a teacher may realize that students will not be able to concentrate on a read-aloud story when another student is tantrumming and may need to move them to a more engaging activity such as choice time. These short-term disruptions to the planned class schedule will pay off in the end as the whole class learns how to ignore and students who are disruptive learn that these behaviors will not get their teacher's or peers' attention.

Limit the Number of Behaviors to Ignore

Whereas some teachers have the problem of ignoring too rarely, others ignore too much or too long. Such teachers effectively ignore their student's initial misbehavior but then they continue to withhold attention, support, and approval for several hours or even days at a time. A related problem occurs when teachers deal with too many misbehaviors at once; whining, yelling, screaming, arguing, and messy work, for example. Ignoring so many things will cause children to feel neglected and leave teachers feeling overwhelmed. Not only will teachers find it difficult to be consistent in their ignoring, but they will find it hard to remember to give attention back to the student for the opposite, positive behaviors.

Select behaviors to ignore and the positive opposite behaviors to give attention.

When using the ignoring teaching tool, it is important that teachers identify specific negative behaviors to focus on. Choose only one or two to systematically ignore at any given time. By limiting the number of misbehaviors this way, teachers can more realistically expect to be consistent in ignoring the misbehavior every time it occurs. As well, teachers will be able to observe and monitor the effects this discipline technique has on the particular behavior.

Certain Student Behaviors Should Not be Ignored

It is important for teachers to select the behaviors they are going to ignore with care. Some teachers ignore all their student's misbehaviors, regardless of the type, severity or the setting in which they occur. Dangerous or abusive behaviors, including hitting, verbal abuse, running away, and damaging property must not be ignored. Bullying a classmate, lying, or stealing, which provide students with immediate benefits while inconveniencing or harming others, should not be ignored either. In these situations a stronger consequence, such as a Timeout to calm down, loss of a privilege, or a work chore needs to be used in order to change the behavior. Ignoring noncompliance will not work because, in this case, the teacher must follow through on the command that she needs her student to follow. Also remember that ignoring an inappropriate behavior will only be effective with those students for whom teacher attention is the primary reinforcement. Thus the teacher will need to have worked very hard at the bottom of the pyramid, building a positive relationship with that student first before ignoring will be an effective tool.

Pay Attention to Positive Behaviors

Some teachers become so engrossed in their teaching that they fail to pay attention when their students speak nicely, share toys, solve a difficult problem, or work quietly. If these positive behaviors are ignored, they will disappear. Teachers often develop a reflex response, reacting to students only when they get into trouble. This negative cycle of paying attention when students misbehave and ignoring them when they are behaving appropriately actually increases the frequency of misbehavior.

If teachers use ignoring, it is crucial that they plan carefully to give attention and praise to prosocial behaviors, particularly those that are the positive opposite of the negative behavior they are ignoring. If a teacher has decided to ignore whining, for instance, he should make a conscious effort to praise the student whenever she speaks appropriately: "I really like it when you use your polite voice." It's important

It's important to remember that as soon as the student stops misbehaving, the teacher should quickly return his attention (within five seconds) and praise some appropriate behavior.

to focus on the positive behavior a teacher wants to see replace the problem one. If a teacher is concerned that a student is grabbing and hitting, she needs to praise him frequently for sharing, staying calm, and keeping his hands to his own body. If a teacher is concerned about a student who is fearful and withdrawn, he needs to praise her for putting up a quiet hand, participating, and helping someone.

Another effective strategy involves combining ignoring and praise in a group of two or three students. When one child is misbehaving, the teacher gives attention to the student demonstrating appropriate behaviors. Imagine a scene in which Peter is throwing Legos on the floor, while Jamal is building something carefully. A teacher's natural instinct is to focus on the child who is misbehaving, "Peter, don't do that." However, this would reinforce Peter's inappropriate behavior. If instead, the teacher ignores Peter and praises Jamal: "Jamal you are putting each block on top so carefully and patiently," Peter will probably begin to behave more appropriately because he sees that cooperative behavior gains teacher attention and misbehavior doesn't. This use of differential reinforcement combining ignore and praise has been shown to improve appropriate behavior and decrease negative behavior (Didden & De More, 1997).

Give Back Teacher Attention As Soon As Possible

Once in a while teachers may be so distressed and angered by inappropriate behaviors that they cannot focus on good behaviors. It's important to remember that as soon as the student stops misbehaving, the teacher should quickly return his attention (within five seconds) and praise some appropriate behavior. Only by combining the withdrawal of attention for inappropriate behaviors with consistent attention for appropriate ones will the teacher be able to reverse the cycle of negative attention for negative behavior. So, just as soon as the misbehavior stops, begin to smile, praise, look at, and talk to the student.

Use Subtle Ignores with Secondary Behaviors

Teachers can be too dramatic in the way they ignore their students. If a youngster begins to sulk, pout or mutter, or roll her eyes, the teacher may make an exaggerated gesture of pulling away and disregarding the misbehavior. This can be almost as reinforcing as giving attention for the misbehavior because it shows the student she has been able to produce a strong emotional response in her teacher.

Although it is advisable to withdraw physical contact, eye contact, and verbal contact when ignoring, it is also important that teachers neutralize their emotional reactions and be subtle. If the student is whining, the teacher should matter-of-factly look away and perhaps comment to another student about something else that's going on. This is effective because it reveals no hint that the teacher is affected in any way by the student's whining.

It is very helpful to use this subtle ignoring for the nonverbal secondary behaviors that often accompany a child's reaction to a teacher's command or request to do something. For example, a teacher has asked two students to clean up their work space before they go out to recess. While they have cooperated with her request and are starting to clean up, they are also moaning, whining, sulking, and sighing as they do the task. Here the teacher needs to focus on coaching and praising their compliance to her request and ignoring the other secondary and less important misbehaviors. "Thanks for starting to clean up!" If, on the other hand, the teacher were to respond to their low grade challenging misbehaviors by saying, "I don't like your attitude and your snotty tone of voice," then s/he would be fueling this response with her attention. Remember it is not necessary, nor realistic, that your students enjoy doing chores or following your directions. It is just important that they do them!

Use subtle ignoring for the nonverbal secondary behaviors.

Conclusions about Ignoring

Teachers who decide to use ignoring must be determined to ignore the student at all costs until the misbehavior stops. Consistency is the essence of ignoring. When a student throws a tantrum it is tempting to

Incredible Years ®

©*Incredible Years* ®

Full size version available:
www.incredibleyears.com/
teacherResources/index.asp

give in. However, each time the teacher gives in, it makes the misbehavior worse because the student learns that she can outlast the teacher. The next time, the tantrum will be louder and last longer. Therefore, it is crucial to continue ignoring until the behavior changes.

It is also important to remember that ignoring is not likely to affect how a student behaves unless a positive relationship has been built up between the the student and teacher. The first task in any plan to change behavior is to increase teacher attention, coaching and praise for positive behaviors. Although ignoring will decrease annoying misbehaviors, it will not increase positive ones. To do this, it must be combined with social approval for good behavior, specific teaching, coaching and practice of positive behavior, and perhaps even an incentive plan.

ENCOURAGE SELF-MONITORING FOR DISRUPTIVE BEHAVIORS

One common problem that all teachers face is the student who blurts out the answer in class instead of waiting and putting up a quiet hand. The teacher's least intrusive teaching tools for reducing this disruptive behavior would be to praise the students who have quiet hands up, answer only students who have a quiet hand up, and occasionally remind students that s/he will only respond to them when they have their hands raised and are quiet. Given that the teacher has taken these preventive steps consistently and the child still is yelling out in class, then it may be necessary to go to a higher level of discipline in the hierarchy such as a planned ignoring or a warning of consequences.

Remember always to have a positive incentive program in place first before using ignoring. Often times a self-monitoring chart can be helpful for inattentive and impulsive children (who act before they think) and prevents the need to use negative consequences. For example, for the students who have difficulty with blurting out responses in class, a teacher can place a picture of a *quiet hand up* at their desks. With this strategy, the student has a picture chart that reminds them of the behavior they are working on and permits them to record every time they put up a quiet hand. The teacher may even want the student to record talking out as well. At the end of the morning the teacher can review the chart to see how many successes the student recorded. Next she can set a goal for how many quiet hands up the student will achieve in the afternoon and offer an incentive for achieving a certain goal. The teacher says, "when you get five quiet hands up and only one calling out you can choose the activity for recess." This strategy is very useful for helping a child learn to monitor his own talking out behavior.

If this is a problem for the whole class, a teacher might consider a quiet hand thermometer. First, the teacher gets a baseline of how often the students are calling out in the morning. Let us say she finds they are calling out 30 times a morning. Next she shows her students a thermometer numbered from 1 to 30 and challenges them to raise quiet hands 30 times. At the same time the teacher is ignoring those who are blurting out responses. The teacher can set up a celebration or incentive for when the class consistently achieves a certain number of quiet hands for three days in a row. (Again teacher expectations regarding the immediacy of an incentive will vary depending on whether the teacher is teaching preschoolers or third graders.)

This type of system can be tailored to different developmental levels and different behavior problems. In the case of preschool children it is probably unrealistic for teachers to be concerned about blurt outs and quiet hands up since it is developmentally normal for preschoolers to be more impulsive and to have difficulty waiting. With this age children, the teacher goal may be simply to encourage students' participation, attention, use of language, or perhaps just sitting still in circle time. Gradually as teachers respond primarily to quiet hands up (or sitting) and reinforce this behavior (and ignore calling out), students begin to learn that this is expected classroom behavior and more likely to get teacher attention.

REDIRECTING MISBEHAVIOR

It's very important for teachers not to ignore students who are withdrawn or off task during classroom activities. While withdrawn behavior is nondisruptive to other students and may be less of a problem for teachers, it is a significant problem for such students because they are not involved in or attending to what they should be doing and therefore not learning what they should be. If the teacher ignores this behavior, it sends the message to the students involved that the teacher doesn't care about their learning and has low expectations for them. On the other hand, punishing a child who is off-task but nondisruptive is unnecessarily severe and may be counterproductive. Instead, the teacher should redirect and re-engage distracted students, giving them the opportunity to become involved in more productive activity.

Many minor or nondisruptive student misbehaviors can be handled unobtrusively by effective use of teacher redirection. This redirection can be nonverbal, verbal, or physical in nature. The advantage of this approach is that it doesn't draw attention to the student's misbehavior from other students and doesn't disrupt the classroom work being carried out. For example a preschool student is complaining that another student took the scissors that she wanted. The teacher might ignore the protests, but say, "Sally, it looks like you need some help getting started. Have you decided what shape you're going to color?" Or a teacher of a 2nd grade student who is clowning around in her seat during math might walk over and say, "Show me how you're going to do this first problem." In both cases, the disruptive or off-task behavior was not given any attention, but the student was directed back to a more appropriate activity.

Tailor behavior expectations according to student's developmental ability.

Use Nonverbal Signals, Prompts & Picture Cues for Redirecting

Many teachers have certain nonverbal signals or prompts that they use consistently and that have a clearly established meaning regarding particular rules for behavior. Examples are an upheld hand with two fingers raised, turning the lights off and on, ringing a bell, or rhythmic clapping; all of which may signal "quiet down." Another creative way for the teacher to indicate to her classroom that she wants their attention is to begin to draw the eyes, ears, and emerging face on the chalkboard or white board. When the teacher finishes drawing the smile on the face all the eyes and ears of the students should be on her. A thumbs up or wink can also quickly acknowledge that students quieted down when this request was made.

Teachers may want to establish special nonverbal signals for particular children to help them remember specific behaviors that are expected of them. One commonly used approach by teachers is the "stare." Catching the student's eye implicitly says, "You need to get back on focus." Although no words are used, this nonverbal and non-confrontive communication redirects the child to pay attention, without drawing attention to him as an overt verbal command would. A teacher might use a signal of "four on the floor" (four fingers pointed down) to remind a child to keep his feet and chair legs on the floor. Sometimes merely walking over to a student and/or placing a hand on the student's shoulder while continuing to teach is an effective way to redirect a student who is off task.For young children, the use of rules stated in the form of pictures or visual cues that symbolize the appropriate behaviors are very powerful ways of redirecting or reminding students about the rules. For example the teacher could have a picture showing quiet work

I can work quietly at my seat and stay in my seat.

Student Name			

©*Incredible Years*®

Full size version available:
www.incredibleyears.com/
teacherResources/index.asp

being done, quiet hand up, or a student staying in seat, so that when some students are talking, out of seat or forget to put up a quiet hand, the teacher can simply point to the visual cue to remind them of the rules for the activity "Remember our rule for asking questions?" Additionally, most teachers have rules posted on the wall. One nonverbal way of redirecting a child is simply to point to the rule on the wall.

Another example of a visual cue is a talking or activity meter that cues children into the teacher's expectations for an activity. For example, if the spinner on the meter is pointing to the red section, it means that students must raise a quiet hand to talk; the yellow section indicates that students can ask peers for help in quiet voices, but must be on-task; the green light indicates choice time when students can use inside voices to talk with each other freely. This approach helps students distinguish between times when they can talk and move about and times when their total attention is required. If a student forgets or a classroom gets too noisy, the teacher can simply point to the red or yellow light signal to remind them to be less noisy.

© Incredible Years®

When teachers first introduce a talking meter, it is important to teach and practice what each color means. For example, "Let's practice what the green inside voices sound like. John and Marius, will you say hello to each other using your inside conversation voices?" "Next, let's hear Sanjay and Marybelle use their quiet whisper voices to see what it sounds like to be in yellow." For a particularly noisy classroom, a teacher might want to use the talking meter in conjunction with a point or sticker system. When the class earns so many points for staying in white or green they can earn a privilege such as 5 minutes of free chat time.

Another kind of nonverbal reminder is the use of reminder cards. Here the teacher does not say anything to the student but passes him or her a reminder card. The card could say, "remember quiet hand up," "now is the time to stop," or "keep working." For use with younger children, use a picture of these messages on the card. This approach is beneficial because it helps the teacher to talk less about the negative behaviors and avoids distraction of other students. Of course, if a teacher is using reminder cards, she is advised to use compliment cards as well. These cards may be given out for the prosocial behavior that is being strengthened.

Other examples of visual or nonverbal prompts are:
- Exaggerated deep breath (calm down)
- Flat palm moved downwards through the air (for quiet down)
- Dark room (lights off and on for transition to recess)
- Thumbs up (good job)
- Wink (working hard)
- Musical sound for transition
- Picture cue—such as red light for "absolute quiet," yellow stop light for "quiet talk while working," green light for "free play"
- The "Stare"—catching the child's eye
- Reminder card (e.g. stop signal, quiet hand up signal, show me five hand)
- Compliment card
- Volume turning down signal with thumb and forefinger (turn down noise)
- Four fingers pointing down (to signal four legs on the floor)
- One finger pointing down and moving in a circle (to indicate turning around)
- Show me five (ears open, eyes on teacher, hands in lap, mouth closed, feet on floor)

| Listening Ears | Inside Voice | Hands to Self | Walking Feet | Eyes on Teacher |

Remember students with attention deficit disorders, impulsivity and language delays are visual learners. Picture cueing and nonverbal signals for rules, routines, and transitions will be very helpful to these students because of their short-term memory problems.

Use Physical Redirection to Practice, Divert, and Diffuse

Young preschool children may need to be physically walked through the motions of the behavior that is expected of them in order to understand the verbal instructions. Even for young children who do process verbal instructions well, walking them through the actual behaviors expected will often help them learn more quickly than if they only receive verbal instructions. For example, if the child is wandering out of circle time, you gently redirect by taking her arm and leading her back to her seat. It may not be necessary to even give a verbal command.

Another type of physical redirect is to ask a disengaged or hyperactive student to do something to help. This might mean asking them to put away the books, collect the papers, tidy up the book corner, or help get the snack ready. Such a request allows the child a legitimate opportunity to move around and engages him in some useful activity, giving him or her a sense of involvement and responsibility. Sometimes it is also helpful to give very fidgety children something to do with their hands, such as knitting or squeezing a rubber ball. These approaches divert and diffuse the disruption before it becomes a problem or gains attention from peers.

Positive Verbal Redirection

There is a real art to redirecting a disruptive student verbally without being confrontational. Sometimes a teacher can signal a child to stop by simply mentioning the student's name while teaching a lesson. This gives minimal attention to the misbehaving child and is often enough to get a child back on track without resorting to consequences.

Try to avoid negative verbal redirections such as, "Didn't you hear what I asked you to do?" or, "You weren't listening and were talking to your neighbor." These redirections do little to help the child become more productive. Instead, for the child who is daydreaming and off task, the teacher might say, "May I see what you have done so far?" For the student who doesn't seem to be listening, the teacher can say, "Jessie will you tell me what the instructions are?" For the student who is chatting, "Face this way please" or, "Having trouble, need a hand?"

One type of ineffective verbal redirection is "why questions." For example a student butts in line and pokes another child and the teacher responds with, "Why did you do that?" Or, a child is procrastinating with her work and the teacher says, "Why is it taking you so long? Why are you out of seat?" Why directions are counterproductive because they draw the teacher into unnecessary dialogue and imply a criticism of the child. Moreover, children don't usually understand why they have behaved the way they did. It is likely that when a teacher asks a child why he did something, he will withdraw or deny the problem. Instead, the teacher should focus on what s/he saw and give direct feedback, "I saw you butting in line. Please go to the back of the line." or "You are having trouble doing your work. You will need to be done before lunch, or you will have to stay in at recess. Do you need any help?"

Of course, one of the most effective positive redirections is through the use of proximity praise. When the teacher praises the students who are working hard, paying attention, and following directions, this praise serves as a reminder or verbal redirection to the students who are not engaged in these behaviors. (See Chapter Five for more details about effective praise and encouragement.)

"Why" directions are counterproductive.

Be Firm and Direct

For some disruptive behaviors, a clear and unambiguously assertive response (without aggression and screaming) is the most appropriate strategy. For example, verbal put downs that are intended to abuse and hurt. If a teacher hears a vicious or loud put-down from a student in her class for the first time, she stops immediately and says firmly, "Jeff! (pause) Those mean words are not okay. We have a rule for polite language and I expect you to follow it. Now, class, back to work." It is not helpful to continue on with a lecture about teasing or disrespectful behavior or to force apologies at this time because students probably need a cool off time before they can learn anything more from the experience. A student who has received this kind of reprimand will need positive feedback as soon as possible for polite, friendly language. If a student engages in repeated bullying, mean, or abusive language towards others, and if direct commands do not work, then teachers will move up the pyramid and give a consequence (see Chapter Eight).

Proximity to a positive peer model can help keep the distractible student on task.

Use Other Students to Help with Redirection

For the highly distractible, hyperactive, or disengaged student, redirecting is a constant process. Such students should be seated nearby the teacher so it is easier to redirect them unobtrusively. However, it is not always possible to arrange this physical proximity because sometimes the teacher may need to work with a small group of children for awhile. When this is the case, it can help to pair the distractible child with another student who is self-directed and focused. Proximity to a positive peer model can help keep the distractible student on task.

Reminders—"Remember our rule for..."

Positive reminders are particularly useful strategies with impulsive or distractible students who have difficulty remembering what is expected of them. For example, the teacher might say to the class at transition times, "Remember, we sit on the mat when we go in class, thanks" or, "Remember, before we leave the class we put our pencils in the container, slide our chairs under our desk, and check the floor for rubbish." For the student who is blurting out or talking loudly the teacher might say, "Remember our rule for asking questions?" or, "Remember the rule for working noise?" or, "Remember our rule for manners?" Reminders given in a positive tone of voice can redirect students quickly away from disruptive behavior back to classroom rules and routines. "Remember" is a nicer way of saying this than "Don't forget" which reminds them of what not to do. These reminders can also be paired with the picture cue cards for the rules discussed in the Proactive Chapter Three.

Calling Students Aside

It is helpful to redirect some off-task students, particularly the attention seeking and oppositional ones, more privately and away from their audience. For example, as the teacher is walking around the room she notices Sally grabbing away the art materials from the other two students at her table. The teacher says, "Sally can I see you a minute?" and as Sally is walking over the teacher resumes her attention to helping some other students and praising their teamwork and cooperation. Once Sally has reached her, she privately asks her, "What is our classroom rule for sharing?" Sally states the rule and the teacher praises her understanding. Then says, "Good. Now I will be watching you for all the times you are sharing." By taking Sally away from her audience, it minimizes the likelihood she will show off, and she will have no audience to perform for. Also the teacher's approach of turning back her attention to other students while Sally is walking over to her is effective because she is avoiding a confrontation, ignoring any secondary nonverbal behavior on the part of Sally (such as eye rolling and sighing), and minimizing the attention given to her disruptive behavior.

CONCLUSION

We have seen that when a student shows minor annoying misbehaviors such as blurting out, butting in, distracting others, talking out of turn, wandering out of seat, or procrastinating at work, teachers can use a variety of teaching tools to redirect and re-engage the student. First, it is crucial that the off task or disruptive behaviors receive little or no attention from the teacher or peers. Ignoring is one of the most powerful discipline tools that a teacher can use. Paired with ignoring, a teacher can use a variety of strategies for redirecting and teaching appropriate behaviors: for example, teachers can ignore the students doing these annoying things and respond to only the students who are putting up a quiet hand or who are working hard, "Thank you Carey for putting up a quiet hand. What is your question?" A teacher can use a rule reminder such as, "Remember our rule for quiet hands up?" She can give a clear direction of the expected behavior, "Hands up without calling out please," or use a nonverbal signal such as demonstrating quiet hand up with a finger on her mouth, or holding up the rules visual cue card. Another option is to take the student aside and briefly review the rule, "What is our rule for respect?" It is also important to teach all the students how to ignore their peers when they are teasing or bothering them or when their friends need privacy to calm down. Using a combination of these proactive discipline strategies will eliminate most annoying or mildly disruptive behaviors in the classroom. For more persistent or unsafe behaviors, other strategies such as logical consequences and Time Out to calm down will be covered in the next chapters.

Like a gardener, teachers are providing sunlight and fertilizer, in the form of attention and encouragement, to the behaviors that they want to encourage. Stray behaviors, like stray branches of vines might be gently redirected or guided back to the trellis. Misbehaviors, or weeds, are covered with a thick layer of mulch and left alone. Without sunlight and attention, these misbehaviors will weaken and eventually stop growing.

TO SUM UP...

Managing Misbehavior: Ignoring and Redirecting

- Choose specific student misbehaviors (low-level attention seeking behaviors) to use a planned ignore strategy.
- When planning to use the ignore strategy, make sure the targeted misbehaviors are ones that can be ignored.
- Praise the opposite prosocial student behaviors (to the negative ones being ignored).
- Avoid eye contact and discussion with student while ignoring.
- Physically move away from student when ignoring, but not too far away.
- Use subtle ignoring especially for nonverbal secondary behaviors.
- Be prepared for testing—remember when first ignoring the misbehavior often gets worse before it gets better.
- Be consistent.
- Return teacher attention as soon as misbehavior stops.
- Combine distractions and redirections with ignoring.
- Limit the number of behaviors to systematically ignore.
- Teach other students how to ignore minor misbehaviors.
- Encouraging self-monitoring when possible.
- Don't ignore withdrawn behavior—use redirections to engage student.
- Use nonverbal signals and picture cues for redirecting.
- Young children benefit from physical redirection at times.
- Positive reminders are particularly useful for impulsive or distractible students.

The Incredible Years®
Teacher Classroom Management Self-Reflection Inventory
Managing Misbehavior—Ignoring and Redirecting

Date: _____ Teacher Name: _____

Teachers learn extensively from self-reflection regarding their classroom management and the teaching strategies they are using that are working or not working. From these reflections teachers determine personal goals for making changes in their approaches to bring about the most positive learning climate they can. Use this Inventory to think about your strengths and limitations and determine your goals.

Setting Limits	1 = NEVER 3 = OCCASIONALLY 5 = CONSISTENTLY
1. I use nonverbal cues and signals to communicate rules as well as words (e.g., pictures of rules such as raise quiet hands, quiet voice, five on the floor, ears open).	1 2 3 4 5
2. I state requests or give directions to students respectively using brief descriptions of positive behaviors desired (e.g., "please keep your hands to your own body").	1 2 3 4 5
3. I use "when-then" or "first-then" commands when possible.	1 2 3 4 5
4. I give children one or two choices and redirections when possible.	1 2 3 4 5
5. I avoid negative commands, corrections, demands, and yelling at students.	1 2 3 4 5
6. I redirect disengaged children by calling out their name with a question, standing next to them, making up interesting games, and nonverbal signals.	1 2 3 4 5

7. I give frequent attention, coaching, praise and encouragement to children who are engaged and compliant following their directions.	1 2 3 4 5
8. I periodically review and practice the classroom rules.	1 2 3 4 5
Differential Attention and Ignoring and Redirecting	
1. I give more attention, coaching and praise to positive behaviors than to inappropriate student behaviors.	1 2 3 4 5
2. I have identified negative behaviors in students I want to decrease and the "positive opposite" of each negative behavior that I will praise, reward and give attention to with my coaching strategies.	1 2 3 4 5
3. I have identified those behaviors I can ignore while keeping the other students safe.	1 2 3 4 5
4. I have worked hard teaching children to ignore their peers when they are laughed at, poked or made fun of.	1 2 3 4 5
5. My ignoring is strategically planned and is done by avoiding eye contact, verbal comments, and physical touch and by keeping a neutral affect.	1 2 3 4 5
6. I use proximal praise strategically (e.g., coach and praise nearby child for behavior I want to encourage) while ignoring the child who is inappropriate.	1 2 3 4 5
7. I use positive self-talk as an approach to staying calm when students misbehave. (write example here)	1 2 3 4 5

8. I start with using the least intrusive proactive discipline strategy when students misbehave. I review my hierarchy of discipline and make sure it is developmentally appropriate.	1 2 3 4 5
9. When using a planned ignore, as soon as a student is behaving appropriately and has calmed down after losing control, I immediately return my attention and encouragement to the student.	1 2 3 4 5
10. I have developed behavior plans that include identifying those inappropriate behaviors to ignore and the positive opposite behaviors to coach, praise and reward.	1 2 3 4 5
11. I help children learn how to self-regulate through specific techniques (e.g., deep breathing, positive self-talk, positive imagery, anger or relaxation thermometer).	1 2 3 4 5
12. I use "positive forecasting" statements to predict a child's success in earning his prize.	1 2 3 4 5
13. I work hard to redirect and re-engage students to other activities when they are frustrated or off task.	1 2 3 4 5
14. I have communicated with parents (via emails or Teacher–to–Parent Communication Home Activities letter) to encourage their modeling and teaching of their children in how to compliment others.	1 2 3 4 5
15. I have shared the classroom discipline hierarchy with the parents of my students.	1 2 3 4 5
Future Goals Regarding Ignoring and Redirecting Strategies:	Total

REFERENCES

Bear, G. G. (1998). School Discipline in the United States: Prevention, Correction and Long-Term Social Development. *School Psychology Review, 2*(1), 14-32.

Brophy, J. E. (1996). Teaching problem students. New York: Guilford.

Didden, R., De Moor, J., & Bruyns, W. (1997). Effectiveness of DRO tokens in decreasing disruptive behavior in the classroom with five multiply handicapped children *Behavioral Inteventions, 12*(2), 65-75.

Gable, R. A., Hester, P. H., Rock, M. L., & Hughes, K. G. (2009). Back to basics: Rules, praise, ignoring and reprimands revisited. *Intervention in School and Clinic, 44,* 195-205.

Hall, R., & Lund, D. (1968). Effects of teacher on study behavior. *Journal of Applied Behavior Analysis, 1*(1), 1-12.

Hyman, I. A. (1997). *School discipline and school violence: A teacher variance approach.* Boston: Allyn & Bacon.

Kalis, T. M., Vannest, K. J., & Parker, R. (2007). Praise Counts: Using self-monitoring to increase effective teaching practices. *Preventing School Failure, 51*(3), 20-27.

Madsen, C. H., & Becker, W. C. (1968). Rules, praise and ignoring: Elements of elementary classroom control. *Journal of Applied Behavior Analysis, 1*(2), 139-150.

Martens, B. K., & Meller, P. J. (1990). The application of behavioral principles to educational settings. In T. B. Gutkin & C. R. Reynolds (Eds.), *Handbook of school psychology* (pp. 612-634). New York: Wiley.

CHAPTER
8

Managing Misbehavior: Natural and Logical Consequences

No matter how consistently you use ignoring, redirecting, warnings, and reminders to deal with inappropriate classroom behavior, and no matter how consistently you reinforce appropriate behavior, there are still times when children will continue to misbehave. This is a necessary part of their developmental drive for independence and their curious exploration and discovery of the limits of their environment. In these cases, their misbehavior needs to be dealt with by imposing a more direct teaching tool from higher on the pyramid. These discipline

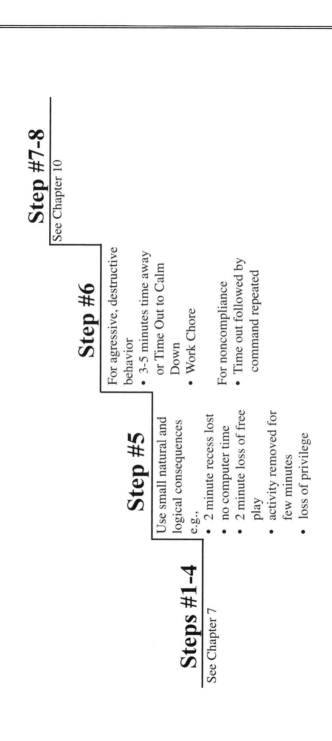

Steps 5-6 of Discipline Hierarchy

Steps #1-4
See Chapter 7

Step #5

Use small natural and logical consequences e.g.,

- 2 minute recess lost no computer time
- 2 minute loss of free play
- activity removed for few minutes
- loss of privilege

Step #6

For agressive, destructive behavior

- 3-5 minutes time away or Time Out to Calm Down
- Work Chore

For noncompliance

- Time out followed by command repeated

Step #7-8
See Chapter 10

"Always choose the lowest, least intrusive first."

tools involve a brief, immediate, and consistent discipline response so that children learn the connection between their own behaviors and negative consequences. In this chapter we will discuss step # 5 in the discipline hierarchy.

A negative (logical or natural) consequence is something the child does not want, such as being last in line, losing recess, getting Time Out in the classroom, missing free time, or loss of a special activity or a privilege. Consequences do not have to be severe to be effective. In fact the key aspect of using this tool is brevity and immediacy, not severity. Consequences are most effective when they are applied immediately, consistently, briefly, and uniformly across all students. This will ensure that students understand and can predict the consequences for their actions, and that they perceive that the teacher uses them fairly. For this reason, it is a good idea to avoid establishing consequences that are delayed or inconvenient to enforce. Classrooms that have clear and predictable discipline hierarchies, as outlined in Chapters Seven, Eight, and Nine allow students to flourish in a safe, predictable environment (Cotton & Wikelund, 1990) that supports their long term social, emotional, and academic development (Bear, 1998) and prevents interference from distracting elements.

Consequences are a way of holding children accountable for their misbehavior. However, students must be familiar with the Discipline Plan in advance so that they can see the negative consequences as the direct result of their behavior. Whenever possible, consequences should be presented as a choice the child has made—for example, "You did not clean up when I asked. You have made the choice to finish cleaning up during the beginning of our snack time."

Consequences are most effective when they are applied immediately, consistently, briefly, and uniformly across all students.

Negative Consequences are:
- consistent
- used uniformly
- applied promptly and briefly after the misbehavior if possible
- convenient to enforce

- presented as a choice child has made
- nonpunitive & reasonable
- related to the behavior
- developmentally appropriate

In the next pages we will discuss several types of logical and natural consequences which have been shown in the literature to be effective in reducing misbehavior (Brophy, 1996; Stage & Quiroz, 1997; Walker, Colvin, & Ramsey, 1995).

NATURAL AND LOGICAL CONSEQUENCES

A natural consequence is some negative outcome that would result from the child's misbehavior without any intervention on the teacher's part. When these kinds of consequences occur, they can be a good learning experience for the student with minimal classroom disruption or teacher effort. For example, a child who refuses to wear a coat to recess would get cold, or a child who intentionally breaks his own pencil or crayons would then need to work with the broken pieces. In a real classroom setting, however, it is often not safe or feasible to allow students to experience the natural consequence of their actions. For example, a first grade student who never does math seat work would eventually experience the natural consequences of not learning math, failing math in school, and not being able to use math skills in real life settings. Clearly, the results of this kind of natural consequence are too long term to be an effective motivator for a child, and teachers must use a more effective immediate consequence for refusing to do school work.

Children's developmental level is another important issue to consider when letting natural consequences take their course. When thinking through the natural consequences that may result from your students' inappropriate behaviors, it's

Because of the cognitive skills involved, natural consequences will work better for school-age children than for preschoolers.

important to be sure that your expectations are appropriate for their developmental age. Because of the cognitive skills involved, natural consequences will work better for school-age children than for pre-schoolers. Very young children will often need teacher intervention to protect themselves from experiencing the negative results of their own impulsive actions. This is because they have not developed the self-regulation skills or world experience to see how their actions will lead to future negative consequences. For example, while it is likely a very effective intervention to allow a 5-year-old to feel cold at recess because she wouldn't put on her coat, it might not be appropriate to let a toddler go outside without adequate clothing. Lastly, in many circumstances natural consequences will be most effective if the child is given a chance to make a different choice soon after experiencing the negative consequence. The child who wouldn't wear a coat to recess might be allowed to go inside to get the coat once she realizes that she really needs it. It is not necessary for her to be miserable for an entire recess for the natural consequence to be effective. The child who ruined the school supplies might be asked to work with them for a brief time, and then would be given the opportunity to earn some new materials so that she could learn to complete her school work in an appropriate manner. Teachers can enhance the effectiveness of natural consequences by calmly making the link between the child's actions and the consequence. "It's your choice to not wear your jacket. You may feel cold if you don't put it on." Or, "I want to let you know that it will be hard to draw with those crayons if they are all broken."

Of course, natural consequences should not be used if children may be physically hurt by them. For example, no child should be allowed to experience the natural consequences of sticking a finger into an electrical outlet, touching the stove, or running in the road.

Examples of Natural Consequences
- If a student forgets her school books or homework, she will not be able to have her paper marked or get a special sticker of recognition that day
- If the student misuses her glue by pouring it all on one art project, there won't be any left for another project

- If the student doesn't come in for snack on time, there might not be any left
- If the student refuses to eat the school lunch, he or she may be hungry later

In a typical classroom setting, teachers more often use logical consequences. A logical consequence is a negative outcome that results from the child's behavior because the teacher set it up that way. This allows the teacher more control over the situation than with a natural consequence. For example, a logical consequence for a student who is throwing toys in the block area is to have to choose another area to play in. A logical consequence for a student who is bothering the other students in his table is to have him move to another table or to work independently for a short period. A logical consequence for pushing to be at the front of the line is to be sent to the back of the line. Logical consequences work best when there is an inherent connection between the misbehavior and the consequence. As with natural consequences, it is useful for the teacher to calmly state the logical consequence for the child's behavior. For instance, "If you spit your milk on the table, I will have to take it away." Or, for a child who points scissors at someone, "If you can't use the scissors safely, then I will remove them." These warnings provide the child with a choice to change the unacceptable behavior and a warning about the consequence if he does not.

Examples of Logical Consequences
- If the student can't use the scissors safely, they will be taken away
- If water is spilled all over the floor, the student will be responsible for cleaning it up
- If the student doesn't wear a bicycle helmet, he'll not be able to ride the tricycle or bike that morning at recess
- If the student can't use a quiet voice in the library, then she will not be allowed to check out a book that day
- If student can't stay at her seat during study time, he will have to sit with the teacher
- If the student doesn't stay in the playground at recess, she will miss 5 minutes of the next recess

- If the student keeps blurting out in class and arguing with the teacher, he will be given an appointment card to stay in at recess to discuss his concerns with the teacher
- If the student breaks a classroom rule, a preferred toy or activity is removed for choice time (e.g., computer time)
- If the student can't stop distracting and bothering other students at his table, then she will need to sit away from the others
- If the student procrastinates and does not do the work in class time, then he will have to do it when other students are doing special activities
- If the student pushes in line at lunch, then she will be directed to the back of the line
- If the student chooses not to work in the place designated by the teacher, he will be kept back at recess to discuss the issue (useful for a larger child who refuses to move)
- If the student continues to call out after warnings and reminders, she has to leave the discussion and work quietly at her desk
- If the student breaks or damages something, he will have to complete a job to 'earn' money to replace it (e.g., sharpen pencils, tidy book shelves, pick up trash in room, clean fish tank)

Logical consequences are most effective for recurring problems where teachers decide ahead of time how they are going to follow through. This approach can help children to learn to make decisions, be responsible for their own behavior, and learn from their mistakes. In the following pages, we will discuss some effective ways to use consequences as well as some of the problems that can occur when using them.

COMMON CONSEQUENCES

Moving the Child

As noted in several examples above, one general category of effective consequences for misbehavior is to take the student away from the situation he/she is disrupting or the situation that is stimulating or reinforcing the misbehavior. This usually stops misbehavior by decreasing the attention it is receiving from other children, and gives the student a chance to calm down and get back on track. A student might be asked to leave the circle area and listen from his desk, to choose another area to play in, to sit near the teacher, or to work independently instead of in a table group. This is different from Time Out in that the student can still continue working and participating in the classroom activities but not at a table with other students. If a child refuses to move after the teacher asks her to, then the teacher could add a consequence by saying, "If you don't go to the table, you will lose your computer time this morning."

Loss of Privileges

Another main type of negative consequence is for the student to lose some privilege. The privilege that is removed may depend on the teacher's assessment of what the child usually likes to do. A consequence will only be meaningful if the student is losing an activity that is enjoyable to him. For one student losing computer time may be very effective, while, for another student, loss of 5 minutes of recess may have much more impact.

Sometimes teachers may specifically set up situations that provide opportunities to both reward and use consequences during the day. For example, teachers may set aside 5 minutes of free time before lunch and 5 minutes of free time at the end of the day. These two times provide a nice break for all students who are following directions, but are also convenient possible consequences for a student who it not cooperating during the morning or afternoon. Students might lose 1 minute of free play for the first rule infraction, 2 minutes for the second, etc... Another creative program was set up by a kindergarten teacher. She allowed all her students to bring in their favorite toy or stuffed animal on Mondays. Students who didn't have a toy on Monday were allowed to pick one out of the teacher's special toy box. The students could play with these special toys before school started and during recess. During the rest of the day they were placed on the top shelf of a book case. If a child broke a classroom rule during the day the teacher would say, "Your bunny will need to stay in for 3 minutes at recess before you can play with him." Thus the students would lose the privilege of playing with their favorite toy as consequence for breaking a rule. The important aspect to this approach is that the special activity is something truly special! Building several small short special times during the day actually allows the teacher more options for instituting a consequence, when needed.

Staying In From Recess or Serving Detention

Another common consequence often used by teachers is to have the student miss recess or, for older students, serve detention. Sometimes students are required to sit and do nothing dur-

It is far more effective to connect this consequence with the student's efforts to repair the situation.

ing these times. This consequence is problematic because it is not connected logically to the misbehavior, denies the child's rights to be socially accountable, and only serves to demonstrate the power of the adult to coerce the child. It is far more effective to connect the experience with the student's efforts to repair the situation. For example, the student might use the time to fix a damaged item, clean up a mess that was made, write an apology, finish the work not completed, or think of a different solution. This can be a very useful way to teach students about responsibility and accountability as well as consequences. In all cases the emphasis should be on how the student can repair or fix the situation rather than on reviewing or rehashing their misdeeds.

Give Appointment Cards for Planned After-Class Chats

A non-confrontational strategy for the older defiant student is to give out teacher appointment cards (which are made up ahead of time with time, place, and reason for appointment). A student who is hostile, sarcastic, and is arguing with the teacher can be given an appointment card telling him when he will meet after class to discuss his concerns. The teacher might say," I can see that what you are saying is important to you so I am going to give you an appointment time when we can talk about it privately when you are calm. At 1:15 today we can meet at my desk to discuss your concerns about...."

This approach has two benefits for the child. First, it avoids a confrontational or public discipline approach in front of the rest of the students and de-escalates or breaks the cycle of negativity between the teacher and student. If the teacher had persisted in discussing the issue at the time the student was dysregulated and being oppositional, her attention could potentially have reinforced the student's misbehavior. Moreover, the discussion would have disrupted the rest of the class. Secondly, at the time a child is misbehaving s/he is usually angry and defensive and unlikely to benefit from a teacher discussion. Instead, teachers should have these discussions at a neutral time when both the teacher and student are calm and use them to collaborate, practice and to develop a plan for coping more effectively with the problem.

There are a number of basic relational skills to remember when having these one-to-one after class chats.

EFFECTIVE AFTER CLASS CHATS

1. Start by acknowledging how the student might be feeling. For example, *"I can see you are upset about missing some of recess time, and I won't keep you long. I need to speak to you about…"*
2. Briefly review the specific problem behavior that occurred in the classroom such as the calling out, butting-in, wandering, being "rude" in tone and attitude and so on. Focus on the positive opposite behavior that is expected. For example, a teacher might say, *"The problem I see is that it is difficult for me to teach and other students to pay attention when you are out of your seat. Would you like to tell me your side of the problem?"*
3. Avoid arguing or haranguing, stay focused on primary issue or rule broken. For example, a teacher might say, *"So the rule is that all students need to be in their desks during work time, and must not get up and talk to other students without permission."*
4. Invite the student's feedback or solution to the problem. *"Can you think of a different way to respond when you get frustrated again? How can you let me know without yelling at me?" "I hear you saying that you are frustrated about how hard the work is. That's good for me to know. Now, we need to think of a better way to solve this problem."*

5. Role play or practice how to respond to the situation using that solution in the future (you can use a puppet for this practice).

6. Work on an agreement about future positive behavior and set up a reward or incentive plan for achieving an agreed upon goal.

7. Finish with brief reminder and separate amicably. For example, the teacher says, *"I appreciate you staying in to talk with me. We all have bad days, and now I understand that you were frustrated. I think we have a good solution that will help you follow the rules. You can use a signal to let me know when you need help. I will try to get to you quickly when I see your signal. If you hurry outside, you'll still have 10 minutes to play."*

USING CONSEQUENCES EFFECTIVELY

Be Sure Teacher Expectations for Student are Age Appropriate

As stated above, the effectiveness of natural and logical consequences depends on children's developmental ability to perform the desired behavior and to understand the link between their behavior and the consequence. For instance, if 3-year-old Alexandra is not ready to be toilet trained, but she is made to clean her underpants, she may feel unduly criticized. Furthermore, if she does not have the developmental ability to use the toilet on her own, then the consequence will not have the intended effect of helping her become trained. For consequences to be effective, children must be developmentally able to understand the link between their behavior and the consequence, especially if the consequence occurs somewhat later. For instance, one very effective natural consequence for a child who won't eat her lunch is to experience hunger later in the day. Children who are three and older will likely learn to eat at lunch time within a few days. Younger children may not be able to understand the connection between eating at lunch and the hunger they feel later.

Be Sure You Can Live with the Choices

When attempting to carry out natural and logical consequences, some teachers find it difficult to allow their students to experience the outcomes of their actions. They are so sympathetic towards their students that they feel guilty for not coming to their aid and may intervene before the consequence occurs. For instance, a teacher tells Angie, a 5-year-old, that the logical consequence of dawdling and not lining up on time will be to miss gym class that day. However, the teacher can't bring herself to let Angie feel the discomfort of missing gym and sends her anyway, even though she is still wandering around the room. Such over-protectiveness can handicap children by making them feel they are fragile and incapable of handling problems or the consequences of their mistakes. Letting children experience and handle the discomfort of their mistake is an important learning lesson. Another possible problem with the above example would occur if the gym class was the teacher's only break during the day. Then she might be reluctant to follow through with the consequence because it would mean that she would also be giving up her own break time.

When using consequences it's important to think about the pros and cons of applying this technique to particular misbehaviors. Be certain that you can live with the consequences and that you are not giving idle threats. In the example above, the teacher should have first considered whether or not she would be willing to follow through and let Angie miss gym if she continued to dawdle. Failing to follow through with an agreed-upon consequence will dilute your authority and deprive your students of opportunities to learn from their mistakes.

The consequences approach doesn't work when the consequences of misbehaviors are too distant.

Consequences Should Be Fairly Immediate

The natural and logical consequences approach doesn't work when the consequences of misbehaviors are too distant. The natural consequences of not brushing teeth would be to have cavities. However, since this might not occur until several years later, it would not be effective. Permitting youngsters not to do homework until the end-of-the-year report card shows they have failed is another consequence that is too delayed to have any influence on their daily study habits. Such long-term consequences may lead children to feel hopeless about their abilities and will not change daily behavior.

For preschool and school-age children it's important that the consequences closely follow the inappropriate behavior. If 7-year-old Dan doesn't bring in his homework, he will have to do it at recess. If 8-year-old Kimmy talks during circle time after repeated warnings, she will lose her computer time for that same afternoon. If 4-year-old Katy is coloring on the table instead of on her paper, the crayons will be removed for the rest of that work period. Each of these consequences will be more effective if the teacher has given a warning before instituting the con-

This plan would likely involve a combination of proactive and positive coaching strategies, praise and incentives as well as a consequence for not doing homework.

sequences. In this way, Kimmy, Dan, and Katy will learn from their inappropriate behavior and will probably behave more appropriately the next time.

Give Student Choices Ahead of Time

Sometimes teachers use consequences in a punitive way, not letting their students know the possible consequences in advance. Eight-year-old Robbie's teacher comes up to him one morning and says, "You haven't completed your homework again, so you're not going to go to the school assembly today." He is given no warning and does not have the choice of deciding to do his homework or miss the assembly. Not surprisingly, Robbie will probably feel resentful and will probably not see himself as responsible for the consequences of his behavior. If homework is a problem for Robbie, then the teacher should set up a reward system ahead of time to support homework completion. Thinking about the teaching pyramid, this system would likely involve a combination of proactive and positive coaching strategies, praise and incentives as well as a consequence for not doing homework. Robbie would understand the positive consequences if he completes his homework (perhaps he can earn extra computer time or a small sticker or prize) as well as the consequence if he doesn't. "Robbie, we have an assembly on Friday. In order for you to be able to go, you will

need to remember to bring in your home-work 4 out of 5 days this week." It is up to the Robbie to decide how to respond; because he understands both the positive and negative consequences, it is fair and predictable.

There are times when a teacher must give a consequence that isn't part of a preplanned system. As long as the student receives a clear and fair warning, these unplanned consequences can still be very effective. For example, Christina has been chatting and distracting other students during quiet work time. The teacher says, "Christina I have asked you twice to work quietly. If you continue to talk out and distract others, you will have to work at a separate table." Christina protests, the teacher repeats the choice and walks away. When Christina settles down the teacher says, "That was a good choice Christina you are working hard now." If Christina had continued to talk, the teacher would have followed through with the consequence. These approaches, which emphasize the language of choice, give students the sense that their behavior is their responsibility and they have some self-control over how to behave. Eventually students understand, through experiencing the consequences, that it is better to respond positively rather than negatively.

It is ideal if the consequences occur on the same day that the misbehavior occurred and should never extend beyond one day after the misbehavior.

Consequences Should Be Natural or Logical and Nonpunitive

Occasionally teachers come up with consequences that are not logically or naturally related to an activity or are too severe. Consider the bus driver who says the student can't come on the bus for two weeks because of misbehaving on the bus one morning. While the bus driver might argue that it is a logical consequence for a youngster who has been misbehaving, this approach is too punitive. When consequences are too harsh or lengthy, children will feel resentful and perhaps even retaliate against such consequences. They will be more likely to focus on the cruelty of the teachers than on changing their own behavior. Instead, the bus driver might say, "if you can't stay seated with your seat belt on in the bus, then you will need to sit up here next to me." Here the child has a choice to make about his behavior. Of course, it would also be important to have an incentive or positive plan in place too for the child's positive behavior staying seated on the bus. At the elementary school

*Consequences
should emphasize
the language of choices
students can make.*

level, it is ideal if the consequences occur on the same day that the misbehavior occurred and should never extend beyond one day after the misbehavior. For preschool children, consequences should occur as close as possible to the misbehavior, certainly within the same day, and are often effective even if they only last a few minutes before getting a new learning trial.

A calm, matter-of-fact, friendly attitude is essential for teachers deciding upon and carrying out consequences. The natural consequence of not wearing a coat when it's cold outside is to become chilled. The logical consequence of misbehaving on the bus might be to miss recess that day. These consequences are not degrading and allow the student an opportunity to make a different decision in the immediate future. Instead, they help children to learn to make better choices and to be more responsible.

Follow Through When Student Objects to Consequence

Sometimes teachers impose a consequence such as staying after school or missing recess for a teacher chat and the student refuses to take the consequence, perhaps by tantrumming in response to the stated consequence or running out to recess instead of following directions and staying in. It is important that the teacher remain calm, since chasing or yelling at the child will reinforce the oppositional behavior. Instead, later in the day, when the child is calm, the teacher can call the student out of class for a discussion and complete the consequence. In this situation it is more important that the certainty of the consequence be enforced rather than the severity or immediacy. For example the teacher explains,

"I explained that you would need to miss recess because you didn't finish your work. Since you did not listen and ran out to morning recess, I am going to have you stay in during your afternoon recess instead."

Involve Your Student Whenever Possible

Some teachers set up a natural and logical consequence program without involving their students in the decisions. This may well cause the children to feel cross and resentful. Instead, teachers should consider this an opportunity to work together with their students to promote positive behaviors, allowing them to feel respected and valued. For instance, if some students are having problems fighting over the computer, the teacher might say, "You seem to be having trouble agreeing on whose turn it is to use the computer. You can decide either to take turns using the computer or it will not be available for use today. Which would you prefer?" Involving students in the decision making about consequences often reduces their testing when there is a problem and enhances their cooperation. Or, let's say Erica is having trouble working quietly with Anna. The teacher might say, "Erica if you're having a problem working here with Anna, would you prefer to work separately?" This message is given as a choice and a chance to choose a better response. If Erica continued to be noisy after this, then the teacher would ask her to move to a different table.

Involving students in the decision making about consequences often reduces their testing when there is a problem and enhances their cooperation.

Be Straightforward and Friendly–Avoid Arguments

Sometimes students vehemently argue or deny that they swore, blurted out, or talked loudly. Teachers need to be careful not to undermine their consequence program by becoming angry, argumentative, or critical with students for being irresponsible or not remembering the rule. This will only reinforce their behavior. Avoid taking their protests as bait and be straightforward, respectful and assertive about the consequences. For example, "Ben I heard you call him a rude name."

Ben denies doing this but the teacher reiterates, "We have a rule for respect and I expect you to use it." Ben continues to argue and deny having said the word and the teacher avoids arguing, "I heard you, go back to your seat, and I'll see you at recess." The teacher walks away allowing the student to cool off. Later the teacher will discuss this incident with Ben and work out what polite language could be used or how he could have used self control to ignore and stay calm. The respect rule will be restated as well as the consequences.

It's important to be straightforward and assertive about consequences, to be prepared to follow through with them, and to ignore students' protests or pleading. Protesting the consequence is a normal and developmentally appropriate limit testing on the part of students. If teachers engage in discussion or arguing, students will feel that they may have a chance of changing the teacher's mind. State the consequence with confidence, and then walk away.

If students refuse to accept consequences, teachers can use Time Out or the loss of a privilege, whichever best fits the situation. After the consequences have been carried out, students should be given a new opportunity to try again, to be successful and to receive praise.

When In Doubt about the Appropriate Consequence, Use Deferment

Sometimes a teacher may be so angry with a child that she can't think of an appropriate consequence. The danger is that in this moment of extreme anger, she will impose a much more severe consequence than necessary. If this happens the teacher should defer making a decision until she can calm down and think through the situation clearly. For example, Cary used rude language and backtalked and her teacher responded, "That makes me very angry, and I need to calm down before I can talk to you about your behavior. Please go to the back of the room and sit at the table until I decide what to do." The teacher then proceeded to pass out the papers and get the rest of the students involved in their work. Then when she was calm she approached Cary and said, "Cary, calling me names hurt my feelings, you know we don't use that kind of language in the classroom. If this happens again you will miss 5 minutes of computer time. Are you ready to go back to work now?"

This teacher's approach is effective because she models a respectful response and as well as how to calm down before trying to solve a problem. If the teacher had threatened Cary, sent a note home, or sent her to the principal's office it probably would have escalated the situation and given more power to the child's misbehavior.

One of the key principles of a classroom discipline plan is that it be respectful, nonhumiliating, and nonconfrontational.

Avoid Group Detentions

Sometimes teachers keep the whole class in from recess for a detention in order to punish a few students' misbehaviors. Teachers should avoid doing this because it erodes the good will of the entire class. Students who are unfairly punished feel let down by their teacher.

Avoid Putting Names on the Board for Negative Behaviors

Sometimes teachers will put a child's name on the board to indicate that the student has misbehaved. They think that this approach serves to warn the misbehaving child. However, this approach is not recommended because it focuses teacher and peer group attention on the misbehaving student and may actually reinforce their negative identity or reputation in the classroom. Public recognition should be saved for positive accomplishments and behaviors, while discipline should be directed to the student as calmly and privately as possible. One of the key principles of a classroom discipline plan is that it be respectful, nonhumiliating, nonconfrontational, limits the amount of attention the misbehavior gets, and when possible, gives the student an option for making a better choice and new learning experience as soon as possible.

Avoid Sending the Child to the Principal's Office

One frequently used consequence used by teachers is to send the misbehaving child to the principal's office. In fact, in some schools teachers will use this strategy as many as 4-5 times a week, even for annoying misbehaviors or student insubordination. It is usually the gradual build up of these minor misbehaviors during the day that leads to the eventual use of an office referral. However, this consequence should not be used for these relatively minor misbehaviors. If used at all, the principal's office should be reserved for misbehavior that is so disruptive that the teacher can't teach at all. In the short run sending a misbehaving child to the office frees the teacher from the stress of the disruptive child for a while, but in the long run it may actually increase the child's misbehavior. Many children get reinforced when they go to the principal's office by the attention of the secretary or the principal or the reaction of their peer group. Moreover, if office referrals are overused, the administrator will be deluged and unlikely to offer any real help to the student. Instead it is likely to be far more beneficial for the child if the teacher continues to use proactive discipline tools such as incentives, warnings, redirection, self-monitoring approaches, ignoring, loss of privileges and in-class Time Outs to manage misbehavior. In addition, sending students to the principal's office to scare them into submission confuses students' perceptions of the role of the principal, who becomes an evil power.

Involving Parents

Another approach that is used by teachers is to threaten a child that his or her parents will be called if she continues to misbehave. This approach is not advised and will usually only work for the child who has a good relationship with his parents and fears their disapproval and disappointment. For the child with multiple family problems and a stressful relationship with his parents, it is unlikely to work and may even result in the child getting excessive punishment from his parents, thus making his defiance worse. These are the children who are practiced at getting punished and almost seem to become immune to it. This does not mean that parents shouldn't be invited in for a meeting to coordinate a behavior plan to help a problem child learn a positive behavior but threats about calling parents should not be used to try to change student behavior.

Avoid Sending the Child Home or At-Home Suspensions

Sometimes teachers believe that at-home suspensions are the most severe consequence they can use for disciplining the student's disruptive and aggressive behavior. While this approach might provide temporary relief for the teacher, it is actually an inappropriate consequence for school behavior for several reasons. First, the consequence is too lengthy and does not allow the child the opportunity to try again and to learn more appropriate behavior. Secondly, it is perceived as a form of abandonment by the student and will severely set back any trust in the relationship between the student, family and teacher. Thirdly, it has the possible ramifications of an angry parent excessively punishing the child for the suspension, particularly if it means the parent's job is jeopardized. Fourth, it is possible that a working parent will be unable to get child care on such short notice and will be forced to leave the child at home unattended. Leaving an aggressive child who has few self-management skills unsupervised at home is highly likely to lead to future behavior problems. The problem has simply been transferred from the school to the streets. Lastly, for a child who is having difficulty in school, staying at home playing on the computer or watching TV may be much more appealing than struggling in the classroom setting, and at-home suspension may actually serve to reinforce the child's negative school behavior and reputation. It is far more effective for the teacher to handle the problem immediately with a brief Time Out to calm down or a form of in-school suspension such as loss of recess or loss of extra school privileges that day or a work chore.

In general, we don't advise at-home suspensions for any child. If a student's behavior is so severe that suspension is deemed necessary, then, in the short term the school should consider an in-school suspension rather than an at-home one. This means that the student is withdrawn from the classroom activities for part of the day and is asked to complete his classroom work by himself. In the longer term, any student who is frequently so disruptive as to require this high level of consequences should be evaluated by a team to institute a comprehensive behavior plan that includes positive behavior strategies as well as consequences. A student who is not successful in the classroom needs more intensive classroom supports, and, in the extreme, may need a different classroom placement.

Avoid Interrogations and Sermons–Be Succinct and Respectful

How often have you encountered a scenario similar to the following. A teacher observes Elonzo throw a handful of dirt at another child on the playground. She calls him over to her and says angrily, "What did you do?" Elonzo, thinking the teacher has not seen the action, replies, "nothing." Now the teacher is even angrier and retorts, "You are lying, I saw what you did, why did you do that?" Elonzo shrugs his shoulders and looks at the floor and says, "So what!" The teacher replies, "Don't you speak to me in that tone of voice. Look at me."

Avoid interrogating a child about what he did. Directly and calmly acknowledge the child's misbehavior and enforce the consequence.

There is tendency for adults to want to make children admit their mistakes and to force them to tell why they misbehaved. Admitting a mistake is extremely hard for anyone to do. This is particularly true when there is a power differential, as with a young child and a teacher. Furthermore, most young children do not really understand why they misbehaved or if they do understand, they may not be able to articulate their reasons. Moreover these sorts of interrogations usually lead to the teacher moralizing and preaching about the misbehavior; words that are quickly tuned out by the child. Finally, in the example above, the teacher is actually teaching her student to be more disrespectful by her own angry tone of voice and blaming attitude.

Teachers should try to avoid interrogating a child about what he did, especially if they directly observed the behavior. Instead, the teacher should directly and calmly acknowledge the child's misbehavior and enforce the consequence. In a discipline confrontation, children generally only hear the first 20 seconds of teacher talk, so teachers should be as succinct as possible. For example, the teacher could say, "Elonzo I saw you hit Ricardo with the dirt, you need to miss the rest of recess and stand next to me." This teacher is modeling respect by remaining calm and polite, and she is not inviting comments or arguments from the child. Even if the child does argue, the teacher should not respond because she has already stated the behavior and the consequence and needs to ignore any protests.

Avoid Emotional Intensity and Escalation

Too much emotional intensity or shouting when disciplining can also escalate children's misbehavior. Taking the example of Elonzo, the

A calm, respectful response to misbehavior is key to a teacher's success in following through with consequences.

teacher might have responded to his lying by lecturing and shouting, "Stop that. Stop throwing dirt! You are in big trouble now. You are getting a detention. Why can't you stay out of trouble for once in your life? What makes you think you can get away with acting like that?" Elonzo probably begins to tune out his teacher at this point and may be thinking to himself that this is just one more teacher who is mean and doesn't care about him. He might even retaliate, "See if I care, you're a lousy teacher and I hate this school." The teacher may react, "Don't you talk to me like that!" and so it continues.

Try to avoid emotional responses to children's misbehavior, for they only serve to escalate the conflict and probably gain the attention of the other children as well as fueling Elonzo's desire to be defiant. Moreover, teachers' shouting models that shouting is an acceptable means of communicating, and will likely unsettle, unnerve, escalate, and overly stimulate children. Instead, the teacher should respond calmly by saying, "I know you probably wish you hadn't thrown that dirt, but you did throw it so now you have to miss the rest of recess. I don't think you will do that again." In this instance, the teacher de-escalates the situation. This calm, non-emotional response to misbehavior is key to a teacher's success in following through with consequences.

Remember to Develop Discipline Plans with a Behavioral Continuum

Sometimes teachers fall into the trap of setting up a comprehensive discipline plan to cure a child 100% of his misbehaviors. This approach is doomed to failure especially in the case of the child with multiple problems, for the expectations for him to change are too high. Let us take the example of Reed, an 8-year-old child who has a low level of tolerance for frustration and frequently storms out of the classroom swearing at the teacher. He then leaves the playground, which results in a school suspension. A teacher who has a behavioral continuum in mind will realize that the first step is for Reed to learn how to stay in the class and a much later step is to manage his profanities. Thus his teacher sets up a discipline plan that rewards him for staying in the classroom each day. The teacher decides to work on profanity later, and she explains to the class that they will ignore his swearing while he is learning to calm himself down. She also gives him a daily pass which permits him to leave the classroom because he is feeling frustrated. During this time he is to go to the counselor's office for 5 minutes and then return to class. If he uses his passes effectively, or if he makes it through the week without needing to use the passes, he is rewarded. Once he is regularly staying in the classroom, then the reward system can be gradually switched to focus on his rude language. In this example we see the teacher planning a discipline approach which uses gradual steps and targets one or two behaviors to encourage at a time.

CONCLUSION ~ THE IMPORTANCE OF
TEACHER SUPERVISION AND CLEAR DISCIPLINE

Remember children with attention deficit disorders, impulsivity, and aggressive behavior disorders have tremendous deficits in their emotional language, social skills, and lack self-regulation management skills. This means that they will need constant monitoring and "scaffolding" by teachers using all the proactive, coaching, and incentive teaching tools outlined in earlier chapters as well as the tools for redirection, warnings, and immediate consequences. This additional supervision and clear discipline can be seen by teachers as an investment not only in the problem child but the classroom as a whole because utilizing these approaches leads to a safe and caring environment. This kind of environment provides optimal social, emotional and academic learning for all students. Nonetheless, these approaches take time, planning, patience, and repetition. Most of all it requires a calm, respectful attitude.

This stage of intervention is the pruning stage, in the gardening metaphor. Teachers work to prune away undesirable behaviors, but are careful not to prune too harshly. Plants that are carefully and lightly pruned grow fully and healthily. Plants that are severely cut down to the ground often do not recover. The same light touch is important when teachers use discipline with children. Teachers must use enough consequences to help the child learn the appropriate behavior, but not so much as to discourage the child from trying again.

TO SUM UP...

Managing Misbehavior: Natural and Logical Consequences

- Consequences do not have to be severe to be effective.
- Follow the "law of least disruptive interventions"—use ignoring, nonverbal and verbal redirecting and warnings or reminders before higher level consequences.
- Make logical or natural consequences immediate, nonpunitive, age-appropriate, nonconfrontive, and short.
- Negative consequences should be tailored to the particular circumstances—something that will deprive that child of something he or she particularly likes (loss of privilege) or something that is inherently connected to the misbehavior (logical and natural consequences).
- Consequences should never be physically or psychologically harmful to the child, nor should they humiliate or embarrass the child.
- When possible, present consequences as choice the student has made.
- Be friendly and respectful but firm—control negative emotions.
- Be prepared for student testing when ignoring or when a negative consequence is enforced.
- Avoid sending students to the principal's office.
- Quickly offer new learning opportunities with immediate teacher attention for prosocial behaviors.

- Make sure the discipline plan is developmentally appropriate.
- Involve parents in discipline plans, but deliver consequences for school behavior in school. Avoid reporting small, daily misbehaviors to parents.

The Incredible Years®
Teacher Classroom Management Self-Reflection Inventory
Managing Misbehavior—Natural and Logical Consequences

Date: _____ Teacher Name: _____

Teachers learn extensively from self-reflection regarding their classroom management and the teaching strategies they are using that are working or not working. From these reflections teachers determine personal goals for making changes in their approaches to bring about the most positive learning climate they can. Use this Inventory to think about your strengths and limitations and determine your goals.

Logical and Natural Consequences	1 = NEVER 3 = OCCASIONALLY 5 = CONSISTENTLY
1. My discipline hierarchy includes some negative consequences at the top step which are non-punitive, applied consistently, brief and are related to the behavior.	1 2 3 4 5
2. I take into account the child's developmental and cognitive stage when using logical consequences to be sure the student understands the relationship between the consequence and the misbehavior.	1 2 3 4 5
3. My discipline plan for my classroom clearly lets students know in advance the possible consequences of particular behavior (e.g., not doing the writing assignment in class results in loss of free time in order to complete the work).	1 2 3 4 5
4. I carry out consequences in a respectful way and help students learn to make good choices and to be more responsible.	1 2 3 4 5

5. I ignore students' arguments, disrespect and protests when giving a consequence.	1 2 3 4 5
6. After following through with a brief consequence, I immediately make an effort to offer the student another chance to try again and to be successful.	1 2 3 4 5
7. I give my students an option to calm down away from the group when I notice they are beginning to dysregulate but have not yet disrupted the class or hurt another child.	1 2 3 4 5
8. If I need to remove a student's privilege, it is non confrontational, relatively brief and occurs as close as possible to the misbehavior occurring.	1 2 3 4 5
9. I avoid putting names on the board for negative behaviors or sending home frowny faces to parents, or sending children to the principal's office.	1 2 3 4 5
10. I involve parents in the behavior plan and focus on the positive opposite behaviors we are giving attention to with coaching, praise and incentives. I do not expect parents to carry out consequences for school behavior at home.	1 2 3 4 5
11. I avoid sermons, interrogations or forcing children to apologize.	1 2 3 4 5
12. My discipline plan starts with an intensive focus on building my relationships with difficult students through child-directed play, coaching methods, praise and incentive strategies.	1 2 3 4 5
13. I follow the 'law of least disruptive interventions' with ignoring, redirections, non-verbal signals and reminders before using a negative consequence.	1 2 3 4 5
14. I use positive self-talk as an approach to staying calm when students misbehave and seek support from my teacher support team.	1 2 3 4 5

Future Goals Regarding Use of Logical and Natural Consequences:	Total

REFERENCES

Bear, G. G. (1998). School Discipline in the United States: Prevention, Correction and Long-Term Social Development. *School Psychology Review, 2*(1), 14-32.

Brophy, J. E. (1996). *Teaching problem students*. New York: Guilford.

Cotton, K., & Wikelund, K. R. (Eds.). (1990). *Schoolwide and classroom discipline*. Portland, OR: Northwest Regional Education Laboratory.

Stage, S. A., & Quiroz, D. R. (1997). A meta-analysis of interventions to decrease disruptive classroom behavior in public education settings. *School Psychology Review, 26*, 333-368.

Walker, H. M., Colvin, G., & Ramsey, E. (1995). *Antisocial behavior in school: Strategies and best practices*. Pacific Grove, CA: Brooks/Cole.

Managing Misbehavior:
Time Out to Calm Down

The student who displays physically or verbally violent behavior—
for example, hitting another child or teacher, screaming so loudly
that other children cannot pay attention, lashing out and pushing over
furniture, or persistently refusing to comply with anything the teacher
requests — needs to be met with an intervention that will stop and
de-escalate the behavior. These tools, taken from the top of the teaching pyramid, are necessarily more intensive than the strategies discussed so far. In Chapters Seven and Eight we discussed how some
commonly used (and disruptive!) discipline strategies such as lecturing
or yelling, putting a student's name on the board, or sending him to the
principal's office have actually been shown to be ineffective (Bear,

1998; Martens & Meller, 1990; Van Houten, Nau, Mackenzie-Keating, Sameoto, & Colavecchia, 1982). In fact, criticizing, scolding, and shouting only results in students learning to shout, criticize, and argue with both teachers and peers. Reasoning with students or putting their names on the board while they are verbally abusive or noncompliant may provide teacher attention that actually reinforces the particular misbehavior or adds to the students' negative self-image. Severe consequences such as sending home or suspending a student for aggressive behavior removes the student from the learning environment and may backfire if the student prefers to be at home. Additionally, sending a child home sometimes results in parental physical or verbal abuse towards the child or parental resentment towards the school because the parents' work schedule has been disrupted. These parental responses serve to compound the student's problems and alienate the parents from the teachers.

The task for teachers is to provide an ethical and respectful approach to discipline: one that teaches that violent behaviors will not be tolerated, serves to help regulate a student who is out of control, establishes positive expectations for future appropriate behavior, and conveys that the student is valued despite his/her mistake. Remember that the word "discipline" means "to teach," so the goal of a discipline plan is to teach the student more appropriate behavior rather that to exact retribution. Ideally a discipline plan should be a whole-school plan and not just an individual teacher classroom concern. All teachers have a role for caring for all students when outside the classroom and schools have a commitment to supporting all teachers in managing students with difficult behavior problems. Thus it is important that all school staff have a consistent discipline hierarchy plan.

Methods discussed in earlier chapters such as effective limit setting, distractions, redirections, ignoring, using logical consequences, and loss of privileges are effective discipline tools for many typical disruptive student behaviors. However, a Time Out or Calm Down strategy is reserved specifically for high intensity problems and unsafe behavior, such as aggression toward peers or teachers

The task for teachers is to provide an ethical and respectful approach to discipline, one that conveys that the student is valued despite his/her mistake.

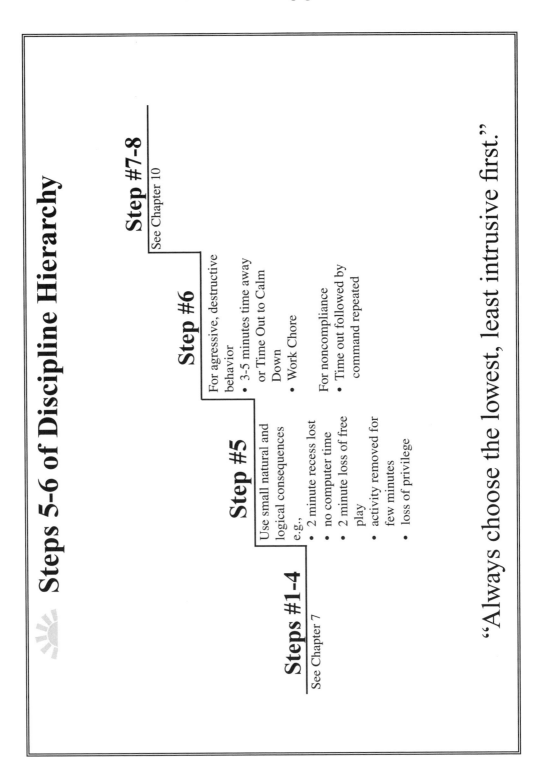

Steps 5-6 of Discipline Hierarchy

Steps #1-4

See Chapter 7

Step #5

Use small natural and logical consequences e.g.,
- 2 minute recess lost
- no computer time
- 2 minute loss of free play
- activity removed for few minutes
- loss of privilege

Step #6

For agressive, destructive behavior
- 3-5 minutes time away or Time Out to Calm Down
- Work Chore

For noncompliance
- Time out followed by command repeated

Step #7-8

See Chapter 10

"Always choose the lowest, least intrusive first."

and destructive behavior. It is also useful for highly noncompliant, oppositional or defiant children (any child who refuses to do what a teacher asks him to do 75% of the time or more falls into this category), since compliance is the cornerstone of a parent's or teacher's ability to socialize and teach a child. Time Out is probably the most intrusive short-term consequence a teacher will employ for disruptive behavior. It can occur in the classroom as a formal, or semi-formal cool off time or it can involve temporary removal from the classroom to another classroom or a specially designated area in the school. Time Out has been well researched and, when used appropriately and strategically for targeted behaviors, effectively reduces aggressive and oppositional behavior (Brophy, 1996; Gardner, Forehand, & Roberts, 1976; Patterson, Reid, & Dishion, 1992; Reinke & Herman, 2002; White & Bailey, 1990).

Time Out is actually an extended form of ignoring in which students are removed for a brief period from all sources of positive reinforcement, especially teacher and peer group attention. When implemented correctly, Time Out offers several advantages over other time-honored disciplinary practices such as lecturing or sending a student home. It models a nonviolent response to conflict, stops the attention the misbehavior is getting, reduces the conflict and frustration, provides a "cooling off" period for both students and teachers, and maintains a respectful, trusting relationship in which children feel they can be honest with their teachers about their problems and mistakes. Time Out is also a time for children to practice the calm down self-regulation strategies they have been taught (e.g., deep breathing, positive self-talk and positive imagery) and to self-reflect on what they have done and consider other solutions. Time Out actually fosters the child's development of an internal sense of responsibility, or conscience. Time Out is more effective than sending a child home because it immediately follows the misbehavior, allows the child privacy to learn to self-regulate, and then quickly returns the child to the classroom to experience a new learning trial and chance to be

A Time Out or Calm Down strategy is reserved specifically for high intensity problems and unsafe behavior, such as aggression toward peers or teachers.

successful. Sending a child home, on the other hand, usually occurs at least an hour after the misbehavior (after parents have been contacted), thus diminishing its power as a negative consequence. Moreover, a student who is sent home has no chance to come back into the classroom and reverse the behavior or repair the situation and be forgiven. Time Out provides the teacher with a chance to teach the student that dangerous behaviors will not be tolerated and will consistently result in temporary exclusion. This protects the rights of the non-disruptive students and helps the teacher teach the aggressive student to practice some self-regulation skills in the heat of the moment.

STEPS TO SETTING UP TIME OUT OR A CALM DOWN TIME

Time Out means different things to different people and, like any discipline strategy, can be open to abuse if the protocols and philosophy of practice are not clearly described before and after its use. As a discipline process it should *never stand alone* and needs a school wide policy that is well-thought-out with back-up and support. Time Out will only work if a strong teaching pyramid foundation has been established including encouragement and coaching, praise and incentives for positive opposite behaviors, and a caring teacher-child relationship.

There are a number of steps in setting up a successful Time Out (Patterson et al., 1992). These steps should be practiced and role played by teachers in order that they have 100% understanding of the process before teaching them to students and carrying out a Time Out with a student.

STEP I: Time Out Location

First you should decide what to call Time Out in your classroom. Time Out has been given many names, such as a "calm down place," "cool-off space," "turtle chair," or the "watching chair." It is important it is not called the "naughty corner" or "naughty seat." Next you need to carefully consider the Time Out location for your class. Preferably it should be a designated area in an empty corner of the classroom that may be marked by a chair, a carpet square, a taped-space on the floor, or any other way that clearly marks the boundaries of the space. While it is important that the area is somewhat removed from the main activity of the classroom, it can be of some benefit if the child in Time Out can see the rest of the class; seeing what peers are doing may serve as an incentive to calm down more quickly. It will likely also be necessary to have another room or classroom that can be used a back-up room in case the child will not stay in the Time Out area (how to use this back up room will be discussed later in the chapter). This room should be a safe place to be alone in, and as boring as possible without toys to play with or access to people to talk to. Although students should not receive any attention while they are in Time Out, there should *always* be an adult nearby to monitor the Time Out. In some cases teachers have made arrangements with another teacher (or a counselor) to use their room as a back-up location for a temporary time until the behavior has been brought under control. Often times a student will not exhibit the same disruptive behaviors in another teacher's classroom. After being sent several times to the back-up room, usually the student will learn that they prefer to stay in the classroom and sit on the Time Out or Calm Down chair.

STEP 2: Types of Behavior that Result in Time Out

You should decide which specific misbehaviors will result in Time Out. Behaviors that are unsafe or extremely disruptive, such as aggressive, violent and destructive behaviors, or verbal abuse to the teacher or peers are good ones to choose. However, the definition of aggression should be clearly defined. All children, especially children ages 2-5 years poke, prod, push and nudge each other at high rates, especially when language development is limited. Using Time Out for these behaviors would result in most young children spending a lot of time in Time Out and would be a misuse of the procedure. These milder physical behaviors can usually be managed with a redirection of the children's activity and a reminder of the classroom rule of hands to own body. For children who exhibit high levels of challenging behavior, it will be important to prioritize which behaviors will receive Time Out. In the beginning, we recommend selecting the most disruptive behavior (i.e., physical violence with desire to hurt another child) to work on. Then after several weeks, when these behaviors have been reduced, you can move on to another aggressive behavior, such as verbal abuse. Consistent defiance or noncompliance from a student is another case where Time Out could be used. Time Out should never be used for minor disruptive behaviors such as calling out, coming late to class, clowning behavior, or defiant attitude.

STEP 3: Time Out length

 A general rule of thumb is three minutes for three-year-olds, four minutes for four-year-olds and five minutes for children five and older. Research has shown in numerous studies that *Time Outs longer than five minutes are not more effective.* However, children should not be let out of Time Out until they have been quiet for about two minutes, signaling that they have calmed down. This means that Time Out may last longer than 5 minutes if the child continues to yell or scream. The most important point is that Time Out is as brief as possible, ends when the child demonstrates that she is calm and regulated, and that the student is immediately given an opportunity to try again, be successful, and receive the teacher's praise.

Some type of visual timer for keeping track of time in Time Out is essential for many children. Most young children don't understand the concept of time, so they may panic when asked to sit still for any period of time. Focusing on a sand timer provides a visual symbol of how much time is left and may actually help a child to calm down.

STEP 4: Sequence of Effective Use of Time Out
For Aggression

When you see an aggressive act, first briefly check on the victim if you can safely do this. This conveys the message that the victim is important and reduces attention to the aggressor. Next give a firm, calm Time Out command to the aggressor. It is important that the student know why he is being sent to Time Out. Here's an example for aggression:

Child hits another child.
> **Teacher:** (*checks the victim first*) I'm sorry that he hit you. You can tell him that you don't like to be hit.

Teacher: (*gives the Time Out command*) It's not okay to hit. You broke our classroom rule and you need to go to the Time Out area to calm down.

Child: (*goes to Time Out*)

For Noncompliance

In the case of noncompliance, the teacher gives the student a warning before giving the Time Out command. This allows the student to make the choice to follow directions. Following is a Time Out sequence for noncompliance:

Teacher: Mary, go to your seat and start working on your math assignment please.(*teacher waits 5 seconds*)

Child: (*still wandering around classroom*) No! I don't want to and you can't make me.

Teacher: If you don't start your math, then you will have to go to Time Out.

Child: I won't do it; you can't make me.

Teacher: Mary, I asked you to start your math assignment and you disobeyed. You made the choice. Go to Time Out now.

In this case there was a command, an "if—then" warning and enforcement of Time Out. This is in contrast to the automatic Time Out for aggression.

STEP 5: Set a Timer

Once your student is in Time Out, you should set a timer for three to five minutes and leave the student alone. It is important not to talk to the student while he or she is in Time Out. Two soda bottles (1 liter each, taped end to end to look like an hour glass) with one bottle filled with sand or water can be turned over to indicate the time passing. When the sand has passed into the second bottle, the Time Out is finished (if the child is calm). Although a visual timer is an excellent way to help children regulate, it is important that the teacher (not the timer) is the one to officially signal that a Time Out is over. The teacher must be attentive to the timer so that she is ready to release the calm child when the allotted time is up. This avoids a scenario where a child is still tantrumming, sees the timer run out, and comes out of Time Out before he is regulated. If the timer runs out and the child is still disruptive, the teacher can calmly reset the timer for two more minutes, saying: "It looks like your body is not calm yet. I'm giving you two more minutes to calm down."

STEP 6: Ending Time Out

Following a Time Out, the main goal is to re-engage the student in a positive activity or new learning trial. We do not recommend that students be asked to explain why they were sent to Time Out, for this draws attention back to the misbehavior and disregulated state. Rather, teachers should be calm, positive or neutral, and should work to help the student reintegrate into the classroom. For the same reason, we do not recommend forcing students to apologize at this time. A forced apology is likely to either be insincere or to start a power struggle over the apology, which undoes the calming effect of the Time Out. Students are more likely to learn empathy and remorse through the modeling of apologies at other times. Occasionally, when two students have had a big fight or misunderstanding, they may need teacher help to resolve an issue. If this is the case, it is recommended that this teaching is done in a neutral problem-solving session with both students when they are calm, but not immediately after the Time Out.

Ending a Time Out for Aggression

Teacher: (*time is over and child is calm*) Mary, your Time Out is over and your body is calm. You can come back to the group.

Teacher: (*Once Mary returns to the group the teacher should look for a chance to re-engage her in the lesson.*) Mary, we're thinking of rhyming words. I'm wondering if you can think of a word that rhymes with "dog."

Ending a Time Out for Noncompliance

After a Time Out for noncompliance, it is important that the student follow through with the teacher's original commend. Therefore, you should repeat the original command after ending Time Out.

> **Teacher:** Mary, your body looks calm. Please come back and start your math assignment now.
>
> **Child:** Okay.
>
> **Teacher:** I'm pleased you are starting your work, you have made a good choice.
>
> (*If Mary refused to start her math, then the entire sequence would have to be repeated.* For example, the teacher says, "Mary, if you don't start your math now, you will go back to Time Out.")

STEP 7: Managing Disruptive Behavior In Time Out

Especially at first, children of all ages are likely to sometimes object to going to Time Out or to be disruptive in Time Out. Many behaviors that occur during Time Out can be ignored as long as the child has gone to the Time Out and is staying in the general Time Out area. For instance, a child who walks to Time Out, but curses and yells at the teacher on the way should be ignored, for any attention to this behavior will prolong it. Once the child is in Time Out, almost all behaviors should be ignored unless the child leaves the general Time Out area or is unsafe. This means that calling out, yelling, crying, whining, threats, and moving slightly away from the Time Out area should be ignored. During this time the teacher can coach the rest of the class to ignore and give privacy to the child in Time Out and praise their cooperative behavior for doing so. (See Chapter Seven for how to teach students to ignore disruptive behavior.)

The teacher can coach the class to ignore and give privacy to the child in Time Out while s/he calms down.

Refusal to go to Time Out: 4- to 6-Year-Olds

Most students under six years of age who refuse to go to Time Out, can be gently but firmly taken to Time Out. At this age, independence is extremely important to children, and they will often choose to do something on their own rather than have a teacher physically help them go there. Following is an example of this sequence:

Teacher: You hit, you need to go to Time Out.
Child:　No! I'm not going.
Teacher: You can go by yourself, or I'll take you there.
Child:　(*Stomps off to Time Out.*)

If the child had refused to go to Time Out after the warning, then the teacher would say, "I'll take you to Time Out" and would gently walk the child to Time Out, holding onto the child's arm. It is important to only use this strategy if you can do so safely. If you are feeling too angry to calmly walk the child to Time Out, or if the child is too big or out of control to move, then you will need another strategy for managing Time Out.

Refusal to go to Time Out: 6- to 8-Year-Olds

Older children are generally big enough that they cannot safely be moved to Time Out. In this case teachers may first try to add on one minute for each refusal to go to Time Out up to seven minutes. At that point a warning should be given to go to Time Out or lose a privilege (for example, missing 7 minutes of recess, computer time, choice time, or another preferred activity).

Teacher: Seth, sit at your seat and start your math problem
　　　　　please.
Child:　No, I don't want to.
Teacher: If you don't start your math assignment, you will go to
　　　　　Time Out.
Child:　I don't care. You can't make me!
Teacher: That's one extra minute in Time Out.
Child:　Who cares? I like it there anyway.
Teacher: That's six minutes now.
Child:　So you can count, huh?
Teacher: That's seven minutes. If you don't go now, you will lose
　　　　　seven minutes of choice time today.

Child: But that's not fair! (*walks to Time Out chair muttering unhappily*)
Teacher: Thank you, you have a made a good choice.

If the student had continued to refuse to go to Time Out, the privilege is removed, and the teacher drops the Time Out instituting the consequence instead.

Child: I don't care if you give me seven minutes!
Teacher: Okay, you will lose seven minutes of choice time later this morning.

At that point, the teacher drops the Time Out and walks away. She should look for the first chance to re-engage the student in some positive learning activity.

Briefer consequences allow the child to have fresh starts and new chances to be successful.

If a privilege such as recess or a computer time or a special privilege is taken away, it is important that it be taken away the same day and only for the same day. Longer punishments, such as taking away recess or computer privileges for the week or missing a day-long field trip, are not more effective. In fact, just the opposite is true—children feel unfairly punished and get caught up in resentments toward the teacher rather than internalizing their role in the problem. Longer punishments remind the child all week of the misbehavior they did on Monday. Briefer consequences allow the child to have *fresh starts* and new chances to be successful. Moreover, if you take away the computer for the week and the child does something else that is inappropriate, you will need to remove a second privilege. A child can quickly fall into such a deep pit that he sees no way to earn himself out of trouble. Moreover, you soon have nothing else to take away. (See Chapter Eight for this discussion.) **Remember the most effective discipline is immediate, quick and followed with a new learning trial.**

STEP 8: Refusal to Sit in Time Out—Use Back-up Time Out Room or Another Class

Whenever possible, keep the child in the original Time Out location because he or she will learn more. However, for the child who initially won't sit in the classroom Time Out or won't settle down after the warning has been given, a back-up room may be useful. This room may be another teacher's classroom or an empty boring room. If the child leaves the Time Out place in the classroom, *calmly return her* with a warning that she will be sent to Time Out outside the class. For example, "If you leave the Time Out area again, you will go to the Time Out room in Mrs. C's class." Remember that the back-up room must be safely monitored and should be set up in advance so that all who come into contact with a child in a back-up Time Out understand not to give the child attention. Time in this alternative Time Out room should be as nonreinforcing as possible.

Seriously Disruptive Behavior

All of the scenarios above assume that the child is still regulated enough that he/she can be ignored or moved when necessary. The majority of children will be able to handle a Time Out with one of the management strategies above. Most children, even when they are very angry, are not likely to exhibit truly dangerous behaviors in a school setting. However, it is important to plan for the small subset of children who are more disruptive during Time Out.

If you have a student who falls into this category, for example, is extremely and repeatedly aggressive when given a Time Out warning, who is too big to move to a safe location, or who becomes destructive to the point where there are safety concerns, then it is important to have a back-up plan for Time Out. In these circumstances, there are several important things to consider. First, no classroom teacher can handle this level of behavior on his/her own. It is important to have assistance so that one teacher can manage the rest of the class, while one (or sometimes two) teacher monitors the child in Time Out. Second, there are no easy solutions to a child who is this out of control, and it is often good to keep several general principles in mind when working out a strategy for managing extreme Time Outs. 1) Continue to minimize the attention given to the child—no talking or looking at the child beyond what is needed to communicate a simple command. 2) Avoid power struggles—don't give a command that you can't follow through on. 3) The goal is to end the Time Out with the child calm and compliant. Within these parameters, some individualization will need to occur, depending on staffing, available space, and the child's specific behaviors.

Ideas for Managing a Very Disruptive Time Out:

1. If the child can be left where she is and ignored, you can start the Time Out wherever the child is, rather than trying to move her to the designated area. You might walk away and say, *"I'll know that you are ready to come out of Time Out when I see you sitting calmly and quietly in the Time Out area."* Now, you can devote your attention to the rest of the class, perhaps gathering them in a different part of the room to distract them with some other interesting idea, and help them as well as yourself ignore the student in Time Out until he/she has moved back to the Time Out area. Notice that strategy serves all three principles above—it minimizes attention to the behavior, avoids a power struggle that can't be won (e.g., trying to move an out of control child), but still sets up the situation so that the Time Out only ends with a calm, compliant student.

2. If the child can't be ignored in place because his behavior is too disruptive or potentially unsafe for other children, you may choose to take the rest of the class out of the room. This is a cumbersome strategy, but can be very effective, and often doesn't need to be used more than a few times. This involves having one teacher take the rest of the class out, preferably for a fun activity.

> **Teacher:** "Would you take the class out for a bonus recess? If John goes and sits in Time Out quickly enough, we may join you when he's done with his Time Out."

Then one teacher stays in the room with the student in Time Out. She should ignore the student completely, seeming to do something else and waiting for him to go to the Time Out area and calm down. If the student tries to leave the room, the teacher may need to stand near the door, blocking the exit, but should still try to adhere to the ignore principles.

Ending a Destructive Time Out

At the end of a Time Out where the student has been very destructive, it is important to have him or her help to repair any mess that was made. The goal here is to have calm and cooperative behavior, not to return the room to pristine condition. For example the teacher says, *"Okay, you are calm and quiet. As soon as we clean up some of this mess, it will be time to go to lunch. You can start with the blocks and I will work on putting these chairs back."*

After the student has demonstrated that he is cooperative and has made an honest attempt to help clean up, he should be re-engaged in a learning activity with the rest of the class. This does mean that the teacher may actually clean up more of the mess than the student, and this is okay.

STEP 9: Initially, Misbehavior Will Get Worse

Remember, when you first use Time Out with a child, the child's behavior will worsen before it gets better. Be prepared for testing.

STEP 10: Who Ends the Time Out?

Sometimes teachers think the student should decide when he or she is ready to come out of Time Out. We do not advocate this approach because in discipline situations it is important that the teacher be in charge of Time Out. The goal should be to return the child to the learning environment as soon as possible.

STEP 11: Teaching Students the Meaning of Time Out and How to Handle Going to Time Out

Before using Time Out as a discipline strategy, it is important to teach students what it means to go to Time Out and how they can manage their own behavior in Time Out. Students will likely have had many different experiences with Time Out in other settings. Some of these experiences may have involved watching a very distressed child being sent to Time Out, some may have involved a very angry teacher or parent, and some Time Outs may have been very punitive and lengthy. Therefore, it is important that students are provided with accurate information about Time Out, as well as coaching on how to calm themselves down while in Time Out. Explanations and role plays about Time Out should include the following points:

a) What behavior will result in Time Out?
b) Where the Time Out area is?
c) How long is Time Out?
d) What behavior is expected in Time Out?
e) Strategies for calming down in Time Out.
f) Coaching other students to ignore a child who is in Time Out and give him or her privacy to calm down.
g) How to rejoin the class.

STEP 12: Prepare Other Students to Ignore Their Peer in Time Out

In addition to preparing students to take a calm Time Out, teachers can teach the other students how to support a child who is in Time Out. If other students are making fun of a student who is in Time Out, this may humiliate the student or the peer attention may actually reinforce the student's misbehavior while in Time Out. Instead peers can be taught to ignore a student who is in Time Out by continuing with the regular class activities and giving the other student privacy. For example, the teacher says to students, *"We are giving Seth some privacy now to calm down. Continue to work on your math problems and I think he will soon join us again."*

TIME OUT ROLE PLAY/PRACTICE

It is helpful to prepare the class for Time Out by practicing the sequence so that students can walk through the process of taking a calm time out and also the process of ignoring a student who is in Time Out. This will help to plant a positive coping model of Time Out in students' repertoires. On page 352 is a sample script of how to role play/practice this scenario to teach children the Time Out steps. Ideally the role play/practice below is done with a puppet who demonstrates how to go to Time Out. Any hand puppet can be used. If a puppet is not available, the part played by the puppet can be acted out with an assistant teacher demonstrating how to go calmly to Time Out. It is very important to model only positive behavior in the Time Out, so that children see this positive coping model. You can use the calm down thermometer described in Chapter 11 to remind children of the strategies they have learned to stay calm.

It is very important to model only positive behavior in the Time Out, so that children see this positive coping model.

STEP 13: Teach Students How To Calm Down Using the Calm Down Thermometer

During circle time teachers can teach students strategies for calming down when they are angry or frustrated. Students are taught how to take deep breaths, use positive self-talk and positive visualization in order to self-regulate and stay calm. It is effective to use imaginary visual methods when doing this teaching such as talking about using a protective turtle shell or a shield while practicing to take deep breaths. Many teachers find that a calm down thermometer is a useful visual aid to illustrate how feelings can change from anger, frustration and disappointment in the hot red zone to feelings of calmness, happiness and relaxation in the cool blue zone. It may be useful to put one of these visual aids on the wall in the Time Out area.

See Chapter 11 for specific more details about helping students learn to regulate emotions and how to use the Calm Down thermometer.

STEP 14: Be Sure Your Classroom Environment is Positive

Remember Time Out will not work unless the teacher has invested in the strategies from the bottom of the pyramid; coaching and developing

CIRCLE TIME LESSON SCRIPT
Role Play
Explain Time Out Using a Puppet

Teacher: Today we're going to talk about one of the important rules in this class. Do you remember the rule about "keeping hands and bodies to ourselves?" Does anyone know why this rule is important?

Child: To keep us safe!

Teacher: That's right! This is an important safety rule. We're going to talk about what happens when someone breaks this rule and hurts or hits someone else. You are all doing such a good job of being safe and gentle with each other, but sometimes children forget or get angry and hit someone else. When that happens, you'll need to take a Time Out until your body is calm and safe again. I'm going to use my puppet friend here to help show you what that looks like. His name is Wally.

Wally: Hi boys and girls, I'm glad to be here.

Teacher: Wally, would you help the children by showing them how to go calmly to Time Out?

Wally: Sure, but this is just pretend because I didn't really hit anyone.

Teacher: That's right—this is just pretend. I'm going to tell Wally to go to Time Out and we'll see what he does. "Wally, you hit someone, you need to go to Time Out."

(Another teacher walks Wally calmly to the Time Out chair and teacher narrates his actions.)

Teacher: Do you see how calmly he is walking? Now his job is to calm down in the Time Out chair for 4 minutes (*vary this depending on age*). Let's see if he says anything to himself while he is in Time Out.

Wally: (*looks at calm down thermometer on wall and takes some deep breaths*) I can do it. I can calm down.

Teacher: Let's say the same thing together that Wally is saying and let's take some deep breaths (*children practice the words and breathing*). These things can help you calm down if you are in Time Out.

Teacher: Now there's one more thing to know. When a friend is in Time Out, we can help him or her by ignoring. That means that we don't look at or talk to him/her. This will give that friend the privacy to calm down. Then when Time Out is over, we can pay attention to our friend again.

Teacher: Wally, you look calm, you can come back now.

Wally: I'm embarrassed that I had to go to Time Out. I'm afraid that no one will like me now.

Teacher: Oh Wally, you just made a mistake. We still like you, don't we boys and girls?

Children Practice: Ask for volunteers from the class to practice taking a calm and quiet Time Out, just like Wally. Coach the child who is practicing to take deep breaths and use self talk (*I can calm down*) or to think of their happy place. Coach the rest of the class to practice ignoring and give the child privacy.

a positive relationship with the student and setting up a classroom environment that is highly rewarding for the child. What makes Time Out an effective discipline strategy is the loss of teacher approval and attention and the contrast between a rewarding classroom environment and the far less rewarding Time Out environment. Research has shown the teachers who are most effective in managing hostile-aggressive students are those that use discipline tools such as Time Out, warnings and loss of privileges sparingly and combine them with a variety of positive strategies (Brophy & McCaslin, 1992; Steinberg, 1996).

STEP 15: Informing Parents about the Use of Time Out

It is important that teachers explain their discipline plan to parents at the beginning of the school year, including when and how they will use Time Out ethically. It is wise to list the specific destructive child misbehaviors that will result in Time Out and to ask parents to sign their permission for its use under these circumstances. Post the Calm Down procedures (or thermometer) on the wall next to the Time Out chair. Ideally this discipline plan should be a whole-school policy applicable to all students in the school.

PITFALLS TO IMPLEMENTING TIME OUT

There are many pitfalls to be avoided in the use of Time Out. On the following pages, you will find some of the problems you may encounter and ways to overcome them.

Criticism and Angry Responses

It can be extremely difficult to keep your cool in the face of blatant noncompliance or aggressive behavior from a student. Sometimes teachers criticize students or accompany Time Out with insulting or hurtful statements. A few examples include "Why can't you do something right for once? Go to Time Out," "I'm fed up! You never listen to me! Go to Time Out," "You've been terrible today. Go to Time Out," "How many times do I have to tell you to stop?" These criticisms are more likely to result in children refusing to go to Time Out or responding in kind. Teachers may then respond with more angry and passionate responses, resulting in an escalation of bickering.

It is understandable that teachers feel hurt and angry when their students misbehave or challenge their authority. However, in order to avoid an escalation of negative exchanges, teachers must decide to refrain from criticisms and be polite and calm at the very time their students are being impolite and agitated. Try to minimize talk about the misbehavior, for this will only escalate your own anger. Try to keep your facial expression neutral. And remember not to lecture a student after a Time Out is completed.

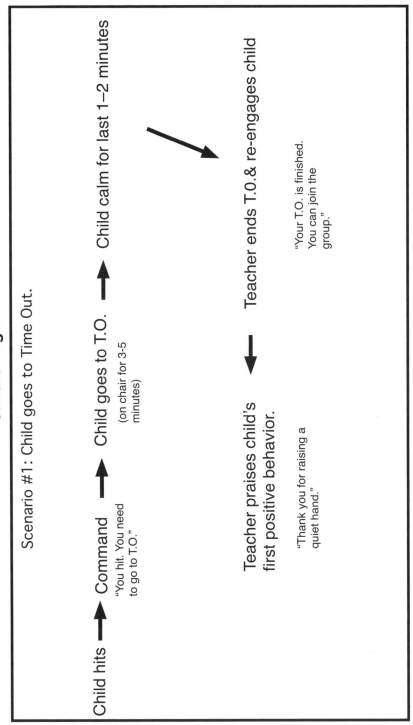

Time Out for Aggression
(In the Classroom)
Children Ages 3–6 Years

Scenario #1: Child goes to Time Out.

Child hits → Command → Child goes to T.O. → Child calm for last 1–2 minutes

"You hit. You need to go to T.O." → (on chair for 3-5 minutes)

Teacher ends T.O. & re-engages child

"Your T.O. is finished. You can join the group."

Teacher praises child's first positive behavior.

"Thank you for raising a quiet hand."

Young Child Resists Going to Time Out
(In the Classroom)
Children Ages 3–6 Years

Scenario #2: Child resists going to Time Out.

Child hits → Command → Child refuses to go to T.O. → Teacher gives one warning.

"You hit. You need to go to T.O."

"You can walk to T.O. like a big boy (girl), or I'll take you there."

↓

Child goes to T.O.

3–5 minutes, last 1–2 minutes child is calm.

*If child refuses, teacher calmly walks child to T.O. with no talking.

↓

Teacher ends T.O. & re-engages child

"Your T.O. is finished. You can join the group."

↓

Teacher praises child's first positive behavior.

"Thank you for raising a quiet hand."

School Age Child Resists Going to Time Out

(In the Classroom)
Children Ages 6-10

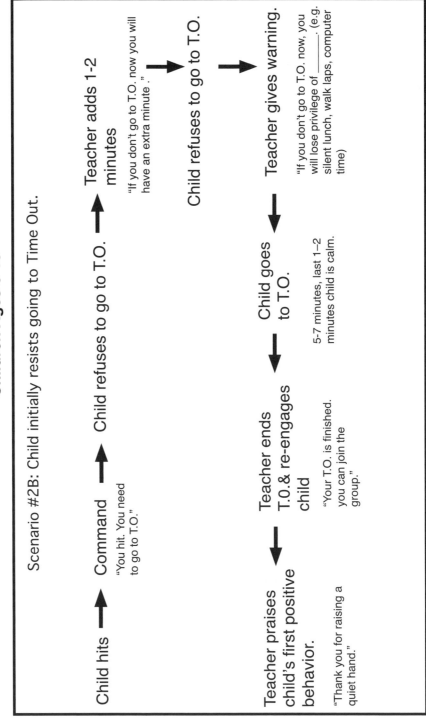

Scenario #2B: Child initially resists going to Time Out.

Child hits → Command → Child refuses to go to T.O. → Teacher adds 1-2 minutes → Child refuses to go to T.O. → Teacher gives warning.

"You hit. You need to go to T.O."

"If you don't go to T.O. now you will have an extra minute ."

"If you don't go to T.O. now, you will lose privilege of _____. (e.g. silent lunch, walk laps, computer time)

Teacher praises child's first positive behavior. ← Teacher ends T.O. & re-engages child ← Child goes to T.O.

"Thank you for raising a quiet hand."

"Your T.O. is finished. you can join the group."

5-7 minutes, last 1–2 minutes child is calm.

School Age Child Refuses Time Out

(In the Classroom)
Children Ages 6-10

Scenario #2C: Child continues to refuse to go to Time Out.

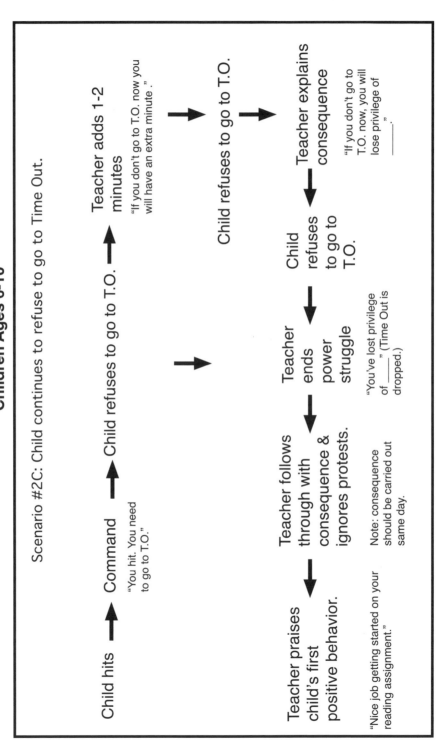

Child hits → Command → Child refuses to go to T.O. → Child refuses to go to T.O. → Teacher adds 1-2 minutes

"You hit. You need to go to T.O."

"If you don't go to T.O. now you will have an extra minute ."

Child refuses to go to T.O. → Child refuses to go to T.O. → Teacher explains consequence

"If you don't go to T.O. now, you will lose privilege of _____ ."

Child refuses to go to T.O. → Teacher ends power struggle → Teacher follows through with consequence & ignores protests. → Teacher praises child's first positive behavior.

"You've lost privilege of _____ " (Time Out is dropped.)

Note: consequence should be carried out same day.

"Nice job getting started on your reading assignment."

Delayed Responses

Sometimes teachers put up with annoying behaviors for a time and then suddenly explode with anger as the limits of their tolerance are reached. "You get into Time Out now!" There are several problems here. First, this means the students don't receive feedback until teachers are boiling with anger and are about to lose control. Second, students receive no warning and consequently have no chance to correct their behavior. Lastly, it may be unclear to a child why he is being sent to Time Out (because the other 10 times he poked his neighbor, the teacher didn't give a consequence). This approach only teaches students an explosive response to frustration.

You may not even be aware of the mounting anger triggered by certain behaviors until you explode. If this is the case, try to think about and monitor your reactions to particular misbehaviors. If you find that certain behaviors elicit a strong emotional response, you may decide that it isn't possible for you to ignore this behavior for very long. This is a good time to present your students with the "Three Strikes Rule." For example, tell them that back talk or arguing three times will result in a Time Out. The first time a child argues defiantly, you might say, *"This is your first strike warning for arguing,"* then, *"this is your second strike warning,"* and finally *"This is the third strike warning. Go to Time Out."* This warns your student that the behavior is inappropriate and alerts you to your mounting annoyance level. With this approach, you are clear about exactly what type of behavior will result in Time Out and you model an effective, calm, and rational approach to a problem behavior. At the same time, you will be looking for opportunities to coach and praise the student for polite and friendly talk.

Expecting Remorse

Some teachers believe that in order for Time Out to be effective, it must result in a child expressing remorse over the misbehavior or looking miserable during the Time Out. They also feel the child doesn't learn from the experience if he doesn't apologize. If these things don't happen, they may mistakenly think Time Out isn't working and stop using it. They may consider a more extreme form of punishment, such as informing a parent or suspension, because those are more likely to result in tears and expressions of remorse. However, as we have seen, excessive punishment, even when it eliminates undesirable behavior in the short run, tends to cause more problems in the long run. Also, these punishments do not teach children to problem-solve or cool down so that they can cope in a more successful way. Tears and apologies may satisfy a teacher's need for "just desserts," but they don't necessarily reflect effective discipline.

Don't be surprised if your students tell you Time Out doesn't bother them, and don't be fooled. They're only bluffing (remember the Br'er Rabbit trick!). Remember, the purpose of Time Out is not to get revenge or produce remorse, but rather to stop the misbehavior and withdraw the reinforcing effects of negative attention from teachers and peers. It provides children with a cooling off period and a chance to think about what they have done.

Prolonged or Abortive Time Outs

It's easy to believe that longer Time Outs are more effective—especially if your students have done something really bad like stealing, hitting, or breaking something. Some teachers add time whenever a student yells or misbehaves in Time Out. This is especially problematic if teachers are giving continual feedback during Time Out, "That is one more minute for that scream," since this attention will actually *increase* the misbehavior. Overly long Time Outs tend to breed resentment in children, and the isolation imposed keeps them from new opportunities to learn from experience, to try again and be successful. Remember, with children, there's no need for the punishment to fit the crime.

The opposite response is also a problem. Sometimes teachers use Time Out for a minute and then let their students out when they bang on the door, cry, or promise to behave. Unfortunately, letting children out when they are still misbehaving reinforces that particular inappropriate behavior. The message communicated is, "If you kick (or cry or promise) hard enough, I'll let you out."

Overly long Time Outs tend to breed resentment and keeps students from new learning opportunities.

The most effective Time Out need only be three to five minutes, provided there have been two minutes of quiet at the end. (Some children take longer to calm down than others.) Initially a disregulated child may have a longer Time Out since the Time Out isn't over until behavior is calm, but this is different than the teacher adding time for each scream. Adding time on for more serious infractions or letting children come out of Time Out prematurely will reduce the impact of Time Out. In fact, these mistakes may even make children's behavior worse.

Overuse of Time Out

Time Out is sometimes used for a variety of behaviors ranging from whining, to yelling and screaming, to out-of-seat behavior, to throwing, hitting and lying. Some teachers report using Time Out 6 to 8 times a day with particularly difficult students. This overuse removes misbehaving children from opportunities to learn or demonstrate good behavior. It doesn't teach them new and more appropriate ways to behave. While frequent Time Out keeps children out of trouble in the short run, in the long run overuse can cause bitterness and make children feel that they can't do anything right.

If you are a "Time Out junkie," make sure you are using it only for selected hurtful or destructive misbehaviors and not for minor disruptive behaviors that could be ignored or redirected such as sulking, whining, calling out, avoiding a task, or minor touching of another student. For example, using Time Out for out-of-seat behavior for the hyperactive, easily distractable and inattentive 6-year-old will undoubtedly result in too many Time Outs and is probably expecting the child to do something she is not developmentally capable of doing. It would be more appropriate for such a child to have a "wiggle space" or "office" where she can go for a few minutes if she needs to move about. When the child is ready, she can rejoin the group without shame. In order to be sure this overuse doesn't happen, teachers need to have a written list of the specific dangerous behaviors that will result in Time Out. While many students may need an occasional Time Out, when a particular student receives Time Out on a regular basis, teachers should keep records about the frequency and duration of the Time Outs so that this information can be used as part of a

Ensure that you are spending more time coaching, encouraging, teaching and practicing the appropriate positive opposite behaviors (to the negative behaviors targeted).

comprehensive behavior plan. If Time Out is working, first the duration of Time Out and then the frequency of Time Out should decrease over time. Most importantly, you must ensure that you are spending more time *coaching, encouraging, teaching and practicing the appropriate positive opposite behaviors (to the negative behaviors targeted)* than you are focusing on negative ones. Time Out will only work if there are frequent positive consequences, teacher attention for appropriate behaviors and a supportive teacher-student relationship.

Lack of Follow Through—Empty Threats

Occasionally teachers threaten Time Out without being committed to following through. They might say, "Do you want a Time Out?" or "You're asking for a Time Out!" or "Are you ready for a Time Out?" These empty threats dilute the teacher's authority. Children come to believe that Time Out won't be used, and the result will likely be an escalation of resistance to Time Out when it is actually imposed.

It is more effective to use an "if—then" statement than an empty threat of Time Out. "If you don't stop on the computer, then you will have to go to Time Out." Then follow through once you have given your student an opportunity to comply. Only mention Time Out if you have the time and energy to carry it out. Otherwise it's better to ignore the misbehavior.

Undermining Time Out with Attention

Some teachers inadvertently give attention (either positive or negative) to students while they are in Time Out. For instance, the child is sent to the principal's office—where the secretary gives him cookies! Timmy yells in Time Out and Timmy's teacher responds to each yell with: "You must be quiet before you can come out." Or a teacher may give a command each time a child leaves the Time Out area: "You need to go back to the Time Out area right now." All these actions defeat the purpose of Time Out and are very reinforcing for children.

There should be *no* communication with children when they are in Time Out. If you are likely to need to intervene for fear that your student will break something, remove any breakable items from the area or find a new location. If your student manages to attract the attention of the other students while in Time Out, you may need to move the area away from the rest of the classroom, move the class to another part of the room, or have the student in another teacher's classroom during Time Out.

Physical Restraint

Sometimes when children repeatedly come out of the Time Out chair/area, teachers will resort to dragging them back to Time Out or physically restraining them in the chair. They may justify such physical restraint by saying that it was used as a last resort, or believe that since it works, it must be all right. Unfortunately this "the-end-justifies-the-means" approach defeats the purposes of Time Out by focusing only on the short-term goals of ensuring compliance and maintaining control. These short-term benefits of physical restraint are far outweighed by the long-term disadvantages: increasing children's aggression and providing a model for a violent approach to conflict situations. Such situations are much better handled by combining Time Out with a loss of privileges, warning that Time Out will be served in another location, or moving the rest of the classroom (see section above for handling challenging Time Outs). Physical restraint is risky and not recommended for several reasons. First the physical restraining and adult attention that necessarily accompanies restraint may actually contribute to reinforcing the oppositional behavior of the child who is being restrained. For some neglected children, physical restraint may be the most intensive adult attention they have had in their lives so they increase their misbehavior in order to get it. Secondly, young children are quite strong and many adults find that when they restrain children they are sometimes holding the children so tightly that they might inadvertently

Physical restraint is risky and not recommended because children don't learn to self-regulate.

hurt them. Certainly physically restraining a child or dragging a child to Time Out is very stressful for the teacher and the rest of the class. Thirdly, physical restraint teaches children to rely on adults holding in order to calm themselves down. Whereas when Time Out is used, the child attributes his eventual ability to calm down to his own behavior and self-control. This ability to calm down alone is a strategy that will be more beneficial to him in the long run. Remember, if you can't reasonably remove a child from his audience, then you remove the audience from the child.

Refusals to Come Out of Time Out

There are several forms of power struggles that can occur during the Time Out sequence. One involves children who refuse to come out of Time Out once it's over. If the child was sent to Time Out for aggression, the teacher can step out of this power struggle by saying, "Your Time Out is over. We're ready for you when you're ready to come back." Then the teacher can ignore and watch for the child to re-engage. Coaxing or scolding at this point will merely add attention to the child's refusal to return to the group.

If the child is rude, disrespectful, or dysregulated when refusing to come back, however, then it is clear that the child isn't really calm and the teacher may say, "You are not calm. I'll come back and check in two minutes to see if you are calm and ready to come out." Remember that a Time Out for noncompliance ends with the teacher repeating the original command. If the child refuses, then a new warning is given, and must be followed up with another Time Out if the child does not comply.

Other Power Struggles

Another type of standoff happens when a teacher refuses to talk or re-engage with the child after Time Out. This is, in a sense, an extended Time Out. As mentioned earlier, this does not teach children how to deal with conflict in an appropriate fashion; rather, it teaches them to withdraw from conflict. Refusing to speak to a student for long periods after misbehavior only escalates tension and anger. In this situation, you should think about what is bothering you, what behavior you expect, and then state this clearly.

OTHER PRINCIPLES OF TIME OUT

Expect Persistence

A child yelling, screaming, swearing and banging on the wall during Time Out can be an exhausting experience for teachers. It's difficult to listen to children misbehaving without feeling anxious, depressed or angry. "Will she ever stop this?" or "What did I do wrong?" or "It can't be good for him to get so upset." Such feelings make it hard to continue Time Out for the full five minutes or to use it again. In a sense, teachers may suffer a "hangover" from trying to use Time Out and avoid its use in the future. If this happens, students have been successful in getting teachers to back down from the rules.

Expect that Time Out will be difficult at times because all students test the limits. If a teacher uses Time Out for hitting, children are likely to hit again several times in order to determine if it is a predictable and consistent response. If they learn that teachers don't always respond to aggression with a Time Out, they may continue to use hitting as a method of handling anger or conflict. In order to remain consistent and cope with the stress of enforcing a difficult Time Out, try distracting yourself or call on the support of another teacher or the principal.

Timeout hangover

Don't Forget Your Student in Time Out

Since teachers must attend to multiple demands in the classroom, it's easier than one would think to forget a child who is in Time Out. This is particularly true if the child was sent out of the classroom, but can even happen when the child is in the classroom Time Out area. This can also easily happen on the playground where there are so many children and few adults to monitor them. It is essential to remember to end Time Out on time to ensure that the child has a new learning trial. This is one of the primary reasons for using a timer to signal the end of Time Out; it will serve as a reminder to the teacher that Time Out is over if the child is calm.

Make Time Out or Calm Down Procedure a Certainty for Aggressive Misbehaviors

Often teachers feel they have no time to carry out a Time Out. They are busy teaching the rest of the class when a student misbehaves. When confronted with stopping the classroom work to implement a Time Out, they decide to overlook or give in to the misbehavior. This makes the use of Time Out inconsistent and usually results in an escalation of inappropriate behaviors during these hectic periods. Remember start by using Time Out consistently, but sparingly, for a few serious misbehaviors. You may experience a few tough days as your students test your commitment to the new rule, but in the long run, your classroom will run more smoothly.

Plan for Time Outs on the Playground and in the Lunch Room

Since unstructured places such as playground recess time and lunch rooms are the places where students are most likely to be aggressive, it is necessary to plan how Time Out will be implemented there. For example, schools might have specially painted benches or places where students are to go if they are given a Time Out. There needs to be adequate staffing in these areas to be sure that Time Outs can be successfully enforced. All Time Outs should be recorded in a monitoring book and followed up with the teacher. For more serious misbehaviors, students may need to be sent to the designated Time Out room in the school.

Support Each Other and Work Together to Manage a Difficult Time Out

Occasionally, while a teacher is doing a Time Out, another teacher or school personnel will disrupt the process by talking to the child or will question the use of Time Out. This makes it difficult to enforce Time Out and will result in the child seeing an opportunity to "divide and conquer."

Research has shown that conflict with students can spread into conflict between teachers. Consequently, if a teacher is doing a Time Out or Calm Down procedure, there should be an agreement that other teachers will be supportive. Teachers who share a classroom should be sure they have discussed, problem solved and agreed on the following before they initiate Time Out:

- Which behaviors result in Time Out
- How to determine who will take the lead in carrying out the Time Out
- Ways for each to show support while supervising a Time Out
- How one teacher can signal to the other that he or she needs help to finish the Time Out
- Acceptable ways to give feedback about the use of discipline
- Where and who will take the student if the Time Out cannot be done in the classroom

Ideally, if a teacher is alone in a classroom and has some difficulties enforcing Time Out there, then a backup team of supportive teachers should be "on call" (with a way to signal the need for help) to be available to assist the teacher and help exit the child from the classroom to an alternative Time Out place. Schools should have a published emergency protocol or "code red" procedure that is used whenever a teacher needs immediate assistance because of a very disruptive student who is a potential threat to someone's safety. If the teacher doesn't have an intercom, then she should have a specially designated code such as a red card which can be given to a responsible student to take to the office to signal help is needed. Specially designated trained teachers need to be available to come immediately to the classroom should the code red be called.

It is important also that teachers do not perceive that calling for assistance is a sign of weakness but rather is the school policy regarding the way the school handles extremely disruptive students. (See Chapter 15 for methods of coping with stress and building a support group.)

Remember There Is No Instant Solution

Some teachers claim that Time Out doesn't work for them. The previously discussed implementation problems may contribute to ineffective Time Out, or it may simply be that a teacher gave up too soon. It's a mistake to expect four or five Time Out trials to eliminate a problem behavior.

Time Out is not magic! Children need repeated learning trials. They need many opportunities to make mistakes and to misbehave and then to learn from the consequences of their misbehaviors. Just as it takes hundreds of trials for a baby to learn to walk, so it takes many trials for children to learn how to behave in a classroom. So remember, even when Time Out is used effectively, behavior changes slowly. Be patient. It will take your students at least 18 years to learn all the mature adult behaviors you'd like to see.

Remember Time Out Does Not Teach Positive Behavior

Time Out is only a short term solution for stopping the aggressive behavior, keeping students safe and making sure aggression is not reinforced with attention. It does not offer students a chance to learn prosocial behaviors. It does not motivate students to do their school work. If the goal in managing classroom behavior is to help children make better choices, learn more acceptable behavior, and to give them opportunities to be successful, Time Out will not, by itself, help further that goal. Rather, it is a last resort when other teaching tools such as coaching, praising, ignoring, redirecting, giving warnings, using logical or natural consequences and removing privileges have not been enough. In addition to using Time Out to reduce aggressive behavior, teachers will need to focus on developing behavior management plans that focus on teaching such students self-regulation and non-violent problem-solving approaches to manage conflict as well as appropriate social skills (see Chapters 11, 12 and 13).

Be Alert to Your Own Need for "Time Outs"

Teachers can be overly sensitive to their student's misbehaviors because they are exhausted, angry or depressed about the lack of apparent improvements in the student's behaviors despite their best teaching efforts. A teacher may also be angry or depressed because of events in his or her personal or professional life that are unrelated to the classroom. A teacher who becomes angry at a student may really be angry at the principal for assigning too many students to the class or for not assigning an aide. Or a teacher may become cross with her students for making noise because she is stressed about a personal situation at home (such as a sick child or a dissolving marriage). Depending on the mood and the energy level of the teacher, a student's behavior can seem tolerable one day and obnoxious the next.

Even the kindest and most well-intentioned teachers get frustrated and angry with their students. No one is perfect. The important task is to recognize the filters and mood you bring to your perceptions of your students, and to have strategies for coping with your own feelings. If you're depressed because of work problems, it may be a good idea take a Time Out yourself, away from the class in order to relax for a few minutes and gain perspective. If you're angry with your principal or co-teacher, you may need Time Out to problem solve. In helping your students to be less aggressive and more able to problem solve and handle conflict constructively, it is vital that you model the use of the calm down strategies to manage your own anger and frustration. When frustrated about a classroom situation you can model for the students the calming self-talk by saying, "I can calm down. We can be patient and figure this out" and take some deep breaths.

Just as we talked about a teacher using a signal to alert school personnel that help is needed with managing a physically dangerous situation, there also should be a safety valve mechanism for a teacher to signal that she needs a "break" or brief Time Out immediately. There must be a "no-blame" climate for this to operate well. For example, a teacher might use the code, "there's a message for me in the office," to signal she needs

Develop your emergency signals for help.

a brief break. Or likewise, if another teacher sees that her colleague's classroom is in chaos, she might use a code signal, "Can I borrow several of your students (the catalysts) for a few minutes?" This short-term colleague support can be immensely helpful to maintain a calm attitude in the face some difficult student behaviors.

CONCLUSION ~ DEVELOPING YOUR DISCIPLINE HIERARCHY

As we have said in Chapter Seven, teachers need to have a classroom discipline plan or hierarchy of consequences for students' misbehavior. We discussed the importance of using the least intrusive teacher interventions such as reminders of rules, redirection, self-regulation prompts, ignoring, and warnings (lower level strategies) to manage most student misbehaviors. However when misbehavior continues despite the use of these proactive discipline tools, then the teacher moves to a higher level in the hierarchy using negative consequences such as taking away privileges, giving work chores, setting up a logical consequence or planned discussions (covered in Chapter Eight). Finally for severe misbehavior such as aggressive or destructive behavior the teacher goes to the top of the teaching pyramid or higher levels on the hierarchy to use the Time Out to Calm Down discipline procedure.

Teachers should make their discipline plan visible in the classroom by posting it on the wall and explaining it to students as well as to parents in their initial orientation meetings.

At this stage in the gardening metaphor, teachers are pruning selectively and checking for aphids which may damage the plant, while at the same time providing extra sunlight, water and fertilizer to strengthen the healthy vines. The gardener checks her gardening plan and makes sure she is leaving enough room for each plant to grow to its full potential. In the next Chapter we will discuss how to assure you have a well organized gardening plan.

Discipline Hierarchies/Steps
For Nondisruptive & Disruptive Behavior

"Always choose
the lowest, least
intrusive first."

Step #8

Give Repeated Opportunities for New
Learning Trials
- Model, coach & practice alternative desired
  behaviors
- Praise replacement behaviors
- Circle Time Lessons

Step #7

Review Behavior Plan
- Check frequency of positive attention for prosocial
  behavior
- Check incentive program is motivating child
- Check that no attention is given during Time Out
- Conference with parent to coordinate home and
  school program
- IEP

Step #6

For aggressive, destructive behavior
- 3-5 minutes time away or Time Out to Calm Down,
  Work Chore

For noncompliance
- Time Out followed by command repeated

Step #5

Use small natural and logical consequences e.g.,
- 2 minute recess lost, no computer time, 2 minute loss of free play
  activity removed for few minutes, loss of privilege

Step #4

Ignore Non Aggressive
Misbehaviors e.g.,
- tantrums, whining

Step #3

As child begins to get upset, coach calm down strategies e.g.,
- deep breaths, talk about feelings, positive visualization, use turtle shell,
  positive self-talk

Step #2

Positive Verbal Redirect
Distractions and
Re-engagement Strategies

Step #1

Nonverbal Cues
Clear rules
Predictable Schedules
Transitions Clear

TO SUM UP...

- Teach students, through role play practice, the procedure for taking Time Out and how to calm down in Time Out (deep breathing, positive self-talk & positive imagery).
- Be prepared for student testing and escalation of misbehavior when first implementing Time Out. Have a plan for how to handle a challenging Time Out.
- Focus on staying calm when implementing Time Out.
- Give 3 to 5 minute Time Outs with 2 minutes of calm behavior at the end.
- Use a timer to help monitor the length of the Time Out. Some children will find a visual time-marker to be helpful. Remember that the teacher (rather than the timer) should release the child from Time Out.
- Reserve Time Out for aggressive and destructive behaviors, and for students with severe oppositional behavior.
- Don't threaten Time Outs unless you're prepared to follow through.
- Ignore child while in Time Out, however, stay nearby to monitor.
- Use nonviolent approaches such as loss of privileges as a back-up to Time Out.
- Follow through with completing Time Out and giving child a new learning trial.
- Support co-teachers' use of Time Out.

- Don't rely exclusively on Time Out—combine with other discipline tools, such as ignoring, logical consequences and problem solving.
- Be sure you are rewarding and coaching the expected positive opposite behaviors.
- Expect repeated learning trials.
- Use personal Time Out to relax and refuel.
- Gain parental support for your discipline plan.

The Incredible Years®
Teacher Classroom Management Self-Reflection Inventory
Managing Misbehavior – Time Out to Calm Down

Date: _____ Teacher Name: _____

Teachers learn extensively from self-reflection regarding their classroom management and the teaching strategies they are using that are working or not working. From these reflections teachers determine personal goals for making changes in their approaches to bring about the most positive learning climate they can. Use this Inventory to think about your strengths and limitations and determine your goals.

Time Out to Calm Down	1 = NEVER 3 = OCCASIONALLY 5 = CONSISTENTLY
1. I have taught my students what Time Out is used for and my students have practiced how to go to Time Out to calm down.	1 2 3 4 5
2. I only use Time Out for aggressive and destructive behavior.	1 2 3 4 5
3. When I use Time Out I am ~ calm, clear, patient, give very little attention to the student in Time Out (but do monitor carefully) and set a timer until 2 minutes of calm is achieved.	1 2 3 4 5
4. When my student is calm and Time Out is over, I immediately re-engage my student to another activity.	1 2 3 4 5
5. I assist other children to learn how to ignore a student in Time Out and to give him or her privacy to calm down.	1 2 3 4 5
6. I have identified a safe place for Time Out that is away from other children and relatively boring.	1 2 3 4 5

7. I help children to practice the words they will use to help themselves calm down in Time Out (e.g., "I can do it, I can calm down").	1 2 3 4 5
8. I use emotion coaching to focus on times when students are staying calm, trying again, and being patient even though it is frustrating.	1 2 3 4 5
9. After Time Out is over I re-engage the student by coaching and giving praise and attention for positive behavior. I do not remind the child of why s/he went to Time Out or force an apology.	1 2 3 4 5
10. I understand that the most effective consequences are immediate, quick, and followed by a new learning trial as soon as possible to help students be successful.	1 2 3 4 5
11. I am firm, respectful and control my negative emotions when engaged in a discipline strategy.	1 2 3 4 5
12. I have explained the hierarchy of the discipline plan to parents of students in my classroom.	1 2 3 4 5
13. I have developed behavior plans, which include behaviors to coach, encourage, praise and reward and those to ignore or use the least intrusive proactive discipline response first. These are reviewed regularly with school staff and by parents.	1 2 3 4 5
14. I have a few logical and natural consequences that I use appropriately. (describe here)	1 2 3 4 5

15. I help parents understand how they can help their children learn some self-calming strategies through phone calls, emails or Teacher-to-Parent Communication Home Activities letters.	1 2 3 4 5
16. I send home only positive notes to parents and if I want to discuss a behavior issue I set up an appointment time to discuss in person with the parent.	1 2 3 4 5
Future Goals Regarding My Discipline Plans:	Total

REFERENCES

Bear, G. G. (1998). School Discipline in the United States: Prevention, Correction and Long-Term Social Development. *School Psychology Review, 2*(1), 14-32.

Brophy, J. E. (1996). *Teaching problem students*. New York: Guilford.

Brophy, J. E., & McCaslin, M. (1992). Teachers' reports of how they perceive and cope with problem students. *Elementary School Journal, 93,* 363-423.

Gardner, H. L., Forehand, R., & Roberts, M. (1976). Time-out with children: Effects of an explanation and brief parent training on child and parent behaviors. *Journal of Abnormal Child Psychology, 4,* 277-288.

Martens, B. K., & Meller, P. J. (1990). The application of behavioral principles to educational settings. In T. B. Gutkin & C. R. Reynolds (Eds.), *Handbook of school psychology* (pp. 612-634). New York: Wiley.

Patterson, G., Reid, J., & Dishion, T. (1992). *Antisocial boys: A social interactional approach* (Vol. 4). Eugene, OR: Castalia Publishing.

Reinke, W. M., & Herman, K. C. (2002). Creating school environments that deter antisocial behaviors in youth. *Psychology in the Schools, 39*(549-559).

Steinberg, L. (1996). *Beyond the classroom: Why school reform has failed and what parents need to do*. New York: Simon & Schuster.

Van Houten, R., Nau, P. A., Mackenzie-Keating, S. E., Sameoto, D., & Colavecchia, B. (1982). An analysis of some variables influencing the effectiveness of reprimands. *Journal of Applied Behavior Analysis, 15,* 65-83.

White, A. G., & Bailey, J. S. (1990). Reducing disruptive behaviors of elementary physical education students with sit and watch. *Journal of Applied Behavior Analysis, 23*(3), 353-359.

CHAPTER
10

Behavior Planning

DEVELOPING A BEHAVIOR PLAN
FOR INDIVIDUAL STUDENTS WITH PROBLEMS

In Chapter Nine we reached the top of the teaching pyramid and discussed the use of classroom management tools that are used sparingly to reduce targeted student misbehaviors. The next important task is for teachers to come back down to the base of the pyramid to review the entire behavior plan and make sure the foundation is still firm with more positive attention, coaching and praise for proscial bevhavior than attention for misbehavior. Then the teacher refocuses on setting up new learning opportunities for teaching children to self regulate, problem solve, manage conflict and make friends. This is step # 7 (review behavior plan) and step #8 (new learning) on the discipline hierarchy.

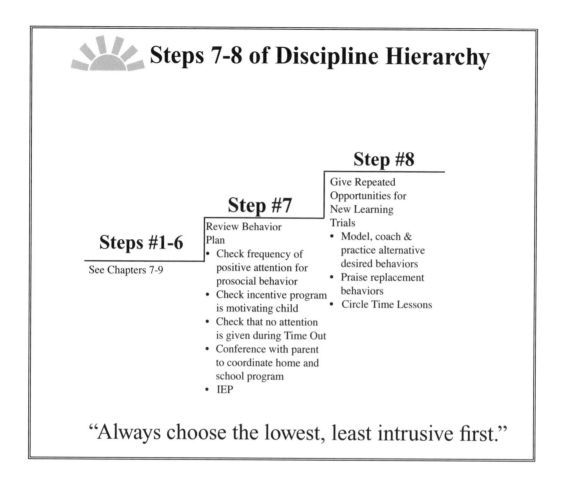

Steps 7-8 of Discipline Hierarchy

Step #8

Give Repeated Opportunities for New Learning Trials
- Model, coach & practice alternative desired behaviors
- Praise replacement behaviors
- Circle Time Lessons

Step #7

Review Behavior Plan
- Check frequency of positive attention for prosocial behavior
- Check incentive program is motivating child
- Check that no attention is given during Time Out
- Conference with parent to coordinate home and school program
- IEP

Steps #1-6

See Chapters 7-9

"Always choose the lowest, least intrusive first."

At this point teachers have all the proactive teaching tools needed to build their students' social, emotional and academic skills and to navigate some of the uncomfortable, but inevitable, aspects of their interactions with their students as they help them learn. Particularly for the chronically misbehaving student (but ideally for all students), it is important to develop an individual behavior plan to help the teacher to be more precise and detailed in how s/he is using specific teaching tools for strengthening particular positive emotional, social and academic behaviors and how s/he follows through with the agreed upon consequences for targeted misbehaviors. These plans can be developed in collaboration with other teacher colleagues and students' parents. The goal is to set realistic goals determined by children's developmental abilities and needs and to scaffold progress on these goals, ideally across school and home settings. Research has shown that classrooms where teachers have developed clear behavior plans have fewer misbehaviors and enhanced student achievement (Walker, 2002; Reinke & Herman, 2002). This chapter focuses on how teachers can set up behavior plans for their students using multiple proactive teaching tools.

DEVELOPING A BEHAVIOR PLAN

Identify Negative Behaviors

First, a teacher should identify the specific behaviors that s/he wants to reduce such as poking, blurting out, profanities, grabbing, interrupting, out of seat behavior, or social withdrawal. It is important that these be defined clearly. For example, what is meant by disrespect? Some teachers might feel that the rolling of a student's eyeballs is disrespectful while others might focus on more overt disrespectful behaviors such as swearing or abusive name calling.

Next the teacher chooses which of these misbehaviors s/he wants to target for intervention first. It is important to start with a small and manageable goal. For instance if the child displays many disruptive behaviors throughout the day, perhaps pick one behavior that happens during circle time and begin with a goal to reduce that behavior. Or, pick a specific time of day, for example, if a child enters the classroom every day in a highly dysregulated state and then continues to be dysregulated during every transition all day long, make a goal to help the student make a successful and calm transition into the classroom every morning. Once the target negative behaviors have been chosen, then observe and record their frequency, intensity and duration, and the occasions or situations in which they occur. For example, are the specific misbehaviors more likely to occur in structured or unstructured times (i.e., on the playground, in the lunch room, or hallways versus the classroom)? Do problems usually happen on particular days, such as Mondays after a stressful weekend at home? Are behaviors more likely to occur in the afternoons than the mornings? Do they usually occur with particular students? Do they occur under particular situations, such as when there is less teacher supervision or during transitions? What are the triggers that usually set the misbehavior off? For example, does the child misbehave when teased, rejected by a peer group, when left out of a discussion, or when a learning task is too difficult or frustrating?

While keeping running records is not easy, this information will be critical for teachers in developing an intervention that is based on the specific needs of the student. For example, if the problem occurs more often in the afternoon, it may be necessary to set up a more frequent incentive program at that time. Or, if the problems occur only in the cafeteria where adult monitoring is minimal, then the intervention may require additional monitoring during lunch times. If the problems primarily occur with particular students, then the teacher will want to set up groupings that separate these children. These records will also enable teachers to monitor any intervention strategies.

Why is the Misbehavior Occurring? (Functional Assessment)

Next formulate a hypothesis about why the child is misbehaving. The following functional assessment checklist will help teachers to understand the student by thinking about why the child may be behaving in a particular fashion. Try to pick the 1-2 most likely reasons for the misbehavior, rather than endorsing many answers. Note that the first four items on the checklist are very frequent causes of child misbehaviors (Scott & Nelson, 1999).

Understanding the child's motivation and self-awareness of the behavior and developmental ability is also key to developing an individualized and appropriate intervention behavior plan for the child. For example, the child with attention deficit disorder or hyperactivity will not have the ability to sit still for long periods of time and may not even be aware of twitching or muttering under his breath. It would be inappropriate to discipline such a child who does not have the developmental ability or capacity to perform a more acceptable behavior. The child who uses the misbehavior to gain power over or attention from others will need an intervention that permits him to earn power and attention for appropriate behaviors rather than for inappropriate behaviors. The child who is easily frustrated may need to learn self-control strategies. The child who misbehaves to avoid a stressful or unpleasant

---

Understanding Your Student's Misbehavior
Functional Assessment

	Yes	No
Child uses the misbehavior in order to get teacher or peer attention	❑	❑
Child is venting frustration with the misbehavior	❑	❑
Child does not have the language skills to use appropriate verbal skills	❑	❑
Child uses the misbehavior to avoid stress or some unpleasant task	❑	❑
Child finds the behavior fun in and of itself	❑	❑
Child is unaware of doing the behavior	❑	❑
Child uses the behavior to obtain power over others	❑	❑
Child uses the behavior to gain revenge because of anger	❑	❑
Child has not been taught other more appropriate prosocial behaviors	❑	❑
Child's home environment or past history has not taught the child predictability or the trustworthiness of adults	❑	❑
Child lacks emotional self-regulation skills due to developmental delays	❑	❑
Child's community/culture/family endorses the behavior	❑	❑
Child's behavior reflects child's feelings of inadequacy and low self-esteem	❑	❑

---

task may need support to complete the task, a modified task, or an adaptive way to signal that he needs a break.

Target Positive Opposite Replacement Behaviors to Increase

For every negative student behavior, the teacher needs to identify a positive opposite behavior to replace it with. For example, for the child who has low self-esteem, is withdrawn, and does not participate in class, the teacher can target efforts to join in play with peers and participate in classroom discussions as the prosocial behaviors to be increased and recognized. For the child who is impulsive, the teacher might identify waiting with a quiet hand up or taking turns as important alternative positive behaviors to encourage. For the child who constantly needs teacher reassurance, the goal might be for the child to do some aspect of the assignment by himself first. For the child who is sad or anxious, the teacher can identify times when the child bravely takes a risk, tries something new or seems happy during an activity. It is important that these targets be achievable (i.e., within the child's developmental capability) and measureable. This step of identifying the positive goals or positive opposite behaviors is key to the eventual effectiveness of a behavior plan. Striving to achieve negative goals, such as the absence of pouting or tantrums or blurting out is not likely to be effective because it does not help the child to visualize the positive alternative.

PLANNING INTERVENTION TOOLS

At this point, the teacher has thought carefully about why, when, and where the misbehavior is occurring and has identified a positive behavioral goal. Now it is time to plan the intervention tools to be used. The goal here is to begin with the bottom of the teaching pyramid and work up. Ideally, the teacher will give the teaching tools at the bottom of the pyramid a chance to work and build a firm foundation before moving up to the next highest level.

Relationship and Proactive Strategies

Since it is often the case that children in need of a behavior plan are frustrating for teachers, it is important to begin the behavior plan with a focus on the teacher-student relationship. Think of all the relationship-building strategies discussed in Chapter Two and pick several to focus on with this student. Perhaps the teacher can find five minutes each day to read with the student, make positive calls home, greet the student at the door, or invite the student to help with a special job. Next, think of the proactive strategies discussed in Chapter

Three. What environmental changes might help scaffold this student to meet the positive goals the teacher has set? Perhaps a different seating arrangement, perhaps an earlier transition warning or special job to do during the transition, perhaps a shorter or more active circle time.

Coaching, Encouragement and Praise

Next the teacher thinks of the specific coaching and praise statements (Chapters Four and Five) that s/he will use to encourage the positive behavior, thoughts or feelings that were targeted to strengthen. For example, "Thank you for raising your quiet hand." Or, "I love the way that you are working so hard. You are focused and calm!" Or, "I'm proud of you for asking her for that in a polite and friendly voice. I know it's hard to wait when you really want something." With this section of the plan, also think of the specific academic, persistence, social, and/or emotion coaching strategies that will support the child's goal. What behaviors will be focused on and described? For example, "I see that you are really sticking with that math problem. You erased your first answer and you are trying again. You are really thinking about solutions and checking carefully." Or, "I heard you ask for that, and now I see that you are waiting patiently for your turn. Your body is so calm and still right now!"

Determine Specific Incentives for Desired Behaviors

Now the teacher is ready to decide if the student would benefit from an incentive strategy (Chapter Six) to further encourage the use of the positive behavior. This may be a nontangible incentive such as extra reading time with the teacher, a few extra minutes of computer time, getting to perform a special task/job, or getting to be first in line. In other cases tangible incentives may be more effective (e.g., a sticker, a prize from a prize box, a positive note home). Understanding the possible underlying motivation for the misbehavior (from the functional assessment discussed above) can help a teacher choose incentives that might be more likely to be effective for this particular student. Understanding the occasions in which misbehaviors occur can also help a teacher determine how often the incentive plan will need to be implemented or what time of day. For example, a young child who disrupts circle every two minutes may need a very small incentive every two minutes (e.g., hand stamp) whereas an older child with a longer attention span might receive a star for completing a set amount of work or for concentrating for 15 minutes. A student who mainly has trouble on the playground can have this specific time of day targeted for an incentive program. When determining specific reinforcers for a student, it is important that a teacher try to involve both the student and his/her parents in the discussion of what would be reinforcing for them.

Select Specific Consequences for Negative Behaviors

Finally, the specific consequences for the misbehaviors must be decided and clearly outlined in the plan. For the child who blurts out but doesn't use profanities, a teacher might decide to use ignoring in combination with praise for waiting with a quiet hand up. On the other hand, for the child who blurts out profanities, the teacher might impose a mild consequence (such as loss of 2 minutes recess or computer time) in combination with points or stickers for polite talk. For the child with impulse control problems, the teacher might decide to use Time Out for hitting, points for cooperation with others, using calm down strategies and social skills training. Remember to use the discipline hierarchy, beginning with lower level teaching tools and moving to higher level ones only as needed.

Once the plan has been agreed upon, a written implementation plan should be drawn up. That is, who will arrange for the incentives, record the data, call the parents, and teach the emotional and social skills. A date should be set to re-evaluate the outcome.

Remember the student on an individual behavior plan is not getting special privileges by being on the plan. Rather the student is being given individual support in much the same way a student with an academic or reading problem would receive additional tutoring.

The following behavior management sheet can be used by teachers in partnership with parents to develop this plan.

BEHAVIOR PLAN

for

_____

Developed by: _____

Date: _____

This plan is to be created by teachers, therapists, or counselors working directly with a student and/or parents, and in collaboration with each other. This plan should be expanded over the year with additional goals and information about successful strategies. At the end of the year, this can become the basis for a transition plan with guidance for next year's teachers The template below provides sample plan examples in the grey boxes followed by space for specific information about the target student's goals and strategies.

I. Identify Negative Behaviors
The following targeted negative behaviors have been targeted to decrease their occurrence:

   For example: interruptions and blurt outs during class; touches other children particularly during large group circle time activities; noncompliance to teacher instructions.

The following behaviors have already been successfully eliminated:

II. Functional Assessment
The assessment indicates why the misbehaviors occur, where and when they occur and the frequency of their occurrence:

III. Targeted Positive Opposite Replacement Behaviors to Increase
The following positive opposite behaviors have been targeted as goals for increasing:

For example: quiet hand up to ask a question; hands to own body; listening and following teacher's directions; being patient when frustrated; using a friendly voice.

IV. Relationship and Proactive Strategies

The following teacher relationship and proactive strategies are particularly effective with this student:

For example: seating child near teacher with back to classroom when doing seat work; picture sequence chart on desk that outlines class schedule to help with transitions; allow for opportunities to move around; nonverbal cues and signals; special one-on-one time with student engaged in child-directed play to promote positive relationship.

V. Coaching, Encouragement, and Praise

The following coaching and encouragement strategies will be used with this student:

For example: teacher attention & frequent verbal praise which clearly describes the positive behaviors s/he has accomplished; persistence coaching for times when s/he is concentrating on reading and working hard to complete the story and/or doing homework.

VI. Specific Incentives for Target Positive Opposite Behaviors

The following incentives are effective in motivating this student and increasing his/her targeted behaviors:

For example: behavior sticker chart which targets positive behaviors which child can earn stickers or coupons for—these are turned in for prizes whenever he/she earns 25; "happy gram" coupons are given for special accomplishments; child likes to earn extra time on computer or chance to be teacher aid—teacher attention is a particularly powerful motivator; child also likes to be a leader of class activities and will work for this privilege.

VII. Effective Discipline for Handling Negative Behaviors

The following proactive discipline strategies are helpful with this student:

For example: clear nonverbal cues and reminders help in redirecting him/ her back on task for non-disruptive behaviors indicating disengagement; warning of consequences often prevents misbehavior from escalating; warning of Time Out for disruptive behaviors such as refusing to follow directions often increases compliance; Time Out to calm down is given for hitting immediately; if he/she can't sit in chair, office is called and he/she went to classroom next door for 5-minute Time Out.

VIII. Parent and Teacher Insights about the Student's Temperament & Interests—Tips for Connecting

The following information is important to know about this student:

For example: Interests—child collects baseball cards, likes computer games, etc. Temperament—likes hugs, squirms and moves a lot and avoids eye contact but absorbs information readily, anxious about new events and sharing self, hates writing but computer helps; Family—has pet dog Ruffie, adjusting to divorce.

IX. Plan for Collaborating with Parents:

The parents would like to be involved in supporting their child's success in school and agreed that the following approaches would be mutually supportive:

For example: behavior sticker chart of positive behaviors sent home each day—child will trade these in for additional incentives from parents; parents will be supportive, positive and hopeful with their child—they will focus on his successes; discipline plan was agreed to by parents and they will avoid punishing bad days at school—as discipline would be administered at the time of misbehavior by teacher at school; telephone calls will be made to mother to tell her of positive behaviors; mother would like to participate in field trips or reading sessions in classroom; parents suggested incentives which they have found motivating for their child; teachers and parents will try to communicate weekly by note, voice mail or e-mail.

Plan discussed and agreed upon (date): _____

Plan to be re-evaluated: _____ (as necessary)

Keep Records of Progress, Reflect and Analyze the Discipline System

As we have seen above, the behavior plan for an individual child involves a combination of different behavior management tools (proactive, incentives and consequences) rather than a single tool. If the plan is working, there should be some reduction in the misbehaviors within several weeks. Although, as was mentioned with the ignoring and Time Out strategies, there will likely be some worsening of misbehavior as the child tests these responses before the behavior will improve. If the misbehavior does not decrease over time with consistent implementation of the plan, then the plan should be reevaluated to be sure the base of the pyramid is sufficiently strong and to determine whether the incentives are not rewarding enough to motivate the child, or the negative consequences are being used too often, or more attention is being given to the misbehavior than to the positive behaviors.

The ability to analyze a discipline plan—to assess whether' it is working to reduce targeted misbehaviors can be more easily done if the teacher has kept good records. Teachers will need a system to keep track of the type of misbehavior, the frequency it occurs, the consequence used, and the effects. The misbehaviors should be graphed for several weeks to determine if they are decreasing with the discipline approach that is being implemented. This record keeping will help teachers to know where students are in the hierarchy of discipline strategies, and will help monitor how often they are experiencing the more severe types of consequences such as Time Out or loss of privileges.

For example, a teacher developed a behavior plan for a child who was aggressive, disruptive, and impulsive at circle time. She began using a variety of positive and proactive teaching tools such as seating him near her, giving him special jobs that let him move around during circle, and giving him praise and hand stamps for sitting. She also decided to give him a Time Out whenever he was aggressive to another child during circle. After tracking his behavior for a week, she noticed that his behavior during the first half of each circle time had improved; he was more attentive and was engaged. She also noticed that by the second half of the circle time, his behavior began to deteriorate; he began bothering other children, and ultimately always ended up hitting another child.

When sent to Time Out, he rolled on the floor at the back of the room, made loud noises, and sang to himself. As soon as the circle time was over, he sat quietly and calmly in his Time Out and was eager to rejoin the group for choice time. This analysis allowed her to guess that this child was likely not developmentally able to sit for an entire circle time and that he might actually welcome the Time Out as a way to take a break from the structure of the circle. She introduced a "wiggle space" where he was encouraged to go when he needed a break from the circle, always welcoming him back after his break with a smile and an opportunity to participate. Gradually, he was able to increase his attention and time in the circle. This teacher's analysis was key to her success with the plan.

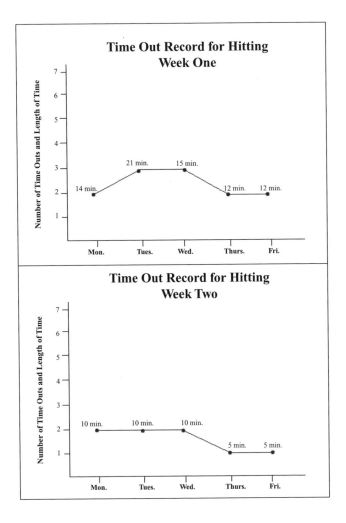

The other important reason to have objective records and charts of the misbehaviors is sometimes on bad days teachers will subjectively think a behavior plan isn't working when it really is. Students on behavior plans still have bad days, but will gradually begin to have more good days. Success is a gradual downward trend in behavior problems and greater distance between the bad days.

Be Prepared for Relapses—Focus on Learning Trials and "Restart Cards"

Sometimes teachers get discouraged and resentful when they have worked very hard to set up an effective behavior plan with a student, it seems to have worked for several weeks, and suddenly the child deteriorates and is right back to her old disruptive behaviors. Teachers may think, "How dare that child do that, after all I have done!" Sometimes these relapses happen because teachers are no longer giving as much positive attention because the child has improved so much. The relapse may be a signal to the teacher that the child still needs this extra approval and support. However, relapses are also a necessary and expected part of a child's learning process! The very nature of children's development is to learn new things, to move to increasing maturity, independence and self-confidence and then to regress to an earlier more immature behavior pattern. This regression helps children to "touch base," to understand that the limits are still there, and then to be able to move forward again. The old adage "two steps forward one step backwards" probably applies to all of us when learning something new, adults and children alike.

This regression helps children to "touch base," to understand that the limits are still there, and then to be able to move forward again.

Moreover, don't assume that the child's regression means he is back to ground zero. Most regressions are a temporary set back that can be turned around more easily than the first time. One way a teacher might handle regressions is to use "restart cards," that is, to give the child an incentive card with the behavior on it he wants to improve. For example, the teacher might say to the child, "Everyone has bad days and you have been doing so well. You will get back on track again quickly. When this card is filled up with stickers for staying in your seat, we will know you are back on track."

Remember children need many learning trials before appropriate emotional regulation and social skills become a stable part of their interpersonal relationships. Children who are hyperactive, impulsive, or learning disabled or children who have experienced family deprivation and environmental stress of some sort will need even more learning trials than children who are by temperament more reflective and attentive or from homes that emphasize emotion and social skills teaching. Nonetheless, with consistent, warm and caring responses from teachers, all young children can eventually learn to be emotionally and socially competent and positive contributors to their classrooms.

INVOLVING PARENTS IN DISCIPLINE PLANS

One key to a teacher's success with a classroom discipline plan will be the degree to which the teacher has obtained parental support for the plan (Christenson, Rounds, & Franklin, 1992). At the initial school orientation, the teacher's standard discipline approach and philosophy should be shared with the parents. This should include both the positive ways that s/he will work to support children's behavioral goals as well as the consequences that will be used and for what types of behavior. Teachers should explain their policies on ignoring, privilege removal, Time Out at parent meetings.

It is also important to discuss proposed methods for communicating with parents about behavior problems that may occur at school (e.g., by phone in the evening). If possible these should be individualized so that they are created with parents' input and modified according to the family situation. Some parents may prefer to communicate via e-mail, others by phone. Ideally the teacher sets up an open line of communication with all parents, before any problem behaviors occur. The communication lines also need to be realistic for the teacher, so teachers should communicate limits on their availability. For example, a teacher says, "I check e-mail once a day, after school, and will try to answer any message within 24 hours. If your message is urgent, please type that into the subject line and I will do my best to answer before I leave for the day."

Where possible, teachers and parents should collaborate to set up behavior plans and determine meaningful incentive systems. This allows parents to reinforce their children's school successes at home. However, school behavior plans should stand on their own and not rely on parents in order to be successful. If plans depend on parents, they discriminate against the child whose parents can't be involved due to mental illness, work schedules, family crises or lack of interest. Plans that do involve parents need to be realistic about how much parents can do at home. For example, families living in a great deal of stress will find it very difficult to carry out reward charts and to monitor behaviors. In these cases, teachers will need to collaborate with parents to determine how much they want to be involved. Regardless, of how involved the parents can be in the behavior plan, it will be important for teachers to give feedback to the parents about how the child is doing with the program and to reinforce their efforts. A special letter with tips for how to encourage specific positive behaviors at home or calls home outlining the positive outcomes their child is making can elicit the parents' encouragement for the child's learning efforts. See website for examples of Teacher to Parent Communication letters.

http://www.incredibleyears.com/TeacherResources/index.asp

How should teachers let parents know of their children's behavior problems at school? Should a narrative description of the child's problem behaviors be sent home with the child?

Often parents want to know about their child's day and want to be closely involved, but are reluctant to bother the teacher with a call; similarly teachers have limited time and may have difficulty reaching parents. When parents and teachers are unable to talk things over, teachers may to resort to sending home impersonal notes about problems, which may foster resentments on the part of parents, and misunderstandings on both sides. Particularly in the case of children who are known to be behaviorally challenging in the classroom, parents and teachers should have a workable, mutually agreed-upon plan for how they will communicate and share information back and forth.

Do not send home daily notes to parents with descriptions of children's problem behaviors in the classroom. Many parents do not know how to interpret these notes. Some interpret them to mean they are supposed to discipline their child at home for his misbehavior at school and respond to the child by being punitive and overly critical. Thus the child receives double punishment. Not only does this reaction from parents damage the parent-child relationship but the parental discipline is so far removed from the actual problem behavior at school that it is unlikely to be effective. In fact, this discipline may create further problems because of the attention given to the child's negative behaviors. Sometimes parents respond to negative notes about their children by becoming defensive and angry and may even blame the teacher for the problem. Consequently we recommend that teachers schedule personal meetings with parents to talk about classroom problems and to collaborate and share with them their discipline plan for the misbehavior.

It is vital for teachers also to be building up a "positive bank account" with parents by sending home "happy grams" and other positive reports for good times and calling regularly to report something positive their child did that day. This positive base will create a trusting relationship between teacher and parents so that if it becomes necessary to discuss a behavior problem, parents will be more open and more able to collaborate with the teacher in addressing the problem.

An additional benefit of sending home happy grams or compliment notes to parents about some positive aspect of the child's behavior or attitude is that it helps the parents focus on the child's successes and focus the child on his or her successes, thus preparing the child to behave in similar ways the next day. See website for Happy Grams and other awards that can be downloaded.

Do not send home daily notes to parents with descriptions of children's problem behaviors in the classroom.

http://www.incredibleyears.com/TeacherResources/index.asp

MOVING BEYOND DISCIPLINE

Repair and Rebuild

Children who are impulsive, oppositional, inattentive and aggressive will need constant teacher monitoring or scaffolding involving redirection, warnings, reminders and consistent follow through with consequences. However, one of the hardest and most important things for a teacher to do when teaching a disruptive student is to move beyond the Time Out and discipline tools to repair and rebuild the strained teacher-student and student-student relationships. This means not holding on to grudges and resentments after consequences have been implemented, welcoming students back as accepted and valued members of the class each day and continuing to teach them more effective ways of problem-solving. It means a philosophy of taking one day at a time, allowing the student a new learning opportunity or fresh start each day, and practicing forgiveness. So instead of saying, "I hope today is not going to be like yesterday, because if you are . . ." the teacher encourages the child and predicts a successful day: " I'm glad to see you, I am sure that you and I are both going to work hard to make it a good day!"

Moving to Self-Management

Initially the teacher will need tight external management and consistent discipline in order to keep the behavior of difficult and aggressive students under control. Indeed research has indicated that teacher use of incentives, differential reinforcement, Time Out and negative consequences result in decreased undesired classroom behaviors and increased positive social skills (e.g., Charlop, Burgio, Iwata, & Ivancic, 1988). However, the eventual goal is to shift away from exclusive teacher management to gradually increasing student self-management skills. This is necessary so that students can become less dependent on teachers to provide direction and incentives for their behavior. Such interventions have the potential for producing more durable and generalizeable behavior gains in situations outside the classroom (Holman & Baer, 1979; Nelson, Smith, Young, & Dodd, 1991; Whalen, Henker, & Hinshaw, 1985).

Certainly one of the central features of many children with behavior problems is the absence of self-reflection or self-management skills. Part of the reason for this is that such children often have distorted self-perceptions and sense of reality (Webster-Stratton & Lindsay, 1999) and make maladaptive self-statements (Dush, Hirt, & Schroeder, 1989). They have difficulty evaluating their own behavior, at times having an inflated sense of their performance and, other times, being very negative about their abilities. They may misperceive others' intentions toward them as hostile, when in fact, the person might have been trying to be helpful. Although the degree of self-management expected of students will vary with the age, developmental ability and temperament of the child, teachers can begin to foster some skills of self-direction even in young preschool children and in children with severe disabilities. Sadly, these skills are seldom taught to students, especially those with behavior problems.

Self-management interventions generally involve a variety of strategies related to changing or maintaining one's own behavior (Shapiro & Cole, 1992). They include self-evaluation and self-reinforcement approaches. For example, teachers can invite children to reflect about how they did that day in order to get a sense of the accuracy of their self-perceptions and self-evaluation abilities. For children who have poor language skills or emotion vocabulary, a teacher might have a thermometer showing the range from calm (blue for cool) to over-excited (red for hot) and ask the child to point to how regulated and calm he thought he was during certain classroom periods of the day (see Chapter 11). This gives the teacher an opportunity to provide students specific feedback on the accuracy of their self-perceptions or to help them remember times when they successfully calmed themselves down and stayed friendly. Often children with behavior problems will focus on their mistakes; however, by reviewing the positive aspects of the child's day, the teacher can help the child to gain more positive attributions.

Working hard

Another self-evaluation approach, particularly for children with behavior problems is to have them complete a form such as Dina's self-encouragement chart (shown in Chapter Five) or Wally's balloon chart that cover certain periods in the day (e.g., reading time, circle time, free play, lunch and so forth). Once the desired behavior has been specified (e.g., quiet hand up, working hard, staying in seat etc.) the student marks his evaluation of his success at accomplishing the task with colors such as green for outstanding, blue for good, yellow for some blurting out, and red for loss of privilege or Time Out. As these are filled out at various time points during the day, it is ideal if the teacher can review them at the end of the day by asking, "Let's see how you did today? What kind of day was it?" The child may respond, "A mainly green day!" The teacher then can reflect, "You're right this was a great green day with only two yellows, I think tomorrow you'll get one more green! Remember what do you have to do to get a green?" Through the use of the balloons and colors the child can reflect on his day at school with the teacher helping him to focus on his successes. If the child is consistently getting more reds and yellows than greens and blues, then the time period for evaluating success needs to be shortened so the child can be more successful and the discipline plan reevaluated.

Self-management interventions also include self-monitoring approaches such as the example in Chapter Six in which a "quiet hand up" sheet or, a "stop, look, think, check" was placed on the students' desks to record whenever they remembered to raise a quiet hand or check their work. The teacher might also challenge the students that if they meet a certain criteria (e.g. 10 quiet hand ups) they can earn a chosen reward.

Stop-look-think-check

In order to prevent discouragement in students who may not think they can meet the challenge or place a ceiling on students who are capable of exceeding the challenge the teacher might use a "mystery challenge." This is when the teacher writes the challenge for accomplishing the task on a piece of paper which is placed in an envelope. When the specified period is completed, the envelope is opened and the students compare their performance against the mystery criteria and earn

© Incredible Years®

rewards depending whether they matched or exceeded the challenge. This approach makes the self-monitoring procedures exciting and results in a high degree of student involvement. Similar programs could be set up for self-monitoring other behaviors such as on-task or "working" behavior or polite language in class or completion of a certain amount of work. The mystery challenge is best used with older children at the point where they clearly understand the behaviors to work on and have been successful at working towards set goals. Preschool children may not under-stand the idea of the mystery challenge and will be confused by changing goal posts.

Teaching children how to internalize positive self-statements is another self-management approach used to modify problem behavior (Meichenbaum, 1993). For example a child with academic difficulties who is off task a great deal of the time may be thinking negative thoughts that perpetuate the problem (e.g., "I hate school," or "I can never do this, it is stupid"). Teaching positive self-statements (e.g., "I can do this eventually, I just need to keep working at it" or "I can do it, I just need to keep trying") can result in improved on task work. (See self-praise in Chapter Five and the use of "I can" cans in Chapter Six.) In Chapter 11 calming self-statements and scripts are described as a method to help students learn how to self-regulate and manage their anger. Finally, social problem-solving training, which is described extensively in the next two chapters, was developed to help children learn the thinking, emotional regulation and social skills involved in making make good choices, assuming responsibility for their own behavior and developing supportive friends.

TO SUM UP...

Preparation is Key

- Do a functional assessment to assess the reason, location, and setting for the behavior problem.
- Carefully plan a hierarchy of discipline tools to be used to manage misbehaviors from the least intrusive to more intrusive.
- Make sure your behavior plan is developmentally appropriate for a particular student.
- Give your behavior plan adequate time and keep records of strategies used and record progress made.
- Be sure you are using more teaching tools from the bottom of the teaching pyramid than the top.
- Get input and support from your teacher colleagues for your behavior plan.
- Expect students to need repeated learning trials.
- Gain parental support for your behavior plan and involve them in goal setting and reinforcing successes at home.

REFERENCES

Charlop, M. H., Burgio, L. D., Iwata, B. A., & Ivancic, M. T. (1988). Stimulus variation as a means of enhancing punishment effects. *Journal of Applied Behavior Analysis, 21*, 89-93.

Christenson, S. L., Rounds, T., & Franklin, M. J. (1992). Home-school collaboration: Effects, issues, and opportunities. In S. L. Christenson & J. C. Conoley (Eds.), *Home-school collaboration: Enhancing children's academic and social competence* (pp. 19-51). Bethesda, MD: National Association of School Psychologists.

Dush, D. M., Hirt, M. L., & Schroeder, H. E. (1989). Self-statement modification in the treatment of child behavior disorders: A meta-analysis. *Psychological Bulletin, 106*, 97-106.

Holman, J., & Baer, D. M. (1979). Facilitating generalization of on-task behavior through self-monitoring of academic tasks. *Journal of Autism and Developmental Abilities, 9*, 429-446.

Meichenbaum, D. (1993). Changing conceptions of cognitive behavior modification: Retrospect and prospect. *Journal of Consulting and Clinical Psychology, 61*, 202-204.

Nelson, J. R., Smith, D. J., Young, R. K., & Dodd, J. (1991). A review of self-management outcome research conducted with students who exhibit behavioral disorders. *Behavioral Disorders, 16*, 169-179.

Reinke, W. M., & Herman, K. C. (2002). Creating school environments that deter antisocial behaviors in youth. *Psychology in the Schools, 39*(549-559).

Scott, T. M., & Nelson, C. M. (1999). Functional behavioral assessment: Implications for training and staff development. *Behavioral Disorders, 24*(3), 249-252.

Shapiro, E. S., & Cole, C. L. (1992). Self-monitoring. In T. Ollendick & M. Hersen (Eds.), *Handbook of child and adolescent assessment* (pp. 124-139). New York: Pergamon Press.

Walker, H. M. (2002). The First Step to Success program: Preventing destructive social outcomes at the point of school entry. *Report on Emotional and Behavioral Disorders in Youth, 3*(1), 3-6, 22-23.

Webster-Stratton, C., & Lindsay, D. W. (1999). Social Competence and early-onset conduct problems: Issues in assessment. *Journal of Child Clinical Psychology, 28*, 25-93.

Whalen, C. K., Henker, B., & Hinshaw, S. P. (1985). Cognitive-behavioral therapies for hyperactive children: Premises, problems, and prospects. *Journal of Abnormal Child Psychology, 13*, 391-410.

Helping Students Learn to Handle their Emotions

Aggression, inadequate impulse control and emotional dysregulation are perhaps the most potent obstacles to effective problem solving and forming successful friendships in childhood. Without help, young children who are angry and aggressive are more likely to experience peer rejection (Asher & Coie, 1990; Asher, Parkhurst, Hymel, & Williams, 1990; Coie, 1990; Rubin, Chen, & Hymel, 1993) and continued social problems for years to come (Campbell, 1995; Campbell, 1990, 1994; Campbell, Shaw, & Gilliom, 2000; Pope, Bierman, & Mumma, 1989). As we noted in Chapter One, research has found that children with emotional regulation difficulties have deficits in social problem solving or conflict management skills (Asarnow & Callan,

Aggressive children are more likely to cognitively misinterpret ambiguous situations as hostile or threatening.

1985; Mize & Cox, 1990). They react to interpersonal conflict situations in hostile and physical ways without pausing to consider non-aggressive or prosocial solutions, and they don't anticipate negative consequences for their aggressive solutions (Asher & Hymel, 1981; Dodge, 1993; Dodge, Price, Bachorowski, & Newman, 1990; Quiggle, Garber, Panak, & Dodge, 1992; K H. Rubin & Krasnor, 1986; Slaby & Guerra, 1988). In short, they have difficulty regulating their negative affect in response to conflict situations.

Such children also have difficulty knowing how to "read" social situations accurately because they distort and/or underutilize social cues (Gouze, 1987; Milich & Dodge, 1984). Furthermore, there is evidence that aggressive children are more likely to cognitively misinterpret ambiguous situations as hostile or threatening (Dodge, 1985; Dodge, 1993; Dodge & Crick, 1990). This tendency to perceive hostile intent in others has been seen as one source of their aggressive responses. Negative social experiences with others, in part the result of children's lack of emotional regulation and social competence, in turn further exacerbate their adjustment difficulties, aggressive behavior problems, and self-regulation difficulties (e.g., Dishion, Patterson, Stoolmiller, & Skinner, 1991; Patterson, Reid, & Dishion, 1992). This cycle also reinforces children's distorted perceptions and social cognitions.

As we will see in Chapters 12 and 13, teachers can help children learn to cope more effectively with conflict situations that provoke anger (e.g. teasing, hitting, disappointment) by teaching them problem-solving strategies and communication skills, and by teaching them to use positive self-statements and other cognitive mediation strategies. However, before students can effectively problem solve with appropriate solutions, they need to be able to recognize and regulate their own emotional responses and to articulate their emotions as well as to read the emotions of the social situations and others more accurately. Teachers can play a critical role in helping students learn to recognize the feelings and thoughts that trigger a problem and learn to manage their anger so they can think about more productive solutions. They do this by helping students to think differently about why an event occurred, preparing them to respond appropriately to situations that typically provoke anger, and encouraging them to employ self-talk and relaxation strategies to keep themselves calm. Teachers also act as powerful models for students whenever they themselves can remain calm and nonaggressive in response to the negative affect and aggression displayed by some students or stressful situations in the classroom.

WHAT IS EMOTIONAL REGULATION?

Emotions are responses to stimuli or situations that affect a person strongly. Emotional responses occur on three levels. The first, and most basic, level of emotional response involves neurophysiological and biochemical reactions to stimuli, including all the bodily processes regulated by the autonomic nervous system: heart rate, blood flow, respiration, hormonal secretions (epinephrine, cortisol) and neural responses (EEG). For example, a person who is angry feels her heart race and her face redden. These responses often occur before a person has a chance to consciously react to an event. The second level is cognitive and affective and involves the language (whether spoken or thoughts) by which a person labels her thoughts about an event or interaction and the feelings associated with it. For example, a child thinks, "He won't share the trucks with me. He doesn't like me, and I feel angry." Or, "Today I get to go to soccer practice for the first time. I'm feeling excited and nervous!" Young children, with emerging language skills, will have difficulty recognizing their thoughts or feelings and may misinterpret another person's intentions or actions because of their cognitive difficulty with perspective-taking. The third level of emotional response is behavioral, where emotions are expressed in a person's actions. This level includes facial expressions and behaviors such as crying, laughing, sullen gazes, withdrawing from, or engaging in verbal or behavioral interactions with others.

Children may differ strikingly in their emotional responses; in the frequency and range of their emotions as well as the ways they express emotion. For example, 7-year-old Billy was sobbing because his soccer team lost their final game, while his teammate, Dan, responded by angrily kicking the fence and hurling a soccer ball at the opposing team members. Still another teammate, Eric, walked off the field and withdrew into himself, sullenly refusing to say anything, while yet another boy shrugged his shoulders and then went to shake hands with the opposing team. Here we have four different emotional responses expressed by a group of similar-aged boys to exactly the same situation. Children also vary widely in the subtlety of their understanding of emotions (both their own and others), in the degree of pleasure they show when they share positive emotions, and in their ability to regulate or control their negative responses to frustrating situations.

Emotional regulation refers to a person's ability to adequately control his or her emotional responses (neurophysiological and biochemical, cognitive, affective and behavioral) to arousing situations. The term *emotional dysregulation* refers to a state when emotional responses are out of control and dysfunctional. While all children are occasionally dysregulated, some children are chronically in this state, like the child with behavior problems whose impulsive anger and aggression are so excessive that he cannot make and maintain friendships and is rejected by peers, or the child whose withdrawal from emotionally challenging situations becomes so habitual that she avoids participation with others, cannot enter into any new learning activities, or persist with the academic task. In these cases, the dysregulation is dysfunctional to their emotional, social and academic growth.

HOW DO CHILDREN LEARN EMOTIONAL REGULATION?

Just like walking, talking, and toilet training, the regulation of emotional responses is a developmental achievement requiring maturation of the

immature brain. This ability is not present in the early years, and it must be learned. The initial regulation must be provided by the environment. Picture the young infant who has a wet diaper, is hungry, or is bored. She expresses her distress in the only way she can, through crying. The infant requires help from the environment to modulate her physiological state and to reduce her internal tension. The parent plays an integral role in helping the infant regulate her emotional arousal: that is, the parent tries to understand the meaning of the baby's cries and then takes the necessary action to calm her. As we all know, some babies are easily calmed and others are more difficult to soothe. This fact suggests that there are individual developmental or temperament differences in infants' ability to acquire emotional self-regulation.

During toddlerhood children are beginning to strive for some autonomy and are driven to explore, but because their language and cognitive development is immature, they can't let others know what their needs are. This results in an escalation of physical and verbal aggressive responses between one and three years of age as toddlers use these aggressive strategies to communicate their wants. The transition period from toddlerhood to the preschool period is accompanied by some beginning maturation in the child's emotional regulatory system. During this developmental period, the burden of emotional regulation begins to shift a little from the adult to the child. One of the most important developmental achievements associated with the emergence of emotional regulation is the child's acquisition of language and communication skills. As children develop language skills, they become increasingly able to label their emotions, their thoughts, and their intentions. And as children become more able to communicate their complex needs and feelings, they can more effectively regulate their emotional responses. In part, this means letting their parents and teachers know what they need or want and having those wishes acknowledged. During this time, preschoolers are also learning to accept that merely expressing a wish will not always result in the outcome that they desire. This means that they will also be working on the important regulation strategies of calming themselves when angry, sad, or disappointed, delaying gratification, and accepting limits. Teachers and parents help in this process by providing support, understanding, and language to talk about these feelings, while at the same time calmly and firmly following through with necessary limits.

There is wide variation in young children's emotion regulation development.

In the transition from the preschool to the school age years, children begin to assume greater responsibility for their own emotional functioning, so that somewhat less adult emotional regulation scaffolding is required. Nevertheless, parents and teachers do continue to have a major role in supporting children's emotional regulation. During the school age years, emotional regulation changes to a more complex and abstract process; whereas in infancy it was primarily reflexive, guided by physiological discomfort, now it becomes more reflective, guided by the child's sense of self, security in the environment, capacity to think ahead to the future, and ability to reflect on another's point of view. Instead of the angry or frustrated preschool child hitting someone or exploding in a tantrum because she can't play with a particular toy, now she will argue with her friend or teacher as to why it is her turn and begin to be able to think about alternative viewpoints. Instead of expressing impatience by wailing, a child may be able to wait and ask again for what he wants. Instead of expressing excitement by running around in circles, a girl will be able to talk about how excited she is. The extreme emotional responses of anger, distress, and excitement have been dampened to some extent by this age. Moreover, as children develop their own capacity for emotional regulation, the internal or subjective aspects of emotion become separate from the external expression of emotion (or affect). Thus we see the school-aged child who can be internally distressed by an event but outwardly express no sign of emotion. During adolescence, there is an upheaval of the child's emotional systems as hormones enter into the picture, challenging the emotional regulation that the adolescent has learned over the years. To the parents and teachers of adolescents, it may seem at times as if the teenager has regressed to the emotional regulatory stage of a preschooler!

WHAT DETERMINES HOW QUICKLY CHILDREN LEARN EMOTIONAL REGULATION?

Just as there is a wide variation in the point at which children start to walk, talk, or learn to use the toilet, some children's neuroregulatory or self-regulatory systems develop at a slower rate than others. We know little as yet about the factors that contribute to these differences in timing. However, research does suggest that there are at least four processes underlying children's growing ability to regulate their emotions:

1. Maturation of the child's neurological inhibitory system. The growth and development of the child's nervous system and brain development provides the necessary neurological "hardware" required for the eventual control of emotions.
2. The child's temperament and developmental status. Some children are more vulnerable to emotional dysregulation due to learning disabilities, language delays, attentional deficits, hyperactivity, or other developmental delays.
3. Parental socialization and environmental support. Differences in the ways that families talk about feelings (their own and others') and regulate their own emotional responses are related to later differences in the ways children express their feelings, their ability to regulate their emotions, and their understanding of the feelings of others. Children who experience chronic stress in their environment, or whose daily lives lack predictability and stability, have more difficulties with emotional regulation and understanding the perspective of others.
4. School and teachers' emphasis on emotional education. Differences in the ways that teachers talk to students about feelings and respond to students' expression of negative emotion in response to conflict situations at school are related to children's ability to regulate emotions.

WHAT CAN TEACHERS DO?

While teachers cannot change the first three factors described above: a child's neurological system or temperament and developmental status, or family situation, it is important for teachers to understand they can have a major impact on students' ability to learn to regulate their emotions and responses through the fourth factor, socialization and environmental support. The following chapter explains some ways that teachers can help their students learn emotional regulation.

These strategies are based on research regarding effective anger man-
agement programs and Piaget's cognitive stages of development (e.g.,
Larson, 1994; Lochman, Lampron, Gemmer, & Harris, 1987;
Lochman & Dunn, 1993; Patterson, 1990; Webster-Stratton, 1990;
Webster-Stratton & Hammond, 1997; Webster-Stratton, Reid, &
Stoolmiller, 2008).

Provide as much stability and consistency as possible

Teachers can support the development of emotional regulation by
providing environmental stability and consistency in the classroom as
well as a supportive and nurturing atmosphere. For example, consistent
limit-setting, clear rules, and predictable routines help children know
what to expect. This in turn helps them feel calmer, safer and more
secure. When children perceive their classroom as a stable, secure
place, and feel that teachers genuinely care about them as individuals,
they begin to develop the emotional resources necessary to deal with
the less predictable world outside.

Accept students' emotions and emotional responses

It is important to remember that when children respond with emotional outbursts, these behaviors are not intentional nor are they a
deliberate attempt to make teaching difficult. Accept the fact that it
is normal for all young children at times to sulk, respond to authority
by yelling, slamming something down, hitting, or to want to withdraw
and be left alone. Understand that some children will more readily
dysregulate or fall apart emotionally than others and that this is not
necessarily a sign of a spoiled, neglected, or abused child. Rather, it
may reflect a child whose temperament is more impulsive, a child with
delayed language skills who cannot express his feelings appropriately,
or a child with ADHD who is so hyperactive and inattentive that he
has missed important social cues. While these emotional responses can
be draining and distressing for teachers, patience and acceptance are
crucial factors in helping scaffold students' ability to learn to cope with
their emotional responses. By tuning in and being understanding of
students' emotional states, teachers can help them tolerate increasing
amounts of emotional tension.

Express your own feelings

One way to help children learn to express feelings and to regulate their own emotional responses is for teachers themselves to use the language of feelings with their students. For example, in the soccer example we discussed earlier, the coach might have said something like this to the boy: *"I understand that it was frustrating to see your team lose after doing so well throughout the whole game. I feel disappointed that we lost. But the important thing is you played a really good game. You were doing your best, kept trying and you were good team members—you all really worked together and you were polite to the other team. I was proud of you."* Teachers who frequently use the language of emotions to express their own emotional states and to interpret others' (nonverbal) emotional expressions and intentions, who talk about feelings so that children learn to identify emotions accurately and become accustomed to talking about feelings, are providing their students with a powerful mechanism for emotional regulation. Their students will be less likely to resort to behavioral outbursts of negative emotions. Research has suggested that children who learn to use emotional language have more control over their nonverbal emotional expressions, which in turn enhances the regulation of emotions themselves. By using the language of feelings and the emotion coaching methods described in Chapter Four, teachers transfer a useful coping skill to their students, model how they cope with particular feelings, and focus on their ability to successfully manage disappointment and frustration. In contrast, teachers who use language to intellectualize their emotions or to talk themselves or their students "out of" a particular emotion will encourage the use of an overcontrolled coping style. For example, "Cheer up and act like a grown up. You lost, but it's just a game. There's no use in being sad about it." This type of comment will teach children to hide, deny, or bottle up their emotions rather than to regulate them.

Avoid "letting it all hang out"

One fad for coping with anger has been to encourage children to let out their feelings by screaming and hitting pillows or punching bags. The theory was that humans were like a boiling tea kettle and needed to release the bottled up anger from their system. However, there is absolutely no evidence that encouraging verbal and physical aggression in any way reduces problems with anger control. In fact, it seems to actually encourage its expression! Thus it is never a good idea to encourage children to behave aggressively when they are angry, not even to toys and other objects. Instead, teachers can encourage appropriate verbal expression of anger and appropriate physical release of tension such as blowing out a deep breath, saying "I'm so mad, but I'm going to control my anger and blow it away," running or walking fast, or jumping up and down. Relaxing or distracting activities such as reading, coloring, stacking blocks, feeding the fish, or helping the teacher with an activity could also be encouraged. These strategies are far more likely to help a child cool off in a productive way.

Encourage students to talk about feelings — Avoid directives about feelings

The fact that children do not talk much about their emotions may be due to both lack of emotional literacy and inexperience and to having experienced their parents' or teachers' disapproval of the expression of emotion or of a certain kind of emotion. For example Billy, who cried when he lost the soccer game, might have been told: "Stop crying like a baby and get mad instead." When adults give directives about emotional expression, children may find it difficult to stay in touch with their true feelings and therefore have problems regulating their emotions. Avoid statements such as, "Don't be sad," or "You shouldn't be angry about that." Instead, label the child's feelings accurately and encourage the child to talk about the emotion: "I see you are sad about that: Can you tell me what happened?" As the child tells you about his experience, listen carefully without judging or giving advice. Sometimes it can be helpful for the teacher to share a past experience that matches the child's. For example, "I remember a time when I dropped the ball and it caused us to lose the game. I felt terrible. But you know I decided to really practice my skills and I became a better team player."

It is important for children to understand that, just as one child likes broccoli and another doesn't, people can have quite different feelings about the same event and there is not a right or wrong feeling for a particular situation. It is also important for them to understand that a person may even have more than one feeling at the same time. The crucial lesson to teach students is that there is nothing wrong with any feeling; all feelings are normal and natural. Some feelings are comfortable and nice inside while others hurt, but they are all real and important. As teachers we are trying to teach children to control their behavior and thoughts, not their feelings. Teachers can help give their students the message that while it is not always okay to act on our feelings, it is always okay to talk about them.

The ability to talk about emotions helps children regulate their negative emotions and behaviors and also gives them far greater power to express affection and concern, to ask for and receive affection, and to achieve new intimacy in their relationships with their peer group as well as their teachers.

A word of caution here: remember in Chapter Four, we talked about the risk of labeling and attending to more negative than positive feelings. When teachers do this, it's likely that children will actually begin to experience higher rates of negative feelings, because they receive the subtle message that these feelings are more important. This can also happen when adults devote much more time to talking about and processing negative than positive experiences. A teacher who is always empathic and ready to sympathize with a child who is sad, mad, or frustrated, but rarely comments on positive emotions, may inadvertently signal to the child that she places more value on the negative emotions. The goal is to pair discussions of negative feelings with gentle suggestions for coping strategies and to make sure to devote even more time to processing of positive emotions. Additionally, it is important to gauge the level of a child's emotional dysregulation before trying to talk about feelings. A child who is unhappy but is able to communicate with a teacher is in a prime state for learning from the discussion. A child who is so unhappy that he or she cannot hear or respond to the teacher's words will not benefit from a discussion. At times like this, it is better to give one brief label to the

The goal is to pair discussions of negative feelings with gentle suggestions for coping strategies and to make sure to devote even more time to processing positive emotions.

emotion and then give the child space to calm down. For example, "I see you are too frustrated to be able to talk now. Let me know when you have calmed down and we can talk about this and figure out a solution." Trying to communicate with a child who is emotionally out of control may exacerbate or reinforce the negative emotion.

USE GAMES AND ACTIVITIES TO PROMOTE FEELING LANGUAGE

Circle time is an ideal place for discussing feelings and playing feeling games. The following are some examples of games you might play with students to encourage the development of feeling language and to help them understand the facial and auditory clues which indicate particular feelings.

GAMES AND ACTIVITIES
PROMOTING FEELING LANGUAGE

Wally's Feeling Wheel Game©
The children sit in a circle and take turns spinning the arrow and watch as it lands on a feeling face. The teacher can then have the children process that feeling in a number of different ways: sharing a time they have had that feeling, making that feeling face, talking about how to cope with the feeling, acting out the feeling, demonstrating how their body looks when it shows the feeling, or using their voice to represent the feeling. This wheel may also be used by children to point to the feeling they have during times when they cannot put a name to the feeling. It can be used when reading books to ask children to identify the feelings of the character in the book at different times. Teachers who don't have a spinning wheel may make a similar game by cutting out pictures of feeling faces from magazines, laminating the

pictures and putting them into a feeling box or envelope. Children can take turns picking feeling faces and then use the ideas listed above to explore the feeling face that they have drawn. These games can also be played with actual photographs of the children themselves in the class showing their various feeling faces.

© *Incredible Years*®

Feeling Dice

Tape a square cardboard box closed (putting some beans or rocks in to make a rattling noise). Decorate each side with feeling faces from a magazine, photographs of children in the class, or faces drawn by the children. Children take turns rolling the dice and discussing or acting out the feelings that are rolled.

Listening Feeling Detective Game

In this game the children close their eyes while one child says something in a tone of voice that may sound happy, angry, frustrated, sad or worried. The children are asked to identify the feeling from the child's voice and say why they think the person may be feeling that way. Here the children are looking for clues to feelings through the sounds of voices.

Watching Feeling Detective Game

In this game the children take turns making faces (without making sounds) and the children try to guess the feeling. Another variation of this game is to show some of the feeling DVD vignettes from the *Understanding and Detecting Feelings Program* in the *Dinosaur Curriculum* (Webster-Stratton, 1990) with the sound track turned off and ask the children to name the feelings of the children on the video. This could also be done using magazine pictures. The key here is to have children focus on the visual clues that provide them with clues to read the feeling. After children have identified the feeling, they might be asked to make their faces look the same way, or talk about what might have caused the feeling.

Making Feeling Masks

In this art project and game give the children paper plates with holes for eyes and ask them to draw a feeling face (without telling anyone what feeling they are drawing). When their feeling masks are completed, the children guess each other's feelings and tell a time when they felt that way.

Food Feeling Games

Children can make edible feeling faces using pita bread or tortillas for the background, peanut butter or cream cheese for "glue," and cut up fruit or vegetables for expressive facial features.

See Dina Dinosaur's Social, Emotional and Problem-Solving Curriculum for more faces for Wally.

CIRCLE TIME
Wally's Feeling Faces Game

This game may be played individually or during Circle Time. Give each student or pair of students an enlargement of Wally's face with cut out mouths representing different feelings (smile, grimace, open mouth excitement, angry snarl). Teachers who do not have the Wally faces template can make up their own version of this game. An internet search for "feeling faces" will yield many different examples of expressive faces that could be used.

   Children listen to the following story and change the facial expressions on their models to match the feelings in the story. Teachers may add to this story to create scenarios representing different emotions or can use the Wally puppet to tell the story.

Wally was having a rough day

1. It all started when a boy in Wally's class called him a monkey face. Look for the mouth that shows how Wally felt when he was called a monkey face.
2. At lunch nobody wanted him to sit at their table. Look for the mouth that shows how Wally felt to be left out.
3. When Wally finished his lunch, he walked by the fifth grade table and accidentally knocked over Mark's milk. Mark, who was a fifth grader, said, "Hey kid! Get over here! I want to talk to you!"

Look for the mouth that shows how Wally felt when he saw the big angry boy.

4. Wally told himself to calm down. "I need to take three deep breaths he said."

Look for the mouth that shows Wally taking a deep breath.

5. Wally told the boy that he didn't mean to spill his milk and said that he was sorry. Then he said that he'd help wipe it up. Mark thought that this was really friendly of Wally and asked Wally if he wanted to play shadow tag with him and his friends.

Look for the mouth that shows how Wally felt to be included with the fifth graders.

After each step, the teacher and children can look around the room to see which mouth different students picked out. Children can talk about the mouths that they picked and the feeling represented.

This game can be played with many variations of feeling stories using situations that are relevant to children in the class. Feeling faces or mouths can be pasted on popsicle sticks so that children can make up plays using the faces as puppets popping up from the theatre to express their feelings. Children can also take turns telling their own stories.

USE GAMES AND ACTIVITIES TO PROMOTE UNDERSTANDING OF THE FEELINGS OF OTHERS

A key dimension to social success is the child's ability to not only communicate his own feelings but also to consider the concerns and feelings of others (Putallaz & Wasserman, 1990). If the child cannot take the perspective of another, he may also misperceive the social cues, mislabel feelings and not know how to respond appropriately. The teacher can use circle time to promote children's discussions of different feelings and perspectives in different situations. The games described below can be used during circle time to help children to think about different feelings and different reasons why people might have those feelings. These games will help children learn empathy skills.

GAMES AND ACTIVITIES
Promoting Understanding of Feelings of Others

Picture Feeling Detective

In this game you can cut out pictures of people and events from various newspapers and magazines (and laminate them). The children take turns picking a picture from the feeling bag and identifying the feeling. Ask the children questions such as:

- How do you think he or she is feeling? Is there another word for that feeling?
- What clues tell you that? (eyes, mouth, teeth, body, etc.)
- Why do you think he or she feels that way?
- What do you suppose happened to make him or her feel that way?
- What do you think will happen next? (predicting)
- What can he or she do to feel differently? (using coping strategy to manage difficult feelings)

Variations of this game can be played with any of the materials listed in the prior box (feeling wheel, feeling dice, and with almost any children's book).

Wally's "How Would You Feel If" Game

Wally (or any other puppet) asks the children to act out how they would feel in the situations listed below. Then depending on the children's level of development and ability to communicate feelings, this exercise can be taken further by asking, "what do you think happens next?" Then ask, "how might you feel then?" and "how do you think the other person feels?" The ability to predict feelings and anticipate consequences is a difficult skill for young children, especially if they do not yet have the words to describe feelings. If this is the case, the teacher should first focus on the child learning the words for communicating feelings and detecting clues to understanding the feelings of themselves and others. The next phase will be to help the children anticipate why they might have these feelings and what they will do to cope with those feelings. The final phase is recognizing the feelings in others, understanding they might be different from their own feelings and learning how to be empathic and offer support.

Wally Asks How Would You Feel If?

- You fall off your bike and hit your head. (sad, hurt, pain)
- You don't get invited to a classmate's birthday party. (disappointment, sad)
- Your mom tells you can have a friend overnight.(excitement)
- A student refuses to let you play on the team with the others. (anger, left out)

- Your teacher says something nice to you. (happy, proud)
- You lost your new baseball mitt. (sad, worried)
- An adult yells at you. (fear, anxious)
- Your sister changes the channel when you have been watching a good program. (anger, frustration)
- A student pushes you and tells you to get out of the way. (sad, anger)
- You get to go to a big waterside. (happy, excited, or afraid)
- You accidentally step in dog poo. (disgusted)
- You don't know anyone at the new summer camp.(afraid, shy)
- Your mother makes lima beans for dinner. (happy, disgusted)
- Your teacher puts your drawing on the board.(proud, embarrassed)
- You have been invited to a party. You love parties but you won't know anyone there. (excited, shy)
- Your parents are divorced. It is time to leave your dad's house. You have had a great time and wish you could stay longer. As you pack you think about your mom and brother at home and can't wait to see them. (sad and excited)
- You solve a problem with your friend. (brave, donfident, friendly)

I feel worried when...

This game can be played when children are old enough to read and write and helps promote empathy and sensitivity to others. Each child is given a slip of paper with the sentence, "I feel worried when..." to be completed. Then they put their anonymous response in a container placed in the center of the circle. Then each student takes a turn drawing out a worry and trying to explain why it would be a worry. The teacher can help the children understand how people have worries about different things. Variations on this game can be played by changing the feeling stem to any other feeling (proud, excited, scared). Each feeling that is explored will expand children's understanding of the range of different responses and feelings that people have. The teacher should also participate in this game so that students understand that adults also have these feelings.

GAMES AND ACTIVITIES
for Promoting Understanding of Changing Feelings

Changing Feelings

Another variation of the "How You Would Feel If" Game is to describe a situation and then ask the children to say, "I used to feel _____ about (situation—see list below) and now I feel _____ about the situation." The point of this game is help children understand that feelings can change over time and are not permanent. It also helps students think of some of the feelings brought on by change.

- Going to school
- Eating lima beans
- Going to the doctor (dentist)
- A brother or sister
- Learning to read
- Helping with chores
- When I moved to a new city
- When my brother was born and got all the attention
- When my parents divorced
- When my aunt died
- Having a bad haircut
- Having to talk in front of class

Wally's Accident Detection Game

In this game the children practice thinking about the difference between an accident and things that are done on purpose. The teacher asks the children to discuss whether they think the following things might have been done as an accident or on purpose. Once the students have discussed the intention involved, the teacher can ask the students to practice or role play the accidental situations and help the students think about the feelings involved and how to offer an apology or repair the friendship. This game is very helpful for students who frequently have hostile attributions about anything that happens to them.

Wally's Accident Detection Game (continued)

- Not watching when you pick up your baseball glove, and picking up your friend's glove instead.
- Throwing a ball that hits another child in the chest.
- Pulling the cat's tail.
- Hiding your sister's candy, which she bought with her allowance.
- Hitting a friend because he hit you.
- Not looking when you reach to get the milk and spilling your brother's milk.
- Calling another child names.
- Sitting at your seat with your feet out and someone trips over them.
- Forgetting to wish your friend happy birthday.

TEACHING STUDENTS SELF-CALMING AND RELAXATION STRATEGIES

To control anger, children must first learn to label their feelings and then to develop self-calming strategies. When they know they have ways to "cool down" their anger or reduce their sadness or manage their fears, they gain a sense of self-control and can prevent the build up of emotions that lead to tantrums and outbursts or tears and withdrawal. The following relaxation and imagery exercises can be used by teachers to teach students some self-calming strategies:

CIRCLE TIME
Games and Activities for Learning to Calm Down

Raggedy Wally and the Tin Man (or Robot Man)

This exercise helps children begin to recognize when they are relaxed and when they are tense. First children practice being the tin man (or a robot) by walking stiffly around the room, tensing up their arms and legs. Then they practice taking three deep breaths ("smell a flower and blow out a candle") to help relax their bodies. As they relax they become a "raggedy Wally" with limp and floppy arms, legs, and head, just like a soft rag doll or cooked spaghetti. The children practice making each part of their body limp until their entire body is limp. Then on a secret cue, they fall to the floor limp and relaxed. During each part of this game, the teacher repeatedly labels the two feeling states "tense" and "relaxed."

Relaxation Imagery

Many children respond well to imagery exercises and these have been described for use in the classroom in a book by Hall (Hall, Hall, & Leech, 1990). The following are two relaxation scenarios from this book, which we have adapted for use with young children. Teachers ask the students to close their eyes and imagine they are lying on a cloud relaxing or in a safe place free from worries. Once students have had frequent practice going to these special relaxation places in their mind, they can be prompted to go there when the teacher notices they are beginning to get angry, anxious, or worried about something. When guiding students through relaxation imagery, it is ideal to have students lying on the floor, in a comfortable position. If this is not possible, they can also sit with their heads down on their desks. The scripts should be read slowly, in a calm and relaxing tone of voice.

CIRCLE TIME: LESSON SCRIPT
Learning to Relax

"The cloud feels soft."

Close your eyes because we are going to imagine we're somewhere else. Take a slow, deep breath…Let it out…Now, one more slow, deep breath…Let it out slowly…Today we are riding on a cloud… The cloud feels so soft…Let your arms hang down so your hand sinks down in the cloud…Let your feet sink down, wiggle your toes a little—how about your shoulders, they're sinking too…We're still lying on that big puffy cloud…The air is warm…Each time I say a part of your body, sink deeper in that soft cloud…(Teacher names various body parts.) Now you can open your eyes. I'd like to know how your body felt when you were floating on the cloud.

Visualizing a safe, relaxing place

Close your eyes…Take a slow, deep breath…Let it out…Take one more slow, deep breath…Let it out slowly and allow your body to relax…For a moment, I would like you to think about something that you're worried about.

Now think about a safe place you can go to where you don't need to worry about anything…Make a picture in your imagination of the sort of place you could go to where you would feel safe… What is this place like? Take a good look around…What sort of things do you like to have in your safe place?…What are the colors like?…What does it smell like?…What do the things in your safe place feel like?…Now, think about actually being in your safe place…What are you doing right now in this safe place?…How are you feeling?…You can stay in this place as long as you want…You can come back to this place whenever you need to…Try to hold onto these feelings as you gently come back to the room.

Note: Sometimes young children will call out their answers in response to the questions posed above. If this happens, sometimes it is better to rephrase the questions as statements.

CIRCLE TIME
Games and Activities

Deep Breathing

Deep breathing is a tried and true method for inducing relaxation. This breathing is most effective if the breaths are drawn in through the nose, held for a moment, and then slowly exhaled through the mouth. It is often difficult for young children to learn this breathing method. One helpful visualization is to have children imagine they are smelling a flower (breathe in through the nose) and then imagine they are blowing out a candle (out through the mouth). Teachers can help guide children effectively through this process by talking softy and slowly as they demonstrate the breaths. *"Smell the beautiful flower and hold it for just a minute. Now I want you to slowly blow out a birthday candle. See how gentle and quiet you can make your breath. This time we are going to try to do this with no noise from our voices. Silently smell the flower and silently blow out the candle."* Other imaginary images can be used for this practice exercise such as blowing up a balloon and letting it out.

Keep a "Happy Book"

Young children who are aggressive often get a lot of attention and discussion of their angry feelings. While this is worthwhile because it helps such children learn to verbalize feelings appropriately rather than acting them out in hurtful ways, it can sometimes result in an overemphasis of teacher attention on the anger emotion. Indeed, many of these children often only recognize their angry emotion and sometimes confuse this emotion with other feelings such as being excited, anxious, worried, sad, fearful or happy. It is important to help children learn to recognize their positive emotions and provide language for expressing a wide range of feelings. For students who are often sad or angry, we find it helpful to focus on times when they are pleased, happy, excited, calm, patient and proud. A teacher might want to start a Happy Book or Journal that includes examples of times when students were happy or celebrated special moments and feelings. Or, students may be asked to write in their journal about ways they coped with a frustrating or disappointed feeling by using a solution that helped them feel better.

See Dina Dinosaur's Triceratops Alphabet Feeling Journal on website:
www.incredibleyears.com/TeacherResources/index.asp

Model emotional regulation—stay calm

How do you handle your own negative emotions? Do you fly off the handle easily? Withdraw in sullen protest? Or, do you model effective self-regulation by verbalizing your feelings and using a calm-down strategy. Teachers should remember that adult modeling is another important factor that contributes to children's ability to regulate emotions. Children who are exposed to frequent displays of uncontrolled anger, frustration, or depression are more likely to express their own emotions in these ways. While much of this modeling is learned from parents, how teachers manage their everyday frustrations in the classroom is also likely to be imitated by students. Teachers can help students by remaining calm and appropriately verbalizing emotions and their strategies for coping. For example, a teacher who is getting frustrated by her students' lack of attention to an instruction for an assignment, might say out loud, "I'd better stop and calm down and relax a little before I continue. I'm getting frustrated because people aren't listening, and I don't want to make things worse. Maybe if I take a deep breath now I'll figure out what it is I need to do next." Or, "I'll be ready to keep going once I calm down. I need a break. Then I'll be ready to deal with this." As always, it is important that teachers model the kind of behavior they expect their students to exhibit.

Teachers should model staying calm, coping strategies and positive emotional states.

In addition to labeling and demonstrating coping strategies for negative emotions, teachers should model talking about positive emotional states. For example, "I'm really proud of myself today. I made a special effort to get up early so that I would be at school in time to set up our activity. It's hard for me to wake up in the morning, but I did it!" Or, "I'm really excited today because my sister is coming into town. I haven't seen her for a long time. It's hard for me to wait till I can go pick her up!" Of course, teachers are human and do get angry, make mistakes and lose their patience with students from time to time. Apologizing to students when this happens does not diminish teachers' authority but rather enhances it. A teacher apology helps students to realize that everyone makes mistakes and can learn from the experience.

One teacher explained to her class her problem with getting cross, "I sometimes feel irritable and angry, and I'd like you to help me during that time. So I am going to put on this hat whenever I feel that way, and I wonder if you can try to be extra quiet during that time." This teacher's approach of asking for help from her students can really foster team spirit in the class.

It is particularly crucial to stay calm yourself when your student's emotional responses are escalating. Sometimes when a child is frustrated or shows increasing tension and anger about something, a teacher responds with additional anxiety or frustration. Instead, the teacher should try to offer calm and soothing words of advice, perhaps even a stroke on his arm or back. Such support often can help children calm themselves enough to able to state how they are feeling.

Teach children positive self-talk about the event

When children experience a negative emotion such as anger, frustration, fear, or discouragement, often there are underlying thoughts that accompany the emotion that reinforce or intensify it, and may even be causing it. These thoughts are sometimes referred to as "self-talk," although children will often express them aloud. For example, a child who is feeling discouraged may say to the teacher or to himself, "I'm just a failure," " I can't do anything right," " I might as well give up," "You don't like me," "You're just trying to make me fail," "I'm the worst in the class," or "No one ever helps me," or "I will kill myself."

In the soccer example, Billy and Eric may have been reacting differently because they are telling themselves different things about the incident. If asked why he cried, Billy might have said, "My dad will be so disappointed with me that we lost the game. I am such a bad player." If Dan were asked why he got angry, he might have said, "It was not fair, the other team was cheating." While Billy responds with negative self-talk, and Dan by blaming the other players, in both cases they were caught up in negative behavioral responses and negative thoughts and

Children can be taught to identify negative self-talk and to substitute positive self-talk.

emotions that might have been averted if they had said something different to themselves such as, "I did my best," "I can do it, it just takes practice, everyone loses sometimes" or "It feels really good to win, but part of the fun is just playing the game the best that I can."

Research indicates that children whose "self-talk" is negative get angry more easily than children whose self-talk is positive. Children can be taught to identify negative self-talk and to substitute positive self-talk. Teachers can help students to combat their inevitable frustrations and insults by thinking or verbalizing thoughts that calm them down, help them control themselves, or put the situation in perspective. For example, when a child is teased by another child, the teacher can encourage her to stay calm by thinking to herself, "I can handle it. I will just ignore him. It is not worth getting upset about. I can stay calm, I am strong." In the soccer illustration above, the teacher might prompt the child to begin thinking this way by saying, "Tell yourself, 'I did my best, my dad will be proud of that,' or, 'We played a great game. Someone has to lose. We are good sports. I am a good team player.'" In this way children learn to regulate their cognitive responses, which in turn, will affect their behavioral and physiological responses.

Learning to use positive self-talk is an extremely difficult process, one which many adults struggle with. Preschool and elementary school aged children will need frequent teacher coaching before they can do this on their own. This is a skill that is worth the effort, however, for it will be useful for regulating negative emotions for the rest of the child's life! Teachers may also find that as they teach children to use positive self-talk, they begin to find it an effective technique for themselves.

Examples of positive self-talk:
    "Take three breaths."
    "Think happy."
    "I'm not going to let it get to me."
    "I am not going to blow my cool."
    "Everyone gets teased at times."
    "I can handle this."
    "I can calm down."

"I have other friends who like me."

"He didn't do it on purpose, it was an accident."

"Everyone makes mistakes. No one is that perfect.
  I'll do better next time."

"With more practice, I'll get it."

"She's just in a bad mood today. She'll be better later."

"I'll calm down and use my brave talk."

"My friends still like me even if I make mistakes."

"I'll feel happier in a little while."

"Just stay cool."

"It's no big deal."

"Take a deep breath."

Teach students the "Turtle Technique" and practice frequently

Teaching students to use positive self-talk and problem-solving strategies (see Chapter 12) provides them with a means of emotional regulation on the cognitive level. However, it is sometimes necessary to help children deal with the neurophysiological/biochemical aspects of emotional arousal. For example, some children, or all children in some situations, may become so physically agitated with a racing heart and rapid breathing that they have no control over their thoughts or behaviors. In these situations, prompts to use self-talk, discuss their feelings, or to problem solve will not be effective; their physiological arousal produces cognitive disorganization that makes conscious thought extremely difficult. In the long run all the strategies discussed in this chapter will help to reduce physiological arousal, but, at times the student may need additional suggestions for how to calm down. Researchers have found that the "turtle technique" is an effective way for children to calm down and a good first step before engaging in problem solving.

It can be very helpful to use a turtle puppet to practice this activity with children. The teacher asks students to imagine they have a shell, like a turtle, where they can retreat when they are getting angry. Students are first prompted to stop their bodies (to halt automatic

1

2 Think STOP

3 Take a slow breath

4 Withdrawing into shell

I'LL TRY AGAIN

5

aggressive response). Then the teacher coaches them to go into their imaginary shells, take three deep quiet breaths, and say to themselves, "Stop, take a deep breath and say 'I can do it. I can calm down.'" As students are taking these slow deep breaths, the teacher asks them to focus on their breathing and to push the air into their arms and legs so they can relax their muscles. As the students continue this slow breathing, the teacher coaches them to repeat to themselves, "I can calm down. I can do it. I can control my anger." Students are coached to stay in their shells until they feel calm enough to come out and try again. Students might also be encouraged to go in their imaginary happy place during this breathing time. Some children will need quite a bit more time than others to get their physiological reaction under control. When students come out, the teacher praises them and gives them feedback for their efforts.

Young children will love the opportunity to practice going into a "real" turtle shell. Teachers might make a turtle shell from a large box, a table with a blanket over the top, or a green blanket. Older children will be ready to visualize imaginary turtle shells, and may enjoy thinking of their shells as imaginary forcefields that no one else can see.

At first these turtle steps are practiced only when children are in calm states. The teacher might ask each student to imagine something that makes him or her angry or may suggest an anger-evoking scenario to act out. It is important that you teach and practice this calming self-talk script with your students frequently because eventually you want the actual words, "stop, take a deep breath, calm down, and think I can do it" to trigger a calming response and internal language within the child when faced with a real-life conflict situation. You might also want to read the book, *Wally Learns a Lesson from Tiny Turtle* to your students or show the Tiny Turtle video vignette from the Dinosaur curriculum to enhance this learning (Webster-Stratton, 1990).

See www.incredibleyears.com/program/child.asp

In addition to the teaching and role play practicing, teachers can model this "turtle technique" themselves for students. For example, a teacher who is getting irritated because students are taking so long to settle in their desks after recess might say, "I'm getting frustrated because students are taking so long to settle down and listen to me. I better go into my shell for a while and calm down. Guess I better use my turtle power and take some deep breaths... I better say to myself, 'Stop, take a deep breath and calm down and think.' Well, I feel better. I better think of another plan. Maybe I will give calm down stickers to those who are sitting in their seats already."

Practice using self-regulation strategies in hypothetical situations

It is important to remember that it will take a long time for students to be able to transfer emotional regulation strategies like the turtle technique from the hypothetical imaginary situations to real-life conflict. It is helpful for children to practice responding to hypothetical situations that normally trigger their angry responses. Once they learn to anticipate such situations and have some practice using strategies for dealing with them, they are more likely to be able to use a regulation strategy when feeling real anger. It is important when doing these practice role plays that an attempt is made to simulate the intensity of feelings that occurs when the situation actually occurs in real life. Through the use of puppets, real examples of conflict situations can be presented. For example, common scenarios are: fights with a sibling over who sits in the front seat, being teased and called names by peers, being yelled at by a teacher or parent, being left out, being bullied, and being prevented from doing or having something they want.

CIRCLE TIME
Detective Hat Game
Practicing Anger Control

The Detective Hat game is fun and an easy way to initiate role play and practice of anger control skills with your students. The questions listed below are designed to practice the following responses: calming self-talk ("Cool down. Take it easy. I can do it. Use my brave talk. If I fight I could get into a lot of trouble. I'm stronger than him; I won't fight."), deep breathing, positive imagery (think of your happy or safe place) thinking about the consequences of fighting or arguing, using your brave talk about your feelings, staying out of a battle and accepting consequences. Scenarios or questions are written on slips of paper and placed in the detective hat. The hat is passed around the circle in time to music. When the music stops, the child holding the hat draws out a paper and reads it to the class. This leads to discussion, role play, and practice of the strategies. Some suggestions for questions include the following:

- What can you think about when you are in your turtle shell?
- Wally's face looks angry—how can you tell if he really is angry?
- Why is it important not to fight?
- A friend makes fun of what you wear to school and then says you are stupid and fat. What can you do to control your anger?
- A kid won't get off the swing and you have already waited 10 minutes and are getting angry. What can you do to stay calm?
- Where are some places you can go to calm down?
- What are some nice thoughts which might help you calm down?
- What usually happens after Time Out?
- Your mother asked you to clean up the living room, and your friend won't help even though you both made the mess.
- A classmate bumps into you and you trip and hurt yourself. (He doesn't say he is sorry.) What do you think to yourself?

- You're playing at a friend's house and s/he doesn't want to do anything you want to do. What can you do?
- A classmate accuses you of cheating on a board game. What can you do to stay calm?
- A classmate teases you because you aren't able to read. How do you know if you are angry?
- A kid grabs your ball away from you. What can you do?
- Your parent tells you, "You're always in trouble, you never help, or share with your sister and you don't try." What can you do to handle your anger?
- Some kids are playing tag but they won't let you play with them. You think they hate you. What can you do about these thoughts?
- Your dad says he won't take you to the baseball game because you fought with your sister.
- You lost the privilege of going on a field trip because of your behavior. What can you do to deal with your disappointment?
- You are playing basketball and are constantly being beaten by the other kids.
- You are having a bad day, what can you do to feel better?

Use calm down thermometer to self-monitor

A calm down thermometer can be a useful way to teach self-control and to monitor a student's mood and self-regulation efforts. Teachers can use the thermometer pictured here or make one together with their students. It is useful to put a strip of Velcro along the side of the thermometer and attach an arrow. This way, students can use the arrow to show where their feelings are on the thermometer. Children often enjoy decorating the thermometer with pictures of calm and angry faces and of a calm-down turtle. Students might add numbers to the thermometer from 1 to 10 with "one" indicating very calm or cool and "ten" indicating very hot. Students and teachers discuss the different points on the thermometer and situations that would lead to feeling "red hot mad"

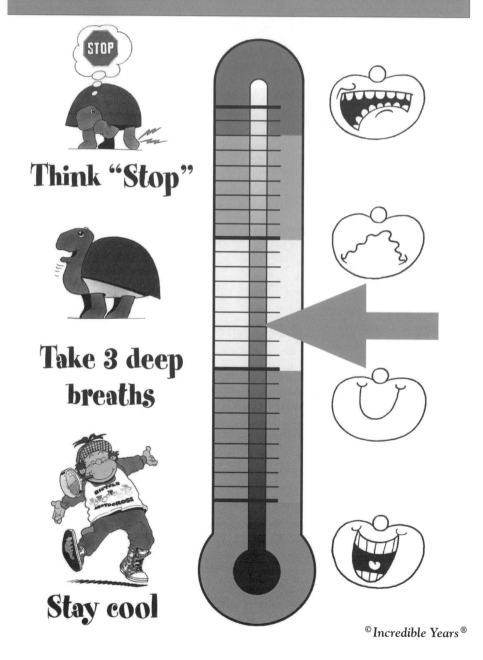

© Incredible Years®

and "cool blue." As with the turtle technique, the thermometer should first be taught and practiced in hypothetical situations—any of the scenarios above could be connected with the thermometer. "Where would your body be on the thermometer if your brother took your model plane and broke it?" Teachers and students then talk about the fact that being at the top of the thermometer means being in the "danger zone" where it is hard to be in control of one's actions. This is not a safe place to be and is likely to lead to making unsafe choices with bad consequences. Next students practice different ways to move out of the "danger zone" (turtle technique, deep breathing, relaxation, calm/happy thought, thinking of happy or safe place or counting to 10). As they practice these techniques, they gradually move the arrow down the thermometer until they have reached a cooler, more relaxed state. At this point, they are ready to talk, process, and problem solve. After students have learned to use the thermometer in hypothetical situations, teachers can begin to direct them to use the thermometer at times of real anger.

CIRCLE TIME: LESSON SCRIPT
Explaining the Calm Down Thermometer

Teacher: Wally has a problem he wants to share with you today. Wally, can you let us know what happened?

Wally: Well, someone knocked down the block tower when I was building and I was soooooo mad.

Teacher: Children, how does that feel when that happens to you?

Child: Mad, that happened to me and I was mad!

Teacher: That is so frustrating. You felt just like Wally did. I think Wally has a trick to share that can help you feel better. Wally, what did you do to stop your anger?

Wally: I have a special trick and it helps me to calm down. I take three deep breaths and then try to change my mad feelings. My mom showed me this thermometer and that helps me remember how to do it. (*Puppet models three deep breaths and how to say "I can calm down."*)

Teacher: Thanks Wally. Now lets take those breaths with Wally as he does it. (*Lead children in taking deep breaths and saying, "I can do it, I can calm down."*) Take a look at this thermometer, what do you notice? (*Children will answer with varied ideas, the colors, the pictures on it. Use this brainstorm to validate their ideas and teach them why the thermometer looks the way it does and how they can use it.*)

Wally: Yeah it has lots of different colors on it. When I am mad I feel red hot! That's when I am mad or frustrated. At the bottom of the thermometer it is blue. It reminds me of cool water.

Teacher: And as you move down the thermometer, you can change your feelings back into happy ones using Wally's trick. Okay, let's try it. Pretend your ice cream just fell off your cone and now you can't eat it. Show me on your faces how you might feel…. I see lots of angry faces. Your mouths are tight, you don't have any smiles. Frances will you come up and show me where the arrow is on the thermometer when you feel mad. Like if your ice cream fell on the ground? (*Child moves arrow.*) Yes! Right at the top, mad and frustrated. Class, let's take deep breaths and see if we can change our feelings just like Wally did in the block area. (*Encourage children to take deep breaths along with you.*) Oh I see some calm faces. How are you feeling now?

Child: Happy, can I move the arrow?

Teacher: Sure.

(*Continue practicing with new scenarios allowing kids to move arrow and then move to small group practice.*)

Help children recognize body cues that signal the build up of tension

The first "early warning" stage of anger or negative emotion is familiar to every teacher or parent. The child grumbles under his breath, looks grouchy, and sulks around the classroom. In the second stage the child becomes increasingly tense, restless, and moody; no matter what is suggested, nothing seems to satisfy or interest him. An explosive outburst may occur at the slightest provocation. The child may shout, curse, or even break something. He usually resists the teacher's efforts at control at this outburst stage and may increase his opposition to anything the teacher says. In the third stage, after the tantrum subsides, depression or remorse may replace aggression; it is the "leave me alone" stage. The child is sad or placid and does not want to interact with his teachers or peer group. In the final fourth stage, the child is ready to resume normal activities and may act as if nothing had happened.

The point for teachers to intervene with suggestions of "turtle technique" or prompting the calming self-talk script or relaxation methods discussed earlier is in the first stage. The second or third stages are the least teachable moments. Often in the first stage children are not aware of their physiological signs of distress nor are they even aware they are becoming angry or frustrated. Consequently, they will not communicate these feelings until they emerge in a full-blown tantrum. Therefore it is helpful for teachers to be alert to the warning stages and help children become more self-aware of these early physiological signals of anger or distress and to encourage them to process these feelings before losing control. You might say, "I can tell by your muttering that something seems to be bothering you. Can I help in any way?" If your student has difficulty expressing herself, you might try to put into words what you suspect the child is thinking and feeling. For example, "I hear you that you seem unhappy. I'm wondering if you are feeling jealous that other students are using the computers first today." Or, you might also ask the child to point to a calm down

Teachers are most effective when intervening at the first stage of anger build up with calm down strategies.

thermometer to indicate how he or she is feeling. Teachers' understanding and concern at this stage can go a long way toward reducing the build up of negative and angry feelings. Once the child learns to recognize the early physiological signs of distress, she can be signaled to use calming procedures such as deep breathing, the "turtle technique" and calming self-talk, positive imagery and relaxation exercises to prevent further escalation.

Another possible time to intervene is in the fourth stage, after the incident is over. At this point, the teacher can lead the child through the feelings, self-regulation, and problem-solving steps. Discussing the event helps promote better understanding in the child of what the triggers are that set him off (e.g., teasing), why it happened, and how he might handle it differently next time. The discussion should include how you and the child each felt about the episode, the causes and early warning signals, alternative ways to solve the problem in the future. Furthermore, once the child and teacher understand what triggered the child's loss of control, they can begin to role play and practice how to handle these stressful situations. During this discussion is it important that the teacher not focus on the child's negative behavior during the event, for this will draw attention to and remind them of images of any misbehavior they demonstrated. Instead, you

want the attention and focus to be on the self-regulation behavior. If the child's outburst resulted in a behavior that needs to be remedied, then that should be addressed calmly and separately, "Okay, your body looks calm. Please clean up the paint that is on the floor." After this is done, then the teacher could process the feelings. "I know that you were really angry that your painting didn't look the way you wanted. That's frustrating. I wonder what solutions you could use if that happens again. Can you think of a way that you could have calmed down? We could practice that together."

Using the puppets can be a very effective way of helping children learn to recognize the early signals of escalating anger and arousal.

Here is an example of a possible script:

CIRCLE TIME: LESSON SCRIPT
Wally teaches about early signals of anger

Wally: I kind of had a problem at school today. It was recess time, you know, and I was out by myself on the playground and I was building some Star Wars stuff out of sand. I was making a big destroyer and a falcon. And when I was out there by myself I saw Tony, Dave and Ian. They're three cool popular guys, and they were walking towards me. I was getting all excited because I knew they had brought their Star Wars toys, and I thought maybe they wanted to come play with me. I was all excited, and when they got over, they started teasing me. They said, "Look at Wally, he has nobody to play with him. Look at the dumb Star Wars stuff he made. Our toys are much cooler." Oh man... I felt my hands ball up in fists and my face get red and I felt like exploding. Then I remembered these feelings in my body were signals that I was getting angry and that I had to stop, think and calm down. Have any of you ever noticed how other people signal when they are getting angry? You know like your parents or teachers?

Students: *(Students discuss what they notice when their parents or teachers or friends get angry.)*

Wally: You know I can always tell when my teacher is angry because his jaw clenches and twitches. What does your body do when you get angry? Does anyone find their fists get tight like mine do? What does your body do when you get angry?

Students: *(Students discuss their own body reactions and what they notice in each other.)*

Wally: Wow you all have body signals that tell you when you are angry. So what are you going to do next time you feel this happening?

(Brainstorm solutions such as going in turtle shell and saying stop, calm down think; or taking deep breath and blowing out a candle, or counting backwards, or thinking of happy place.)

Praise students' efforts to regulate their emotions

Teachers should be sure to praise students for handling their frustration without losing control of their anger. For example, "I am really pleased that you kept trying and working hard even though you were losing." Research has shown that aggressive and impulsive children receive more critical feedback, negative commands and less praise than other children, even when they are behaving appropriately (Hawkins, Smith, & Catalano, 2004; Reinke & Herman, 2002; Stormont, Smith, & Lewis, 2007). In essence, they train their teachers not to praise or reinforce them for their positive behaviors because their emotional responses are so exhausting to deal with. However, they need positive feedback even more than other children, for when they are praised, they are likely not to notice or process it. This means teachers will have to work extra hard to catch all the patient behaviors to reinforce when they do occur.

Aggressive children need coaching and praise even more than others when they are calm and patient.

It is particularly important for teachers to use persistence and emotion coaching discussed in Chapter Four to highlight behaviors involving self-control with difficult tasks, appropriate expression of feelings (be they positive or negative), and control of emotional outbursts in frustrating or disappointing situations. Teachers should reinforce any calm, purposeful activities following a disappointment or frustrating event. For instance, "That was great, you have incredible patience muscles. You calmed yourself down, you made a good choice," or, "That was cool. You were patient and kept trying even though you were getting frustrated with that difficult math assignment." Students can also be taught to reinforce themselves with self-praise and positive self-talk: "I did a good job," or, "I stayed really calm, I am strong inside me. I was patient with myself and it paid off in the end. I made a good choice."

Teacher praise will help a student change a negative self-image to that of a person who is able to handle emotions. It's not necessary to wait until a student has become fully capable of emotional regulation. The "language of becoming" will express confidence in the student's future success. For example, "You are becoming a courageous person who can really control your anger (or fears) well. You are very strong inside." Teachers can help make this vision a reality.

Use Time Out for inappropriate emotional angry outbursts

No matter how proactive a teacher is with emotional support for students, there will be times when a student's anger escalates to the point where he or she is not in control. At these times the student may hit or lash out at another student or the teacher, or may have such a violent tantrum that the teacher feels the class is not safe. At this time, it is appropriate for the teacher to impose some structure that will allow the child to calm down safely. Remember that no amount of teacher comfort, scolding, or processing will penetrate when a student is emotionally out of control. When this happens, a Time Out to calm down will help the child regain emotional control and will reinforce the idea that there are limits and consequences for behaviors that are not safe. When giving a Time Out to a child who is out of control, the teacher should make a calm and direct statement: "Josh, your body is not safe. You need to take a Time Out to calm down." See Chapter Ten for details on enforcing Time Out to calm down.

Appropriate expression of negative feelings

As mentioned earlier, children need to know that all feelings are okay —anger, anxiety, sadness and other negative feelings are unavoidable and they are normal, but that there are different ways of expressing those feelings, and that they have a choice in how they express them. Children should be taught to put their negative feelings into words in ways that are assertive but not hostile. Teachers can help them learn the difference between sticking up for their rights and attempting to hurt someone else, and can praise them when they express difficult emotions in appropriate ways. For example, "I hate you. You are stupid" may accurately reflect how the child is feeling at the moment, but "I'm so mad at you because you ripped up my picture" is a more appropriate way to express the feeling and the problem. In addition, the other child's response to the first statement is likely to be escalating anger, while the second statement may begin to trigger remorse or empathy. In the long run, children who learn to make this type of "I" statement will have healthier adult relationships.

Work collaboratively with parents

Teachers will have even more success in helping students regulate their emotions if their parents are also using feeling language and the anger management strategies with their children. Teachers can communicate some of this content through parent letters that explain how some children mislabel feelings and why it is important for parents to accurately label their children's feelings. For example, the letter might ask parents to notice times when their children appear excited, happy, proud, worried, angry, calm, patient, frustrated, and sad and label those feelings. It is important that parents be encouraged to talk about happy, satisfied, relaxed and pleasant feelings, and not only angry, sad or frustrated feelings. In fact, more positive feelings should be modeled than angry or negative feelings. It is also important that children know that they are not to blame for their parents' negative feelings and that parents express confidence in children's ability to manage their disappointment or anger or sadness about a situation. Homework assignments can help parents and children explore feelings. For example, take turns labeling the feelings in magazine pictures, write down a happy thought for each person in the family, read a book and talk about the feelings of the characters. It is also important for parents to understand the Turtle Technique and to be able to coach children to go into their turtle shells, "stop, take a deep breath, calm down and think." Then whenever parents notice a child starting to get angry and out of control, they can cue their child's de-escalation responses. Encourage parents to stay with the exact scripted words, for it will be more effective in helping the child to become calm. When teachers and parents work together to support the use of these anger management strategies, children will have the necessary environmental support to learn to regulate their emotions. See website for examples of Teacher-to-Parent Communication letters about anger management.

http://www.incredibleyears.com/TeacherResources/index.asp

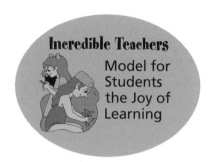

TO SUM UP...

**Helping Students Learn to Regulate their Emotions
and Control their Anger**

- Use feeling talk with your students and encourage them to talk about feelings to build their feelings literacy vocabulary.
- When talking about negative feelings, also focus on coping. strategies or positive thoughts to manage these feelings.
- Give more attention to positive feelings than negative feelings.
- Acknowledge individual developmental differences in students' ability to regulate emotions.
- Use games and activities to teach the language of feelings and to promote understanding of differences in others' feelings.
- Use Time Out to calm down for destructive or hurtful behavior.
- Teach children self-regulation skills such as positive imagery, use of happy place, deep breathing, and positive self-talk strategies.
- Teach the "Turtle Technique" or Calm Down thermometer for regulating emotions.
- Practice anger management responses to hypothetical conflict situations.
- Model emotional self-regulation skills in the classroom for students.
- Elicit the support of parents in managing anger and teaching children to coach and express their feelings and ways to self-regulate.

The Incredible Years®
Teacher Classroom Management Self-Reflection Inventory
Helping Students Manage their Emotional Self-Regulation

Date: _____ Teacher Name: _____

Teachers learn extensively from self-reflection regarding their class-room management and the teaching strategies they are using that are working or not working. From these reflections teachers determine per-sonal goals for making changes in their approaches to bring about the most positive learning climate they can. Use this Inventory to think about your strengths and limitations and determine your goals.

Emotional Regulation Skills	1 = NEVER 3 = OCCASIONALLY 5 = CONSISTENTLY
1. I use emotion-coaching and persistence language (e.g., patience, persistence, trying hard, sticking with it, concentrating, staying calm, waiting for a turn) to promote emotion literacy and self-regulation of emotions.	1 2 3 4 5
2. I model self-regulation strategies such as taking deep breaths, using positive self-talk, using anger thermometer, thinking of happy place and positive forecasting and imagery for my students.	1 2 3 4 5
3. I prompt children to take deep breaths and use coping self talk such as "I can do it, I can calm down."	1 2 3 4 5
4. I promote identification of feelings in self and others through the use of photographs, posters and games (bingo) that portray people in various emotional states.	1 2 3 4 5

5. I help children understand how peers feel by pointing out facial expressions, voice tone, body language or words to label their feelings.	1 2 3 4 5
6. I teach specific emotional literacy words by labeling feelings or positive feelings responses of others when children share, trade, wait or help them (i.e., help children see the connection between their behaviors and others' feelings).	1 2 3 4 5
7. I model appropriate feelings language by modeling emotional expression throughout the day (e.g., "I am getting frustrated now, but I can calm myself down by taking a deep breath or using my turtle technique.").	1 2 3 4 5
8. I use books and stories of common childhood scenarios to practice talking about the characters' feelings and thoughts.	1 2 3 4 5
9. I use puppets, pretend games, imaginary stories and drama activities to set up problem scenarios and children practice talking about their feelings.	1 2 3 4 5
10. I talk to parents of my students to help them understand how to teach their children emotion language.	1 2 3 4 5
11. I have developed behavior plans that target emotion language and self-regulation calm down steps for children according to their developmental abilities and target goals.	1 2 3 4 5
12. I pay more attention to positive emotions than negative emotions.	1 2 3 4 5
13. When I talk about negative emotions, I combine this emotion language with a coping thought or feeling (e.g., "you seem frustrated with that math problem but are staying patient and keep trying").	1 2 3 4 5

Future Goals Regarding Use of Emotional Self-Regulation Skills:	Total

REFERENCES

Asarnow, J. R., & Callan, J. W. (1985). Boys with peer adjustment problems: Social cognitive processes. *Journal of Consulting and Clinical Psychology, 53*, 80-87.

Asher, S. R., & Coie, J. D. (1990). *Peer rejection in childhood.* Cambridge: Cambridge University Press.

Asher, S. R., & Hymel, S. (1981). Children's social competence and peer relations: Sociometric and behavioral assessment. In J. D. Wine & M. D. Smye (Eds.), *Social Competence* (pp. 125-157). New York: Guilford Press.

Asher, S. R., Parkhurst, J. T., Hymel, S., & Williams, G. A. (1990). Peer rejection and loneliness in childhood. In Asher & J. D. Coie (Eds.), *Peer rejection in childhood* (pp. 253-273). Cambridge: Cambridge University Press.

Campbell, S. (1995). Behavior problems in preschool children: A review of recent research. *Journal of Child Psychology and Psychiatry & Allied Disciplines, 36*(1), 113-149.

Campbell, S. B. (1990). *Behavior problems in preschool children: Clinical and developmental issues.* New York: Guilford Press.

Campbell, S. B. (1994). Hard-to-manage preschool boys: externalizing behavior, social competence, and family context at two-year followup. *Journal of Abnormal Child Psychology, 22*(2), 147-166.

Campbell, S. B., Shaw, D. S., & Gilliom, M. (2000). Early externalizing behavior problems: Toddlers and preschoolers at risk for later maladjustment. *Development and Psychopathology, 12*, 467-488.

Coie, J. D. (1990). Adapting intervention to the problems of aggressive and disruptive rejected children. In Asher & J. D. Coie (Eds.), *Peer Rejection in Childhood* (pp. 309-337). Cambridge: Cambridge University Press.

Dishion, T. J., Patterson, G. R., Stoolmiller, M., & Skinner, M. L. (1991). Family, school, and behavioral antecedents to early adolescent involvement with antisocial peers. *Developmental Psychology, 27*(1), 172-180.

Dodge, K. A. (1985). Attributional bias in aggressive children. In P. C. Kendall (Ed.), *Advances in cognitive-behavioral research and therapy* (Vol. 4, pp. 73-110). Orlando, FL: Academic Press.

Dodge, K. A. (1993). Social-cognitive mechanisms in the development of conduct disorder and depression. *Annual Review of Psychology, 44,* 559-584.

Dodge, K. A., & Crick, N. R. (1990). Social information processing bases of aggressive behavior in children. *Personality and Social Psychology Bulletin, 16,* 8-22.

Dodge, K. A., Price, J. M., Bachorowski, J. A., & Newman, J. P. (1990). Hostile attributional biases in severely aggressive adolescents. *Journal of Abnormal Psychology, 99*(4), 385-392.

Gouze, K. R. (1987). Attention and social problem solving as correlates of aggression in preschool males. *Journal of Abnormal Child Psychology, 15,* 181-197.

Hall, E., Hall, C., & Leech, A. (1990). *Scripted Fantasy in the Classroom.* London: Nichols Publishing.

Hawkins, J. D., Smith, B. H., & Catalano, R. F. (2004). Social development and social and emotional learning. In J. E. Zins, R. P. Weissberg, M. C. Wang & H. J. Walberg (Eds.), *Building academic success on social and emotional learning: What does the research say?* (pp. 135-150). New York: Teachers College Press.

Larson, J. (1994). Violence prevention in the schools: A review of selected programs and procedures. *School Psychology Review, 23,* 151-164.

Lochman, J., Lampron, L., Gemmer, T., & Harris, S. (1987). Anger coping intervention with aggressive children: A guide to implementation in school settings. In P. A. Keller & S. R. Heyman (Eds.), *Innovations in clinical practice: A source book* (Vol. 6, pp. 339-356). Sarasota, FL: Professional Resource Exchange.

Lochman, J. E., & Dunn, S. E. (1993). An intervention and consultation model from a social cognitive perspective: A description of the anger coping program. *School Psychology Review, 22,* 458-471.

Milich, R., & Dodge, K. A. (1984). Social information processing in child psychiatric populations. *Journal of Abnormal Child Psychology, 12*(3), 471-489.

Mize, J., & Cox, R. A. (1990). Social knowledge and social competence: number and quality of strategies as predictors of peer behavior. *Journal of Genetics Psychology, 151*(1), 117-127.

Patterson, G., Reid, J., & Dishion, T. (1992). *Antisocial boys: A social interactional approach* (Vol. 4). Eugene, OR: Castalia Publishing.

Patterson, G. R. (1990). Some comments about cognitions as causal variables. *American Psychologist, 45*(8), 984-985.

Pope, A. W., Bierman, K. L., & Mumma, G. H. (1989). Relations between hyperactive and aggressive behavior and peer relations at three elementary grade levels. *Journal of Abnormal Child Psychology, 17*(3), 253-267.

Putallaz, M., & Wasserman, A. (1990). Children's entry behavior. In A. S.R. & C. J.D. (Eds.), *Peer Rejection in Childhood* (pp. 60-89). Cambridge.: Cambridge University Press.

Quiggle, N., Garber, J., Panak, W., & Dodge, K. A. (1992). Social-information processing in aggressive and depressed children. *Child Development, 63*, 1305-1320.

Reinke, W. M., & Herman, K. C. (2002). Creating school environments that deter antisocial behaviors in youth. *Psychology in the Schools, 39*(549-559).

Rubin, K. H., Chen, X., & Hymel, S. (1993). Socioemotional characteristics of withdrawn and aggressive children. *Merrill-Palmer Quarterly, 39*, 518-534.

Rubin, K. H., & Krasnor, L. R. (1986). Social-cognitive and social behavioral perspectives on problem-solving. In M. Perlmutter (Ed.), *Cognitive perspectives on children's social and behavioral development. The Minnesota Symposia on Child Psychology* (Vol. 18, pp. 1-68). Hillsdale, NJ: Lawrence Erlbaum Associates.

Slaby, R., & Guerra, N. (1988). Cognitive mediators of aggression in adolescent offenders: 1. assessment. *Development Psychology, 24*, 580-588.

Stormont, M., Smith, S. C., & Lewis, T. J. (2007). Teacher implementation of precorrection and praise statements in Head Start classrooms as a component of a program-wide system of positive behavioral support. *Journal of Behavioral Education, 16*, 280-290.

Webster-Stratton, C. (1990). *Dina Dinosaur's Social Skills, Emotion and Problem-Solving Curriculum.* Seattle, WA: 1411 8th Avenue West.

Webster-Stratton, C., & Hammond, M. (1997). Treating children with early-onset conduct problems: A comparison of child and parent training interventions. *Journal of Consulting and Clinical Psychology, 65*(1), 93-109.

Webster-Stratton, C., Reid, M. J., & Stoolmiller, M. (2008). Preventing conduct problems and improving school readiness: Evaluation of the Incredible Years Teacher and Child Training Programs in high-risk schools. *Journal of Child Psychology and Psychiatry 49*(5), 471-488.

Teaching Students to Problem Solve

Why is it Necessary to Teach Students to Problem Solve?

Young children often react to their problems in ineffective ways because their cognitive brain development is immature. Common childhood responses to problems are to cry, tantrum, yell, hit, bite, become destructive, withdraw, become anxious, avoid the situation, tattle, lie, steal, or make up imaginary stories about what happened. These responses do little to help children find satisfying solutions to their problems. In fact, they often create new ones. But research shows that children continue to use these inappropriate strategies either because they have not been taught more appropriate ways to

Teachers have a key role in teaching social problem-solving skills to all children, but particularly those who are aggressive, impulsive, anxious, or fearful.

problem solve or because their inappropriate strategies have been inadvertently reinforced by parents', teachers', or other children's responses in the past (Hawkins, Smith, & Catalano, 2004; Knutson, DeGarmo, Koeppl, & Reid, 2005; Ostrander & Herman, 2006).

It also has been shown that children's temperament influences their ability to learn more effective problem-solving skills. In particular, children who are hyperactive, impulsive, inattentive, and aggressive are more likely to have cognitive difficulties with social problem solving (Asarnow & Callan, 1985; Beauchaine, Neuhaus, Brenner, & Gatzke-Kopp, 2008; Webster-Stratton, 1985). Such high risk children perceive social situations in hostile terms, generate fewer prosocial ways of solving interpersonal conflict, and anticipate fewer consequences for aggression (Crick & Dodge, 1994; Dodge & Price, 1994). They act aggressively and impulsively without stopping to think of non-aggressive solutions (Asher, Parkhurst, Hymel, & Williams, 1990; Putallaz & Wasserman, 1990; Rubin, Chen, & Hymel, 1993) or of the other person's perspective. On the other hand, some children are more easily able to employ appropriate problem-solving strategies, and play more constructively and cooperatively with others. Consequently, these children are better liked by their peers and more successful in interactions with parents and teachers (Rubin & Krasnor, 1986; Shure, 1997; Spivak, Platt, & Shure, 1976). Teachers have a key role in teaching social skills to all children, but particularly those who are aggressive, impulsive, anxious, or fearful. These children need extra support to think of more prosocial solutions to their problems and to evaluate which solutions are better choices and more likely to lead to positive consequences. In essence, these high risk students are provided with a thinking strategy that corrects the flaws in their decision making process and reduces their risk of developing ongoing peer relationship problems.

Curriculum-based lessons can be applied in the classroom to support general social skill and cognitive-problem solving development for all children, while particularly targeting high risk students. Including both high risk and typically developing students in social skills lessons will support the overall positive social and emotional climate in the entire classroom. The risk of the high risk students experiencing social rejection and negative stereotypes will be reduced, and classroom social cohesion, empathy among students, and cooperative learning will increase. Moreover, the more socially competent children will learn to be more understanding, helpful and empathic to those with more difficulties solving social problems.

Indeed it is the job of both teachers and parents to prepare today's children to be responsible citizens who are capable of thoughtful decision making and coping with interpersonal conflict carefully and sensitively, particularly when under stress. As has been pointed out by Gardner and others, (Gardner, 1993; Ladd, Kochenderfer, & Coleman, 1997), interpersonal and intrapersonal intelligence are as vital to healthy functioning as mathematical competence. Children's successful development into adulthood is dependent on their ability to use critical judgment, effective decision making skills, and perspective-taking regardless of their innate ability, and cultural or family background. The teaching of these skills early in life can serve to protect against or prevent the onset of problem behaviors such as drug abuse, pregnancy, school drop out, violence, suicide, and delinquency (Coie, 1993).

What Empirical Evidence Is There for Problem-Solving Approaches?

Reviews of social skill and cognitive problem-solving instruction programs for children have generally shown promising results (e.g., Beelmann, Pfingste, & Losel, 1994; Durlak, Weissberg, Dymnick, Taylor, & Schellinger, 2011; Schneider, 1992; Weissberg, Kumpfer, & Seligman, 2003; Brown, 2008). One of the first pioneering programs called *I Can Problem Solve* (ICPS) was developed by Shure and Spivak (Shure, 1994; Spivak, et al., 1976) for children in preschool through sixth grade and has been evaluated over a period of 30 years (Shure, 1997). Results have shown short-term improvements in interpersonal as well as academic behavior. Other programs such as Skillstreaming (Goldstein & Pentz, 1984; Miller, Midgett, & Wicks, 1992) and

Results indicated enhanced generalization and maintenance when training was provided to the parents as well as the children.

Social Problem Solving (Camp & Bash, 1985; Weissberg, Jackson, & Shriver, 1993; Weissberg & Greenberg, 1998) and others (e.g., Battistich, Schaps, & Wilson, 2004; Elias & Tobias, 1996; Zins & Elias, 2006) have also reported significantly improved social skills and cooperative strategies for resolving interpersonal conflict. However follow-up studies of these and other similar programs have revealed that the effects will only generalize across settings and be long lasting if they are ongoing, integrated into the classroom environment, and involve partnerships with parents. Several studies have reported that when training highly aggressive young children with conduct problems in problem-solving strategies, the results indicated enhanced generalization and maintenance when training was provided to the parents as well as the children (Kazdin, 1995; Kazdin, Esveldt, French, & Unis, 1987; Kazdin, Siegel, & Bass, 1992; Webster-Stratton & Hammond, 1997; Webster-Stratton, Reid, & Hammond, 2004).

Teacher As Model

Undoubtedly, teachers are already teaching their students more appropriate problem-solving tactics without realizing it, especially if students have opportunities to observe teachers problem solving in the classroom. It is a rich learning experience for students to watch a teacher resolving conflict with a student or a colleague and evaluate the outcome of the solutions. For instance, a teacher who has a very small budget to buy all the classroom supplies for the year might share the problem-solving process with his students. Together they could think through the possible solutions, discuss how to prioritize needs, and how to decide which solution will lead to the best outcome. Students also learn much by observing how teachers react to daily hassles and problems in the classroom and how they encourage on-the-spot problem solving between students who are experiencing conflict. Teachers can further this learning by thinking out loud and modeling positive problem-solving strategies. For example, when presented with a frustrating situation such as a computer that breaks down or paint that gets spilled all over the floor, a teacher might think out loud so students can hear, "How can I solve this? I need to stop and think first. This is frustrating, but I need to stay calm. I'll take a big breath. What plan can I come up with to solve this problem?"

TEACHING PROBLEM-SOLVING STEPS THROUGH GAMES, PUPPETS AND HYPOTHETICAL PROBLEM SITUATIONS

Clearly there are many skills involved in social decision making; however, based on the problem-solving literature (D'Zurilla & Goldfried, 1971; Spivak, et al., 1976) researchers have suggested that, for children, the process of problem solving can be divided into at least 7 steps and presented as the following questions.

1. What is my problem? (Define the problem and feelings involved)
2. What is a solution? (Begin to brainstorm solutions)
3. What are some more solutions? (Brainstorm alternative solutions)
4. What are the consequences? What happens next?
5. What is the best solution or choice? (Evaluate consequences of solutions in terms of safety, fairness, and good feelings and make a good choice)
6. Am I using my plan? (Implementation)
7. How did I do? (Evaluating the outcome and reinforcing efforts)

For children between the ages of three and five, the primary focus will be placed on the first through third steps of identifying problems and generating possible solutions. The later steps of evaluating and implementing appropriate solutions are more easily done by children ages 6 to 10. Younger children first need to develop a broad repertoire of possible positive solutions to choose from. Then they can begin to understand that some

For children between the ages of three and five, the primary focus will be placed on the first three problem solving steps.

solutions may have more satisfactory outcomes than others. The ability to think ahead to possible outcomes for each solution and evaluate the best solution requires a level of cognitive development that will be particularly difficult for hyperactive, inattentive, and impulsive children who react in the moment and also for any child in the preoperational Piagetian stage of cognitive development where fantasy and reality are often confused (Piaget & Inhelder, 1962).

Methods and strategies that can be used by teachers to teach each of the problem-solving steps involved in decision making are highlighted next.

1 What is my problem?

©*Incredible Years*®

STEP ONE: What is my problem? How do I know I have a problem?

A fun way to begin problem-solving discussions with students is to ask them to pretend they are "detectives" who are trying to solve a problem. Teachers can encourage students to put on their imaginary detective hats to try to solve some hypothetical problem scenarios.

The first step in helping children understand whether they have a problem or not is to coach them to pay attention to their feelings. If they are feeling uncomfortable (sad or angry or fearful), this will be an important clue that there is a problem to solve. They should be encouraged to pay attention to their Feelings Fingerprints (Elias & Clabby, 1989); the unique way their body signals them they are in distress. The signal may be sweaty or clenched palms, stomachaches, a racing heart, a red face, tears, or a tight jaw. Labeling the bodily sensations involved in the problem situations is an important initial step for it serves as a detective clue or "trigger" that problem solving is needed. Once students have recognized and labeled their own feelings, then teachers can help them learn how to accurately define the problem. For example, the problem may be defined as, "I feel angry because a classmate won't share the basketball with me" or, "When they won't let me play with them, I feel frustrated and mad."

Another aspect of this problem definition process also involves encouraging students to think about the feelings of others in the situation. For example asking, "What do you think the boy who has the basketball feels?" Some students may not attend to or have difficulty reading the feeling cues or fingerprints of others in a situation or may misinterpret others' feelings, leading to inappropriate decisions. Moreover, some students may have a limited range of ability to label emotions; that is, they only have words for emotions such mad and sad. For such children to become effective problem solvers, their feeling vocabulary will need to be expanded to include other feelings such as pride, worry, calmness, stress, excitement, fear, confusion, embarrassment, and disappointment. (See Chapter 11 for a discussion of how to enhance emotional literacy.) Once children have labels for a range of feelings, they have a way to describe what they are feeling and to regulate their emotional response to their problems, rather than just reacting or being overwhelmed by them.

STEP TWO: Brainstorm a Solution

After the problem has been defined, the next step is to invite students to generate as many different solutions, options, or choices as they can. This brainstorming process teaches students flexible thinking and creates an attitude that encourages students to realize that there is often more than one reasonable way to solve the problem. During this stage of the process, solutions are not evaluated, so teachers avoid criticizing or editing any ideas, no matter how silly or inappropriate they may seem. Instead, teachers encourage imaginative thinking and try to model creative solutions. Teachers can praise the thinking process and student

© *Incredible Years* ®

2 What is a solution?

efforts to solve the problem. In particular, it is helpful to praise for their *different* solutions (e.g., "Good, that is a different idea! We have four possible solutions now.") because it will encourage a broader variety of solutions rather than variations of the same idea.

STEP THREE: Brainstorm More Solutions

If students are having difficulty finding a solution, teachers might suggest some ideas. Teachers can help children build a repertoire of common

3 What are some other solutions?

social solutions such as: walk away, wait for a turn, say please, do something else fun, trade, offer to share, ask for help from parent or teacher, talk about your feelings, ignore, ask politely, calm down, admit mistake, apologize, give a compliment, take a deep breath, and forgive yourself. As children learn each of these solutions, the solution can become part of a problem solving detective kit that children can refer to when they have a problem. (*Preprinted, laminated solutions cards, sample pictures shown below, come in Wally's Detective Solution Kit with the Incredible Years' Dinosaur Curriculum. Or teachers and students can also make their own classroom set of solution cards, perhaps illustrated by the students.*) When students are working with real or hypothetical problems, they can be prompted to check the solution kit to find a solution that might work.

Ignore Wait and take turns Share

Sometimes older school age children can be prompted to think about their goals when generating solutions. For example, "What do you want to have happen? Picture how you want this to end up." Games, puppets, stories, and practice role plays will add to student enjoyment and engagement in the problem solving process. The following are a few games that teach problem-solving steps one and two, and three (identifying the problem and generating solutions).

CIRCLE TIME SCRIPT
The "Suppose Game" to Practice Solutions

In the Suppose Game a student chooses a 'suppose card' from a folder. On this card is picture and description of a problem situation to solve. The student reads the suppose card (or has it read to him by the teacher if he can't read) and the class then generates possible solutions. Some examples for questions for this game are suggested below and teachers can add to the scenarios by using common problems that occur at school every day. More of these problems may be found in two colorful children's books, *Wally's Detective Book for Solving Problems at School* and *Wally's Detective Book for Solving Problems at Home* (Webster-Stratton, 1998).

The Suppose Game

Here are some examples of suppose card problem situations for this game: (these are excerpted from the *Dinosaur Curriculum*, a video-based program for teaching young children empathy, social skills and problem-solving developed by Webster-Stratton, 1990).

- Suppose a child much younger than you started hitting you. How would you feel? What would you do?
- Suppose a boy had been playing for a long, long time with the computer, and you wanted to play with it. How would you feel? What would you do?
- Suppose there was only one piece of pizza left and you and your sister both wanted it. How would you feel? What would you do?
- Suppose you broke your dad's favorite lamp. How would you feel? What would you do?
- Suppose you are constantly teased and bullied by another child at school. How would you feel? What would you do?
- Suppose you want to meet a new friend. How would you feel? What would you do?

- Suppose your teacher made you stay in for recess because you called a classmate a name but she had not seen that the other child had called you a name first. How would you feel? What would you do?
- Suppose you ripped a brand-new pair of pants that your father bought you for a special event. How would you feel? What would you do?
- Suppose you really want a cool pair of shoes that you saw in a store, but your mother says they are too expensive. How would you feel? What would you do?
- Suppose a cupcake you have been saving disappeared and you see icing on your sister's mouth. How would you feel? What would you do?
- Suppose another child calls you a baby for playing dolls or says you are ugly. How would you feel? What would you do?
- Suppose you ask another child to play with you and he or she refuses. How would you feel? What would you do?
- Suppose your brother wrecks a model you've been working on for two weeks. How would you feel? What would you do?
- Suppose your best friend has a new friend whom you don't like. How would you feel? What would you do?
- Suppose there is a group of "popular" kids, but they are kind of bossy and don't let you play what you want to play with. How would you feel? What would you do?
- Suppose there is a group of kids who form a club but they don't invite you to join them. How would you feel? What would you do?
- Suppose you have trouble with reading and sometimes stutter and the other kids laugh and tease you. How would you feel? What would you do?
- Suppose you play chase on the playground, but it starts getting rough and there is pushing and shoving. How would you feel? What would you do?
- Suppose the child sitting next to you jostles your papers and kicks you under your desk. How would you feel? What would you do?
- Suppose there is a group of children playing jump rope and you want to join in. How would you feel? What would you do?

Once the students have discussed possible solutions to a suppose card problem, teachers can ask them to role play or act out their proposed solutions. For example, if the students have suggested 'find something else to do' as a possible solution to the situation of the boy who won't share the football, the teacher can set up a role play practice to show what this looks like. One student can be chosen to be the football player who hogs the ball and another student to be the classmate who wants to play football.

Have students practice positive solutions, not inappropriate behaviors.

Students will love participating in these 'plays' and acting them out helps students to see exactly what behaviors are involved in carrying out the solution and to practice the appropriate language. Sometimes teachers are reluctant to do role plays at first, but they soon realize that these active practice sessions are far more important to a student's actually learning and applying problem-solving behaviors and thinking than theoretical discussions or lectures. Examples of how to structure role plays will be discussed below. One key principle is not to have students act out negative behaviors, rather focus their practice on the positive solutions. If teachers use each suppose card to generate and act out multiple solutions, it is likely that only a few scenarios will be covered in each teaching session. For preschool children, the teacher may want to only focus on one problem card in a circle time.

Use puppets to role play and act out the problem situations

Puppets are an extremely effective teaching technique for engaging children and bringing problem solving discussions to life. We suggest using largish, life size puppets (preferably puppets with moving mouths) who visit the classroom on a regular basis to ask the students for help solving particular problems. Puppets such as Wally Problem Solver, Molly Manners, and Tiny Turtle, can present a problem for

discussion in one session and then come back the next session to tell students what happened when they tried out their ideas. Puppets can also share with the students how they coped with a difficult situation. Here are some examples of the problems which puppets like Wally and Molly can bring to students for their help solving. Note: While this book refers frequently to Wally and Molly, any other puppet (including animal puppets) can be effectively used when working with children.

CIRCLE TIME PROBLEMS FOR DISCUSSION

Wally and Molly and their friends Ask Students for Help Solving these Problems

Telling and listening

- Wally is afraid to bring his homework (or his behavior chart from his teacher) home because he hasn't done well. What solution can Wally use?
- Wally has a fight in the school yard with other children who won't let him play with them. What should he do?
- Molly and Wally fight over what channel to watch on TV and end up being sent to Time Out. How can they solve the problem? What are some solutions?
- Molly is not invited to a birthday party when most of her classmates are going. How does she feel? How can she solve this problem? What is a solution?
- Wally takes his friend's baseball glove because his parents won't buy him one. What is another solution?
- Oscar the Ostrich hides his head in the sand and is afraid because his parents fight—he is sure they are fighting because of him. How can Oscar solve his problem?
- Tiny Turtle is afraid of an adult who gets angry at him. What solution can Tiny use to solve his problem?
- Wally tells a lie because he is afraid he will get into trouble. What is different solution?
- Wally is teased about the way he looks and doesn't want to go to school anymore. How can Wally solve this problem?

Here is a sample script for how Wally would present the last problem to the students.

 CIRCLE TIME: LESSON SCRIPT
Wally Gets Teased

Wally: Today the kids at school were teasing me and calling me a monkey face!

Teacher: How did that make you feel?

Wally: I felt so mad, I called them names back!

Teacher: How did you feel about that solution?

Wally: Not so good because they called me a dummy, and said I couldn't play with them.

Teacher: I wonder if there was a different solution that might have worked better? Do you want to ask these kids for their ideas?

Wally: I guess so—but I bet they never get teased.

Teacher: Oh I think all kids get teased sometimes.

Wally: Really? Well how do you kids feel when you are teased?

Teacher: (*encourages students to label their feelings*)

Teacher: Well I guess those feelings are clues there is a problem. Right? Can anyone state Wally's problem for us?

Children: He was feeling really mad because other children were teasing him.

Wally: Wow! You really listened to my problem. You're right I was mad because they teased me.

Teacher: That's right. So now let's see if these children can come up with some solutions, or ideas, to solve your problem. I'm pretty sure they'll be able to help. They are good problem solvers!

(*encourages students to generate solutions - such as ignoring, walking away, being humorous in response, taking a deep breath and calming down, explaining feelings*)

Teacher: Wally these kids are great problem-solving detectives, look at all the solutions they came up with.

Wally: Can we practice some of those ideas because I'm not sure I know how to do them?

Teacher: Okay let's pick two students who will show you how to react when someone teases you. And Wally you can be the one to tease okay? (*two students volunteer*) Children, Wally is going to pretend to tease you and you will show him how to say "please stop" and then you can ignore and walk away.

Wally: Yeah, I want to make sure you know this is just pretend, right? I wouldn't really call you names.

Students: We know that, Wally!

Teacher: Okay, let's all say "ready, set, action" to start our pretend play.

Wally: Neaner, neaner, you are a monkey face!

Students: (*Role play some of the solutions that were discussed. The teacher will need to coach younger students how to do each solution.*)

Wally: Wow that was cool—I didn't get any reaction from either of you when I teased—it wasn't much fun. I'm going to try that next time someone teases me. I'll let you know what happens.

Next Session

Wally: Hey you know what someone was teasing me again and saying I was stupid and couldn't even kick a ball and you know what I did?

Teacher: Tell us Wally.

Wally:	(*Wally demonstrates*) Well, I was feeling really mad and I knew I was supposed to say how I felt about the teasing, but I just couldn't do it so then I took some big breaths so I could calm down. And I thought to myself, "I'm not going to pay any attention to him, I can be stronger than him." I walked away and found someone else to play with.
Teacher:	How did you feel about that?
Wally:	Oh it was so cool, I felt so powerful.
Teacher:	(*to students*) How do you think Wally did?

Use the Wally Detective Books or other Books to Practice Solutions

There are a variety of resources teachers can choose from to teach problem solving. Many children's books are good resources for problem situations (including the two from Incredible Years, *Wally's Detective Book for Solving Problems at School* or *Wally's Detective Book for Solving Problems at Home*). When using books for problem solving, teachers don't have to use the exact words in the story. Teachers might begin reading the story to set up the problem, show the picture of the scene, and then pause to let the children discuss the problem and possible solutions. Sometimes a teacher might ask students to look first at the pictures in a book to see if they can guess what the problem is. The point is to present the class with an example of a problem that is relevant to their experiences, so existing stories or problems can be tailored to children's particular strengths and weaknesses and their developmental level. Teachers can explore the character's feelings

Present the class with an example of a problem that is relevant to their experiences.

with students and help them define the problem, brainstorm solutions, and practice them in role plays to see how they work out. The following is another problem solving script using one of the problems taken from Wally's detective book.

CIRCLE TIME: LESSON SCRIPT
Waiting for a Turn on the Computer

Teacher: Boys and girls, today I have a special book that can help us learn to solve problems we may have at school. I am going to share a picture and I want you to look for clues that Wally and his friend are having a problem. Can you see anything on their faces that tells you they are having trouble?

Child: He looks mad.

Teacher: Wow! You are really looking carefully. Does any one notice something on his face that tells you the boy with the red hair looks mad?

Child: His mouth looks mean. His eyebrows are pointy.

Teacher: Put your thumbs up if you agree. How about Wally? How is he feeling?

Child: He looks sad. He has no smile.

Teacher: Sounds like Wally and his friend are mad and sad. Those are feelings that let you know you are having a problem. Let me tell you what is going on in this picture. Big Red here has been using the computer for a long, long time. Wally really wants a turn. What can Wally do?

Charles: He can ask him for a turn.

Tanisha: He can wait.

Peter: He can find another toy.

Teacher: Okay, let's act out that first idea of asking for a turn. Charles and Tanisha I'd like you to show the class what that looks like. Charles, Tanisha is using the computer you would like a turn. When we say, "ready, set, action" you are going to ask for it, using polite words. Tanisha, if you were feeling really friendly when Charles asked for a turn, what would you do?

Tanisha: I'd let him have a turn.

Teacher: Yes, that would be such a friendly thing to do, to share the computer. Let's see what that looks like.

Charles: (*teacher whispers words in child's ears if needed*) Can I have a turn on the computer?

Tanisha: Okay. (*she stops and lets him use the computer*)

Teacher: Solutions that are fair and safe are thumbs up solutions! Put your thumbs up if you think asking is a fair solution. Looks like you all agree. Let's try another solution for Charles if Tanisha wasn't ready to stop her work on the computer. This time Tanisha is going to politely say that she isn't done yet. (*Continue acting out waiting, asking again, doing something else, staying calm by deep breathing etc.*)

Notice that this role play is structured so that no negative behavior is acted out. Even when the role play demonstrates that Tanisha is not ready to share, she is prompted to communicate this in a friendly and polite way. Acting out negative behaviors in front of the class will provide a powerful negative image that is hard for children to resist.

Pass the Detective Hat Game For Practicing Generating Solutions

Another circle time game that can be used to present hypothetical problem situations for students to solve is to play "pass the detective hat game." This game was described in Chapter Eleven for practicing anger control. Hypothetical problem situations and questions (such as those shown above) are written on small pieces of paper and placed in a Sherlock Holmes detective hat. The children sit in a circle and the hat is passed around the circle while the music is on. When the music stops, the child who has the hat in his lap gets to choose a problem from the hat and try to answer the question. If the student can't answer the question, he can ask a friend to help him. The puppets and teachers also participate in this game by helping to read the problems for nonreaders, modeling appropriate inner talk out loud, adding additional solutions, and role-playing. For example, the teacher or puppet might say, "Let's see, I have a problem. I am being teased and I don't like it —what can I do? Johnny suggested I could ignore her and Anna suggested I could ask her to stop. Those are two good solutions—does anyone have any other ideas?" Here are some ideas for the detective hat game for practicing solutions.

CIRCLE TIME
Detective Hat Game
for practicing generating solutions

- A friend comes to you and wants to know what to do when he is teased.
- What is a solution?
- How do you know when you have a problem?
- Someone took your skipping rope without asking. What are some solutions?
- You want to ride on the swing that your friend is using. (It could be book, TV show etc.) What are some solutions?
- You are sitting next to someone who keeps bothering you by touching your hair and whispering in your ear. What are some solutions?
- The other kids are playing ball and you want to join them. What are some solutions?
- You are presenting your project in front of the class and one of your friends starts making faces at you. What are some solutions?

Include some jokes in the detective hat so sometimes the student gets to ask the class a joke rather than present a problem.

STEP FOUR: What are the consequences of the solutions? What is the best plan?

After generating many different solutions or possible choices, the next step is to look at what would happen if a particular solution were carried out. For instance, if a student suggested "grabbing" or "hitting" in order to get the football back, he is helped to consider the possible outcomes. For example, the teacher says, "Imagine what might happen next if you did grab the ball away." Students will likely picture such things as losing a friend, getting into trouble with the teacher, or getting into a fight. This discussion should be carried out in a noncritical way, even though the solution proposed is inappropriate. If students feel criticized for their solutions, they may avoid suggesting ideas in the future. Young children will process consequences at a very basic level, perhaps categorizing solutions into thumbs up and thumbs down solutions, or friendly and unfriendly solutions. Older children will be able to start to

4 What happens next ? (consequences)

think through more nuances of solutions including the possibility that sometimes a prosocial solution doesn't result in the desired consequences. For example, asking a friend politely for a toy may mean that the friend shares; however, it's also possible that the friend will say that he is not done yet, and he might even be rude! Often, children are surprised or upset when things don't go according to their plan. Part of learning to problem solve involves realizing that often the first solution doesn't work and that it's not always possible to know the outcome of a particular solution until it's tried. However, it can become burdensome for students to go through the exercise of evaluating every single solution that is suggested. Teachers can be selective about this, evaluating a few examples of both prosocial and negative solutions.

5 What is the best solution ?

STEP FIVE: What is the best solution or choice?

After reviewing possible outcomes of a few solutions, the next step is to help the students decide which one or two might be the best choice to try. By phrasing it as a choice the student must make it gives them the responsibility for solving the problem.

CIRCLE TIME
Detective Hat Game
For Evaluating Fairness and Feelings of Solutions

In this game scenarios are placed in the detective hat to help students learn about the concept of fairness. The hat is passed around the circle and when the music stops, the child holding the hat draws out the paper, reads the scenario and tries to answer the question about the solution proposed, whether or not it is fair, and how each person feels about the situation. This game helps children evaluate their solutions in terms of fairness and feelings and is more appropriate for primary grade students. Some examples suggestions for questions include the following:

Molly Says: Is it fair or not?
- One person is watching TV and another comes in the room and changes the channel. Is that fair? Why?
- There is one piece of pizza left and two children. One child takes the piece of pizza. Is that fair? Why?
- A brother and sister are going to camp and there is only one camera. The girl insists she should have the camera. Is that fair? Why?
- You want to read a book, but someone else is reading it and won't give it to you. Is that fair? Why?
- One student refuses to do what the teacher asks her to do, so she loses recess privileges. Is that fair? Why?

Choosing the best solution involves students asking themselves three questions: Is the solution safe? Is it fair? Does it lead (eventually) to good feelings? If the solution meets these criteria, then the children are encouraged to try it out with a role-play practice session.

CIRCLE TIME: LESSON SCRIPT
Felicity Steals Something

Felicity: Well I came today because I have a problem that I was hoping to get some help with.

Teacher: These kids are great problem-solvers, I bet they could help.

Felicity: I did something at school this week, and I need to talk about it. My friend Ruby had a stuffed bear in her locker. I really wanted one like that so I just took it! She was really upset because it was her special animal.

Teacher: What happened then?

Felicity: Well the teacher asked, "Who took Ruby's bear?" and I didn't want to tell so I lied and said, "not me." I really thought I would get in big trouble if she found out it was me, and I was so worried. I knew I shouldn't have taken that animal, but I thought I would lose Ruby as a friend if she found out it was me. And the teacher would send a note home and I would definitely get in trouble and be grounded.

Teacher: Well, that does sound like a big problem, Felicity. It was brave to share your problem with these children. I can see that you're feeling worried about the choices you made. Let's think about that choice and about its consequences. Does anyone remember what questions Felicity could ask to think about the consequences of her solution?

Students: *(brainstorm why students think her solution might not be the best one in terms of safety, fairness, and good feelings)*

Felicity:	I see, so I made one problem into two problems because I lied. My first choice to take the bear wasn't fair to Ruby and it won't lead to good feelings, and then I lied. That's not fair and I know that will also lead to bad feelings! What should I do now?
Students:	*(generate solutions such as admit mistake, tell teacher and Ruby, apologize, give back animal)*
Felicity:	Are you disappointed in me—do you think I'm really awful because I did that?
Teacher:	Well you know, Felicity, everyone makes mistakes sometimes. How do you students feel about Felicity now?
Students:	*(tell her how they feel)*
Felicity:	Well I'm worried I won't be strong enough to admit my mistake. Can we practice doing that?
Teacher:	Sure let's have some actors to play the parts of the teacher, Ruby, and Felicity. *(student role plays in front of class admitting mistake to Ruby and teacher and experiencing consequences)*
Felicity:	Okay let me try it now and see how I do? "Ruby I am really sorry I took your bear, here it is back. I shouldn't have taken it and I want to make it up to you. Would you like one of my toys for a while? Do you think we can still be friends?" *(turns to students)* Well, how did I do?

Practicing What to Do When a Solution Doesn't Work!

As stated above, even when students use prosocial solutions, there is no guarantee that the outcome will be positive. It is important for students to practice how they will respond if their solution does not result in success. The ability to try another solution is an important real life social skill! For example, even though the student asked politely to play basketball, the other child still did not want to give up the ball and would not let him play with him. This student might then need to wait patiently until the child was done with the ball, find another activity, find a friend to play with, look for a toy to trade, or make a plan to play with the ball another day. All of these strategies involve self control, but students who have been taught to look for another solution when the first one doesn't work will be better able to stay calm in these situations. Here are some hypothetical scenarios where a first solution doesn't work. These can be presented by a puppet or used in a pass-the-hat game.

CIRCLE TIME
Detective Hat Game
Scenarios for Practicing What to Do When Solutions Don't Work

- You ask your friend politely to play a game with you and s/he says s/he doesn't like that game. What solution will you use next?
- You ask your friend who is bothering you to stop whispering (or ignore the whispers and touches) but s/he still continues. What will you do next?
- You wait patiently to get a turn with the computer but the other child is taking too long. What solution will you use next?
- Your mom is asking you to set the table and your favorite TV show is coming on. You ask her if you can set the table after the show and she says 'no.' (This teaches waiting and thinking about another's perspective and feelings.)

For the problem situations listed above you can practice some of the following solutions: thinking about another's perspective and feelings, asking again politely, waiting, ignoring, walking away, doing something else fun, thinking helpful thoughts, using calming self-talk, or asking for help.

6 Can I use the plan?

STEP SIX: Implementation of problem-solving skills

The next step when engaged in hypothetical problem-solving games is for the students to think of a situation where they might use the agreed upon solution. This can also happen when a teacher observes a similar 'real-life' problem occurring and can prompt students to use a solution to try solving the problem. For example, students might complain that a classmate is hogging the computer, or another student is in tears because she has been excluded from the hopscotch game. While it may be tempting for teachers to tell students what to do or to implement an immediate consequence for the child who is teasing or not sharing, walking students through the problem-solving steps is likely to lead to better long-term learning. Problem solving in the midst of real-life conflict is much harder than problem solving in a hypothetical or neutral situation. Children may be so angry and upset that they cannot think clearly and are not able to problem solve. A teacher may be able to calm them through discussion, so they can come up with some solutions or it may be the case that there needs to be a brief cooling off period before the problem can be addressed. Occasionally a problem is so distressing that it is best discussed later when both the teacher and the students have had time to calm down and gain some perspective.

Once students have learned the problem-solving steps and practiced them with hypothetical problem situations, they will be ready to discuss their own personal problems. Instead of the teacher bringing up hypothetical problems to discuss, s/he can begin the class by asking, "does any one have a problem today that they want help solving?" It won't take long before students are looking forward to these discussions because they know this is a time when they can share their difficulties and get some ideas for how to cope with them. It can be helpful to setup a problem solving station in the classroom. This area might have pictures of prosocial solutions and templates for students to record their problems. Students can use this space individually to think about or write about a problem. Alternatively a pair of students who have a problem might be coached to go together to the problem solving station to discuss and pick a solution for their problem.

STEP SEVEN: Evaluating Outcome How often do teachers and parents say, "Joey makes the same mistakes over and over again. He doesn't seem to learn from experience or remember what happened the other times?" The reason for this is that some children lack the skill of using the past to inform the future. They do not know how to recall past experience or to see how those experiences apply to what is happening now. This is why the seventh step is so important because it helps students learn how to evaluate how successful they were in solving a problem (whether hypothetical or real-life) and whether they might use it again in the future. Thus it encourages them to rethink the past event and anticipate whether this would be a good choice in future situations. Teachers can help students evaluate the solution and its consequences by asking the same questions that they asked themselves when they were choosing a good solution:

7 How did I do?

1. Was it safe? Was anyone hurt?
2. Was it fair?
3. How did you feel about it and how did the other person feel?

Is your solution safe?

Does your solution lead to good feelings?

Is your solution fair?

*Coach and praise
students for their
problem-solving efforts.*

If the answer to any of those questions is negative, then students can be encouraged to think about a different solution. For example, "Okay so that was not the best choice because it led to bad feelings. Sam is still really mad at you and it seems like you feel badly about that. Let's think of a better choice for next time." Finally, one of the most important aspects of this process is to reinforce the students for their efforts at problem solving. Teachers must coach and praise the problem-solving process and encourage students to self-praise. It will be a long time before students are able to skillfully use all the problem-solving steps smoothly, so it is important that this coaching and encouragement come at all stages of the process. For example, a teacher says, "Sheila, you used your words to say that you are mad that Johnny won't share. You are recognizing your feelings and talking about the problem!" "John, I see that you asked Sydney for that when you wanted it. That's a great way to try a friendly solution." "Mark, I am impressed with you. I know it wasn't easy to apologize after you lost your temper. It wasn't right to yell at those boys, but it takes a strong person to admit a mistake. I'm proud of you for doing that."

MAKING PROBLEM SOLVING MORE EFFECTIVE

The following section focuses on some of the problems teachers may encounter when they try to teach problem solving to their students. It also includes some effective ways to be successful.

Discover The Student's View of the Problem First

Sometimes teachers are too quick to come to a conclusion about what exactly they think is the student's problem. For instance, Juan's teacher may decide that he is having trouble sharing. It may be that from Juan's point of view, the problem is that his friend grabbed the ball away from him in the first place and wouldn't let him join in the game. Or perhaps Maria shared the crayons with her friend but then the friend refused to give them back. If the teacher makes a quick decision about the problem, s/he may focus her energies in the wrong direction. By misinterpreting the situation, she may lecture Juan or Maria about sharing. This can lead to the child's resistance to the problem-solving process. A child who is blamed for something he didn't do (or believes he didn't do) will likely become upset about unfair treatment. If the child is preoccupied with the injustice of the situation or is plotting how to retrieve the crayons or ball, he or she won't hear a word of his teacher's good ideas.

The first task is to try to understand the problem from the student's point of view. Teachers can ask questions like, "What happened?" "What do you see as the problem?" or "Can you tell me how you feel about it?" This kind of question helps the student to clarify the problem in his or her own mind, but also insures that the teacher won't jump to the wrong conclusion about what's going on. In the previous example, Juan's teacher might say, "Now I understand what the problem is. You shared the ball, but your friends played with it too long and wouldn't give it back. And that made you mad." In order for children to learn anything from a problem, it is important that the solution be relevant to their perception of the situation. When a student believes that the teacher understands his point of view he is more likely to be motivated to deal with the problem cooperatively.

Encourage Students to Come Up with Multiple Solutions

Sometimes teachers believe that telling their students how to solve a problem helps them learn to problem solve. For example, two children may have trouble sharing a tricycle on the playground and the teacher responds by saying, "You should either play together or take turns. Grabbing is not nice." Or, "You must share. Lamar will get mad and won't be your friend if you don't share. You can't go around grabbing things. Would you like that if he did it to you?" The problem with this approach is that the teachers lecture or tell their students what to do before they have found out what the problem is from the student's viewpoint. Moreover, telling a student what to do (or what not to do) does not help her to think about the problem and how to solve it. Lastly, in this type of situation, a direct command to share is likely to be met with resistance because the solution is teacher-imposed and leaves the students no control over how to respond.

It is more effective to guide students into thinking about what may have caused the problem than to tell them the solution. To help students develop a habit of solving their own problems, they need to be encouraged to think for themselves. They should be urged to express their feelings about the situation, talk about their ideas for solving the problem, and anticipate what might happen if they try a particular solution. Teachers can offer a few solutions to expand their repertoire of solutions once students have had a chance to talk about their own ideas.

Guided Problem Solving

Another problem occurs when teachers think they are helping their students to resolve conflict by telling them to work it out for themselves. This might work if students already have good problem-solving skills and ideas about solutions but, for most young children, this approach will not work. For example if two children, Max and Tyler, are fighting over a book, working out the problem themselves will probably result in continued arguing and Tyler, the more aggressive child, getting the book. Therefore, Tyler is reinforced for his inappropriate behavior because he got what he wanted, and Max is reinforced for giving in because the fighting ceased when he backed down. In this case, the teacher could have guided the two boys through the problem-solving steps, supporting Max for speaking up and encouraging Tyler to use a prosocial solution.

TEACHER-STUDENT SCRIPT
Ineffective Teacher Problem Solving with Student
"It's Mine!"

Two children are fighting over a basketball and each are grabbing it.

Teacher: I've told you a million times not to grab each other's toys.

1st child: But it's mine.

2nd child: She took it. I had it first.

1st child: No you didn't.

Teacher: Can't you two learn to play together? You must learn to share!

Fighting resumes.

TEACHER-STUDENT SCRIPT
Effective Teacher Problem Solving with Student

"She Hit Me"

Tina is crying and holding her arm.

Teacher: Who hit you?
Tina: Sarah.
Teacher: What happened? (*Teacher elicits Tina's view of problem.*)
Tina: She just hit me.
Teacher: Do you know why she hit you? (*Teacher encourages Tina to think of causes.*)
Tina: Well, I hit her first.
Teacher: Why?
Tina: She wouldn't let me look at her book.
Teacher: That must have made you angry. How do you think she felt when you hit her? (*Teacher helps Tina think of the feelings of others.*)
Tina: Mad.
Teacher: I guess that's why she hit you back. Do you know why she wouldn't let you look at the book? (*Teacher helps Tina to see the point of view of the other child.*)
Tina: No.
Teacher: How can you find out?
Tina: I could ask her.
Teacher: That's a good idea. (*Teacher encourages Tina to seek facts and discover the problem.*)

Later.

Tina: She said I never let her see my books.
Teacher: Oh, now you know why she said no. Can you think of something you could do so she'd let you look at the book? (*Teacher encourages Tina to think of solutions.*)

Tina: I could tell her I won't be her friend if she doesn't give it to me.

Teacher: Yes, that's one idea. What would happen if you did that? (*Tina is guided to think of consequences of solution.*)

Tina: She might not play with me again or be my friend.

Teacher: Yes, that's a possible result, do you want her to be your friend?

Tina: Yes.

Teacher: Can you think of something else so she would still be your friend? (*Teacher encourages further solutions.*)

Tina: I could trade her one of my books.

Teacher: That's a good idea. What might happen if you did that?

In this example, Tina's teacher helps her to think of why she was hit and define the problem. When she learns that Tina hit first, she does not lecture or offer advice, but helps her student to think about Sarah's feelings. Through problem solving she encourages Tina to consider the problem and alternative ways to solve it.

CIRCLE TIME SCRIPT
Real Life Problem Solving with Student
"She won't let me play with her."

Lizzie: (*runs in classroom from recess crying*) Kimmi's not going to be my best friend. I hate her! She wouldn't let me play with her.

Kimmi: No I didn't say that, I didn't! She's a liar!

Teacher: I can see you are both upset and feel bad. I think you both need to calm down first before we can find out what the problem is and see what we can do to fix things? (*teacher may direct children to separate seats for a few minutes or schedule a time at lunch to discuss the issue later*)

> **Teacher:** Remember our rules for problem solving? (*reviews rules of no put downs, no interruptions*) Okay Lizzie you first, what do you see as the problem? (*Lizzie states problem*) How do you feel? Kimmi what do you see as the problem? (*states problem*) How do you feel? What do you think you can do to solve the problem? (*if they can't think of any ideas refer them to the problem-solving solution kit*)

If there is too much emotional arousal the children won't be able to solve the problem. So the teacher in this example reassures them and allows cool off time first. The teacher may want to use the problem-solving cue cards for the steps as they work through the problem.

Be Positive and Fun

Sometimes teachers try to be helpful by telling their students when their solutions are silly, inappropriate, or not likely to be successful. This can make them feel ridiculed and they'll probably stop generating solutions. Another type of problem occurs when teachers become obsessive about this process and force their students to come up with so many solutions and consequences that the discussion becomes confusing.

Avoid ridiculing, criticizing, or making negative evaluations of your students' ideas. Instead, urge them to think of as many solutions as possible, and to let their imaginations run free. If they have a short attention span or become bored, not all the solutions have to be looked at in detail regarding the possible consequences. Instead, focus on two or three of the most promising ones.

Ask about Feelings

When some teachers problem solve, they avoid discussing feelings. They focus exclusively on the thinking style, the solution, and the consequences. Yet, they forget to ask their students how they feel about the problem or how the other person in the situation may have felt. It is also important for teachers to be aware of their own feelings. Hearing a student report that she has been sent off the playground for hitting someone may provoke feelings of anger, frustration, or helplessness in the teacher. It is important for the teacher to stay calm and in control of her own emotions before trying to help the student.

Teachers can encourage students to think about their feelings in response to a problem or to a possible outcome of a solution. Students can also be coached to consider the other person's point of view in the situation. For instance, a teacher might ask, "How do you think Julie felt when you did that? How did you feel when she did that?" Students can be urged to discover what someone else feels or thinks. "How can you find out if she likes your idea? How can you tell if she is sad or happy?" This will help students to be more empathetic and, because they try to understand other people's feelings and viewpoints, results in more willingness to problem solve, compromise and cooperate. A teacher who shares his own feelings about the problem will help students feel understood. "I'm feeling sad for you right now. I know it's not easy to be teased, and I am sorry that you had to experience that. Let's think about what to do."

Encourage Many Solutions

Sometimes teachers begin to evaluate students' solutions before the brainstorming process is finished. They may criticize a poor solution or encourage a student to try the first prosocial solution that comes up. Instead, it is useful to encourage students to think of many possible solutions without comments from them as to their quality or potential effectiveness. Teachers can praise the thinking and brainstorming process, "Wow, you are thinking of a lot of solutions. It's good to have a lot of options before you pick the best one." Teachers can also expand a child's list of solutions by offering a few of their own. However, these should be offered as suggestions, not as orders. Research has shown that one difference between a well-adjusted and a poorly-adjusted child is that the well-adjusted one is more likely to think of a greater number of solutions to problems. The goal, then, is to increase students' ability to generate numerous ideas.

Use Open-Ended Questioning and Paraphrasing

Using open-ended questions will maximize a student's thinking about the problem. Teachers may be tempted to ask "why" questions ("Why did you do that?") or multiple choice questions ("Did you hit him because you were angry or because he was making fun of you or...") or closed-ended questions ("Did you hit him?"). These approaches should be avoided because they result in a "yes" or "no" answer or close off discussion because students feel defensive or blamed. Instead teachers might ask "what or how" questions such as, "What happened?" "How are you feeling?" "What other feelings do you have?" or "What do you think the other person feels?" These open-ended questions will be more likely to engage the child in the problem-solving process.

Paraphrasing or reflecting back to the student about what they are saying also helps them feel listened to and valued for their ideas. The advantage of paraphrasing is that teachers can rephrase some of their statements into more appropriate language. For example when the child was asked how he felt, he responded, "He's really stupid." This can be paraphrased as, "You sound really angry with him." This will help them eventually to develop better problem-solving vocabulary.

Using Picture Cues and Solution Cards to Prompt Students

Sometimes young children are overwhelmed by verbal problem-solving strategies. Cue cards such as Wally's problem-solving steps shown earlier are useful non-verbal cues to help children remember the steps and to organize their thinking. It is helpful to show these cards frequently or post them on the walls in the classroom so that teachers can easily refer to them as an appropriate situation arises. In addition, solution cards that depict a variety of possible solutions can be put in a brief case or file labeled "Problem Solving Detective Manual." Teachers can refer students to check the solution cards when they are having difficulty coming up with a solution to a real-life problem.

©Incredible Years®

Make Solution Detective Notebooks

Teachers can strengthen students' problem solving discussions by utilizing some of the ideas they have suggested in writing journals and homework exercises. For example, school age students could be given a homework exercise to write about (or draw a picture of) a problem that happened and what solution they used to solve the problem. From these drawings and discussions teachers can compile a classroom solution detective manual that can be viewed by parents and other students and teachers in the school.

Think about Positive and Negative Consequences

When teachers discuss the possible consequences of solutions, they occasionally focus on negative ones. For instance, a teacher and boy may be talking about outcomes of a proposed solution that hitting his friend may allow him to get the ball he wants. One obvious consequence is that the other child will cry, be unhappy, and get the hitter in trouble with his teachers. Most teachers would predict this consequence. However, many would overlook the fact that hitting or grabbing *might* work to get the desired ball. It is important to be honest with students and explore both the positive and negative consequences. If hitting or grabbing works in the short run, the child then needs to think about what effect such behavior might have on his friend's desire to play with him in the long run. By evaluating all of the possible outcomes, students can make a better judgment about how effective each solution is.

Model Your Thinking Out Loud

It is helpful for your students to observe daily problem solving that goes on in the classroom. Students can learn by watching teachers decide who is going to pick up the supplies, write the weekly note home, or decide where to take a field trip. There are countless opportunities for children to observe teachers discussing a problem or conflict, generating solutions, and then working together to evaluate what the best solution might be. It is also helpful for them to see teachers evaluate a solution that may not have worked out well and to hear a plan to try different strategy for the future. Research suggests that this opportunity for children to observe adults resolving conflict is critical, not only for developing their problem-solving skills, but also for reducing their stress and anxiety about unresolved issues.

Focus on Thinking and Self-Management

Often teachers believe that the objective of problem solving is to come up with the best solution to a particular situation. While this would be nice if it happened, the real purpose for going through this process with students is to teach them a thinking strategy and a method of self-management rather than generating the "correct" solution.

Therefore when problem solving with students, teachers can focus on *how* they are thinking rather than on specific conclusions. The goal is to help them become comfortable thinking about conflict, develop a knowledge base for generating good solutions or choices, and understand strategies for thinking ahead to the possible consequences of different solutions. These cognitive social problem-solving skills will eventually lead to self-management when faced with real-life conflict. The following are two approaches to responding to a very dependent and insecure student. In the second example, notice how the teacher helped the student to become more independent and secure with the problem-solving approach.

CIRCLE TIME SCRIPT
Ineffective Problem Solving with Student
"But I want help now!"

Marty: Teacher, I need help with this.

Teacher: I can't, I'm busy.

Marty: Please, Teacher, please help me?

Teacher: I have to get this done first, I'll work with you later.

Marty: Please? I want you to work with me now. I can't do it!

Teacher: Just go work by yourself while I finish this. You have to learn how to work by yourself. You can't have everything the minute you want it.

Five minutes later.

Marty: Teacher, are you finished yet?

Teacher: I'll tell you when I'm finished, don't bother me or I won't help you at all.

Effective Problem Solving for Promoting Student Self-Management

Marty: Teacher, will you help me?

Teacher: I'm working with Anna right now. When I finish working with Anna, then I can help you.

Marty: Please teacher, please help me now.

Teacher: I can't help now as I am in the middle of something with Anna.

Marty: But I really need help! I can't do it!

Teacher: Can you think of something different to do while I finish this? (*Teacher helps Marty think of alternative activity.*)

Marty: No.

Teacher: You're just teasing me. What part of it can you get started?

Marty: I could draw something.

Teacher: Yes, that's one thing you could do.

Marty: Or, I could do the other part of the page and leave this section for later.

Teacher: Yes, now you've thought of two good solutions. You are getting to be a pretty good thinker when you have a problem. And when I'm finished with Anna, I'll come over and help you with the part that is causing you difficulty.

Emotional confrontation can be avoided when both Marty and his teacher recognize the problem and each other's point of view. Marty can learn to accept what he cannot have and to wait for what he wants if he is guided to think about how his teacher is feeling and if he feels his teacher understands how he is feeling.

Make Your Puppets Come Alive

As we have discussed, puppets are very helpful for teaching children problem-solving concepts. Young children are enthralled with puppets and will talk about painful or sensitive issues with them more easily than with an adult. The children won't notice if the teacher is not a trained puppeteer— the important thing is to be fun and playful with the puppets. The puppets become "real" for the children so each puppet must have a name, an age, personality, special interests and a family situation. Teachers can use several different puppets to represent different temperaments (shy or impulsive) and family situations (for example, adopted, living with single parent, or living with two parents). The puppets should be subject to the same classroom rules and discipline as the students. They can be used to model earning a special privilege for successfully solving a particularly difficult problem, for handling frustration appropriately, or coping with a learning difficulty. In order to keep their personalities alive, puppets can change clothes, be involved in holidays and celebrations, and sometimes go out on the playground or eat lunch with the class.

Hold Regular Class Meetings or Circle Times

It is important to have protected time to devote to teaching social skills and problem solving. Just as reading and math have set times in the school day, regular weekly class meetings or Circle Times should be used to teach the problem-solving steps and to discuss problems that may be identified either by the teacher or students. These meetings are more effective sitting on the floor (or on small chairs) in a circle or semicircle format away from desks. For younger children, the teacher will usually direct the agenda for these meetings, first teaching students basic problem-solving steps, then systematically teaching a variety of friendly solutions, and then putting these solutions into practice with hypothetical solutions that the teacher (and puppet) present to the class. The teacher will choose problems that are relevant to the children, but will not usually solicit student input into what problems are discussed.

Older children can start to take more responsibility for the content of the problem-solving sessions. Teachers will still want to make sure that students understand problem-solving steps and a repertoire of friendly solutions, but then students can help direct the content. When starting these meetings the teacher should discuss with the students the "ground rules" for the circle time meeting. For example saying, "Remember what our rules are for our detective circle meeting time?"

Classroom Meeting or Circle Time Rules

Listening Ears

- One person speaks at a time
- Listen and look when another is speaking
- One problem will be discussed at a time
- No "put downs" allowed when sharing opinions (about anyone: parents, teachers, or other students)
- Keep hands and feet to yourself
- Meetings will last no more than 30 minutes
- Everybody's suggestions for solutions are welcomed
- Anyone has a right to pass
- When talking about a problem, do not use another student's name unless the two students have agreed to present the problem together

Once the ground rules have been reviewed, then the teacher and students set the agenda by asking who has a problem they want to discuss. If there are several students with problems, then one or two are chosen for that meeting and the others scheduled for subsequent weekly meetings. For older children (who can write) it can be helpful to have a "problem solving box" in classroom. Students can write out their concerns or ideas for the circle time discussion and put them in the agenda box during the week. Teachers can make it clear that everything won't be discussed right away, but this is a way for teachers to know what students are concerned with.

When the agenda or problem to be discussed has been settled, the students discuss their feelings about the problem and go onto to suggest possible ways to solve the problem. Students are encouraged to express their ideas for solving the problem as a suggestion. For example, "Would it help if you...?" or, "I have a suggestion." Sometimes it is helpful for the person speaking or sharing a suggestion to hold a special speaking object (e.g. stuffed bear such as Talking Ted or a toy microphone) and then everyone in the group knows who is speaking and who is listening. When finished sharing her ideas, the speaker passes the microphone to the next child to speak. Any child who does not want to speak may say "Pass" and hand it on. Sometimes children who find it difficult to speak out will allow Talking Ted to speak on their behalf. During Circle Time it is important that the teacher value all opinions, summarize what children have said, avoid interruptions or criticisms and follow the Circle Time rules just as the other students do (e.g., teacher raises quiet hand up to ask a question). It is important that students feel safe during Circle Time to say what they feel.

It can be helpful to have a "problem solving mailbox" in the classroom.

Occasionally the teacher may want to ask for help with a problem. Problems can be anything from playground issues, teasing and bullying, to issues such as cheating, put-downs in the classroom and noise levels. For example, one second grade teacher was worried about put-downs in her classroom so she brought it up at the class meeting. She began by saying, "In our class we have a politeness rule, and we use language that helps people feel good about themselves and respectful to others. This means we have a "no put-down zone" in our classroom. But I have noticed some put-downs being used, and I wondered if it is possible that some of you don't realize that these words are put-downs. First I would like to talk about some examples of put-downs?" The class goes on to list put downs such as, "gee you're a idiot, weirdo, nerd" or, "that's a dumb idea," or, "your mother's a dog-face." Some students may not see these put-downs as hurtful but as something funny. The teacher continues the discussion by asking the students how they would feel if they were called these names. The class is prompted to discuss why someone speaks this way. Next she asks the class to brainstorm other more appropriate ways of communicating disagreement. Eventually she may suggest the idea of a "put up" rule. She might plan with her class that she will give a sticker whenever she notices someone giving a "put up" to a classmate. Finally, she will ask the students to practice or role play with each other different ways they can give put ups.

Put Up Rule

Invite Others to Circle Time

During Circle Time students, teachers, puppets, and guests can be encouraged to bring up problems for problem solving. Some problems or situations are too sensitive for students to be open about. These are the issues that puppets can raise. For example, issues around bullying, stealing, being afraid of a teacher or parent, or being touched in unwanted places can be presented by Wally or Molly puppets. Lunch time and recess problems can also be brought up in circle time. For example, the lunch time and recess supervisors or bus drivers should be encouraged to come to these meetings to bring up problems regarding table manners or sportsmanship or bus behavior for the students to help solve. Finally, asking parents to join Circle Time occasionally can help promote collaboration and build strong links between home and school.

Set Up Activities to Practice Problem Solving and Reinforce Prosocial Solutions

It is essential that teachers provide small group cooperative activities to practice the concepts discussed during circle time or in classroom meetings. See Chapter 13 for descriptions of some more of these activities. The teacher's role during these activities is to coach and praise the children whenever they use appropriate problem-solving strategies.

Praise and More Praise—Issue Personal or Classroom "Challenges"

Throughout the day, in class, on the playground and in the cafeteria teachers should look for students who are making good choices and effectively problem solving and pause to praise the children's use of these strategies. For example a teacher might say, "Wow, you two worked that problem out like real detectives! You are getting very good at solving problems and staying calm." Teachers can also issue either a personal challenge or classroom challenge to meet the goal of achieving a certain number of good solutions. For example, "I am going record every time I see someone problem solving and making good choices. When the class gets to 50 we will have a celebration." An individual challenge might also be effective, "Mathew, I am going to give you a personal challenge—when I notice you coming up with 10 different good solutions, you will be admitted to the detective club, level one." Mathew might be given a punch card with numbers on it that he can have punched whenever he is observed making good choices. Or, he might wear a detective wristband which permits the teacher to stamp it for each time he uses a safe solution.

Involving Parents

Children will learn these problem-solving steps even better if parents are informed of them and can reinforce their occurrence at home. Teachers can send home newsletters and pictures explaining the problem-solving steps and encouraging parents to use this terminology at home whenever there is a conflict. For example, when a brother and sister are arguing, parents can trigger the problem-solving process by ask-

I'm good at helping!

© *Incredible Years* ®

ing, "What is the problem?" "What are some solutions?", "What do you think would happen if you did that?", "Are there any other solutions?" and, "What do you think is the best choice?" (based on being fair, safe and leading to good feelings). Parents using the school problem-solving terminology at home will cue children into using this thinking process when they are becoming upset. Of course, if teachers can offer actual workshops to train parents in problem-solving strategies this will lead to even greater assurance that parents will understand how to use the process at home. Finally, teachers can give problem-solving homework assignments that ask children to discuss particular problems with their parents. For example the Dinosaur curriculum uses a detective activities manual that includes student home activities that are to be completed in discussion with parents or a guardian. For example, one such home activity is as follows, "Freddy and Felicity seem to be fighting a lot over things like who gets sit in the front seat, or who gets to watch a particular TV program and their mother gets angry at them when they fight. Talk to your parent about ways they could solve this problem and bring your ideas to class." The children's books, *Wally's Detective Book for Solving Problems at Home* and *Wally's Detective Book for Solving Problems at School* (Webster-Stratton, 1998) are given out to children to read with their parents at home. These books provide a rich array of solutions to choose from when children are faced with a variety of common problems. Teachers can offer parents a workshop to learn how to use these books successfully with their children by talking about only one or two problems in a sitting and using puppets to practice their solutions. Finally, there are some brief letters or simple tips for parents that teachers can send home to help them teacher their children to problem solve. See web site for teacher-to-parent communication letter.

☀ **http://www.incredibleyears.com/TeacherResources/index.asp**

CONCLUSION

Teaching these social problem-solving steps is no harder than teaching any other complex set of academic skills such as long division or geography or reading. First teachers teach the step-by-step procedures and then they provide modeling, repeated practice, and reinforcement with different situations. Gradually with time and practice and persistence these "scripts" will become automatic for students, and with ongoing experiences they will be broadened and integrated. Just as with academic subjects, there is no expectation these skills will all be mastered in one grade or one course but will require continued instruction and infusion into classroom content throughout the student's education. Moreover, just as some students have more difficulty with a particular academic subject, some children have more difficulty with reading social cues, understanding how to solve problems, and expressing their feelings. With persistent coaching and encouragement on the part of the teacher, students will come to perceive themselves as competent decision makers and will be armed with the necessary skills for meeting the challenges of adolescence and adulthood.

TO SUM UP...

- Use games and puppets to present hypothetical problem situations for students to practice the problem-solving steps and learn the vocabulary.
- Help students clearly define the problem and to recognize the feelings involved.
- For preschool children, primarily focus on generating and learning a variety of different solutions.
- Be positive, creative, and humorous.
- For primary or elementary age students, focus on thinking through to the various consequences of different solutions.
- Help children anticipate what to do next when a solution doesn't work.
- Model effective problem solving yourself.
- Remember it is the process of learning how to think about conflict that is critical, rather than getting the correct answers and choosing the best solution to try out.

The Incredible Years®
Teacher Classroom Management Self-Reflection Inventory
Teaching Students to Problem Solve

Date: _____ Teacher Name: _____

Teachers learn extensively from self-reflection regarding their class-room management and the teaching strategies they are using that are working or not working. From these reflections teachers determine personal goals for making changes in their approaches to bring about the most positive learning climate they can. Use this Inventory to think about your strengths and limitations and determine your goals.

Problem-Solving Skills	1 = NEVER 3 = OCCASIONALLY 5 = CONSISTENTLY
1. I help students identify a problem emotion that indicates they have a problem to solve.	1 2 3 4 5
2. I help students stay calm so they can talk about the problem. If needed, I prompt them to take deep breaths and use self talk such as "I can do it, I can stay patient and solve this problem."	1 2 3 4 5
3. I help students with problem-solving difficulties to work with other students who are good problem-solving detectives.	1 2 3 4 5
4. I promote students motivation to be problem-solving detectives with special rewards for using effective solutions.	1 2 3 4 5
5. When children have a problem, I encourage them to check out the classroom problem-solving solutions detective kit.	1 2 3 4 5

6. I encourage students to write stories about how they have solved problems (or to dictate stories so I can write them down if they are unable to write).	1 2 3 4 5
7. I model problem-solving language myself throughout the day (e.g., "I am getting frustrated now, but I can calm myself down by taking a deep breath and thinking of my happy place").	1 2 3 4 5
8. I provide opportunities for children to practice solving problems by setting up conflict scenarios for them to solve (e.g., one student wants to be on the computer but someone is using it; or one student has a favorite toy and another student wants it; or a child feels left out of a game).	1 2 3 4 5
9. I teach specific problem-solving solutions in circle time or individually with children (e.g., practicing asking for something, apologizing, taking turns, waiting, asking teacher or a peer for help, sharing, complimenting, ignoring, doing something else).	1 2 3 4 5
10. I use persistence, emotion and social coaching with students.	1 2 3 4 5
11. I teach specific problem-solving steps by helping them follow the sequence of : 1) define the problem, 2) think of solutions, 3) ask what would happen next? 4) evaluate the best choice, and 5) choose the best solution to try out.	1 2 3 4 5
12. I use books and stories of problem-solving scenarios to practice the problem-solving steps.	1 2 3 4 5
13. I use puppets, pretend games, imaginary stories and drama activities to set up problem scenarios and children practice solving the problems by acting out their solutions.	1 2 3 4 5

14. I have developed behavior plans that target problem solving steps and specific solutions they can learn according to their developmental abilities and target goals.	1 2 3 4 5
15. I am teaching the parents of my students to understand how to teach their children to problem solve through personal meetings, emails, or Teacher-to-Parent Communication Home Activities letters.	1 2 3 4 5
16. For parents of students with emotional-regulation difficulties I meet with them to share the problem solving strategies and how to use emotion coaching methods.	1 2 3 4 5
Future Goals Regarding Problem Solving Training:	Total

REFERENCES

Asarnow, J. R., & Callan, J. W. (1985). Boys with peer adjustment problems: Social cognitive processes. *Journal of Consulting an Clinical Psychology, 53*, 80-87.

Asher, S. R., Parkhurst, J. T., Hymel, S., & Williams, G. A. (1990). Peer rejection and loneliness in childhood. In S. R. Asher & J. D. Coie (Eds.), *Peer rejection in childhood* (pp. 253-273). Cambridge: Cambridge University Press.

Battistich, V., Schaps, E., & Wilson, N. (2004). Effects of an elementary school intervention in students "connectiveness" to school and social adjustment during middle school. *The Journal of Primary Prevention 24*, 243-262.

Beauchaine, T. P., Neuhaus, E., Brenner, S. L., & Gatzke-Kopp, L. (2008). Ten good reasons to consider biological processes in prevention and intervention research. *Development and Psychopathology, 20*, 745-774.

Beelmann, A., Pfingste, U., & Losel, F. (1994). Effects of training social competence in children: A meta-analysis of recent evaluation studies. *Journal of Abnormal Child Psychology, 5*, 265-275.

Brown, W. H., Odom, S. L., & McConnell, S. R. (2008). *Social competence of young children: Risk, disability and prevention.* Baltimore: Paul H. Brookes Publishing Co.

Camp, B. W., & Bash, M. A. S. (1985). *Think aloud: Increasing social and cognitive skills—A problem-solving program for children in the classroom.* Champaign, IL: Research Press.

Coie, J. D., Watt, N. F., West, S. G., Hawkins, D., Asarnow, J. R., Markman, H. J., et al. (1993). The science of prevention: A conceptual framework and some directions for a national research program. *American Psychologist, 48*, 1013-1022.

Crick, N. R., & Dodge, K. A. (1994). A review and reformulation of social information processing mechanisms in children's social adjustment. *Psychological Bulletin, 115*, 74-101.

D'Zurilla, T. J., & Goldfried, M. R. (1971). Problem solving and behavior modification. *Journal of Abnormal Psychology, 78*, 107-126.

Dodge, K. A., & Price, J. M. (1994). On the relation between social information processing and socially competent behavior in early school-aged children. *Child Development, 65*, 1385-1397.

Durlak, J. A., Weissberg, R. P., Dymnick, A., B., Taylor, R. D., & Schellinger, B. (2011). The Impact of Enhancing Students' Social and Emotional Learning: A Meta-Analysis of School-based Universal Interventions. *Child Development, 82*, 405-432.

Elias, M. J., & Clabby, J. F. (1989). *Social decision making skills: A curriculum guide for the elementary grades*. Gaithersburg, MD: Aspen.

Elias, M. J., & Tobias, S. E. (1996). *Social problem solving: Interventions in schools*. New York: Guilford.

Gardner, H. (1993). *The multiple intelligences: The theory in practice*. New York: Basic Books.

Goldstein, A. P., & Pentz, M. A. (1984). Psychological skill training and the aggressive adolescent. *School Psychology Review, 13*, 311-323.

Hawkins, J. D., Smith, B. H., & Catalano, R. F. (2004). Social development and social and emotional learning. In J. E. Zins, R. P. Weissberg, M. C. Wang & H. J. Walberg (Eds.), *Building academic success on social and emotional learning: What does the research say?* New York: Teachers College Press.

Kazdin, A. (1995). Child, Parent and Family Dysfunction as Predictors of Outcome in Cognitive-Behavioral Treatment of Antisocial Children. *Behavior Research and Therapy, 3*, 271-281.

Kazdin, A. E., Esveldt, D. K., French, N. H., & Unis, A. S. (1987). Problem-solving skills training and relationship therapy in the treatment of antisocial child behavior. *Journal of Consulting and Clinical Psychology, 55*(1), 76-85.

Kazdin, A. E., Siegel, J. C., & Bass, D. (1992). Cognitive problem-solving skills training and parent management training in the treatment of antisocial behavior in children. *Journal of Consulting and Clinical Psychology, 60*, 733-747.

Knutson, J. F., DeGarmo, D., Koeppl, G., & Reid, J. B. (2005). Care neglect, supervisory neglect and harsh parenting in the development of children's aggression: A replication and extension. *Child Maltreatment, 10*, 92-107.

Ladd, G. W., Kochenderfer, B. J., & Coleman, C. (1997). Classroom peer acceptance, friendship, and victimization: Distinct relational systems that contribute uniquely to children's school adjustment. *Child Development, 68*, 1181-1197.

Miller, M. G., Midgett, J., & Wicks, M. L. (1992). Student and teacher perceptions related to behavior change after skillstreaming training. *Behavioral Disorders, 17*, 291-295.

Ostrander, R., & Herman, K. C. (2006). Potential developmental, cognitive, and parenting mediators of the relationship between ADHD and depression. *Journal of Consulting and Clinical Psychology, 74*, 89-98.

Piaget, J., & Inhelder, B. (1962). *The Psychology of the Child.* New York Basic Books.

Putallaz, M., & Wasserman, A. (1990). Children's entry behavior. In Steven R. Asher & John D. Coie (Eds.), *Peer Rejection in Childhood* (pp. 60-89). Cambridge.: Cambridge University Press.

Rubin, K. H., Chen, X., & Hymel, S. (1993). Socioemotional characteristics of withdrawn and aggressive children. *Merrill-Palmer Quarterly, 39*, 518-534.

Rubin, K. H., & Krasnor, L. R. (1986). Social-cognitive and social behavioral perspectives on problem-solving. In M. Perlmutter (Ed.), *Cognitive perspectives on children's social and behavioral development. The Minnesota Symposia on Child Psychology* (Vol. 18, pp. 1-68). Hillsdale, NJ: Lawrence Erlbaum Associates.

Schneider, B. H. (1992). Didactic methods for enhancing children's peer relationships: A quantitative review. *Clinical Psychology Review, 12*, 363-382.

Shure, M. (1994). I Can Problem Solve (ICPS): *An interpersonal cognitive problem-solving program for children.* Champaign, IL: Research Press.

Shure, M. B. (1997). Interpersonal cognitive problem solving: Primary prevention of early high-risk behaviors in the preschool and primary years. In G. W. Albee & T. P. Gullotta (Eds.), *Primary Prevention Works* (pp. 167-188). Thousand Oaks, CA: Sage.

Spivak, G., Platt, J. J., & Shure, M. B. (1976). *The problem solving approach to adjustment.* San Francisco: Jossey-Bass.

Webster-Stratton, C. (1985). Mother perceptions and mother-child interactions: Comparison of a clinic-referred and a non-clinic group. *Journal of Clinical Child Psychology, 14.*(4), 334-339.

Webster-Stratton, C., & Hammond, M. (1997). Treating children with early-onset conduct problems: A comparison of child and parent training interventions. *Journal of Consulting and Clinical Psychology, 65*(1), 93-109.

Webster-Stratton, C., Reid, M. J., & Hammond, M. (2004). Treating children with early-onset conduct problems: Intervention outcomes for parent, child, and teacher training. *Journal of Clinical Child and Adolescent Psychology, 33*(1), 105-124.

Weissberg, R., Jackson, A., & Shriver, T. (1993). Promoting positive social development and health practices in young urban adolescents. In M. J. Elias (Ed.), *Social decision making and life skills development: Guidelines for middle school educators* (pp. 45-78). Gaithersburg, MD: Aspen.

Weissberg, R. P., & Greenberg, M. (1998). School and community competence-enhancement and prevention programs. In I. Siegel & A. Renninger (Eds.), *Handbook of child psychology: Child psychology in practice* (Vol. 4). New York Wiley.

Weissberg, R. P., Kumpfer, K. L., & Seligman, M. E. P. (2003). Prevention that works for children and youth: An introduction. *American Psychologist, 59*, 425-432.

Zins, J. E., & Elias, M. J. (2006). Social and emotional learning. In G. G. Bear & K. M. Minke (Eds.), *Children's needs III: Development, prevention, and intervention* (pp. 1-13). Bethesda, MD: National Association of School Psychologists.

CHAPTER 13

Peer Problems
and Friendship Skills

F ew teachers need to be convinced that a positive social classroom
climate and peer friendships provide an important context for achieving
optimal student learning. Through the successful formation of friendships,
children learn social skills such as cooperation, sharing, and conflict management (Howes, 2000). Friendships also foster a child's sense of group
belonging and connectedness and begin to facilitate children's empathy
skills; that is, their ability to understand another's perspective. The formation
of friendships, or their absence, has an enduring impact on children's
social, emotional, and academic adjustment in later life (Burgess,
Wojslawowicz, Rubin, Rose-Krasnor, & Booth-LaForce, 2006). As noted
in earlier chapters, research has shown that peer problems such as isolation, rejection, and aggression are predictive of a variety of problems
including depression, poor academic achievement, school drop out, and

other psychiatric problems in adolescence and adulthood (Cairns, Cairns, & Neckerman, 1989; Kupersmidt & Patterson, 1991; Ladd, 1990; Ladd, Kochenderfer, & Coleman, 1997; Lau, Fung, Ho, Liu, & Gudino, 2011).

Why do some children have more difficulties making friends?

For some young children, making friends is not easy. It has been found that children who have a more difficult temperament, including hyperactivity, impulsivity, and inattention, have particular difficulty forming and maintaining friendships (Brown, Odom, & McConnell, 2008; Campbell, 1994; Pope, Bierman, & Mumma, 1989). Their inadequate impulse control leads to aggressive responses, poor problem solving, lack of empathy and a failure to consider the potential consequences of their actions. These children also have significantly delayed play skills that include difficulties waiting their turn, making suggestions in a friendly way, accepting others' suggestions, and collaborating in play with peers (Webster-Stratton & Lindsay, 1999). It has been found that children with poor conversation skills are more likely to be peer-rejected (Asher & Coie, 1990; Coie, 1990; Olson, 1992). They have difficulty knowing what to say to initiate a conversation and how to respond positively to the overtures of others. As a result, they have difficulty joining in groups (Putallaz & Wasserman, 1990). Children with social difficulties often misjudge what is expected of them in social situations. They may be impulsive or disruptive when entering a group, have trouble sharing and waiting their turns, or make inappropriate or critical remarks. Consequently, their interactions are often annoying to other children. Other children may be threatened by how easily impulsive children become emotionally upset or aggressive. These peers may respond by isolating, rejecting, or making fun of them. Young impulsive children who are having these kinds of peer difficulties also report internal distress, such as loneliness and low self-esteem (Asher, Parkhurst, Hymel, & Williams, 1990; Asher & Williams, 1987; Crick & Dodge, 1994). These self-perceptions contribute further to their social difficulties by causing them to be overly sensitive to peer comments, to lack confidence in approaching other children, and eventually to withdraw from interactions and group activities. Their isolation results in fewer and fewer opportunities for social interactions and fewer chances to learn more appropriate social skills. The end result can be a negative reputation among classmates and other peers, social isolation, and eventual disengagement from the learning process.

A major challenge for teachers is to prevent peer rejection and exclusion and to promote effective social skills and positive friendships for all children. Teachers are even more important than parents in this endeavor because parents are often not present to help when their children are having difficulties in large peer groups. In this chapter we discuss ways teachers can teach some of the specific social skills, covered in many social skills curriculum, which research has suggested are important for children to learn in order to develop good friendships (Bear, Richards, & Gibbs, 1997; Bierman, Miller, & Stabb, 1987; Elias & Tobias, 1996; Greenberg, Kusche, Cook, & Quamma, 1995; Gresham, 1995, 1997; Grossman, et al., 1997; Knoff & Batsche, 1995; Webster-Stratton, 1990, 1999; Webster-Stratton & Reid, 2003).

A major challenge for teachers is to prevent peer rejection and exclusion and to promote effective social skills and positive friendships.

Teaching children how to initiate peer interaction and enter a group

One of the first social skills to teach young children is how to enter a conversation or begin an interaction with peers. Some children are shy and afraid to initiate or join in when a group of students are already engaged in an activity. Other children have trouble because they are overly enthusiastic. They abruptly barge into a group of children engaged in play without asking or waiting for an opening. As a consequence, they are frequently rejected by the group. Both types of children need to learn how to approach a group, wait for an opening in the conversation, and politely ask to join in. Teachers can teach these group entry skills by role playing practice scenarios where a child wants to join a group of children in play. As we discussed in the prior chapter for teaching problem solving, we find the use of large life-size puppets (Wally and Molly) during Circle Time to be an engaging way to model and coach appropriate group entry skills. The following is an example of a circle time script you might do with your students.

CIRCLE TIME: LESSON SCRIPT
Initiating Group Entry

Teacher: Boys and girls, Wally (*puppet held by the teacher*) has a problem that he needs your help with.

Wally: Well, here's what happened. I was out on the play ground and some other children were playing with marbles. It looked really fun and I wanted to play, but they were so busy that they didn't notice me. I wasn't sure how to get them to let me play. Can you help show me what to do?

Children: *Teacher helps children give Wally ideas.*

Teacher: Those are some good ideas, and there are some important things to do when you want to play with children who are already playing. I think we can act out some solutions that will help Wally. I need three actors to pretend be playing with this game. (*Teacher has puzzle, game, or blocks, depending on age of children.*)

Teacher: Let's pretend that you two are playing with these blocks and, Mindy, you want to join in. The first thing you can do is watch so that you understand what they are playing.

Wally: Oh, wow—that's a good idea. Mindy is really watching. That means she'll understand their game better. I think I can do that.

Teacher: The next thing that Mindy can do is to give a compliment or say something nice about their game. Mindy, can you try that?

Mindy: "Gee, that's looks like a fun game." (*Teacher could prompt these words if child didn't know what to say.*)

Wally: "Wow, Mindy just gave a friendly compliment. I bet you boys and girls like hearing her kind words."

Teacher: So, Mindy, after you've watched for awhile, you can ask politely if you can play. Let's try that.

Mindy: "Would you mind if I played with you?" (*asks permission*)

Wally: "That was great. Mindy is asking politely and in a friendly way if she can play, and she is waiting patiently to hear the answer. I think this seems like a really good way to ask to join in. I bet those two children will let her play!"

Playing Children: "Okay, we've just started."

Wally: That was friendly. Seems like Mindy could ask them what she should do to play with them.

Mindy: "Thanks, which piece do you want me to use?" (*asks how to join in*)

Teacher: "Wow! Mindy even asked what she should do in the game so that the other children can share their ideas with her."

Wally: You really helped me figure this out. I think I understand now. First I'll watch and wait. Then I'll give a compliment. Then I'll ask to play and listen for an answer. And when I start playing, I'll find out how I can join in without messing up their game. I'm going to try that tomorrow when those children play marbles again!

Alternative Variation:

Teacher: "You know, Wally, that worked really well the first time Mindy tried. I know that sometimes kids aren't ready to play when you ask. Could we see what you would do if they didn't want you to play? (*Teacher sets up new role play and let's children know that this time they will say the child can't play. However, it is important to coach the children to use a polite response when saying no. The teacher should have them practice friendly ways of responding before starting this role-play. It is also likely that Wally or the teacher will need to coach the child who is joining in—helping him or her to remember the steps.*)

Child from class

John: (*approaches the group, pauses and watches students play basketball for a while*) "Gee, great shot." (*compliments and waits for response from peers*)

John: (*pauses for awhile and watches them play*) "Would you mind if I played with you?"

Children: "I'm sorry, we're in the middle of a game. Maybe you can play when we're done."

Teacher: "That was a very polite way to say no to John. I wonder what he will do?"

John: "Okay, maybe another time. When you're done, if you want another game with me, that would be fun." (*accepts decision and finds something else to do*) "Let's see maybe I'll ask Freddy if he wants a game of marbles."

Teacher: "John accepted their answer and is finding something else to do. That can be a hard decision, but John is being really strong!"

Change Roles: This time another student can play the role of asking to join in the play. Wally can be one of the peers who is already playing the game, or he can take the role of coaching the student to go through each step (watch, compliment, ask to play, accept response).

This role play practice emphasizes the four steps of entering a group of children (1) watch from the sidelines and show interest; (2) continue watching and say something nice about children playing; (3) wait for a pause in game before asking to join in; and (4) ask politely to join in and accept response. As children are learning these steps, it is important for the teacher to clearly define each step and coach it during the role-play practices. For example the teacher says, "Okay, first you are going to just watch the other children to see what they are doing. When you know what they are doing, try to think of something friendly you could say about their game and give a compliment." Younger children may need the teacher to provide the words for the compliment. For example teacher says, "You can say, 'You are really good at playing ball.'" Older children may be able to come up with their own script, but the teacher should still label the steps. After children have learned the basic steps of polite ways to join a group, it is important to rehearse coping responses if their requests are denied (scenario 2, earlier). Research indicates that about half the time children are turned down in their requests to join in play with others. Therefore it is important to prepare them for this possibility so that it is not a crushing event, and so that they can look for another group to play with.

About half the time children are turned down in their requests to join in play with others.

Teach young children how to play with each other

While all young children will need encouragement and coaching to initiate social interactions, children who are impulsive, inattentive, hyperactive or socially isolated will need more intensive help. Children with Attention Deficit Hyperactivity Disorder are delayed in their interactive play skills and many have not learned the principles of asking politely, waiting, or cooperation and balance in give-and-take relationships. An impulsive five-year-old's social and emotional development may look more like a toddler or three-year-old. These children often lack the cognitive and developmental skills necessary for good cooperative and reciprocal interaction.

For these children, social skills must be broken down into explicit teaching, where each skill is presented and practiced during a structured circle time or small group lesson. Teachers might begin by asking students questions to elicit their ideas about what friendly behavior is. For example asking, "What makes a good friend?" or "How do you play with friends?" will help children to brainstorm their ideas about how a good friend behaves. Next ask for a child to volunteer to demonstrate some of these specific friendly behaviors (helping, sharing, waiting) using blocks or Legos. This demonstrating can be done with the teacher and child, two children, or a child and a puppet. Before the role-play begins, the rest of the class is asked to notice (perhaps by putting up a thumb) each specific friendly behavior. Students of different ages can focus on developmentally appropriate skills. For example younger students will focus on asking, sharing, helping, waiting, being polite (please and thank you), and taking turns. Older students, who have mastered these basic skills, will focus on making friendly suggestions, listening and responding to an idea, giving compliments, asking for permission, agreeing with someone, compromising, giving up a turn, and being flexible.

CIRCLE TIME SCRIPT
Playing with a Friend

Teacher: Boys and girls, Wally (puppet held by teacher) came today to show you how he plays with his friends. I need one of you to be his friend. (*teacher sets up blocks or puzzle or cooperative activity*)

Teacher: Let's see the friendly thing Wally does first.

Wally: (*is building a castle out of duplos*) Would you like some of my duplos and horses? (*offers to share*)

Student: Yes, I want the big horse and barn please.

Wally: (*hands his friend his barn and horse*) Here's the black horse and my brown horse is running in the field.

Teacher: FREEZE ACTION! Who saw something friendly here? (*child identifies sharing, or teacher prompts them to say that sharing occurred*) How did that make Wally's friend feel? Can someone else come up and show me what sharing looks like?

Continue with Wally modeling how to share, wait, take turns, trade, offer to help, suggest an idea, accept an idea etc. The pacing of this practice will depend on the age of the children. Younger children may spend an entire lesson on the concept of sharing, with several children role playing the same behavior. Older children may move quickly through these simpler behaviors and then practice some of the more complicated social skills listed above (suggesting, compromising).

Once this friendly play has been modeled for the students and practiced in Circle Time, then teachers can set up a semi-structured situation where small groups of students practice what they have learned with unstructured and cooperative toys (such as blocks, Lincoln Logs, drawing materials). It is usually best to pair up more socially competent children with a child who has fewer skills. During these play periods teachers will need to pay particular attention to social coaching strategies discussed in Chapter Four and focus on praising children with delayed social skills whenever they notice them taking turns, sharing, asking politely and waiting. Since this is a labor-intensive activity, it is immensely helpful to have trained teacher assistants and parents to help provide individual coaching and encouragement during these small group practice times. Teachers can also use socially skilled students (or trained students from older grades) to be "coaches" and ask them to notice and praise all the friendly behaviors exhibited by other children.

I'm good at listening!

©Incredible Years®

Teaching children how to follow directions

Part of learning reciprocal play involves accepting the ideas and directions of another child. Children who are noncompliant and impulsive have difficulties accepting directions from their friends as well as their parents and teachers. The teacher can help students learn the skills of listening and following directions by playing various directions games. For example, teachers may play Wally (or Simon) Says and ask students to follow directions given by the puppet: "Wally says put your hands on your head. Wally says put your hands in your lap. Wiggle your fingers." It is important that teachers highlight the students' cooperative behavior by giving praise for listening carefully and following the directions. Later children may take turns giving the directions, so that students have experience following the directions of their peers.

Ask me how I shared.

©Incredible Years®

Other following direction games can also be played. Younger children may be given a number of colored shapes or specific objects (car, boat, train) or Wally's clothes and his body to dress and given directions to follow. "Find your green circle and put it on top of your red square." "Drive your car around the boat." "Make a line with the car in front, the boat in the middle, and the train at the end." "Put Wally's glasses on and his snow hat." Again, each time students follow a direction, teachers respond with praise and encouragement. Older students can be given more complicated instructions and praised for their good listening and memory skills.

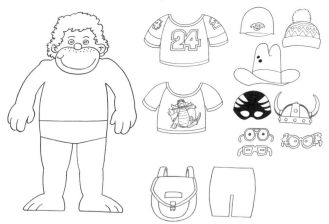

See Dinosaur Curriculum for a wide variety of Wally's clothes.

CIRCLE TIME: LESSON SCRIPT
Following Directions

Teacher: Boys and girls, Wally (*puppet held by teacher*) came today to show you how he listens and follows directions. I need one of you to be his friend and give him some directions.

Wally: I am listening carefully to what you ask me to do.

Student: (*Teacher whispers a direction in student's ear to ask Wally—"Wally put your right arm in the air."*)

Wally: (*puts up his right arm*)

Teacher: FREEZE ACTION! Who saw Wally listen? Okay now we are going to play a game where Wally gives you a direction. You have to listen carefully because when he says, "Wally says touch your nose, you follow his direction ~ but if he doesn't say 'Wally says' you don't do what he asks. Okay let's try that....

Continue with Wally giving directions and teacher praising students for listening carefully.

Note: Older children will enjoy the challenge of listening carefully and only following the directions when "Wally says." For younger students the focus should be on listening and following each direction Wally gives (without the trick of "Wally says").

Teaching children how to talk with friends

As we noted earlier, poor conversation skills have been linked repeatedly to poor social competence and peer rejection (Coie, 1990; Coie, Dodge, & Kupersmidt, 1990; Ladd, 1990). On the other hand, training in conversational skills has been found to enhance unpopular children's social functioning (Bierman, 1989; Ladd & Asher, 1985). Through role plays and games, teachers can practice and coach students in learning effective conversation skills such as introducing oneself, listening and waiting to talk, asking another child's feelings, taking turns in conversation, suggesting an idea, showing interest, praising someone, saying thank you, apologizing, and inviting someone to play. Teachers should focus on only one or two of these conversation skills at a time by first practicing and then praising and rewarding them whenever they occur in the classroom, lunchroom, or playground.

CIRCLE TIME: LESSON SCRIPT
Introducing Oneself

Teacher: Boys and girls, Molly (*puppet held by teacher*) is new to our class and she came today to show you how she introduces herself to new friends. I need one of you to be a new friend she wants to meet. (*teacher works Molly puppet*)

Molly: (*approaches child*) Hi, I am Molly and just started school today. What is your name?

Teacher: Did you see how Molly said her name and then asked her new friend's name? That's a good way to get to know someone!

Student: (*says her name*)

Molly: I like to play with puzzles, do you like that? Would you like to do a puzzle with me?

Teacher: FREEZE ACTION! Who saw what Molly did to introduce herself? Do you know the names of everyone in this class? (*ask for some students to tell their names*) Okay what did you notice what Molly did to find out what her new friend likes to do? Was she friendly?

Continue with Molly demonstrating questions she could ask her new friend or things she could share about herself such as her favorite game, sport, animal, color etc.

CIRCLE TIME: LESSON SCRIPT
Making Friendly Suggestions

Teacher: Boys and girls, Wally (*puppet held by teacher*) came today to show you how he listens to friendly suggestions. I need one of you to be his friend and give him some directions. (*teacher blocks or puzzle or cooperative activity*)

Wally: (*is building a castle out of duplos*) I am listening carefully to what you ask me to do.

Student: (*Teacher whispers a direction in student's ear to ask Wally*—"Wally would you put a blue block on top?")

Wally: "That's a good idea. I'll put the blue block on top."

Teacher: *FREEZE ACTION!* That was a really friendly suggestion. Who saw Wally listen? Okay now we are going to play a game where Wally gives you a suggestion and you listen to him.

Continue the game with Wally and the students taking turns giving friendly suggestions and listening to each other.

For older students, this game can then progress to teaching how to make a friendly counter-suggestion or politely refuse a suggestion.

Teacher: Wally, sometimes when someone makes a friendly suggestion, you might have your own ideas and you'd rather not follow their suggestions. Has that ever happened to you?

Wally: It sure has! The other day, I was drawing a picture and my sister, Molly came over and said that I should draw a house and a tree on my picture. I had the idea of drawing a whole sky scene with a rainbow, a sun, birds, a hot air balloon, and an airplane. I didn't want to draw the house. I was kind of frustrated with Molly for telling me what to do.

Teacher: Boys and girls, do you have an idea about how Wally could have politely told Molly about his plan? I wonder what Molly could have done then?

After the children talk about possible solutions, this scene could be acted out in a variety of ways showing a polite refusal, a counter-suggestion, a compromise, accepting a friend's refusal.

Here are some games and activities teachers can use to practice "friendly talk" and listening skills.

CIRCLE TIME
Games and Activities
for Teaching Friendly Talk

Compliment and Sharing Circle Time

It is often satisfying to end the day or the week with a compliment circle time. At this time the teacher asks for a volunteer (or can pull a name out of a hat) to say one nice thing about something friendly or kind a classmate has done that day. Each child is given a turn and asked to choose a different student to compliment so that everyone gets a turn. The children are encouraged to say, "I'd like to say "well done" to . . . because . . ." With young children, it is helpful to pass a stuffed animal to the person who is to receive the compliment as a tactile accompaniment to the friendly words. This works particularly well for children with limited language skills because they can still indicate a compliment by passing the bear to someone. The teacher can then help prompt or model the friendly language, "I see you are passing the bear to Jordan. You can say, "Jordan, you are my friend. I like you."

Praising

A regular sharing Circle Time can build students' sense of trust and group cohesiveness. Students can bring an object from home to share or teachers may have a selection of sharing questions that are drawn out of a special box. Some examples of questions to begin this process are, "What is the luckiest thing that ever happened to you?" or "What is your favorite animal or food?" or "What do you like to do on a rainy day?" Gradually, over time the questions can become more personal such as asking, "Tell us a time someone helped you this week" or "Tell a time when you were really angry but you stopped yourself" or "Tell us about something kind that you did." A sharing circle activity can be used to start the afternoon or as a mode of transition.

Guided Block Building Game

Pair up students. Have each pair divide two identical sets of large wooden blocks into two piles. Put a cardboard screen between the two piles of blocks so that one child cannot see the other child's blocks. Ask one student in the pair to make a structure with the blocks, narrating the steps as he builds. Ask the other student to try to make an identical structure, relying on his peer's verbal instructions. The second student will need to ask questions and receive help from the first student in order for this to happen. The first student will need to be supportive and specific to help his peer complete the task. (This game could be played with a number of different materials: play dough, paper and crayons, or other art supplies.) This game helps the children learn how to ask questions, listen, take turns in conversation, suggest ideas and be helpful.

Twenty Questions Game

Guess What? Make a file of pictures compiled from interesting magazines. Then ask a student to pull a picture of a secret object from the file. Then tell the other students they have 20 "yes" or "no" questions in order try to guess what the secret object is.

Secret Animal

The names of animals (or pictures for younger children) are written on sticky labels. A label is placed on a child's back without letting him or her see the name of the animal. The rest of the class is allowed to see the animal name. The student with the hidden label asks questions to find out what animal is on his back. "Is my animal a mammal?" "Does my animal live in the water?" Peers provide friendly responses to these questions. Depending on the age of the children, teachers may provide hints and ideas for questions. This game relies on teamwork to answer the questions and keep the hidden animal a secret until it is guessed.

Clay modeling: Guess What?

In this game one child makes something out of clay and the other children ask questions to guess what he is making.

Telling and listening

Molly's Listening Game

Pair up students and ask them to talk about a topic such as their favorite sport, a time when they were happy, something exciting, a favorite movie, or their family. Each student has one minute to speak while the other student listens with ears and eyes. After the speaker stops, the listener says a few words summarizing what the speaker said. Children return to the circle and take turns sharing something interesting about their partners.

Suggestion Game

Older students work in groups of 3-4 and are given materials (poster board and markers, collage materials, other art supplies) to complete some joint project. Students are told to take turns making a friendly suggestion to the other members of the group. Each suggestion must be accepted by the other students or politely responded to with a counter-suggestion, and a compromise reached. Students who have not had prior practice with this activity will likely need a great deal of initial coaching to be successful.

CIRCLE TIME
Detective Hat Game
Practicing Friendly Talk

Put some of the following questions into a detective hat and ask students to volunteer to pick out questions to answer and role play (or pass the hat in a circle and stop the music to indicate a student's turn). These questions are directed at helping students practice friendly conversation skills such as: being polite when interrupting someone, asking permission of parents, asking for help, telling yourself to wait, learning how to successfully join in a group of children and thinking of someone else's point of view.

(During circle time, children practice different friendly responses.)

- Your parents are talking and you want to ask them if you can go over to your friend's house for the night. (Your friend is on the phone.) What will you say?
- Your teacher is talking to you after school, and your mother is waiting in the car pool line to pick you up. What will you say?
- Your mom is on the phone and you want to ask her if you can go to the ball game with a friend. How can you interrupt?
- You want to sit in the front seat next to your father, but your sister got there first. What can you say?
- Some kids are playing a board game. You want to play but they are half way through the game. What can you say?
- Someone has hidden your lunch box so you don't have anything to eat for lunch. How would you explain this to your teacher?

- There are two games of football going on in the yard and the other game is getting muddled up with yours. How could you sort out the problem in a friendly way?
- The new boy in your class is standing by himself on the edge of the playground. How could you include him in your game?

Another Idea to Promote friendship

Pass a hat that contains all the students' names. The name each student picks out is their secret friend for the day. The teacher can give various instructions such as:

"Watch your friend and look for one friendly thing that he or she does today. At the end of the day, share that friendly thing in compliment circle."

OR

"Draw a picture of your secret friend. Under the picture, write a sentence about something he or she is good at."

OR

"Do a secret good deed for your friend sometime during the day. Share your good deed at the closing circle."

Use discussions and cooperative learning activities to teach children friendship skills

It is helpful for teachers to have regular discussions with their students about friendship and what it means to be a good friend. Concepts such as helping, sharing, apologizing, forgiving, complimenting, and being a good team player are key ideas for students to understand. These discussions should be held regularly (e.g., once a week), perhaps with students sitting in a circle on the floor. In these class meetings teachers can read stories about friends who face problems in their relationships. For example, a child who is unco-ordinated but wants to be on his friend's baseball team, or the friend who is being excluded by some other kids, or the child who doesn't know whether or not to forgive a friend who said something mean to him. These stories can prompt teachers to ask questions such as, "What would you do if you saw your friend being left out by a group of children?" or, "What would you do if your friend wanted to play on your soccer team, but you knew he was pretty clumsy?" Concrete examples from the classroom and playground should be used to help students think of ways they can counteract social isolation and bullying.

Carefully planned cooperative activities create mutual positive dependence among group members.

In addition to classroom discussions about friendships, it is also important to incorporate games and cooperative learning activities that help students practice friendly behaviors such as sharing, helping, and teamwork. Carefully planned cooperative activities, where the focus is on the performance of the group, create mutual positive dependence among group members. When each member of the group is given responsibility for every other member's learning of the prescribed task, students begin to feel responsible for each other. In fact, if practiced frequently, group projects can create cohesiveness that extends to an entire classroom. Small group cooperative learning activities also help prevent peer rejec-tion. Below is a list of cooperative activities that encourage practice of friendly behavior. The group size for each of these activities should vary according to the age and temperament of the child and the number of adults available to supervise. The teacher should team up the more hyper-active and impulsive children with calmer and more reflective students. Students who are isolated or who tend to be victimized should be placed with positive, friendly students. Some children may require coaching in pairs before they are ready to join larger groups of children. Children with friendship difficulties will need more teacher supervision and coaching than more socially competent children. For each of the activities listed below it will be important for the teacher to circulate and reinforce the targeted friendship skills.

GAMES AND ACTIVITIES
for Cooperative Learning

Blindfolded Maze Drawing

Students work in pairs and are given a maze to complete. One child is blindfolded and the other child is asked to give directions that help the blindfolded child move his pencil through the maze. The friend may also guide the child's hand through the maze if it is too hard to follow verbal directions. For young preschool children, the teacher can make the maze on the floor with masking tape and have the friend physically lead the blindfolded child through the maze. Each child takes turn being blindfolded. This activity is designed to help children experience being helped by someone and to understand that one of the things involved in friendship is trust. A variation of this game can be to build an obstacle course out of chairs, cones, bags, tables and to guide the blindfolded person around the obstacles.

Paper Chain

Students are given strips of paper and tape. They color their own link (or may be asked to put a secret message on the link) and then the group links the chain together. This activity is designed to teach the concepts of sharing, cooperation and teamwork. Teacher Social Coaching during this activity is essential.

Cooperative Art Poster

Students are divided into groups of 4 to 6 per table. The teacher instructs them to make a poster together and encourages them to share and decide together how they want their poster to look. They are given art materials (e.g., large poster board, glue, glitter, paint, scissors, stickers, magazine pictures) but each table's supplies are limited so that children are forced to negotiate. During this activity the teacher coaches praises children for appropriate asking, sharing, discussing ideas, helping each other and waiting their turn. This activity helps children practice all the skills of cooperation.

Cooperative "Favorite Things" Poster

Students are divided into groups of 4 to 6 per table. On each table is a variety of magazines and pictures and one poster board. Each table of students is asked to make a poster that shows their group's favorite animals and foods. In order to accomplish this task they need to ask each other questions and share their own likes and interests. This activity promotes cooperative skills, encourages self-expression and builds friendships by helping children get to know each other better.

Cooperative Tinker Toys/Legos/Clay Modeling

Students are divided into pairs for this activity and asked to plan and make something together with Tinker Toys, Bristle Blocks, Legos or Clay. They are encouraged to be friendly by taking turns, complimenting each other, sharing, asking for pieces, making friendly suggestions, problem solving and so forth. As children become more skilled, teams of three or four children will require more negotiation and sharing.

Tallest Tower

Pair the children up, give them paper, scissors, tape and a variety of old cereal boxes, toilet paper rolls, and egg cartons. Ask each pair to make the tallest, strongest and most beautiful tower they can together.

Design a Class T-shirt with a theme

Children discuss the theme for the t-shirt and then execute the design together. The design might be scanned into the computer and printed on special iron-on decals, or each child can draw his own version of the design on his shirt. Older children may enjoy making compliment t-shirts: each child in the class uses fabric pens to write a compliment on every other child's t-shirt.

Share a chair

In pairs, have children devise as many ways possible to both occupy one chair with their feet off the floor.

Friendship Mobiles

Each child makes their own mobile, which is hung in the classroom. This mobile is made out of long strips of a paper (4" by 6") with holes punched in the ends and hung with yarn. On each of these mobiles is the student's name, favorite color, favorite thing to do, a positive characteristic about the child from the teacher, and two positive things other children have said about that student.

Draw a Group Body

The class or small groups of children draw a group body. One child makes the hands, another the shoulders, another the ears, and so on. A variation on this theme is to pair up children and have them trace each other's bodies on large drawing paper. Next to each person's body drawing the teacher writes positive comments that the children say about that person.

Cooperative Story

As a group, the children tell a cooperative story. The teacher might begin the story: "One day, in a time far away, there lived two children, a boy named Marcus and a girl named Annika. These children weren't ordinary children. In fact, they had a secret power...." At this point, the children take turns adding 2-3 sentences to the story. The teacher records the story on a large sheet of paper, and then reads the story out loud after each child has had a turn.

Telephone Game

The teacher begins a secret message on one side of the circle. The children take turns whispering the secret to the next child in the circle. The teacher might give a small bonus reward to the class if the secret message is accurately passed around the whole circle.

Use role-plays to handle typical relationship problems

In addition to Circle Time discussions and cooperative practice activities with students, teachers can help their students learn how to respond to typical friendship problems through guided role plays and practices. Again the use of puppets can make this an engaging learning process for students. The following are some examples of scenarios you might enact with your students during circle time meetings.

CIRCLE TIME: LESSON SCRIPT
"He's teasing me."

Teacher: Wally was teased on the playground and he wants to talk to us about how he handled it. So, I am going to pretend to tease Wally so he can show us what he did. (*It is important that the students are not asked to act out negative behavior, so the teacher or a teacher assistant must act out the role of the teaser and Wally's response.*)

Teacher: "Wally, you have funny face, you look like a monkey, you are so wiggly, always jumping and you can't even kick the ball!"

Wally: "That's so old it's got mold on it." or "I fell off my dinosaur when I first heard that."

Teacher: Wow! you just stayed so calm! You didn't let it bother you. In fact, you told a joke! That is one way to respond to someone who is teasing. What's another way you would respond. Can anyone think of a way to tell the teaser to stop?

Student: Wally could say, "Stop, that's mean. I don't like that!"

Teacher: Those are good strong words. It's important to let someone know that you don't like to be teased! Would you like to practice that with Wally? We can pretend that Wally is teasing, but it's just pretend. Wally wouldn't really tease you, right Wally!

Wally: That's right—I really like you, but we can pretend so you can show what you would say. Let's say "ready, set, action" so we'll know it's pretend.

Wally: "Neaner, neaner, you are a slow poke!"

Student: That's mean. Stop! I don't like that.

Wally: I'm sorry. I'll stop teasing you.

Teacher: Great job using strong words! I'm wondering if anyone has ever tried walking away and ignoring if someone teases. That's a really hard thing to do, but it's such a strong solution! Does someone want to try that? (*Gets student volunteer and coaches student to ignore and walk away when Wally teases.*)

Wally: "You are like a turtle, just so slow, I'm faster than you!"

Student: Ignores and walks away. (*He is taking deep breaths*)

Wally: "I wonder why I can't get a response from him? I usually do. Why is he ignoring me? I can't get a response from him. He's pretty powerful. What is this breathing stuff? Well this is no fun—I guess I'll give up."

Teacher: Wow—ignoring a teaser is a fantastic idea. How did you keep up that ignoring?

Second Student: I just told myself I could do it! I kept trying to think of something else.

Teacher: You have really strong ignoring muscles. WOW. Terrific now we have three solutions to being teased. Does anyone have a different idea for what to do? (*discuss when to get help from an adult or how to tell person you don't like being called that name before walking away*) or, How does it feel to be called an unpleasant name? (*explore feelings*) What can be done to stop the name calling?

In the above sample script, the emphasis is on speaking up for oneself, staying calm, using humor to disarm the teaser and ignoring. Students may come up with other funny responses to take the fun out of teasing. Of course, it is also important to emphasize the importance of not teasing back.

CIRCLE TIME: LESSON SCRIPT
"They won't let me play with them!"

Wally: (*looking upset and tearful talks to students*) I need your help with a problem today. I feel terrible. I wanted to play with some other kids on the playground and they wouldn't let me. They said I was too clumsy to play soccer. I don't know what to do. Do you have any ideas?

Teacher: Wally, that must feel terrible

Wally: Yeah, it's rotten, I feel like no one likes me.

Teacher: (*asks students*) What should Wally do now?

Students: (*brainstorm possible solutions*)

- think a happy thought
- take deep breaths to calm down
- find another friend to play with
- accept their decision and remember all kids get left out sometimes
- tell them how you feel
- wait and ask them again later

Teacher: Okay let's practice some of those ideas. Who wants to try first?

The students would then go on to role play and demonstrate how they would respond when told by other children they would play with them.

CIRCLE TIME: LESSON SCRIPT
Handling a put down

Wally: (*looking upset and tearful talks to students*) You know sometimes I find my school work really difficult, I know it's not as neat as some people's. But today Katie came up and she said, "You know Wally, your writing looks just like squashed flies. It's rubbish! Just look at mine. I've finished already and the teacher has given me a star."

Teacher: Oh, how did that make you feel Wally?

Wally: It made me feel as if I wanted to give up trying and run home to my mom.

Teacher: (*asks students*) What should Wally do now?

Students: (*Brainstorm possible solutions. Older students might be asked to write their ideas on cards which are randomly picked for role plays and discussion.*)

- say to yourself, "If I keep trying I know that my writing will get better"
- think about what you are good at—"I'm not good at writing but I am good at painting"
- tell Katie how you feel
- recognize the put down and tell yourself that children who give put downs aren't very happy inside
- remember some children think that being a put downer will make them popular, but it doesn't
- think about something else

Teacher: Okay let's practice some of those ideas. Who wants to try first?

Other Ideas for Scripts for Puppets Regarding Relationship Problems

- Wally knows that someone is saying mean things and lies about him behind his back.
- Molly's friend tells someone else something that Molly told her was private and not to be shared.
- Molly's friend breaks a promise.
- There is someone in your class that always wants to be first.
- There is a student in the class who is shy, has no friends and feels really lonely. Ask students to discuss ways to make new friends and to help someone who may be lonely.

Student Generated Problems

In preschool and kindergarten, the teachers will present the problem-solving scenarios, often based on common problems that are observed between students in the classrooms. In older grades, the teachers can continue to present problems, but students can also become active participants in this process. Teachers might have a "problem report" form available for students who would like some help solving a social problem. Class guidelines should be set for these problem reports including that they are anonymous (teachers can work with the group to help everyone understand why it's important not to use names on the report). During problem-solving circles, the teacher can pick out a problem to read to the class. It is important that the teacher is the one to read the problem out loud so that he or she can help to make the participants unidentifiable, if necessary. Then the class can work with Wally to generate and act out solutions to the problem.

Another Circle Time Activity

Have cards with compliments and put-downs on them. Ask children in circle time to read a card out and put it in the appropriate pile (compliment or put-down pile). Ask them to explain why they think it is a compliment or put-down. ("Your work is rubbish" versus "Thank you for helping me to find my coat.")

CIRCLE TIME
Detective Hat Game
Practicing Friendly Social Skills

The Detective Hat game is an easy way to initiate role-play and practice of friendship skills. Here are some examples of questions you might put in the hat. They are designed to practice the following skills: sharing feelings; saying something friendly; helping someone else; and telling teacher.

- How could you help a child who won't share?
- You see your friend being left out of a game and even bullied and pushed way by some kids on the playground. What should you do?

- Your friend just lost his new shoes. What can you say?
- Your dad seems angry and says he's having a bad day. What can you say?
- One of your friends is being left out by the other kids. What can you say or do?
- You notice someone crying on the playground. What can you say or do?
- Share a time you helped someone.
- One of your friends is kind of a poor loser. Whenever his team loses he throws a fit and sometimes he cries. He seems to want to win at all costs. He cheats and breaks the rule and one time he even said the other team got a foul when they didn't and then argued with the coach. He hogs the ball all the time. How can he be a good sport?
- One of your classmates never wants to try anything the other kids are doing. She goes off by herself all the time and stays alone. What can you do to help?
- Your best friend wants to play with someone else. What can you say?
- You want to apologize to a friend for something you have said. What can you say?

Apologizing

©*Incredible Years*®

Empathy training

A key aspect to a child's social success is his or her ability to begin to consider the concerns, goals, and feelings of others. If a child cannot take the point of view of another person, then s/he may misperceive social cues and not know how to respond. While the development of empathy takes years, and all children are self-centered and "egocentric" at this age, it is still possible for teachers to promote children's awareness of others' feelings and perspectives.

The following game can be played to help foster empathy skills.

CIRCLE TIME
Detective Hat Game
Practicing Thinking of Other's Feelings

This time the detective hat game is directed at helping children understand the importance of apologizing, explaining, complimenting, being friendly, being honest, having good sportsmanship, offering to help fix the situation, and resisting peer pressure and temptation. Here are some sample ideas for questions for your hat:

- You've been playing checkers with a friend and lost the game. How do you feel? What does your friend feel? What can you do?
- You yelled at a friend when he broke your model. How does your friend feel? What can you do?
- You lost your new jacket and it is the second time you have lost it. How do you feel? How are your parents going to feel? What can you do?
- You forgot to do the chores you mom asked you to do. How does your mom feel? How do you feel? What can you do?
- Your friend wants you to bike down to the store to get some candy, and your parents have said you are not to go beyond the front yard. What can you do?
- Your brother keeps some candy in his desk and you want a piece. What can you do?
- You are only allowed to watch 1 hour of TV per day. Your favorite show comes on, but you've already watched an hour of TV. Your dad asks you how much TV you've watched. What can you say?
- You broke a family rule by eating a Popsicle in the living room and some of it stained the couch. Your mom seems mad and asks you if you ate a Popsicle in the living room. What can you do?
- One of your classmates is having trouble learning to read. How does he feel? What can you say or do?

Teaching students problem solving and conflict resolution

Starting a friendship is one thing; keeping a friend is another. The key skill to sustained friendship is knowing how to resolve conflict. In the absence of this skill, the most aggressive child usually gets his or her way. When this happens, everyone loses. The aggressive child may learn to abuse friendships and will experience rejection by peers for the aggression, while the passive child learns to be a victim. See Chapter 12 for a discussion of the ways teachers can help their students learn how to settle disagreements and problem solve, an important aspect of keeping friends.

Teaching students to use positive self-talk

When children experience peer rejection or a disappointment, often they have underlying negative thoughts that reinforce and intensify the emotion. These thoughts are sometimes referred to as "self-talk," although children will often express them aloud. For example, a child who tells you, "I am the worst kid, no one likes me, I can't do anything right" is engaging in negative self-talk which s/he is sharing with you. Some children will be able to verbalize these feelings and beliefs, while other children may feel them but not have the words to express how they feel. Teachers can teach children to identify negative self-talk and to substitute positive self-talk in order to help cope with their frustrations and to control angry outbursts. For example, when a child's request to play with a friend is refused by another child, s/he can say to herself or himself, "I can handle this. I will find another friend to play with" or "I can stay calm and try again" or "Count to 10. Talk don't hit" or "Stop and think first." In this way children learn to regulate their cognitive responses, which in turn will affect their emotional and behavioral responses. Positive self-talk provides children with a means of emotional regulation with their peers.

Again, using a puppet such as Wally can help to verbalize self-talk and teach students how to turn negative self-talk into more positive coping self-statements. Here is a sample scenario you might try:

CIRCLE TIME: LESSON SCRIPT
Feeling Left Out

Wally: Sammy is having a birthday party and he didn't ask me. I don't think he likes me. No one likes me. I feel so lonely. What should I do?

Teacher: Can you all help Wally think of some positive thoughts that will help him feel better. What could he say to himself?

Students: (*generate self talk that is more positive*) He can only ask a few friends, it doesn't mean he doesn't like me. I have other friends. I'm a good friend and I can ask someone to play with me as well, then I won't feel lonely.

This is an extremely hard exercise for most children. Typically children will respond with solutions of behaviors that Wally could engage in. Teachers will need to provide examples of positive self-talk to illustrate the concept.

Praise and establish reward programs for children with social difficulties

Students who have particular social difficulties such as shyness, anxiety or, conversely aggression and inattention, may need the extra support of an incentive program to help strengthen particular friendship skills. Teachers should start by choosing one or two social behaviors to increase such as joining in play for the shy child, or waiting and taking turns for the impulsive child. These specific behaviors should be practiced with the student and then listed on a chart. This chart may placed on the child's desk or kept nearby so that it is readily accessible to the teacher. The student then receives praise and a sticker, stamp, or point each time he or she exhibits the positive behavior. When praising, teachers should wait for a natural break in the interaction so as not to disrupt the conversation and play activity. Teachers can praise both children in the interaction for their cooperative behavior and talk about how they are becoming good friends. For example, "You two are cooperating and working very well together! You are being very friendly with each other and helping each other make this a cool structure. You look like good friends." Older children will likely prefer to keep these incentive systems private, while younger children may be proud to be praised in front of their peers. Each day the student's chart and progress can be reviewed. Once these first one or two social skills have become reliable and consistent, additional social behaviors can be substituted.

Collaborating with parents

Parents have relatively few opportunities to see their children in settings where they are with large groups of children. Behavior in the classroom may be very different from behavior at home. While the child might be doing well when a single friend comes to visit at home, s/he may still have substantial peer problems in larger group settings. It is important for teachers to discuss children's social needs with their parents. For the child with some social difficulties, it is important to collaborate with parents to identify a few positive social skills to work on. For example, a teacher may have set up a classroom chart to encourage a child to cooperate with peers. At the end of the day this "friendly report card" can be sent home with the child, and the parents can add checks earned at school to their home reward chart. For example, earning 5 checks at school might equal an extra story time or a special activity at home. It also is ideal if the teacher can have an incentive program at school. For example, each day the child earns an agreed-upon number of checks s/he gets to choose a special activity such as extra computer time with a friend, or leading the lunch line, or leading a class discussion. When students are struggling in one area, it is important for teachers to highlight the student's strengths so that peers see him or her in a positive light. For highly distractible children, it is helpful to assign a school counselor, aide, or teacher as a "coach." This coach would meet with the child 3 times a day for a brief 5-minute check-in. During this check-in, the coach would review the child's behavior chart and praise any successes in interactions with peers. S/he would also review to make sure the child has his or her books ready and his or her assignments written out in his or her notebook for the rest of the morning. At lunch s/he would review expectations for lunch period or recess and again, before going home, would review the day's positive behavior as well as see that the child had his or her behavior chart, books, and homework ready to take home. This additional scaffolding will help strengthen the learning and can be gradually withdrawn as the child experiences success.

Encourage parents to invite classmates home

Often parents don't know who their children's friends are at school and which classmates play particularly well with their child. Teachers are in the best position to help parents know which classmates are positive role models and have interests and a temperament that complements their child's temperament or nature. Encourage parents and children to invite classmates over after school or on weekends. However, in some instances (especially with hyperactive or withdrawn children) you will need to help parents understand that when friends are invited over, this play time should not be unstructured or unmonitored. Rather, help parents understand the importance of planning the visit with their child and doing some cooperative activities such as building a model with Legos, working on a craft, baking cookies, or playing basketball. Parents should be encouraged to be present during these interactions so they can help coach friendly play and assure they are successful events. Furthermore, setting up these cooperative activities will help children practice and learn appropriate social skills and develop closer friendships. Parents should be cautioned to avoid letting the children spend their time watching TV or playing computer games as there will be very little social interaction and less chance to get to know each other. For shy or hyperactive children teachers may want to recommend to parents that their children's first play visits be relatively short and structured with close parental coaching so that interactions don't get out of control and the children part having had a good time.

Encourage parents to use social coaching in their one-on-one play time with their children at home

It is helpful for teachers to provide parents with information on the importance of parent-child play. Teachers can emphasize the value of social coaching during "child-directed" play time between parents and children. Remember the descriptive commenting and coaching strategies described in Chapters Two and Four. This information should also be shared with parents so that they learn how to use their attention and language to encourage their child's academic, persistence, social, and emotional development through play.

CONCLUSION

Specific teaching of friendship skills builds on the scaffolding provided by social and emotion coaching and problem-solving lessons. At this point students are able to integrate all the behaviors, feelings, language, and thought patterns that have been discussed earlier. This is a bit like learning to do division after the student has a foundation in addition and subtraction or learning to put together grammatically correct sentences in a new language after the basic vocabulary has been learned. Gradually with developmental progress, practice, and persistence these "friendly communication scripts" will become automatic for students, and used when they can stay calm and regulated. Just as with academic subjects, there is no expectation these skills will all be mastered in one grade or one course but will require continued instruction and infusion into classroom content throughout the student's education. Moreover, due to students' particular family backgrounds and their developmental stage some children will have more difficulty making friends than others and will need additional support in this learning.

TO SUM UP...

Coping with Peer Problems and Teaching Friendship Skills

- Teach students how to introduce themselves, enter groups, how to play cooperatively, and how to talk politely with friends through discussions and circle time role plays and practices.
- Set up cooperative learning activities and games to help students practice friendship skills.
- Use social and emotion coaching strategies.
- Prompt children to notice students who are being friendly and helpful.
- Model social skills as teacher and through the use of puppets.
- Remind or cue children to use their calm down strategies and positive self-talk.
- Praise and establish reward programs for target social behaviors for students with social difficulties—identify the positive opposite behavior to the misbehavior you are reducing.
- Collaborate with parents to promote specific children's social skills at home.

The Incredible Years®
Teacher Classroom Management Self-Reflection Inventory
Ways I Promote Friendships
and Cooperative Learning Teamwork

Date: _____ Teacher Name: _____

Teachers learn extensively from self-reflection regarding their class-room management and the teaching strategies they are using that are working or not working. From these reflections teachers determine personal goals for making changes in their approaches to bring about the most positive learning climate they can. Use this Inventory to think about your strengths and limitations and determine your goals.

Social and Friendship Skills	1 = NEVER 3 = OCCASIONALLY 5 = CONSISTENTLY
1. I prompt children to help their peers to take deep breaths and remind them of their brave talk (e.g., "I can do it, I can be patient, I will feel better") when they are angry or frustrated or sad.	1 2 3 4 5
2. I promote identification of friendship behaviors through the use of photographs, cooperative games, and stories that portray people helping each other in difficult situations.	1 2 3 4 5
3. I prompt students to recognize how their peers are being friendly by pointing out their cooperative behavioral actions and how this is making them feel (e.g., "your friend is praising you for figuring out the answer to that problem and is proud of you").	1 2 3 4 5 1 2 3 4 5
4. I teach specific social friendship behaviors by commenting upon students who are sharing, waiting their turn, helping someone, trading, apologizing, complimenting, making a friendly suggestion, staying calm).	1 2 3 4 5

5. I model friendship behaviors by naming them when I use them with students throughout the day (e.g., "I am going to be your friend and share my pencil with you, I can wait for you to listen, I am sorry you are feeling sad and want to help you, together our classroom can be a team.").	1 2 3 4 5
6. I provide opportunities for children to practice social skills with each other.	1 2 3 4 5
7. I teach specific social skills in circle time or individually with children such as practicing asking, apologizing, taking turns, waiting, helping, sharing, using words, and teamwork.	1 2 3 4 5
8. I strengthen social skills in my classroom by using social coaching language.	1 2 3 4 5
9. I have identified targeted social skills I want to teach individual students to learn according to their developmental needs on their behavior plan.	1 2 3 4 5
10. I have targeted the positive opposite social behavior to give attention to for every negative behavior I want to decrease.	1 2 3 4 5
11. I encourage children's cooperative behavior by giving them classroom jobs, encouraging them to help each other and giving them choices.	1 2 3 4 5
12. I use puppets, pretend games, imaginary stories and drama activities to set up problem scenarios and children can practice solving the problems by acting out their friendship solutions.	1 2 3 4 5
13. I talk with the parents of my students to help them understand they can encourage their children to learn social skills and to help them identify good classmate matches for play dates at home.	1 2 3 4 5

14. I have developed behavior plans that target social skills according to their developmental abilities and target goals. I have coordinated these efforts with the children's parents so they can praise them at home.	1 2 3 4 5
Future Goals Regarding Strategies I will use to enhance social competence in my students:	Total

REFERENCES

Asher, S. R., & Coie, J. D. (1990). *Peer rejection in childhood.* Cambridge: Cambridge University Press.

Asher, S. R., Parkhurst, J. T., Hymel, S., & Williams, G. A. (1990). Peer rejection and loneliness in childhood. In S. R. Asher & J. D. Coie (Eds.), *Peer rejection in childhood* (pp. 253-273). Cambridge: Cambridge University Press.

Asher, S. R., & Williams, G. A. (1987). Helping children without friends in home and school *Children's social development: Information for teachers and parents.* Urbana, IL: ERIC, Clearing House on Elementary and Early Childhood Education.

Bear, G. G., Richards, H. C., & Gibbs, J. C. (1997). Sociomoral reasoning and behavior. In G. G. Bear, K. M. Minke & A. Thomas (Eds.), *Children's needs II: Development, problems and alternatives* (pp. 13-25). Bethesda, MD: National Association of School Psychologists.

Bierman, K. L. (1989). Improving the Peer Relationships of Rejected Children. In B. B. Lahey & A. E. Kazdin (Eds.), *Advances in Clinical Child Psychology* (Vol. 12). New York: Plenum Press.

Bierman, K. L., Miller, C. M., & Stabb, S. (1987). Improving the social behavior and peer acceptance of rejected boys: Effects of social skill training with instructions and prohibitions. *Journal of Consulting and Clinical Psychology, 55,* 194-200.

Brown, W. H., Odom, S. L., & McConnell, S. R. (2008). *Social competence of young children: Risk, disability, and intervention.* Baltimore: Paul H. Brookes Publishing Co. .

Burgess, K. B., Wojslawowicz, J. C., Rubin, K. H., Rose-Krasnor, L., & Booth-LaForce, C. (2006). Social information processing and coping strategies of shy/withdrawn and aggressive children: Does friendship matter? *Child Development, 77,* 371-383.

Cairns, R. B., Cairns, B. D., & Neckerman, H. J. (1989). Early school dropout: Configurations and determinants. *Child Development, 60,* 1437-1452.

Campbell, S. B. (1994). Hard-to-manage preschool boys: externalizing behavior, social competence, and family context at two-year followup. *Journal of Abnormal Child Psychology, 22*(2), 147-166.

Coie, J. D. (1990). Toward a theory of peer rejection. In S. R. Asher & J. D. Coie (Eds.), *Peer Rejection in Childhood* (pp. 365-398). Cambridge: Cambridge University Press.

Coie, J. D., Dodge, K. A., & Kupersmidt, J. B. (1990). Peer group behavior and social status. In S. R. Asher & J. D. Coie (Eds.), *Peer rejection in childhood* (pp. 17-59). New York: Cambridge University Press.

Crick, N. R., & Dodge, K. A. (1994). A review and reformulation of social information processing mechanisms in children's social adjustment. *Psychological Bulletin, 115,* 74-101.

Elias, M. J., & Tobias, S. E. (1996). *Social problem solving: Interventions in schools.* New York: Guilford.

Greenberg, M. T., Kusche, C. A., Cook, E. T., & Quamma, J. P. (1995). Promoting emotional competence in school-aged children: The effects of the PATHS curriculum. Special issue: Emotions in developmental psychopathology. *Development and Psychopathology, 7,* 117-136.

Gresham, F. M. (1995). Social skills training. In A. Thomas & J. Grimes (Eds.), *Best practices in school psychology—III* (pp. 39-50). Bethesda, MD: National Association of School Psychologists.

Gresham, F. M. (1997). Social Skills. In G. G. Bear, K. M. Minke & A. Thomas (Eds.), *Children's needs II: Development, problems and alternatives* (pp. 39-50). Bethesda, MD: National Association of School Psychologists.

Grossman, D. C., Neckerman, H. J., Koepsell, T. D., Liu, P., Asher, K. N., Beland, K., et al. (1997). The effectiveness of a violence prevention curriculum among children in elementary school. *Journal of American Medical Association, 277,* 1605-1611.

Howes, C. (2000). Social-emotional classroom climate in child care, child-teacher relationships and children's second grade peer relations. *Social Development, 9*(2), 291-204.

Knoff, H. M., & Batsche, G. M. (1995). Project ACHIEVE: Analyzing a school reform process for at-risk and underachieving students. *School Psychology Review, 24,* 579-603.

Kupersmidt, J. B., & Patterson, C. J. (1991). Childhood peer rejection, aggression, withdrawal, and perceived competence as predictors of self-reported behavior problems in preadolescence. *Journal of Abnormal Child Psychology, 19*(4), 427-449.

Ladd, G. W. (1990). Having friends, keeping friends, making friends, and being liked by peers in the classroom: Predictors of children's early school adjustment? *Child Development, 61*(4), 1081-1100.

Ladd, G. W., & Asher, S. R. (1985). Social skill training and children's peer relations: Current issues in research and practice. In L. A. L. & M. M. (Eds.), *Handbook of social skill training* (pp. 219-244). New York: Wiley.

Ladd, G. W., Kochenderfer, B. J., & Coleman, C. (1997). Classroom peer acceptance, friendship, and victimization: Distinct relational systems that contribute uniquely to children's school adjustment. *Child Development, 68*, 1181-1197.

Lau, A. S., Fung, J. J., Ho, L. Y., Liu, L. L., & Gudino, O. G. (2011). Parent training with high-risk immigrant Chinese families: A pilot group randomized trial yielding practice-based evidence. *Behavior Therapy, 42*, 413-426.

Olson, S. L. (1992). Development of conduct problems and peer rejection in preschool children: a social systems analysis. *Journal of Abnormal Child Psychology, 20*(3), 327-350.

Pope, A. W., Bierman, K. L., & Mumma, G. H. (1989). Relations between hyperactive and aggressive behavior and peer relations at three elementary grade levels. *Journal of Abnormal Child Psychology, 17*(3), 253-267.

Putallaz, M., & Wasserman, A. (1990). Children's entry behavior. In A. S.R. & C. J.D. (Eds.), *Peer Rejection in Childhood* (pp. 60-89). Cambridge: Cambridge University Press.

Webster-Stratton, C. (1990). *Dina Dinosaur's Social Skills, Emotion and Problem-Solving Curriculum*. Seattle, WA: 1411 8th Avenue West.

Webster-Stratton, C. (1999). *How to promote children's social and emotional competence*. London, England: Sage Publications.

Webster-Stratton, C., & Lindsay, D. W. (1999). Social Competence and early-onset conduct problems: Issues in assessment. *Journal of Child Clinical Psychology, 28*, 25-93.

Webster-Stratton, C., & Reid, M. J. (2003). Treating conduct problems and strengthening social emotional competence in young children (ages 4-8 years): The Dina Dinosaur treatment program. *Journal of Emotional and Behavioral Disorders, 11*(3), 130-143.

CHAPTER 14

Partnering with Parents

The importance of teacher collaboration with parents

There is convincing evidence that parent involvement in children's learning and the quality of parent-school interactions have positive effects on children's academic achievement, social competence and school engagement (Battistich, Schaps, & Wilson, 2004; Domina, 2005). On the other hand, lower levels of parental involvement and poor parent-teacher relationships are associated with increased child externalizing and internalizing problems (Battistich, Solomon, Kim, Watson, & Schaps, 1995). The highly acclaimed book, *A New Generation of Evidence: The Family Is Critical to Student Achievement*, opens by saying, "The evidence is now beyond dispute. When schools work together with families to support learning, children tend to succeed not just in school, but throughout life" (Castro & Bryant, 2004; Henderson

*Schools can best
serve the needs
of their students
by becoming more
family-centered.*

& Berla, 1994; Hindman, Skibbe, Miller, & Zimmerman, 2010; Kohl, Lengua, & McMahon, 2000; Webster-Stratton, Reid, & Hammond, 2004). Realizing that students' cultural backgrounds, economic conditions, and home environments can profoundly affect their adjustment to and performance in school, schools are finding that they can best serve the needs of their students by becoming more family-centered and more focused on students' emotional and social needs as well as academics (Cappella, Frazier, Atkins, Schoenwald, & Glisson, 2008). Some innovative schools are providing nonacademic services to children and their families, such as evidence-based parent education classes and parent resource rooms, courses for parents to become classroom aides, GED classes, employment training workshops, and groups to help children learn appropriate social skills, problem-solving, and anger management strategies (Storch & Crisp, 2004). Schools such as these demonstrate that the relationships between home and school are beginning to change in fundamental ways.

Despite the evidence for the importance of family involvement on student motivation and academic performance, home-school partnerships are often fragile. It can be hard for teachers to systematically encourage and form partnerships with parents, and parents do not always participate even when they are encouraged to do so. Several major barriers to family involvement exist in schools. The first barrier is that teachers may feel too stressed by classroom demands to be able to devote the time needed to forge relationships with parents. Large classes mean that teachers have little time to spend with individual students, let alone with their parents. It is true that it takes extra time and effort to learn about students' families, their culture, interests, past experiences with school, parenting styles, and life stressors. Furthermore, in light of the pressing academic demands on teachers' time and energy, administrators may not support their involvement with family members.

A second barrier to parent involvement in children's schooling is misunderstandings between teachers and parents. Teachers may believe that parents are not interested in participating in their children's education. Parents, in turn, can feel intimidated by teachers and school administrators, and feel they lack the knowledge to help educate their children. Parents may have had negative school experiences themselves, leading to negative feelings about schools and a lack of trust in teachers. Overall changes in demographic and employment patterns may further complicate the development of strong home-school partnerships. As the population becomes increasingly ethnically diverse, teachers and parents may come from different cultural and economic backgrounds, leading to contrasting values and beliefs. Disadvantaged and minority families may face language and literacy barriers, have no access to transportation to schools, have no experience asking teachers questions, or fear attending school functions at night if they live in dangerous neighborhoods. Such families may feel so overwhelmed by the stress in their lives, that they have little energy to be involved in their children's education. Moreover, the rise in the number of dual-worker families and single parent working families means there is less time for parents to spend on school involvement. Such barriers, be they lack of confidence, poverty, divorce, illness, or job stress may contribute to parents' lack of involvement with teachers and unfortunately reinforces teachers' perceptions that parents are not interested in forming partnerships with them.

A third barrier is that some teachers lack confidence or skill to reach out to families. Working collaboratively with parents to effectively problem solve a challenging academic or behavioral issue takes specialized interpersonal skills; skills that teachers may feel uncertain about, especially when first starting their careers (Epstein, 1992). Teachers may not have had training in dealing with family issues, conducting therapeutic interviews, coping constructively with a parent's anger or frustration, using effective communication and negotiation strategies, and conducting successful parent conferences (Burton, 1992). After all, most teachers entered the teaching profession to work with children; working with the parents of these children may feel like an enormous leap outside of their comfort zones. Studies have shown that there is scant

Working collaboratively with parents to effectively problem solve a challenging academic or behavioral issue takes specialized interpersonal skills.

attention in teacher education programs on how to build relationships and partnerships with parents (Chavkin, 1991). Teachers need concrete skills, knowledge, and positive attitudes about family involvement in order to effectively work with parents. This training must emphasize more than traditional parent-teacher conferences; recognizing the additional assistance (e.g., parent education classes and support services) and encouragement that families need in order to help their children in school. Evidence suggests that such assistance may be essential for many minority and economically disadvantaged parents, for whom school involvement is often an intimidating and difficult proposition.

For teachers to be successful at collaborating with parents, they must recognize the intrinsic worth of families as contributors to children's learning and be willing to reach out beyond the traditional roles of teachers. Successful partnerships between teachers and parents will result in the development of educational programs that support each student's individual emotional and academic needs. These teacher-parent partnerships will also result in teachers who feel less stressed and more valued and supported by their students' families.

WAYS TO PROMOTE PARENT INVOLVEMENT

Start Before School Starts

Parent involvement efforts need to start even before school starts. Teachers need to reach out right away to get to know families. One way to do this is to send home a "welcome" greeting to all parents and incoming students, asking families to complete interest surveys regarding children's favorite activities and family interests. Teachers who know ahead of time that a particular student has a history of problems in school should make a special effort to establish positive communication with the child and his or her parents before the first day of class. This might be done through a phone call, in-school meeting, or in rare occasions, a home visit. The purpose of this communication is to welcome the child and parents to the classroom, reassure parents of your commitment to working with their child, and to build a relationship that can later form the foundation of positive problem solving as the need arises.

Before school starts teachers should also communicate their class-room philosophy and discipline to all parents. This might be done in a letter that is sent to parents and also communicated during an initial orientation meeting. The letter might include:

- teacher philosophy of positive classroom management and discipline (teaching prosocial skills and emotional regulation, consistent class rules, emphasis on positive behaviors, incentives, and consequences)
- some information about the teacher
- teacher commitment to parent involvement
- teacher homework policy
- how and when teacher can be reached (by phone, email, or office hours)
- parent's need for interpreter or translation of written material
- invitation to first parent meeting at the school

Establish a Positive Base With Positive Notes and Phone Calls

Teachers should start sending home good behavior messages at the beginning of the year through positive notes and phone calls. These can include messages about and something special a child has accomplished or to share how the teacher feels about the student's positive behavior. Teachers can ask the parent to share the content of the call or note with their child. When teachers take the time to build up this positive relationship, parents realize how much teachers are invested in their child's learning.

Most parents report they only hear from teachers when there is a problem or at the pre-scribed parent-teacher conference times. When communication is prescribed or negative, it's easy to see why partnerships with parents fail. Parents learn to become wary of any messages from the school, and may start avoiding school phone calls and stop reading notes from teachers. Instead, teachers should take every opportunity to show families they care. Each teacher will find different ways

Teachers should take every opportunity to show families they care.

to build these relationships; for example: birthday cards, special award notices, get-well cards, thank you notes, e-newsletters, classroom blogs, an answering machine with a daily recorded message, and good news phone calls. Teachers may need to devise a system to keep track of these positive calls and notes to be sure that there is regular communication with every parent in the classroom. In every classroom, there will be parents who naturally return these messages and make communication easy. Teachers should be sure to recognize those parents who are helping by volunteering time in class, chaperoning on field trips, donating supplies and food, and helping children return home activities. Other parents will be harder to reach, and these are the ones who need more teacher attention and effort. This extra effort will pay later dividends for parents, teachers, and students. Students flourish when parents are involved in their schooling and teachers will find that positive relationships with parents are crucial in the event that there is a behavioral or academic concern that needs parental involvement or input.

Weekly Classroom Newsletter

The more teachers can tell parents about the curriculum and what is going on at school, the more involved parents will be. A weekly newsletter is an excellent way to communicate classroom activities, goals for students' learning, ways parents can enhance learning at home, and reminders of the upcoming events. In these newsletters teachers can invite parents for lunches at school and suggest ways they might participate in the classroom that week. These newsletters can be sent home with students, e-mailed to parents, posted on a school or classroom blog, and posted outside the classroom. The key to making these newsletters effective is for teachers to have a relatively easy and time-efficient way of writing the letters and for parents to be able to receive the letters in an accessible format. In schools where families do not speak English, translations of at least some key material will be important. Since these newsletters can be time consuming for teachers, it may be possible for teachers to find creative ways of obtaining help to prepare them; a parent volunteer might write and format the letter, using a few notes provided by the teacher. In older elementary school classrooms, students might even be involved in producing the newsletters.

On the IY web site teachers can find a set of *teacher-to-parent and parent-to-teacher communication* templates and parent letters that teachers can use throughout the year. Some of these notes leave room for teachers to write a short note to parents, others are prepared letters that cover topics such as classroom and family rules, academic, persistence, social and emotion coaching, teaching children to give compliments, helping children learn to calm down, and teaching problem-solving strategies.

☀ **http://www.incredibleyears.com/TeacherResources/index.asp**

Brown Bag Lunches or "Office Hours"

In addition to the 'back to school' nights and regularly scheduled parent-teacher conferences, it is also important to set up regular informal mechanisms for parents to communicate with teachers. Some teachers schedule brown bag lunches once or twice a month with parents. These are times when any parent can come with a sack lunch and join the teacher for an informal question and answer period. Other teachers may want to establish one particular day a week or month that they are available in the classroom after school for informal parent meetings. It is important to realize that a portion of working parents will not be able to take advantage of these times because of work schedules. While it goes above the call of duty for teachers to occasionally be available in the evenings or on weekends, this may be the only time that a few parents are able to connect with the teacher. Phone calls or e-mails may be useful ways for these parents to stay involved.

Home Visits

A home visit is probably the most personal way for a teacher to show her concern and caring for a student. For parents, it's an opportunity to meet the teacher in their familiar surroundings. For students, it is a chance to see that their parents and teacher are working collaboratively and to show off something special about their home lives. And for the teacher, it provides a better perspective about the student's family life and will contribute to a strong positive relationship. Except in a few special school programs, home visits are not usually a paid part of a teacher's workload. This may make visits impractical in many cases. However, for students who are truly struggling, or if all other means of communication with parents have failed, this occasional home visit may be a crucial key to making contact with an otherwise inaccessible family.

Parent Education Groups

In some schools teachers are joining with school counselors, school nurses, and educational psychologists to offer group parent education classes. These classes are an opportunity for teachers to develop joint plans with parents regarding students' needs. These classes also help parents understand the ways they can support their children's education by working with their children at home. Parent groups are also a way for parents to get to know teachers and to let them know their concerns and what family situations may be influencing their children's emotional, social and academic learning. When parent groups involve teachers as co-leaders, long-lasting partnerships are developed which serve to empower each other as well as the children.

Several studies have been done with the Incredible Years Parent Programs showing the impact of school-based parent intervention programs on children's school readiness and learning. These studies have also shown that children of parents who were involved in these parent programs showed significantly improved social competence, emotional literacy, problem solving and reduced behavior problems when compared with children in schools that did not offer these programs (Reid, Webster-Stratton, & Hammond, 2007; Webster-Stratton & Reid, 2009; Webster-Stratton, Reid, & Hammond, 2001; Webster-Stratton, et al., 2004).

The Teacher-Parent Partnership Model

The ideal relationship between the teacher and parent is based on a collaborative partnership. This is in contrast to a hierarchical relationship whereby the teacher is assumed to be the expert who dispenses advice or commands to parents. Meaning "to labor together," collaboration implies a reciprocal relationship that uses the teacher's and parents' knowledge, strengths, culture, and perspectives and considers them of equal importance. The teacher is usually more knowledgeable about teaching principles,

**Sample Teacher-Parent Script
"Get Acquainted Meeting"
Script in September**

Teacher: Hello, Ms. Jones, I'm Ms. Parks, thanks for taking the time to come in and get acquainted. I've enjoyed working with Takisha these first two weeks of school. (*Recognize parents' efforts to meet with you.*)

Parent: It's nice to meet you early in the year. Takisha's been telling me about how much she likes circle time. She's so excited about circle time that I don't hear about the rest of the day. I'd love to know what else is on the schedule so I can ask her questions about the rest of her day.

Teacher: Well, circle time is the way we start the day. It's a good opportunity for kids to talk about themselves. We also do calendar and talk about the weather and Friday is Takisha's show and share day. (*Explains daily schedule.*)

Parent: Oh, that's good to know. I didn't know she could bring things in to share.

Teacher: Yes, I really like the children to bring in something inexpensive, like a book they've been reading, or a small toy, or a momento from somewhere they've been, or something about your family or culture. And you are welcome to come as well. (*Welcome parents to classroom.*)

Parent: Oh, she has a favorite story I read her about her the holidays we celebrate. I'm sure she'll want to bring that.

Teacher: That sounds good and we could read that at story time. After circle time the kids get to choose their first center. All of the centers have pre-reading or pre-math activities.

Parent: I'm wondering, what center does Takisha usually choose? She doesn't really know any math and she can't she read.

Teacher: Oh, I've noticed she loves the manipulatives table. That's a center where there are boxes of coins or stones or blocks and the children can make patterns or count or sort the pieces. It looks like they're just playing, but actually what they're doing is getting comfortable with the concept of numbers. After their first center activity, they all switch, and the children have a chance to work at one of the other centers. Then we have a snack and a 20 minute outdoor recess.

Parent: You know, sometimes Takisha is shy with other kids in the neighborhood. Is she making friends here during free play and recess?

Teacher: I haven't noticed any problems but thanks for alerting me. I'll keep an eye out for how things are going for her. If she has any trouble I'll let you know and we can talk about how to help her. For now she seems to be joining in well with the others. Maybe I can share with you who might be a good friend to set up a play date with—would you like that? (*Acknowledges parents' concerns and lets her know she will work with her concerning this possible problem.*)

Parent: What can I do to help Takisha do well this year?

Teacher: Next week I'll be sending home a list of books for parents to read with their kids. It would be great if you and Takisha could read together for 10 minutes every night. I have the books in the classroom if you'd like to borrow them, and I know most of them are available at the library. By reading together I mean you reading to her or just looking at pictures together and talking about what might be going on in the pictures. You don't have to get her to sound out the words. Just let it be a fun, enjoyable time for you both. If she tells you a story when she looks at the pictures, you can write it down and make a story book of her own where she is the author. Children love to think of themselves as writers and the first step is to encourage their story telling. (*Shares something the parent can do at home to support her child's learning.*)

> **Parent:** That will be easy, she loves looking at picture books and talking about the pictures. Thanks for taking the time to meet with me. If there's anything I can do to help or if there's anything I should know about Takisha's progress, please call me.
>
> **Teacher:** It was great meeting you. I know you work full time, but if there's ever a day that you'd like to come observe or help out in the class, I'd love to have you. Also you an email me any time or leave a message on my answering machine, I usually do my call back calls in the evening —is that a problem?
>
> **Parent:** Not at all and I love the idea that we can communicate by email. Sometimes I work very late.
>
> **Teacher:** I think Takisha's going to have a good kindergarten year.

curriculum, and overall child development and learning while the parent is more knowledgeable about the child's temperament, likes and dislikes, culture, family stresses, and emotional needs. Accepting the notion of complementary expertise creates a relationship between parents and teachers that is mutually respectful and supportive. In this nonblaming and nonhierarchical model, the teacher promotes collaboration through reflection, summary of suggestions made by parents and their goals for their children, reinforcement, support and acceptance, humor and optimism, encouragement of parent participation and sharing of her own ideas, key learning objectives and developmentally appropriate goals.

EFFECTIVE COMMUNICATION WITH PARENTS

Tips for Setting Up Successful Meetings

The key to successful collaboration with parents is the teacher's use of effective communication and problem-solving or negotiation skills. The following discussion includes some of the blocks to effective communication between teachers and parents and some ways to overcome them.

Involving Parents from the Start—Speaking Up

It doesn't matter if it is the first week of school, or even the first day of school, teachers need to contact parents as soon as they become aware of a child's academic or behavioral problem. This is at the core of successful collaboration with families. Sometimes teachers try to avoid conflict, disagreement or disapproval from parents by not talking with them about their children's behavior or learning problems. They may avoid setting up parent meetings and asking for help with the child with the hope that the child will eventually improve or outgrow the problem. However, if the child continues to misbehave, teachers may begin to store up grievances and even though they haven't called the parents for help, they may even begin to blame them for the child's misbehaviors. The teacher in the following example clearly has been storing up a lot of resentment.

> **Teacher:** I've had it! I've tried for three months with this child. Nothing seems to help. I can't do this with a large class. I don't get any support from the parents. I never see his parents at the school and I don't think they care. If they don't care, why should I care?

There are several reasons why teachers need to speak up and contact parents at the first sign there is a problem. First, if teachers don't involve parents in planning in regard to a student's behavior problems they may come to feel resentful of the parents for their lack of recognition of their efforts. (Of course, parents can't support teachers if they don't know what is going on.) Second, by involving parents early in the planning the teacher may discover there are other family factors that have a bearing on the child's misbehaviors such as a divorce, death in the family or some other family crisis. Understanding a particular child's family circumstances will help to put his behavior (and his family's) into perspective so that the teacher can focus on ways to increase his feelings of security during what may be an unpredictable or stressful situation at home. Third, if teachers wait too long before talking with parents, they may find that when the meeting finally occurs parents are angry that they haven't been informed about the problem. This can damage future collaborative efforts. Indeed, one of the most common complaints among parents is that teachers wait too long before contacting them about a school problem.

Sometimes a teacher does not speak up with parents because he or she fears being punished or criticized by the parents for not being a competent teacher. These individuals may think it is a sign of inadequacy to ask for help or to admit to a parent that they need their help in managing a child's problems. They may believe in the "good teacher" myth, that is, good teachers should handle all of their students' problems on their

Most competent teachers will involve parents from the outset in collaborative planning with some mutually agreed upon goals.

own without the help of parents. Rather, just the reverse is true. It is the most competent teachers who will involve parents from the outset in collaborative planning regarding a student's difficulties and develop a solution-focused behavior plan with some mutually agreed upon goals, wherein parents can support teachers' teaching efforts at home.

Call Parents and Offer Flexible Time Choices

The first thing a teacher must do when there is a problem is to call or e-mail the parents and set up an appointment date to arrange a meeting with them. Teachers may need to be persistent in making this contact (both mothers and fathers) and shouldn't give up after one or two tries. Teachers may need to call at work or at home during the evening, send a note home with the child, or send an e-mail. Remember that this contact will be much easier if you have already established a positive relationship with the parents. Teachers should make these contacts with the knowledge that it is their professional duty to do so. (Would a doctor hesitate to call a parent about a medical problem?)

Once the teacher reaches the parent, she should express a positive, caring attitude and explain that the call is because of her concern for the child. A brief summary of a positive behavioral goal will be more effective than stating the problem negatively. For example, the statement, "I am calling because I am concerned about how to help Jessie learn to get along with the other students" will be much easier for a parent to respond to than "Jessie has been hitting and fighting with other students. We need to do something about this." It will be useful for the teacher to share that she already has some strategies for addressing the child but that she would like the parent's insight into additional ideas. The teacher expresses confidence in being able to work the problem out together. Teacher tries to be as flexible as possible with potential meeting times and be sensitive to the fact that some parents have jobs that do not allow them to be away from work, even to attend school meetings. For very highly stressed families, sometimes a home visit may be the only way to have a successful meeting.

Welcome Parents

Once a meeting is scheduled, teachers should remember that parents feel very vulnerable when they are asked to attend a meeting about a difficulty that their child is having. For some parents, this may feel like they are being called to the Principal's office. The initial welcome when parents first arrive can be key to the success of the meeting. Teachers can set a positive tone by providing a friendly welcome, thanking the parents for coming, and checking about the scheduled time to meet: For example, "I am so pleased you could manage to meet with me. I have an hour scheduled for us. Does that still work for you?"

Use "I" messages instead of "You" messages

Positive "I" messages communicate what the teacher wants or feels. They're a way to be clear about an issue without having a destructive effect. "You" messages and negative "I" messages tend to blame, criticize or pass judgment, and they often generate anger or humiliation. The following examples highlight the difference between positive and negative messages.

Teacher
to Parent: Your child is always late for school and he has missed a lot of days. What is going on? Why can't you get him to school in the mornings? (*"You" message focuses on blaming parent.*)

Alternative
I am concerned that Carla is arriving late in the mornings and missing so much school. I wonder if there is a way we can work

together to help motivate her get to school on time. (*"I" message focuses on teacher's feelings and desire for change.*)

**Teacher
to Parent:** Dan is a real problem in this class. He is hitting other kids and other parents are complaining. He is wild and disruptive and irresponsible. I can't get any teaching done. What is going on at home with Dan? (*This message focuses on criticizing child or something at home*)

Alternative
I'm concerned about Dan's hitting in class. I would like to work with you to develop a plan to help him learn to be more cooperative. (*"I" message focuses on concern and what teacher wants and does not blame.*)

**Teacher
to Parent:** I'm not at all pleased with Sally's progress in reading. (*critical "I" message*)
Alternative
I would like to work together to figure out how we can help strengthen Sally's reading progress. (*positive "I"message*)

Begin with a statement of concern

In the positive "I" statement examples, the teachers began by letting the parents know that they cared about the child and that his or her welfare and education is of primary concern. This type of introductory statement expressing concern will set the tone for the entire conversation.

Be brief, clear and specific

Collaborative problem-solving will be most effective when teachers focus on positive behavioral goals for children rather than focusing on the problem behavior that is occurring. These positive goals can be stated clearly and briefly. For example, "I'd like to help Dan learn to use words to express his feelings and to help him keep his hands to himself when he is frustrated." It is not necessary to recount episode after episode of a child's problems to prove a point about how messy or irresponsible a student has been. Instead, the teachers can describe

Focus on positive behavior goals to replace problem behaviors.

the problem or behavior clearly and briefly and focus on the positive outcome that is desired. The positive "I" messages in the above examples illustrate this. Teachers should also avoid vague statements such as, "She's not behaving," or "Her attitude isn't good," and judgmental comments such as, "Your child is mean," or "Your child is lazy." These give no useful information and will alienate the parent.

Ask for feedback

Sometimes it may not be clear if the parent has understood the teacher's point of view. If this happens, teachers might ask, "Am I making sense?" This is much more effective than rambling on and on, and it assures the parent that his or her comprehension of the situation is important.

Avoid too much speaking up—Be selective

Speaking up does not mean teachers should be insensitive about where, when, or how they express feelings. First of all, it is important to ask: "Do I have a legitimate issue to discuss or am I in a bad mood?" "Am I overreacting?" "Am I really interested in solving anything?"

Describe steps taken to solve problem

It is important for parents to recognize that teachers have already thought about the problem and have taken appropriate action to deal with the situation. It will be reassuring for parents to know teachers are not calling them in lieu of solving the problem themselves. For example, the teacher might say, "I had a meeting with your son about his yelling out and swearing in class. We reviewed the rules of the classroom discipline plan. In addition, I am giving him extra attention and praise for polite talk. But I would also like your input and to coordinate a plan with you at home if that is possible?"

Active Listening—Obtaining Parental Input

Another of the most frequently voiced complaints by parents about teachers is that they don't feel listened to and respected by teachers. Unfortunately, instead of listening and allowing parents to speak up about their child's problem, teachers sometimes respond to parents' concerns with interruptions, questions, arguments, criticisms, and advice. Some parents report they feel confronted with a "know it all attitude" when teachers lecture to them about what to do or how to feel. In fact, few people really know how to listen, nor understand its potential power for building a strong relationship. Moreover, whenever a person doesn't feel listened to, it is likely that he or she will either restate the problem again and again or withdraw totally from the relationship. For instance in the following examples the teachers deny the problem or provide instant advice:

> **Parent:** I am having a frustrating time reading with Billy. He gets mad when I correct him and doesn't seem to want me to read with him.
>
> **Teacher:** Well, maybe you shouldn't correct him so much. (*provides instant solution*)
>
> **Or**
>
> **Parent:** Billy doesn't seem to have any friends. He never gets invited to any birthday parties.
>
> **Teacher:** Don't worry about it. It happens to all children sometime. (*deny problem*)
>
> **Or**
>
> **Parent:** You need to understand I am a single mother. I work. I don't have time to deal with this.
>
> **Teacher:** Don't you care about your child? (*blaming*)

Listening attentively is one of the most powerful ways teachers can support a parent. However, due to teachers' busy schedules, it is rarely done and often undervalued. Listening means giving the parent "the floor," allowing him or her to state feelings or ideas without interruptions. However, good listeners are not passive, merely nodding their head with a blank expression or listening while continuing to mark student papers. Instead, teachers listen by watching parents closely, using appropriate facial expressions, asking open-ended questions in an effort to understand the situation and reflecting on their thoughts and feelings. Here are some tips to become an effective listener.

An Effective Teacher Listener

- Maintain eye contact. Stop whatever work you are doing.
- Make sure there are no physical barriers between you and the parent. It's best to sit next to each other or in a circle. Don't sit at your desk with the parent on the other side.
- Give the parent a chance to finish speaking before responding.
- Listen to both the content and feeling of what the parent is saying. Every message has both a content component, which is the actual information that is conveyed, and a feeling component, which is the nonverbal message.
- Express interest by asking open-ended questions about the situation. Ask what the parent thinks is causing the problems.
- Feedback: Summarize and then paraphrase in your own words the content of the message and the feelings expressed by the parents. This is not a judgment about what the parent has said and is not agreeing or disagreeing. This simply lets the parent know you understand.
- Validate: Try to see the problem from the parent's point of view. Let the parent know that his or her point of view is a valid one. Validation can help reduce the gap that may exist between teacher and parent. It is important to admit that there are views that differ from your own and that, given a different position, the perspectives might alter.
- Encourage the parent to continue.

Note: Of course it is also important for the teacher to give some thought about when he/she is available to communicate with parents. If the teacher is walking out to the parking lot, is in the middle of setting up for a class event, or is in a rush to get home it will be difficult to communicate effectively. Instead, teachers should let parents know a good time for communicating with them about their children's needs.

In the next examples the teacher shows how s/he is listening carefully to what the parents are saying.

Parent: I am having a frustrating time reading with Billy. He gets mad when I correct him and he doesn't seem to want me to read with him.

Teacher: I'm glad you came to talk to me about that, it must be frustrating for you especially as I know you are eager for him to do well in school. Tell me more about what happens when you read together. (*validating feelings and asking questions to understand problem*)

Or

Parent: Billy doesn't seem to have any friends. He never gets invited to any birthday parties.

Teacher: I'm glad to know about that. Billy must be feeling very lonely. What does he say about friends at school? (*reflecting child's feelings and gathering further information*)

Or

Parent: You need to understand I am a single mother. I work. I don't have time to deal with this.

Teacher: I understand how overwhelmed you must feel. (*validating feelings*)

In these instances, the parent's feelings were validated as the teacher tried to see the problem from the parent's point of view.

Some teachers mind-read, believing they know the parent's motives or opinions without first checking them out. Rather than making assumptions about what a quiet family member is thinking or feeling during a meeting, a teacher might encourage him or her to talk. This can be done by discussing things that are of interest to the parent, asking directly for an opinion from this person, or by sharing a relevant experience. A teacher might tell a parent about some aspect of coping with his own children if it is relevant to the situation. It is important to think about the perspective of the quiet parent. Sometimes it is useful to think about how the parent might see an issue, then validate this feeling. You might say, "I can see how that must have hurt your feelings," "That would have made me cross too," or "Yes, I feel frustrated when my son does the same thing," or "The change in culture must be very confusing to him and to you."

Be Polite and Positive and Edit Complaints

As teachers listen, they may feel some frustration with a parent's seeming lack of involvement with or interest in their child, or may disagree with their style of parenting, or be angry about critical remarks. Even so, it is essential that teachers remain positive and avoid criticisms of the parent. Put-downs will evoke anger, resentment, defensiveness and guilt, or depression in the parent, and undermine effective communication and problem solving. Here are some examples of teacher put-downs.

> **Teacher**
> **to Parent:** You are too harsh in your discipline.
> *Or*
> If you spent more time with your child he wouldn't misbehave so much.

A professional attitude is extremely important in the effective resolution of a situation, and teachers can make a conscious decision that they will be polite no matter how anyone else is acting. The fact that a parent is rude and angry does not make it acceptable for the teacher to behave that way. Teachers won't always feel polite, however, so they will have to learn to do a bit of editing before speaking. Here are some tips to help become a good editor.

Communicate what you are able and willing to do

Teachers can edit out statements referring to what they can't do.

> **Parent:** Why can't you do more individual work with my son?
> **Teacher:** I can't. I've got 32 kids and other kids that are worse than your son! I've got a million things to do and can't take the time for one student. (*Focus is on what she cannot do, which creates opposition.*)

Alternative
I would like to give him more attention. Perhaps on Fridays at lunch I can meet with him individually for 20 minutes until we can see about a tutor possibility. (*Edit focuses on what she can do.*)

Focus on the positive

Complaints about parents should be edited. Imagine a situation where a teacher set up a behavior plan at school and sent home daily behavior reports to the parents. The parents had agreed to set up a star chart at home and to give the child a special reward for getting 10 positive notes home from the teacher. The teacher finds out that the parents didn't manage to set up the star chart. She is furious because she has put so much energy into the classroom program and feels it is being sabotaged by the parents. This teacher no longer feels like continuing the positive calls home or sending home notes until the parents have completed their part of the bargain.

This kind of thinking on the part of the teacher creates a stand-off and it is the child who will lose out in the end. Thus it is important that teachers not take parents' failures to follow through personally. It is also important that teachers take responsibility for continuing her part of the behavior plan and supporting the child in the classroom, regardless of whether the parents are able to follow through at home. Teachers may not feel that their efforts are being recognized at first, but over time, they may find that parents become more involved as they begin to trust that teachers really do go the extra mile for their child. Students' learning should not be jeopardized because parents are not able to be involved in their education.

Think about the child's needs and point of view

Teachers should try to enter into parent meetings with a focus on the perspective of the family and child. This means thinking about what the student needs or what might be going on for his family. For example, "I wonder if the parents are nervous about meeting me in a school, perhaps they would prefer a home visit?" Or, " Johnny's mother is so stressed out because of she lost her job. It's so hard being a single mother of 4 children. I bet she doesn't have the energy to do a star chart or even to get the stickers. I could offer to set up a chart for her, or maybe even set up a plan that gives the rewards at school."

Focus on Fixing the Problem

Sometimes effective communication is hindered by blaming. This occurs when people place the responsibility for a problem with someone else. They may directly accuse others of creating the problem or they may do this more subtly. Here are some common examples of blaming as reported by parents.

> **Teacher:** Your daughter gets her own way and you never discipline her. That's why she's such a behavior problem. You're not tough enough.
>
> *Or*
>
> **Teacher:** I think you spank her too much. That's why she's so aggressive.
>
> *Or*
>
> **Teacher:** You are not attached to your child, If you were she would not have these problems.
>
> *Or*
>
> **Teacher:** Your child is the most aggressive child I have ever seen. He is really crazy and I've handled tough kids before— but not like your child.

Blaming sets people against each other in battle rather than uniting them to solve a problem. When teachers talk to parents, it is important to focus on fixing the problem not the blame. Following teachers' meetings, parents often report that they felt blamed by the teacher for their children's behavior problems at school. However once parents realize that teachers are primarily interested in working together to solve their child's problems (and not to blame them) they will soon become partners. For instance, the teacher says to a parent, "The problem seems to be that Gillian is overly aggressive. Let's decide how we both want to handle these problems in the future so that we can be consistent with each other. I know if we work together we can help her be more cooperative." This approach emphasizes collaboration and consistency is more likely to lead to a successful outcome.

A Problem Is Always Legitimate

A parent may bring up an issue with the teacher, only to have it dismissed by the teacher as not being a serious problem. For instance, parents may be concerned that their child is acting aggressively at home or is overly anxious about school work. However, the teacher doesn't believe there is a problem in the classroom and therefore doesn't see the value of discussing it. Here are some examples of denying or discounting a problem.

> **Teacher:** Don't worry about it. His behavior at school is fine. There are a lot worse kids than him.
>
> *Or*
>
> **Teacher:** That is normal behavior for his age. It's not a problem. You expect too much of him for his age.

Although the teacher may not see an issue as a problem for the child at school, the parent does. Therefore, in the interest of good collaboration with parents, teachers need to address the situation and cooperate to help resolve it. Active listening and validation will allow teachers to better understand the parent's point of view.

Focus on Realistic Changes

Statements such as, "Nothing works with this child," "He's just like his brother who was always in trouble," "He'll never change," "I'll try but it won't do any good," communicate a hopeless message that all efforts toward change are futile. It can also be communicated by subtle cues, such as one- or two-word replies. "I don't know," "I guess," or "Whatever," spoken in a passive, depressed voice, indicate lack of hope as well as implying a lack of interest. Hopelessness can even be indicated nonverbally by deep sighs or eye-rolling.

If teachers or the parents feel a sense of hopelessness when tackling a problem, there must be a shift to focus on changes that can realistically be made. Although no major problem can be resolved in one discussion, each one does have a workable solution. This is an important attitude to convey. For instance, teachers might communicate an attitude of hope by saying: "Okay, we are going to have to be patient with him as it takes time to change. He's been through a lot. First let us talk about how we will manage the hitting behavior and then we will talk about what social skills we want to teach him. We want to develop a short-term and a long-term plan. "

Stop Action, Refocus and Stay Calm

Occasionally when teachers or parents are trying to discuss a problem, they end up "unloading;" that is, dragging in all sorts of gripes about the child. They may even go on to list every misbehavior the child has done over the past two months. Pretty soon both parties feel overwhelmed and angry.

> **Teacher:** He's irresponsible. He hits other kids, he doesn't listen, he runs around and won't stay in his seat. He so disruptive that I can't teach the other kids. He's always interrupting me in class and then doesn't do what I ask him to do. He's driving me wild!

Teachers can call a stop action, or truce, and halt all discussion when they realize unloading is occurring. This might be a statement such as, "I need to stop talking about this right now, and start again when we have some time to calm down," or "I think we should reflect on this awhile and set up another meeting to continue our planning." (Note the use of "I" messages. When a meeting is cut short, it is important to set another time in the near future to continue the discussion.)

Get Feedback

People become defensive when they feel they are being blamed, whether or not they actually are being accused, and whether or not they really are to blame. They may react by becoming angry or argumentative, making excuses, becoming distraught and crying, or withdrawing and refusing to participate in further discussion.

> **Mother:** You seem to have a lot of aggression in your classroom. My son has told me several times about being hit by several boys.
>
> **Teacher:** (*He thinks she is saying he can't control the classroom and reacts defensively.*) You don't have 30 kids all day without any help. There is bound to be some hitting — all young kids do that.

Studies have shown that there are two filters whenever two people are talking. One affects how a person communicates and the other affects how the message is received. It is important for teachers to try to become aware of these filters and how they may alter how they talk to parents and the way they hear what is said to them. For instance, if a teacher feels he is being blamed or criticized, it is a good idea to stop the discussion and get feedback about what the parent meant. For instance, the teacher in the above example could attempt to clarify what the parent meant by asking a question.

> **Teacher:** Are you concerned that I am not managing the aggression? (*asks for feedback*)

Dealing with Parental Resistance and Complaints

Teachers sometimes find themselves suggesting possible solutions to parents only to be met with "yes-buts" from them. Yes-butting occurs when every attempt to make a suggestion or state a point of view is discounted because something is wrong with it. It is easy to feel defeated or rejected when this occurs: "I'm wrong again. Nothing I say is acceptable to this parent." This results in, "What's the use of trying to help? This parent doesn't care about her child, why should I care?" The parent who yes-buts is often unaware of rejecting the teacher's views.

> **Teacher:** I think we should get a tutor for Andrea to help her with her reading.
>
> **Mother:** Yes, that's a good idea, but it would never work. You know she wouldn't do the extra reading at home and it would be a waste of money. (yes, but)

Teacher: Well, maybe you could do the individual tutoring with her yourself?

Mother: I don't have time to do extra home work with her. Isn't that the teacher's job? (*defensive*)

Teacher: Don't you care about your daughter's success in school? (*critical*)

It is important that teachers remain positive and confident rather than become critical with the parent. Sometimes parents react defensively to a teacher's advice because they feel the teacher doesn't really understand their situation or when their own ideas have been discounted. Therefore, before coming up with a final plan, it is always important to be sure that the teacher has listened carefully, validated the parent's point of view and has invited the parent's solutions to the situation.

Another distressing situation for a teacher is to be on the receiving end of complaints or criticisms by a parent. This is usually unanticipated and almost always hurtful. Consider your responses to the following parental comments:

Parent: Why am I hearing about this problem now? You should have been helping her sooner in the year.

Or

If you knew how to teach, my son wouldn't be having these problems.

Or

Your homework is so uninteresting, no wonder she doesn't want to do it.

Or

My son has never had difficulties before in class, it must be something you are doing wrong. He says you don't do anything to stop the kids from picking on him.

It is important to maintain a professional and respectful attitude and not to react defensively or angrily, otherwise the cycle of criticisms will continue. Teachers need to recognize that they're dealing with a parent who is highly distraught about their child. Parent anger may be diffused with one of the following strategies:

A Respectful Teacher

- Admit a mistake if there is one.
- Listen attentively to the parent without being defensive.
- Show concern by getting more information about the complaint.
- Refocus the negative complaint into a positive recommendation for dealing with the situation. For instance, instead of saying, "Don't you care about your daughter's success?" the teacher could say, "Yes I will give her extra attention at school but I think she could do with help outside of school. I know you want her to be successful. Since I know how busy you are at work, I wonder if there is another way we can provide her with some extra tutoring?"

The following are some other examples of ways you can respond to the parental criticisms presented above.

Teacher: You have reason to be angry about that. I was not aware she was struggling with her reading and I wish I had been.

Or

Yes I should have contacted you sooner. You have reason to be upset. (*admit mistake*)

Or

That really concerns me. Can you explain more what you mean? (*show concern*)

Or

I hear what your saying? How can we make the homework more interesting for her? (*refocus on positive*)

Or

Can you tell me more about how the kids are picking on him?
Are there other times where he felt I did nothing to help him?
(*get more information*)

Agree on Mutual Goals and Brainstorm Solutions

Once the issue or problem has been discussed and both the parent and teacher feel they have expressed their views and been listened to, the next step is for them to agree upon their common goals and to share possible solutions. The teacher can ask the parents if they have any suggestions for how to solve the problem. The teacher also shares her ideas for what she has already tried and what she thinks will be helpful to the child given the new information from the parents. Then the teacher and parents should work out a plan of exactly what the teacher will do at school and how the parents will be involved. For example, the teacher might say, " Here's what I will do at school, I will set up a reward program to help him remember to listen and not blurt out in class. Then I will send home a note each day to let you know how many stickers he has earned that day. You can record these on your sticker chart at home, and when he gets 25 of them perhaps plan a surprise."

Express Confidence

Whenever there is a problem with a child, parents are probably anxious. They need to know they are dealing with a confident teacher who has the ability to handle the situation and to work together with them and with their child to teach him or her alternative prosocial behaviors. Teachers can let the parents know they are confident of their eventual success and that with the extra support at school and at home they believe the problem will be resolved.

Plan Follow Up

It is important to plan a follow-up meeting or phone call to review the success of the planned intervention. If the parents have computers for email communication or cell phones for texting, these are useful ways to give weekly feedback on progress their child has made before the next scheduled meeting. The follow up plan is vital if parents are going to believe in the teacher's commitment to their child.

> **Teacher:** I've had a lot of experience with children like Robbie. I know that by working together we can get results. I will contact you in two days to let you know how things are progressing. Let me know if anything else comes up that I should know about Robbie.

Sample Meeting Script with the Parent to Discuss a Problem

Teacher: It's good to see you again Ms. Parks. You said you wanted to talk about a problem. (Welcome parent)

Parent: Yes, I'm concerned because Takisha is refusing to sit down for our reading time at home. She's always seemed to like reading with me in the past. Now she just says, "I don't want to do it. I hate reading." Last week she even threw her book across the room. I'm not sure if I should force her to sit down and listen or if I should just let it go.

Teacher: How long has this been happening? (*Listen and get information about problem.*)

Parent: It's just been in the last two weeks. Did anything happen at school?

Teacher: You know, about three weeks ago a new girl joined our class. She's a little older than the other kids and she's just begun reading some single words. She's been struggling with reading, and I've been praising her a lot each time she reads a new word. Perhaps I haven't been noticing Takisha's progress as much as I was. (*Suggests an idea.*)

Parent: Well Takisha is really fond of you. If this new girl is getting a lot of attention from you, Takisha may be feeling left out. At home when her cousin is over, Takisha sometimes sulks if her cousin gets more attention than she does.

Teacher: I wonder if some other children are also feeling a little left out. Maybe I went a little overboard in making the new girl feel welcome. I guess I need to make an effort to praise each child's special abilities more often.

Parent: That's a good idea. I think that would help Takisha at school. What do you think I should do about her reluctance to read with me at home?

Teacher: Maybe you could do reading in a little different way for a while. I have some CDs of some children's books that you could listen to. I know that in the past Takisha has liked dinosaur books. I have some great CDs of some of those. Also, if you have a DVD player, I do have movies of some of the other books that we have in the classroom. You could listen or watch the story and then go to the book to see the pictures. This might help Takisha feel less pressure to read. And perhaps you could just read to her and not ask her to read for a while so it is a fun time for you both. Also anytime you want to come in to class and read to the children you are welcome. We have reading times twice a day. (*Offer something she can do to help and invite her participation.*)

Parent: Well, I don't have any way to play CDs, but I do have a DVD player. Maybe we'll start with that. Now that I know how she might be feeling, I'll praise her more for listening and coming up with ideas.

Teacher: Oh that's a great idea. Also, it might be good not to give her tantrums and resistant behavior too much attention. Why don't we talk this coming Monday about how Takisha's doing. I'm glad you brought this to my attention so quickly. Takisha asks such great questions during circle time. I really love having her in the classroom. (*Be positive about solving the problem and support parent.*)

Parent: Thank you very much for taking the time to meet with me. I feel better now that I know what's going on. Shall I call you on Monday or do you want to call me?

Teacher: Could I call you in the evening, because it's hard for me to call during the school day? (*Plan time to talk again.*)

Parent: Yes, any time after 6:30 would be fine.

CONCLUSION

Involving parents in their child's education requires a commitment to families, a proactive plan for involving parents that is carefully crafted prior to school starting, and teacher time set aside for communicating and collaborating with parents. It is a process that is demanding and time-consuming, sometimes frustrating, and often rewarding. For the already overworked teacher, it can seem difficult to know where to carve out any extra time for this collaboration work during the day. However, the value of this approach for children's social, emotional, and academic growth cannot be underestimated. In long run this commitment to work with parents may actually save time, for it can lead to more positive relationships with students, less stressful classrooms and more support for both teachers and the family. For the child it will make all the difference.

TO SUM UP...

Teachers Partnering with Parents

- Make a plan for parent involvement before school starts.
- Send home regular positive notes and make positive phone calls, emails or text messages.
- Set up informal and formal mechanisms for parents to communicate with teachers.
- Don't store up grievances; call a meeting with a parent when a child misbehavior first occurs.
- Express your concern for the child's optimal learning.
- Be brief, clear and concise when describing a behavior problem and focus on the positive opposite behaviors that the child will be taught.
- Ask for parent feedback and suggestions for solutions.
- Don't interrupt, argue, give advice; listen attentively and validate parents' concerns.
- Stick to the point and avoid unloading multiple gripes.
- Edit: be polite and positive.
- Focus on fixing the problem and avoid blaming.
- Recognize the parent's point of view.
- Take one step at a time in goal setting.
- Get and give feedback.
- Stay calm and patient.
- Stop and call a Time Out if anger mounts.

- Make positive recommendations for solutions in collaboration with parents.
- Plan a follow-up with parents.
- Encourage ongoing conversation.

The Incredible Years®
Teacher Classroom Management Self-Reflection Inventory
Partnering with Parents

Date: _____ Teacher Name: _____

Teachers learn extensively from self-reflection regarding their classroom management and the teaching strategies they are using that are working or not working. From these reflections teachers determine personal goals for making changes in their approaches to bring about the most positive learning climate they can. Use this Inventory to think about your strengths and limitations and determine your goals.

Building Positive Relationships with Parents	1 = NEVER 3 = OCCASIONALLY 5 = CONSISTENTLY
1. I set up opportunities for parents to participate or observe in classroom.	1 2 3 4 5
2. I send home regular newsletters to parents and positive notes about their children.	1 2 3 4 5
3. I have a regular call schedule for calling parents to give them positive messages about their children.	1 2 3 4 5
4. I have regular posted telephone hours or times parents can reach me.	1 2 3 4 5
5. I schedule parent evenings/meetings to share classroom activities with parents and to present ideas for carrying over classroom activities at home. (e.g. coaching methods)	1 2 3 4 5
6. I consider parents' for ideas, materials and support for classroom activities.	1 2 3 4 5

7. I recognize the importance of partnering with parents and collaborating in order to develop strong connections with children.	1 2 3 4 5
8. I encourage parents to share aspects of their culture and traditions with the classroom and with me.	1 2 3 4 5
9. I share students behavior plans with parents and invite their participation in goal setting and discussing ways to enhance their learning at home.	1 2 3 4 5
Future Goals Regarding Involving Parents:	Total

REFERENCES

Battistich, V., Schaps, E., & Wilson, N. (2004). Effects of an elementary school intervention in students "connectiveness" to school and social adjustment during middle school. *The Journal of Primary Prevention 24*, 243-262.

Battistich, V., Solomon, D., Kim, D., Watson, M., & Schaps, E. (1995). Schools as communities, poverty levels of student populations, and student's attitudes, motives, and performance: A multilevel analysis. *American Educational Research Journal, 32*(3), 627-658.

Burton, C. B. (1992). Defining family-centered early education: Beliefs of public school, child care, and Head Start teachers. *Early education and development, 3*(1), 45-59.

Cappella, E., Frazier, S. L., Atkins, M., Schoenwald, S. K., & Glisson, C. (2008). Enhancing schools' capacity to support children in poverty: An ecological model of school-based mental health services. *Administration and Policy in Mental Health, 35*, 395-409.

Castro, D. C., & Bryant, D. M. (2004). Parent involvement in Head Start programs:The role of parent, teacher and classroom characteristics. *Early Childhood Research Quarterly, 19*, 413-430.

Chavkin, N. F. (1991). Uniting families and schools: Social workers helping teachers through inservice training. *School Social Work Journal, 15*, 1-10.

Domina, T. (2005). Leveling the home advantage: Assessing the effectiveness of parental involvement in elementary school. *Sociology of Education 88*(5), 233-249.

Epstein, A. (1992). School and family partnerships. In M. Alkin (Ed.), *Encyclopedia of Educational Research* (pp. 1139-1151). New York: MacMillan.

Henderson, A., & Berla, N. (1994). *A new generation of evidence: The family is critical to student achievement.* Columbia, MD: National Committee for Citizens in Education.

Hindman, A. H., Skibbe, L. E., Miller, A., & Zimmerman, M. (2010). Ecological contexts and early learning: Contributions of child, family, and classroom factors during Head Start, to literacy and mathematics growth through first grade. *Early Childhood Research Quarterly, 25*, 235-250.

Kohl, G. O., Lengua, L. J., & McMahon, R. J. (2000). Parent involvement in school conceptualizing mutliple dimensions and their relations with family and demographic risk factors. *Journal of School Psychology, 38*(6), 501-523.

Reid, M. J., Webster-Stratton, C., & Hammond, M. (2007). Enhancing a classroom social competence and problem-solving curriculum by offering parent training to families of moderate-to-high-risk elementary school children. *Journal of Clinical Child and Adolescent Psychology, 36*(5), 605-620.

Storch, E. A., & Crisp, H. L. (2004). Taking it to schools: Transporting empirically supported treatments for childhood psychopathology in the school setting. *Clinical Child and Family Psychology Review, 7*, 191-193.

Webster-Stratton, C., & Reid, J. M. (2009). A school-family partnership: Addressing multiple risk factors to improve school readiness and prevent conduct problems in young children. In S. L. Christenson & A. L. Reschly (Eds.), *Handbook on school-family partnerships for promoting student competence* (pp. 204-227). Seattle Routledge/Taylor and Francis.

Webster-Stratton, C., Reid, M. J., & Hammond, M. (2001). Preventing conduct problems, promoting social competence: A parent and teacher training partnership in Head Start. *Journal of Clinical Child Psychology, 30*(3), 283-302.

Webster-Stratton, C., Reid, M. J., & Hammond, M. (2004). Treating children with early-onset conduct problems: Intervention outcomes for parent, child, and teacher training. *Journal of Clinical Child and Adolescent Psychology, 33*(1), 105-124.

Managing Personal Stress

At times, all teachers feel angry, depressed, frustrated, or guilty when dealing with difficult students and difficult classes. Upsetting feelings are to be expected and are even essential and beneficial. They signal the need for change and problem solving and provide motivation. Danger arises, however, when these feelings are so overwhelming that teachers are immobilized by depression or lose control of their anger. The challenge is not to avoid these feelings or to eliminate conflict, but learn to cope with emotional responses to conflict in a manner that provides more self-control.

Researchers (e.g., Seligman, 1990) have demonstrated a clear relationship between what we *think* about a situation, how we *feel* about it, and how we *behave and relate to individuals in the situation*. To see how this works, let's consider the various ways a teacher might react to this situation. The classroom feels like it is in chaos. It is noisy. The teacher is trying to teach while two children are shouting across the room and two others are chatting away privately. Another student wanders in late, and a classmate yells, "hey, you are late!" Annoyed with the noise, the teacher might think to himself, "This class is impossible, inconsiderate, irresponsible, and lazy. It's a constant hassle to settle them down before I can teach." As the teacher thinks these negative thoughts, his anger mounts, and he begins criticizing the students and yelling at them. On the other hand, he might view the situation as hopeless or think that he is to blame: "It's all my fault for being a poor teacher. There is nothing I can do." In this case, he is more likely to feel depressed and tentative, and to avoid making a request or disciplining the students. If, however, he kept his thoughts focused on his ability to cope and to be calm, he might say to himself: "Some of the class is not focused this morning. I'm going to need to change my pacing here, get the group's attention, and remind students of the talking rule." This would facilitate more rational and effective responses to the students' misbehaviors.

The truth is that we become angry not because of an event itself but because of the view we take of it. Most teachers are aware that some days a noisy classroom is not bothersome and other days it is very irritating. The purpose of this chapter is to help teachers identify the negative self-statements that increase their distress, and substitute coping responses during periods of conflict. You will see the parallel to the work teachers are doing with children in Chapter Eleven.

STEP 1: Be Aware of Your Negative and Positive Thoughts

Thoughts are always present and are under the individual's control, and no one else's. Since these thoughts are always there, they frequently become background noise, are taken for granted, and are often not even consciously processed. It is important for teachers to learn to pay attention to their thought patterns, to recognize maladaptive and stressful thoughts, and substitute positive coping responses. Imagine the following scene:

You have a difficult class. It seems like you are putting out brush fires all day. The noise level feels like the playground. One boy constantly gets up and wanders around the classroom, stopping to interfere with a classmates work. Other students giggle and chat privately rather than listen to your teaching.

What are your thoughts now? They're probably negative.

STEP 2: Decrease Your Negative Thoughts

After becoming aware of negative thought patterns, the next step is to decrease them. There are four ways to do this.

1. Thought interruption

The first step is to stop the negative thought as soon as it surfaces. A teacher might say to herself, "I am going to stop thinking about that now." Some teachers wear a rubber band on their wrist and snap it every time they have a negative thought to remind them to stop it. "Stop worrying. Worrying won't help anything."

2. Reschedule worrying or anger time

Constantly reviewing the anger and worries caused by a particular student or class of students is very draining. It is helpful to actually schedule in a brief period (10-20 minutes) during the day to review and process negative feelings about a particular situation. For instance, a teacher might tell himself that at 9:30 p.m. he will think about the frustrating circumstances and allow himself to feel as angry as he wants. During the rest of the day, he will stop these thoughts and save them for the scheduled break. The challenge is not to allow these thoughts to interfere with his mood, work, or play until the scheduled time. The idea is not to stop thinking about unpleasant things altogether but to control when the thinking is done so that a pervasive negative mood doesn't take over the whole day. Paradoxically, teachers are likely to find that when they begin their scheduled anger/worry time, the intensity of the problems has diminished somewhat. This may mean that the teacher is able to more constructively problem-solve during this worry time instead of fuming or ruminating or catastrophizing.

3. Objectify the situation

The third approach to stopping negative self-talk is to ask whether specific thoughts or actions are helping to reach a desired goal:

- What is my goal? (*To reduce the noise level of the classroom and have a wandering child sit in her seat.*)
- What am I doing now? (*Getting frustrated and angry.*)
- Is what I'm doing helping me reach my long-term goal? (*No, we're arguing and I'm yelling.*)
- If it isn't, what do I need to do differently? (*Think more positively and come up with a plan. For example, I will start by focusing on the students who are sitting and attending. Perhaps I can adjust my lesson plan to give the whole class a change of pace.*)

This is similar to the "turtle technique" for helping children manage anger (Chapter 11). Teachers can briefly withdraw into an imaginary shell to assess their mood, thought, and behavior. Then they come out again with a new strategy or plan. It is ideal to use this "turtle technique" before losing control, but all teachers lose their temper sometimes. Sometimes, an angry response or explosion slips out before the teacher is consciously aware of being upset. As teachers become more aware of situations that trigger negative emotions and the thoughts that signal emotional escalation, they will be able to interrupt the anger sequence at earlier stages, before the anger explodes.

Teachers can briefly withdraw into an imaginary shell to assess their mood, thought, and behavior.

4. Normalize the situation

Another way to objectify a situation is to normalize it by remembering that all teachers have difficult and conflictual days with their students and all students have behavior problems. Moreover, all teachers and children sometimes have feelings of guilt, depression, anger, and anxiety. Normalizing these thoughts will take away some of their power. Then the goal is to stop the negative ones. A teacher might say to herself, "I'm feeling uptight, but that's natural," or "Lots of teachers feel discouraged at times. This feeling will pass."

STEP 3: Increase Your Positive Thoughts

Reducing negative thoughts won't automatically increase positive ones. Here are six steps to help increase your positive thoughts.

1. Dispute negative self-talk

Combat self-talk that contains should, ought, and must statements or generalizations that include words such as awful or terrible. Instead of thinking, "I should be a better teacher," a teacher might think, "Why do I feel I have to be the perfect teacher? I'm doing a pretty good job." The negative thought, "My students are horrible!" might be replaced with, "These children are wound up today. Mondays are a challenge for everyone." The thoughts normalize and objectify the misbehaviors. This is not an easy skill to learn. At first, teachers will likely need to do this kind of thinking after the fact. Teachers can think back to situations where they felt out of control, identify the negative self-talk, and think of ways to dispute it next time they encounter that situation.

2. Substitute calming or coping thoughts for negative ones

Another approach is to replace upsetting thoughts and negative self-statements with alternative calming ones. If a teacher is thinking about a particular student in hostile terms, "He is misbehaving because he deliberately likes to get me upset," she can practice thought-stopping and try to substitute thoughts that emphasize her ability to cope, "I'm going to help him learn to control himself," "It's up to me" or, "He is misbehaving because he has not been taught social skills, so it is my job to teach him those skills. I can be the one to make a difference."

3. Time Projection

The idea here is to think more positively by mentally traveling forward to the time when the stressful period will have ended. For instance, a teacher might say to himself, "I've had other students like this and after several weeks on a consistent behavior plan, they were much improved." This strategy helps teachers to remember that all feelings and situations are transient and that both the difficult situation and the negative feelings surrounding the situation will go away eventually (although often not without some type of plan or intervention). In some cases situations are likely to change quickly (e.g., a three year old who is tantrumming to get his way will stop in a few minutes if the teacher ignores). In other cases, the situation may need more intervention, patience, and effort from the teacher (e.g., a student who is reacting to home stress such as a divorce or a student with a long history of problematic behavior). However, it is still important to acknowledge that the problems will lessen as time goes by, and as efforts are made to ameliorate the situation. Time projection recognizes stressful feelings, allows teachers to see a more satisfying future, and reminds one that psychological pain is not fatal.

Teachers can also remind students of the temporary nature of the problem. The teacher could say to the seven-year-old who is frustrated because she cannot read, "Next year at this time you will be reading. Won't that be great!" Or another example, "This is a tough time now, but you won't always feel so sad."

4. Think and verbalize self-praise thoughts

A fourth way for teachers to think more positively is to give themselves a pat on the back for their accomplishments. Many people don't give themselves credit for what they do, particularly for the difficult job of teaching, and then they belittle themselves when things don't work out right. Every teacher does many effective things in the course of the day, even on a day that feels like it didn't go well. It is important to acknowledge daily accomplishments! For example a teacher might think, "Today was rough, but I stayed patient with Marius during that first tantrum," or "Sanjay actually read a whole page today for the first time."

5. Humor

Humor helps to reduce anger and depression. It's important for teachers not to take themselves too seriously. At times when teachers are at their most frustrated, it can be helpful for them to step back and gently poke fun at themselves, "Oh yes, I'm perfect. I never lose my cool." Occasionally a teacher may be able to use kind humor to turn around a negative mood for herself and for a student. A teacher might say, "Oh my goodness—look at us. We are both red in the face. I think we're going to turn purple and explode! I would hate that to happen because it would make a mess!" Accompanied with a warm smile and laugh, this could diffuse the situation for everyone. Although this takes a light and strategic touch, when it works, it can be almost miraculous. Being able to laugh at oneself can alter a negative mood. It is also an excellent skill for teachers to model for students. It might be helpful for teachers to keep a private "funny moments" journal to record some of the more outrageous classroom behaviors that occur during the day. Students can also be helpful aides in using humor—the class might keep a "joke jar" to use at times when the level of classroom frustrating is rising. One teacher that we know had a silly hat that she wore when she was starting to feel frustrated. This served as a light hearted signal to the class that her temper was fragile, and the class was given the goal to help her be able to take the hat off again when things felt back under control.

6. Model coping self-talk and self-praise

As teachers are learning to use coping and self-praise thoughts when confronted with a problem, it is useful to state these thoughts out loud. Teachers are powerful models for their students. During the day there are countless opportunities for teachers to model out loud for their students how they thought about and coped with a difficult situation. By observing these responses students will eventually learn to use them as well. For instance, it is circle time and the teacher says to the students, "I'm really proud of the way we all coped well with the disappointment about the field trip being canceled. I told myself not to overreact, that these things happen sometimes. I made a plan to see about a different field trip we can do. I feel good about that." Here the teacher is modeling not only how she stopped herself from overreacting but also how she praised herself for her control.

All teachers will find that there are times when they are discouraged. Behavior change takes practice and time.

Of course, all teachers will find that there are times when it is difficult to use self-control techniques. Relapses and problems are to be expected. It is important to think in terms of small gains and not to belittle gradual progress. It takes practice to become proficient and teachers must learn to praise the effort and give themselves credit for trying.

Examples of teacher calming, coping, and self-praise thoughts

- I don't like it when he acts like that, but I can handle that.
- My job is to stay calm and help him learn better ways to ask for what he wants.
- I can help her learn better ways to behave.
- She's just testing the limits. I can help her with that.
- This isn't the end of the world. He's a bright child and I'm a caring teacher. We will make it over this hump.
- He really doesn't do that much anymore. This is a temporary setback.
- I shouldn't blame my impatience on him. I'll talk to him about it.
- I am doing the best I can to help her learn more positive behaviors.
- I can develop a plan to deal with it.
- I need to stick to the issue, and not take this personally!
- He doesn't really understand what those swearing words mean. I'm not going to let it upset me.
- He is swearing because he's looking for a reaction. If I can ignore and stay calm, the words will lose their power.
- I shouldn't be so hard on myself. No one expects perfection. Take one step at a time.
- Look for positives, don't jump to conclusions.
- We're getting through this—each day gets better and better.
- I can cope.
- No one can make me mad; it's up to me.
- I can't control her behavior right now, but I can control my thinking and my anger.
- I'm a good teacher.
- I am trying hard and will persist.
- I need to stay focused on the primary issue and not the secondary annoying misbehaviors.

The following sections focus on some particular problems to watch out for when learning to use self-control techniques, and suggestions for dealing with them.

Refute Negative Labels and Focus on Specific Behaviors

"He's thoughtless." "That class is always..." or, "That class never..." Negative labeling, which categorizes either a individual child's personality or an entire classroom, is destructive. A label implies that a child always behaves in a particular way and is incapable of changing. Because Jamal is often oppositional, the teacher labels him as "irresponsible," "inconsiderate," "lazy," or "spoiled." Teachers who have learned to view the world in this extreme manner will quickly become frustrated, angry, and blaming whenever they are in an upsetting situation with that person or classroom.

It is important to avoid focusing on a single problem behavior as though that reflects the student's entire personality. One way to keep from labeling a student is to refute this negative thinking by asking: "Is this always true?" "Is this totally accurate?" or "Can I think of a time when this is not true?" Most likely the behavior is only true for the moment or for some portion of the time. Next, teachers should try to isolate and define the specific annoying behavior and come up with a coping self-statement. For instance, when Jamal's teacher catches herself thinking that he is lazy, she could say, "Okay, that's not a fair label. He's not really lazy. Right now he is not listening and following directions. I need a plan to help him listen and do what I ask."

Avoid focusing on a single problem behavior as though that reflects the student's entire presonality.

Avoid Personalizing

Sometimes teachers assume they know the reason why a student behaved in a certain way and slip into the trap of taking student behaviors personally. They forget that student behavior has many causes, most unrelated to a personal vendetta against the teacher! Unfortunately, these assumptions can become self-fulfilling prophecies. For example, two children are fighting over the toys while the teacher is trying to get the snack ready. The teacher mind-reads, "They're being loud on purpose. They want to make me mad!" Or, a teacher comes back from a meeting and finds her classroom in a shambles. She mind-reads, "No one cares about me... They dislike me." This kind of negative mind-reading is bound to increase resentment and anger towards the students and aide.

Teachers should focus on being facilitators of change, not victims of the situation.

Rather than speculating about motives, teachers should focus on specific positive opposite behaviors they need to teach the students. There is a high possibility of error when assuming another person's motives. Instead of the teacher thinking, "They are doing it on purpose to get me mad," he might say to himself, "I don't know what has upset them today. I'll ask them and see what we can do about the problem." In this example, instead of mind-reading the teacher asks them about their problem. In the second example the teacher might tell herself, "I need to talk with my aide about teaching the kids to put away the toys." Both teachers have avoided mind-reading and focused on the behavior they want to change. They've chosen to see themselves as facilitators of change rather than as victims of the situation.

Avoid Negative Time Projection

Individuals who mind-read often engage in fortune-telling. They predict a dismal future by assuming that because an event occurred in the past, it will continue to occur. For instance, six-year-old Andy has been stealing small things at school. His teacher thinks, "He'll become a delinquent and drop out of school!" Other examples of fortune-telling are, "He'll never stop," "She'll never change," "Oh no, it's starting again. It will be just the same as last time." This kind of gloomy prophesying causes teachers to feel depressed, act passively, or withdraw from helping their students behave more appropriately. Moreover, making negative predictions about the future sets up a self-fulfilling prophecy. If teachers are convinced their students will never behave any better, then they probably won't.

A more positive way of thinking about Andy's stealing would be, "I can help him learn not to steal." This focuses on coping effectively with the problem and results in the child receiving more hopeful messages about his capabilities. If prophecy is to be helpful, one must mentally travel forward to a time when the stressful period will have ended and predict a positive outcome. The harried teacher who has 34 students in her classroom, four of them with significant behavior problems, might say to herself, "This class is challenging and needs more monitoring! I will ask for an aide in the classroom and set up an incentive program to teach them social skills. Then in a few months it won't be so difficult." Making a positive prediction will remind you that there'll be a more relaxed future.

Thought-Stop and Substitute Coping Thoughts

Sometimes teachers catastrophize, imagining the worst possible outcome or exaggerating the importance of a negative event. If a teacher was trying to do math with a small group of students while the other students were out of seat and yelling, he would be catastrophizing if he said to himself: "I'm totally overwhelmed. I can't stand it. They're driving me crazy! My class is too big. Nobody gives me any support." This kind of thinking heightens anger and leads to explosive outbursts by convincing teachers that they're out of control.

Teachers can recognize exaggerated statements by looking for phrases that include words such as *always, never, everybody,* and *nobody*. These words are a signal to use thought stopping and substitute coping thoughts such as, "Stop! It's not always like this. This is a tough afternoon, but I can be in control of my anger. If I stay calm, I can deal with this."

Avoid Absolutes and Set More Flexible Standards

Self-talk that includes *should* and *must* implies that one has a right to something and that it is intolerable if it doesn't occur. The first part of this may well be true, but the second part causes the difficulty. Circumstances don't always allow for the ideal, and to react as if the resulting situation is unfair may invite emotional upset. Teachers might feel they have a right to have students who behave respectfully and appropriately at all times or to have peace when they are teaching. This kind of attitude on the part of teachers is the basis for a lot of anger and stress when working with sulky students who challenge their authority. By expressing preferences in the form of absolutes, they feel victimized when their wishes aren't met. The resulting sense of injustice and the desire to punish or set things right sustains anger and fuels further conflict. Consider Sally, a first grade teacher who is having trouble in the classroom with Jessie, who is hyperactive and noncompliant. She thinks, "He shouldn't embarrass me like this, he must respect me. It isn't fair. I don't deserve a student like this who is causing my classroom to be out of control." Sally is thinking in terms of being victimized by her student and, therefore, she is more likely to find her anger escalating as well as her desire for revenge. "He deserves to be punished." The combination of anger with a desire to punish can lead to an aggressive reaction rather than a coping response. These kind of moralistic beliefs will lead teachers to feel that they have the right to classrooms that are free from misbehaviors, rather than accepting that these behaviors are normative, occur in every classroom, and are part of the teaching experience.

Effective teachers remain flexible and learn from their mistakes.

Teachers can work to rewrite absolute beliefs into more flexible thoughts. In a sense, this means learning to expect unpredictability and mistakes as a part of life and to understand that humans are imperfect and fallible! In the above example with Sally and Jessie, Sally could say to herself, "He's a little squirrely today. Must be an off day. All children do this from time to time." or "I like respect, but it takes time to get it with these kids. I'm not going to get stressed out about this." Another tactic would be to mentally dispute all self-talk that includes *musts*, *oughts*, and *shoulds*. "Who says children should treat teachers fairly?" "What makes me think my students should be perfect when many students aren't!" or "Who says I ought to be perfect?" Many teachers find that challenging the "should" they set for themselves can lead to a refreshing release from unattainable standards for their own behavior.

Think about Long-Term Goals

Teachers who feel victimized by their students often move quite quickly from thinking, "This isn't fair! I don't deserve this!" to thinking, "This student deserves to be punished." Their impulse to punish is really a desire for revenge, which their anger serves the purpose of justifying. They may think they are in control of the situation, even though their anger is out of control.

It's hard to let go of anger, especially when a teacher feels that he is the victim of unfair treatment. Anger can make teachers feel righteous, energized, and powerful. Giving up anger can be difficult because it is sometimes confused with passive defeat and loss of power. In such situations, it is useful to think in terms of long-term goals rather than the short-term satisfaction of getting revenge. A teacher might say to himself, "In the long-term, it is better for Jason to see me cope by taking charge of my anger." Another constructive self-statement would be, "The long-term cost of letting my anger explode would be far greater than the momentary satisfaction of showing him I won't be pushed around."

Objectify and Normalize

A different type of upsetting self-statement occurs when teachers blame themselves for their problems with their students. When confronting a problem, they say to themselves, "I'm a total failure as a teacher, I can't do anything right." Or they may focus on their situation and say, "If only I had a smaller classroom, maybe he would behave better," or "It's because I don't have kids myself that I'm having these problems." In these instances, teachers generalize and interpret problems with their students as a reflection of their teaching skills or their life style. Not only does this oversimplify a complex problem, it makes them feel hostile and passive, and may eventually cause a teacher to withdraw or quit.

Teachers who are falling into this self-criticism trap must work to depersonalize self-critical thinking by remembering that ALL children have behavior problems and that students' behavior difficulties are probably less a reflection of their teaching style than of many students' need to test the limits of their environment as part of their developmental drive to explore and be independent. Instead of being self-critical, these teachers need to remember to objectify the students' specific problem behaviors and think about a plan.

- How can I help my students learn more positive behaviors?
- What is my goal for this student?
- Is what I'm doing helping him learn how to manage his emotions and social interaction?
- If it isn't, what do I need to do differently?

Teachers should also be aware that their own life-circumstances may make them more vulnerable to self-critical thinking at times. Stressors such as divorce, death, chronic illness, unemployment, or a move often weaken teachers' internal resources and clear thinking. The goal is not to avoid or deny your personal stresses but recognize situations that may contribute to maladaptive thinking and responses.

Teachers who are self-critical will need to work particularly hard to learn to replace their critical thoughts with self praise. Many people are reluctant to praise themselves, perhaps because they feel it is self-centered or vain. However, just as it is good to compliment other people, it's also good to do the same for oneself. Some examples of self-praising thoughts are: "I'm a good teacher," "I try hard," "I'm proud of myself for taking charge of the situation," "I'm making progress and I think I can help this student," or "It's getting better each time I do this."

Avoid Blaming Parents and Focus on Being Calm and Using "I" Messages to Receive Support

Occasionally when teachers are frustrated with their students, they blame the parents for the problem. A teacher might think, "I have done so much for this student. I'm getting no support from his parents. Why should I care if they don't! It's their fault for not backing me." Or, "If they were more involved with their son, I wouldn't have these kinds of problems." Teachers who make this type of blaming self-statement are highly likely to find themselves in conflict with the parents, which, in the end, will make it more difficult to help the student.

Teachers may also fall into the trap of attributing a particular student trait to the parent or to the family, "Johnny is aggressive, just like his dad" or "You are in trouble just like your brother was." This kind of thinking is a "trait-trap," implying that a student's behavior is innate and can't be changed. Often this type of thinking can become a self-fulfilling prophecy. It's likely to be verbalized in anger or despair, and students are taught that they're expected to imitate their parents' or siblings' undesirable behaviors.

Thoughts that blame the parents for the way the student is behaving are not productive and must be stopped. Teachers can work to substitute positive coping thoughts about parents as well as children. For example, "I wonder why John's father is so hard to reach. It would be good for me to understand more about what's he's dealing with at home." Or, "I am guessing that things must be pretty stressful for Mary's family. I know that they care about her, but it seems like they're dropping the ball right now. They probably need support." It is also helpful for teachers to focus on positive things about the parents of their students. For example, "I know Angie's mother missed that last teacher conference, but she makes sure that Angie is here on time every day and her homework is always in her back pack."

Focus on Coping

At times teachers' self-statements are defeatist and discouraged. The teacher who has worked hard setting up a behavior plan with a difficult student, but finds he continues to misbehave may say to herself, "I'm tired of this. Why try at all? Nothing will work" or, "I can't deal with this. He's just not capable." Or a teacher may be uncomfortable with her own ability to change and says to herself, "This praising stuff doesn't feel like me. I'm a yeller!" The adoption of a defeatist attitude usually results in withdrawal from the problem, avoidance of discipline, and a simmering level of annoyance or anxiety. Eventually, the teacher will either explode with anger or become depressed and give up trying. Moreover, saying that a child is not capable of learning or a teacher is not capable of changing all too often becomes a self-fulfilling prophecy.

A more useful coping response is to think about what you can do to help your students. You might think, "This is frustrating, and I'm tired but I can cope," or "No one can make me mad or make me give up. The choice is up to me." Other coping thoughts include, "Stay calm, it could be worse," or "He will get better, it just takes time and practice." The teacher whose self-statements reflect her stress about her ability to change her teaching strategies can counter these by saying, "Stress in changing one's teaching style is normal, I can cope with it. It will get easier with practice."

The Importance of Obtaining Colleague Support

Obtaining the support of colleagues can be a valuable way of coping with the stress of teaching or a difficult day in the classroom. Without ongoing colleague support, teaching can become a lonely and stressful profession. Arranging regular meetings with other teachers to "let off steam" and express some of the frustrations and failures of teaching is an important coping strategy. Such meetings provide support to teachers because their situation is normalized when they recognize that other teachers have similar problems. It is also cathartic—up to a point. However, just whining and complaining without action planning can lock teachers into self-defeating dialogue, "It'll never change," and stifle problem solving. Therefore it is important in these teacher support meetings to follow a healthy sounding off (without labeling students and classes) with a structure that involves colleague support and problem solving.

Teacher support teams help teachers to be confident, reflective and solve problems.

Teachers can follow the problem solving format described in Chapter Twelve to work on problems together. The active support and help of colleagues in solving a difficult classroom situation or a particular student problem can take some of the pressure off the teacher's feeling that s/he is totally responsible. Moreover, it can reduce teacher attitudes of inadequacy and increase the emphasis on effective coping strategies.

Sometimes teachers will not ask for support from their colleagues regarding a classroom management issue because they think that admitting a problem suggests to other teachers that they are weak or ineffective. Such negative thinking is unrealistic and needs to be challenged because all teachers struggle at times and can benefit greatly from the feedback and reinforcement of others. Without such colleague feedback, there is the danger that teachers will become inflexible, stop learning, and fear innovation. Conversely with supportive nonjudgmental colleague feedback, teachers will be confident, willing to take risks, reflective, and supportive of others.

CONCLUSION

Often people state that a particular event or person made them feel angry or depressed. Although this is not a conscious attempt to avoid responsibility, it tends to put them in a victim role. Such people rarely feel they have any influence over their emotions, and they alternate between holding in their feelings and exploding with rage. However, control over emotional reactions is all internal, and is under the control of the individual. Each teacher can learn to become aware of his or her internal states, belief, attributions, and feelings. This leads to an active decision making process about how to feel about, think about, and respond to stressful situations. Although this is a hard process to learn, it is empowering for it frees the teacher to be proactive about his or her responses to the daily ups and downs in the classroom.

TO SUM UP...

- Refute negative labels that may come to mind.
- Avoid speculations about intentions.
- Paint a positive future.
- Use thought-stopping when tempted to catastrophize and substitute coping thoughts.
- Normalize behavior and use flexible standards.
- Get control of your anger.
- Avoid being be self-critical; instead objectify and use self-praise.
- Support parents or others involved in teaching the student and seek their support.
- Focus on coping.
- Use humor and be positive.
- Reschedule anger or worry times.
- Model positive, coping self-talk.
- Set up regular support meetings with other teachers.

REFERENCES

Seligman, M. (1990). *Learned Optimism*. Sydney: Random House.

CHAPTER 16

Helping Your School
Become Bully Proof

Carl, aged 8 years, is hyperactive, impulsive and inattentive. He fidgets constantly in class, rocking back and forth in his chair, his hands and feet always moving. He often mumbles to himself in an effort to focus on the teacher's directions. His teacher finds his body movements distracting and is critical of his failure to follow through on directions. He is regularly teased and jeered at because of his "odd" behaviors. Few of his peers will play with him. At recess, he is isolated, barred from participating in group games. A small group of older boys once made a game of taunting him, calling him names, and pushing him around. Another time they attacked him on the way home from school and tied him up, calling him their "pet monkey." Recently at school he has started to become verbally abusive with younger children.

Mary frequently comes to school smelling like feces, and even though she is five years old, he still has toileting accidents. She is ashamed about this problem and is always anxious lest it occur at school. At recess and lunch time, she is ridiculed by other children. They call her a "baby," tell her she is stupid, and whisper to each other when she is near. She has never been invited to participate in group games with the other girls in her class, nor has she ever been invited to a classmate's birthday party. She is often found alone in a corner of the playground. In conflict situations, she cries easily and withdraws.

Robbie, aged 6 years, is sent to the principal's office by his teacher almost daily for inappropriate language and unruly behavior, both of which disrupt classroom work. On the playground he frequently starts fights with other children. Nevertheless, he seems to have a small cadre of peers who follow him around, are attracted to his self-confidence, and excited by his bravado and bold language. Robbie has been sent home from school several times for aggressive behavior; each time he receives severe spankings from his father for his misbehavior. Sometimes his older brother hits him as well for making his father angry. Robbie's father is an alcoholic and on several occasions when drunk he has verbally and physically abused Robbie's mother. Robbie has witnessed this violence. Robbie's mother is frequently depressed and withdrawn. Perhaps as a result, she seems unconcerned about Robbie's schoolwork and behavior and rarely communicates with his teacher. Frustrated with Robbie's behavior, his teacher is critical of his parents' apparent lack of concern.

What is bullying and why does it occur?

A person is being bullied or victimized when he or she is exposed, repeatedly and over time, to negative actions on the part of one or more other persons (Olweus, 1993).

Bullying among children is one of those hidden areas of social interaction, like physical and sexual abuse, that has thrived because of secrecy on the part of those involved and neglect on the part of professionals.

Most bullying occurs at school and most of it is hidden from school staff (Dodge, Coie, Pettit, & Price, 1990). Out of a combination of shame and fear of retaliation, victims will rarely report the bullying incident. They also may not want to admit to difficulties at school for fear of worrying their parents, especially if their family is under stress or has experienced some trauma.

Bullying is defined as repeated attacks (physical or verbal) upon someone who has less power by someone who has more power, either by virtue of physical strength, age, social status or sheer numbers. This definition distinguishes the bully from the child who may occasionally hit or call another child names, but does not do this to the same person repeatedly and over time, and from the child who attacks another child of approximately the same psychological and physical strength. Bullying may be overt (direct, obvious) or covert (indirect, hidden) (Loeber & Schmaling, 1985). Covert bullying includes spreading rumors, social ostracism, and manipulation through friendships. It is a problem that may cause long-term damage to the victim and bully alike. In the scenarios described above, the children are victims of bullying. Carl experiences overt physical and verbal bullying at school, Mary is the recipient of overt verbal bullying at school, and Robbie participates in overt physical and verbal bullying towards peers and is the recipient of physical bullying at home. All three children are also experiencing covert forms of bullying, including social rejection. All types of bullying can be destructive to children's well being, though in different ways; moreover, they are interrelated and often occur together in the same relationships (Olweus, 1989, 1993).

Surveys have indicated that as many as 15% of school children—1 out of 7 students—are occasionally involved in bully/victim problems; 3% of children report they are bullied once per week or more often (Olweus, 1993; Tremblay, et al., 2000). The frequency is higher for children in elementary school (kindergarten to grade 5) than for children in middle school, especially for physical bullying. Boys are more likely to experience overt forms of bullying and girls more indirect forms of bullying. Evidence suggests that boys are more likely than girls to be either victims or bullies. The most common situation is for a group of two or three students to repeatedly harass one individual.

Research (e.g., Farrington, 1992; Fox & Boulton, 2005; Smith, Schneider, H., Smith, & Ananiadou, 2004) suggests that certain personality characteristics may put children at increased risk for being bullied. Typical victims are often more anxious and insecure than their peers. They are likely to be more cautious, sensitive, and quiet; they may suffer from low self-esteem, and have a negative view of themselves and their situation. When attacked by other students, they usually will cry and withdraw rather than retaliate. They may perceive themselves as failures for being unable to handle their problems; they may feel stupid and ashamed of this, and may even come to think they deserve the bullying. When victims report bullying to adults, they are sometimes ordered to "stand up for themselves," further reinforcing their guilt and self-concept of social incompetence. Although they may have a positive attitude toward schoolwork, they have a negative view of their ability to form friendships. It is typical for them to be without a good friend in class. Traits associated with victimization for boys are smaller than average size, less than average physical strength, perceived lack of physical attractiveness, and poor communication skills. There is a second category of victim, the so-called "provocative" victim. These children have both anxious and aggressive behavior patterns, and are sometimes hyperactive and impulsive. Their aggressive, disruptive behavior "provokes" other children into bullying behavior. It is important to realize, however, that this type of victim does not cause the bullying and is in no way responsible for it, although he or she can be made aware that bullying is a possible response to his or her aggression (Cook, Williams, Guerra, Kim, & Sadek, 2010).

Typical bullies have a strong need to dominate others and to control social interaction (Cook, et al., 2010; Olweus, 1978; Pulkkinen & Tremblay, 1992). They are often aggressive toward adults as well as peers. Bullies may be impulsive as well. Physical strength and a confident appearance are associated traits, along with a positive self-image. They often have well-developed communication skills so that they are slick at talking their way out of trouble. Insensitive and lacking in empathy, they may even feel their victims deserve their treatment. If they have been reared in a home where the atmosphere is primarily critical and harsh, they may have a hostile attitude toward their surroundings, including school, and toward authority figures. Bullying may be only one aspect of a general pattern of antisocial behavior. Furthermore, bullying during the elementary years is a predictor of delinquency later in adolescence.

There is a second category of bully, the more passive bully, the follower or "henchman." These children do not take the initiative in bullying but participate on the sidelines. They may support the bullying by jeering or laughing at the victim, cheering the bully on, or engaging in the name calling and exclusion, even though they may wish the bullying wasn't happening.

Research on bullying suggests that family factors are of considerable significance in the development of the personality of the child who bullies as well as the child who is at risk for being bullied (e.g., Loeber & Farrington, 2001). The victim often enjoys a secure home life and close relationships within the family. He or she may feel insecure about meeting parental expectations. Bullies, on the other hand, are likely to come from problematic homes characterized as lacking in warmth, with a low level of home supervision and monitoring. Studies have found that parents of bullies are likely to be overly punitive and use physical violence as their method of discipline. There may be an increased frequency of alcoholism and drug abuse in the family and a greater likelihood that such children have witnessed spouse abuse. They may have been rejected by a significant adult. Another commonly associated parenting style is permissiveness towards children's behavior, including aggression, and failure to set appropriate limits or consequences when aggression occurs. Too little involvement, too much freedom, and violence in the home are key contributors to the low self-esteem, low empathy skills and escalating aggression that create a bully (Cook, et al., 2010; Loeber & Schmaling, 1985).

It must be emphasized that family factors, although important, cannot account for all cases of bullying. Bullies and victims do not always come from the types of families described above. The temperament of the child also plays a part in the development of what psychologists refer to as "aggressive reaction pattern" or bullying

The temperament of the child also plays a part in the development of "aggressive reaction pattern" or bullying.

There is a clear relationship between "teacher density" and the amount of bullying.

(Olweus, 1993). Aggressive children have been shown to be more likely to be impulsive, hyperactive, inattentive, distractible, and irritable; temperamental traits which make it more difficult for them to learn problem solving and appropriate social skills. They turn to bullying because they lack the skills for dealing appropriately with social situations.

The conditions at school also have a role in accounting for bullying; specifically the degree of supervision during recess, lunch and other breaks (Olweus, 1993). Research has found a clear negative association between "teacher density" and the amount of bullying; that is, the greater the number of teachers supervising at recess or in the lunchroom or other breaks, the lower the incidence of bullying. Studies where students have been interviewed about teachers' responses to bullying have indicated that both the bully and the victim felt that teachers did little to stop the problem. This perception led them to conclude that teachers were unconcerned, and that they would be allowed to continue their behavior (Olweus, 1993; Smith, et al., 2004).

What can teachers do?

Every child has the right to an education free of aggression and humiliation. No child should be afraid to go to school for fear of being bullied, and no parents should have to worry about their child being bullied. This means that no child should be allowed to bully another child. If a child is prone to bullying, he or she should be provided with the kind of guidance, coaching and constraints that will teach him or her to be a responsible member of the school community, and he or she should be held accountable for any bullying by having to face consequences. Research has shown that whole-school anti-bullying programs that include teacher and parent involvement can be effective in reducing its occurrence and create a safer learning environment (Farrington & Welsh, 2003; Smith, et al., 2004; Snyder, 2001; Tremblay, Mass, Pagani, & Vitaro, 1996). In fact, the basic classroom management principles discussed in the earlier chapters regarding building a strong foundation of positive relationships, coaching, praise and rewards coupled with proactive discipline and an emphasis of social and emotional curriculum will all contribute to a safe environment and enhanced social and emotional competence and a reduction in bullying incidents. In this chapter we will review some of the specific steps that can be taken to reduce bullying and strengthen a supportive peer group. What steps should be taken to ensure this?

1. Understand the early signs of possible bullying

Early detection of bullying is an important aspect of prevention. Everyone in the school community needs to be made aware of the indicators that a child may be falling into a victim role or developing into a bully. Here are some of the signs:

Signs of child falling into a victim role

- reported incidents of being the object of derogatory remarks
- repeated experiences being made fun of, laughed at, degraded, belittled
- a pattern of being dominated by others
- getting pushed, shoved, punched, hit, or kicked and being unable to defend one's self adequately
- having books and/or money taken, damaged or scattered around
- having bruises, cuts, torn clothing with no explanation
- being excluded from peer group activities at recess or during breaks
- frequently being the last to be chosen for team activities
- hovering near teachers during recess or breaks
- difficulty speaking up in class
- appearing anxious or insecure at school
- reluctance to go to school
- being a "loner"—having no close friends
- never inviting classmates home after school, or never being invited over to others' homes or to parties

Signs of child becoming a bully

- generally negative attitude and oppositional toward school authority figures and parents
- high frequency of antisocial behaviors such as lying, stealing, swearing, hitting
- having a tough "bravado" demeanor
- having a strong need to dominate others by threats or bragging about one's physical prowess
- having difficulty following the rules and tolerating delays or refusals
- repeatedly taunting, teasing, name calling
- low empathy for others and a refusal to assume responsibility for one's actions
- associating with other antisocial peers

2. Establish conditions at recess and other breaks that discourage bullying

Most bullying at school occurs during recess or other breaks. Thus schools and teachers need to be sure there is adequate supervision during recess and other breaks (lunch time, bathroom breaks bus rides) so that bullying cannot occur. Schools with higher teacher density during recess have lower levels of bully/victim problems. However, simply increasing the presence of teachers during these times is not enough; teachers must know how to intervene early, quickly, and effectively in bullying situations and must be ready and willing to do so. Teachers and staff may need to cue themselves to identify bullying for what it is. Even if there is only a suspicion that bullying is taking place, it should be acted upon. Rather than thinking, "They're just goofing around," "It's all in fun," or, "He's not trying to be mean," the teacher's guiding rule should be, "Better to intervene too early rather than too late." A consistent response from

Teachers need to intervene early and effectively.

teachers and playground supervisors gives students a clear message that bullying is not acceptable and that those in charge will support the victim or potential victim. Potential bullies need to know that power (i.e., the school authorities, teachers, parents) will always be used to protect the potential victim.

A teacher who observes bullying needs to intervene by:

- imposing an immediate consequence on the bully (whatever is specified on hierarchy discipline plan).
- speaking on behalf of the victim, modeling, and encouraging victim's use of an assertive response.
- reporting the incident to the classroom teacher and parents of the students involved.

The school schedule and the school environment can be set up in such a way as to discourage bullying. Since a good deal of bullying takes the form of older children being aggressive against younger and more vulnerable children, schools should try to schedule recess at separate times for older and younger students and for special education students. Furthermore, since bullying tends to occur more frequently in certain parts of the playground and in bathrooms, these areas should receive extra monitoring. A well-equipped and attractive outdoor environment with structured activities at recess can help reduce bullying by inviting more positive activities.

3. Have clear class rules about bullying and regular classroom discussions about these problems

Along with school-wide discipline policies and programs, individual classrooms can be a place for education about bullying. As we have discussed in Chapter Three, the proactive teacher has explained and posted classroom rules about friendly behaviors for all to see. For example, the following three rules set clear standards regarding overt and more covert forms of bullying:

- Bullying or hurting other children is not permitted. Friendly behavior is expected by all.

- Students will try to help children who are bullied by seeking help from an adult.
- Students will include students who are often left out, by inviting them to play with them and participate in activities.

Students should be praised for following the rules; in particular, students who are easily influenced by others should receive appreciation for not reacting aggressively and for standing up for others who are bullied.

It is important for teachers to have regular class meetings about bullying and friendly behavior. Some general examples of this are provided in Chapter 13. These discussions should be held regularly (e.g., once a week), perhaps with students during circle time. In these class meetings teachers can clarify and reiterate the consequences of breaking the rules. They can read stories about bullies and victims (e.g., being teased, left-out, bossed around, etc.) where the bully is presented as anxious and insecure beneath a tough surface and where students learn to empathize with the victim. Along with the stories, role plays can help children think about ways of responding assertively without becoming aggressive themselves, and can help the class explore the feelings of the bully, why he might be acting that way, and what the bully should do instead to make friends. Concrete examples from the classroom and playground should be used to help students think of ways they can counteract social isolation and stop bullying. It is important to discuss verbal bullying and covert bullying so that students realize that even passively observing from the sidelines is being an accomplice to the bullying. Students can then be prompted to discuss and practice how they can help a child who is being victimized, rather than standing on the sidelines.

Empower students to report bullying.

Because students may feel that if they tell the teacher about a bullying incident they will be perceived as tattlers, teachers need to counteract this attitude by telling students that reporting bullying is following the school's rules. Moreover, tattling on behalf of another child who needs help can be defined as being compassionate, friendly and sensitive to the feelings of the weaker child. The goal is to have students understand that both victims and bullies need help, and that only if incidents are reported will that help be forthcoming. For instance, suppose that a student is frequently ostracized by the other students at recess. The teacher could use puppets to act out the situation in circle time meetings.

CIRCLE TIME: LESSON SCRIPT
Bullying

Teacher: Boys and girls, Wally came today because he saw a problem on the playground. He needs your help to solve this because it's a serious problem, isn't it Wally?

Wally: Yes! There is a girl in my class named Felicity and I don't know her very well. She just moved here and is pretty quiet. Every day at recess some other girls are going over to her and are saying mean things about her and about her family. Felicity looks really sad and tries to go away from them, but they keep following her. One of the girls even pulled her hair and pushed her yesterday. I wanted to tell those kids to stop, but I was afraid that they'd start saying mean things to me.

Teacher: Wow, Wally, that is a big problem. I'm really glad that you told us about it. Boys and girls, what do you think Wally should do?

(Key points for this discussion: 1. Wally needs to help Felicity by telling an adult. 2. Label the teasing/aggressive behavior as bullying. 3. Suggest that Wally look for ways to include Felicity and be her friend. 4. Explore Wally and Felicity's feelings. 5. Discuss reasons why the other girls might be bullying. 6. Discuss things that Felicity could do to help herself. As students discuss these options, the teacher can guide them and role-play/practice some of the solutions. Remember that the students should not act out the bullying behavior.)

Cooperative learning activities in the classroom, where students work in small groups, with teacher providing social and emotion coaching methods also help prevent bullying. It is important that the teacher split up the more aggressive children and put them in different groups with assertive, socially skilled students (who will not accept bullying) and not with victims. Students who are isolated or who tend to be victimized should be placed with positive, friendly students. Carefully planned cooperative group activities, where the focus is on the performance of the entire group, create mutual positive dependence among group members and by extension a feeling of cohesiveness in the whole classroom. When each member of the group is given responsibility for every other member's learning of the prescribed task, students begin to feel responsible for each other, an attitude which is contrary to that of the bully or the passive bystander.

4. Special intervention for victims

The goals of intervention for victims are to build children's self-confidence, to rebuild their sense of security at school, and to establish a feeling of being accepted or, ideally, liked by at least one or two classmates. Teachers can pair up victimized children with more popular children and foster friendship opportunities. They can also give these children extra attention and coaching for targeted social behaviors and emotions.

Another aspect of intervention with victims is teaching them the importance of letting their teacher and parents know about incidents of bullying. Often children will not want to tell adults for fear of getting the tormentor in trouble and then experiencing retaliation. They may even convince their parents not to tell the teacher. They need to be helped to understand that in the long run this secrecy is *more* harmful to them because it allows the bully's behavior to continue. Children who are victimized need to learn to report incidents. Teachers and other school authorities, for their part, need to give the victim the message that it is not his or her fault for being harassed. They need to assure children that they will get adequate protection against retaliation or continued harassment from bullies.

It is also important that the victim learn to avoid or ignore the bully when possible as well as to know how to stand up to aggression:

with verbal assertiveness, not aggression. Research has shown that bullies don't continue bullying children who respond assertively to their efforts to control or isolate them. Teachers can model this assertive behavior for the child. For example, when an incident occurs on the playground the teacher might say to the child who has been bullied, "Tell Robbie that you don't like being hit and not to do it again." During class the teacher can also present role-play scenarios for children to practice assertive responses to bullying behavior. During these role plays children can also be prompted to talk about the victim's feelings of humiliation, helplessness and worthlessness.

5. Special intervention for bullies

The goal of intervention for bullies is to stop the bullying and replace this behavior with appropriate social interactions. This involves teaching social skills and non-violent methods of expressing feelings and resolving conflict. It also involves increasing their empathy for others and their acceptance of children who are different.

Intervention begins with clear limit-setting; the message that bullying will not be tolerated. If a teacher even suspects there is a problem, s/he needs to take action immediately by talking with the suspected bully and victim. The message should be given clearly: "We don't allow bullying in our class/school and it must stop." The teacher needs to impose a negative consequence for the bullying behavior. Whenever bullying occurs, immediately send the bully to Time Out for 5 minutes to calm down and give attention to the victim (so that the bully's behavior is not inadvertently reinforced with teacher attention). Afterwards, focus on the positive opposite behaviors targeted for the bully to receive teacher coaching, so the bully learns which behavior is more likely to give him attention. (See Chapter Nine for information on Time Out.)

The bully will likely try to minimize his contribution to the problem and may even blame the victim, saying, "He started it" or, "It was her fault!" It is important for the teacher not to engage in an argument about who started the bullying. Bullies are often very good at talking themselves out of problem situations. If allowed to tell their version of the story, they may humiliate the victim. Don't waste time on "getting to the bottom of things"—it diverts the focus from the bullying behavior to the circumstances. Instead, calmly impose the consequence. Remember the message is that bullying will not be tolerated, under any circumstances. If you are in doubt about who did the bullying (a rare situation indeed) send both children to Time Out, saying, "It looks like both of you may have been doing some bullying, so both of you need to go cool down and think over how you could have behaved differently."

Loss of a privilege (an alternative to Time Out) can also be an effective discipline approach for bullying. The privilege might be removal of some part of recess or some special privilege that the student values, like computer time. Teachers should set up a discipline hierarchy for their classrooms defining the consequences for bullying.

If bullying is going to be met swiftly with negative consequences, teachers will need to observe and closely monitor playground behavior, in particular extra supervision for children with a history of bullying (actual or suspected). This will mean that the lunch time or playground supervisor will need to position himself/herself close to the suspected bully, and to be visible to everyone. This will not only ensure safety of victims but will discourage others from becoming involved because they will not want to be the object of similar supervision. Sometimes teachers have a negative attitude toward recess supervision because they don't want to be seen as police officers; or they may stay inside at recess because they feel they need a break from the students. While teachers do need breaks, recess is not the appropriate time to take these breaks. Failure to adequately supervise recess, lunch time and the loading of buses means that the weaker students will be left to the mercy of bullies; without adequate supervision, intervention will not happen, and lack of intervention implies silent condoning of the bullying. Attentive supervision is effective not only for helping the bully realize his behavior is inappropriate, but also for assuring the safety of potential victims.

Although immediate consequences are necessary to protect the victim and stop the behavior, a teaching comprehensive behavior plan is still needed; one that uses the whole pyramid and includes positive interventions along with the consequences. Bullying is an extreme form of many of the negative behaviors that have already been discussed in earlier chapters. It will be easier for the bully to change his behavior if he feels accepted and liked by teachers and peers. This means that teachers must overcome their frustration with the bullies and work to develop relationships with them (Chapter Two). They must also work to foster positive relationships between the bully and peers (Chapter 13). Teachers need to be careful to coach, praise and reward these children whenever they are behaving cooperatively with teachers and peers, being sensitive to others' requests, assuming responsibility for their behaviors, and—especially—reacting in non-aggressive and calm ways in a poten-tial conflict-provoking situation (Chapters Four and Five). Children who are engaging in bullying behaviors likely have social skill deficits and may not be as motivated by social praise and encour-agement, so teachers may need to incorporate incentives for being friendly into their behavior plans (Chapter Six). Children who bully others are not easy children to develop relationships with; teachers will need to make an extra effort in this regard. It has been said that the children who most need love will ask for it in the most unloving ways; the same can be said for the chil-dren most in need of encouragement, coaching, praise and positive attention. In summary, intervening with a bully will take the entire array of teacher positive management skills, positive dis-cipline, and social skills coaching that this book covers.

Intervening with a bully will take the entire array of teacher positive management tools in the teaching pyramid.

How can a teacher help change a child's negative reputation in the classroom, school and community?

While it is important to deal firmly and consistently with bullying behavior, it is also important to avoid contributing to the creation or continuation of bullying behavior. Children even as young as age five may have developed a negative self-image and may have established a reputation in the school (and perhaps the community) as the "bully" or "problem child." In some instances, even before children have started school, teachers have been warned of particular students they will have who have been labeled as "difficult" or "disruptive." Once school starts such reputations are often reinforced by the reactions of other students,

"You're always in trouble," or "You're bad, the teacher doesn't like you," or "You can't come to my birthday party because my parents say you are a troublemaker." If a teacher doesn't control this type of comment, this child's negative reputation may expand beyond the classroom to the school and to the community of parents. It can snowball, beginning with a child's complaint to his parent that he was hit again by Bobby on the playground, compounded by parental anger towards Bobby and even towards his family if the parent blames them for Bobby's aggression. Sometimes it even leads to parents' blaming the teacher for allowing hitting to occur at school. When parents hear that their child and other children have been bullied or hit by a particular child, they may rally other parents to complain to the Principal, asserting that the child doesn't belong in that classroom. This kind of "lynch mob" mentality is detrimental not only for Bobby's future growth but for all the students' relationships in the classroom as well as for the school community. It is, in essence, a form of adult bullying of an already troubled child. If successful, it sends the message that the school community has no broad-based responsibility where everyone helps each other. It will result in a declining sense of community, fewer supports for teachers, an increasing alienation of families and children with particular difficulties and an erosion of positive relationships between the teacher and students. Teachers need to remember that although bullying behavior is unacceptable, the bully is a child in the school community who needs help to change his or her behavior patterns. This bully is desperately in need of all the help and support that the school can provide.

What can schools and teachers do to prevent this ripple effect?
Establish school policy and philosophy

Clear school policy has a vital role in preventing bullying and helping children who become involved in bullying incidents. School policies should communicate a clear message to students, parents and teachers that bullying will not be tolerated and will be handled firmly. Policies should clearly set forth the rules and specify what will happen if the rules are broken. It is not recommended that bullying be handled by sending children home or suspending them. Bullying that is happening at school should be dealt with at school (with parental involvement).

Since victims may be afraid to bring up their experiences with bullying for fear of retaliation from the bully, the school should set up a procedure enabling students to call the school counselor anonymously. The counselor can encourage the child who is victimized to also talk with his or her teacher and parents, and can involve relevant persons in providing help for the victim. If school policies have not been set up the teacher can advocate for their implementation and if they are in place teachers can help explain them to families.

Educate families so they can talk to their children about bullying

The school has an important role in educating families about the meaning of bullying, both for the bully and the victim. This educational effort can take place through the use of special workshops and through regular parent meetings. Bullying is a multifaceted problem rooted in a variety of interrelated factors such as the child's temperament, social behavior, communication skills, level of self-esteem, and self-confidence, in addition to family, school and societal influences. Rather than blaming some single source such as society, the family or the child, schools can be proactive, focusing on preventing bullying regardless of the factors which may have contributed to the problem in the first place.

The school should provide comprehensive training to help prevent as well as treat the socialization difficulties that lead to bullying. This training needs to go beyond individual teachers' efforts with individual students; it should be part of an effort involving the entire school and families. Supportive education and training in social skills, problem solving, empathy training and esteem-building address the root causes of bullying and have long-term payoffs for the school.

It is important for schools and teachers to elicit parent support in making it clear to their children that bullying is unacceptable. Parents can be encouraged by teachers to introduce the issue with their children by talking about the problem and asking them if anyone in their class is often "picked on" or left out. Parents can

Training in social skills, problem solving, empathy training and esteem-building address the root causes of bullying and will have long-term payoffs for the school.

increase their children's understanding of the problem by explaining the concepts of passive participation in bullying and of "covert" bullying (excluding the child). Parents might attempt to determine whether their child has sympathy for the victim and whether s/he would be willing to do anything to help the student. Parents should encourage their children to report bullying to teachers, explaining why "tattling" is not wrong but actually helps the bully (and potential victims) in the long run. Parents can strive to develop their child's empathy for the victim and involve their child in ending the victimization by inviting a "victim" to a picnic or after school play time.

Changing the Child's Reputation in the Classroom—Promoting a Sense of Classroom as Family

For the child who has already established a negative reputation in the classroom as a bully or trouble-maker, the teacher will need to define strategies and formulate a plan for how to change this child's reputation. For example, the teacher can do this by working especially hard to develop a positive relationship with this child. The teacher may begin noticing or commenting on particular strengths this child has that refute his aggressive image, "Bobby, you are good friend—you are sharing nicely and being very gentle with that toy. Josh seems to be enjoying playing with you." The teacher may set up formal compliment circle times each day where students give compliments to each other on a regular basis. The teacher may ask the other students to notice the particular times when Bobby is helping and cooperating. In other words, the teacher is helping the other children know that Bobby is working hard on learning a particular behavior (e.g., to ask and not grab or hit) and trains them to notice it when Bobby is helpful and uses his words well—a major step in changing their perceptions of him. The teacher can then praise the children for noticing Bobby's successes, so that the children become engaged and excited for Bobby's successes as he learns to manage his anger more appropriately. This same strategy can also be used by the teacher for other children who are having particular difficulties such as learning to read, or to do math, or spelling. In other words, the teacher is creating a classroom environment where children learn there are individual differences in each others' cognitive, behavioral and social abilities and where they are invested in helping their friends achieve their own "personal goals." A sense of community is created in the classroom when children are learning to appreciate and applaud each others' accomplishments. Thus they are developing meaningful relationships with each other.

Promote friendships

The teacher can help parents know about particular friends who work well with Bobby. These friends might be encouraged to invite Bobby over to their houses or vice versa. It is important that students with negative reputations develop one or two good friends in the classroom, friends who are popular and socially appropriate, not friends who have similar difficulties with aggression. Teachers can help mastermind these relationships by making strategic assignments of groups for group cooperative projects or field trips and by noticing when children are being good friends with each other. For example, "You two are working well together, Jimmy is a good friend."

Open communication with parents

If there is a child in the classroom known to all the parents as aggressive, the teacher needs to be sure that s/he calls the parents whenever there is an incident involving their child and the aggressive child. The teacher can explain the situation to the parents before it escalates (or they hear about it from someone else) and let the parents know that s/he is carefully monitoring the child with aggressive tendencies. Teachers will need to reassure parents that their child will be safe. The teacher might also elicit the parents' support in this endeavor by telling them how they are handling the problem in the classroom through collaboration with the parents, social skills and problem-solving training and assertiveness training for all the children. The teacher's optimism and confidence in how she explains her interventions in the classroom and her belief that she will be successful are key ingredients to engendering parental support and patience. The teacher might also point out the dangers of such a child feeling ostracized by his peer group and talk about the child's unique strengths and contributions to the class. Finally, it can also be very helpful for parents of other children in the classroom to realize that in addressing the "problem child's" behavior through strategies such as class meetings, special training, compliment circles, and peer reinforcement, not only is that child being helped, but all the children are learning how to handle conflict in relationships in appropriate ways. Excluding or kicking a child out of class—and disposing of the problem—teaches children nothing about problem solving, managing conflicts and developing relationships.

Mutual responsibility between home and school

As noted above, schools have an important responsibility for informing families about the extent and causes of the problem. The message to families can be that because of the potential seriousness of bullying, the school is going to focus on even minor cases of bullying and social isolation; moreover, the school should advise parents that this monitoring may initially result in increased contact from administrators or teachers until the problem has been resolved. Conversely, schools need to ask parents to communicate openly with them, to stay involved, and to contact teachers if they suspect their own or another child of bullying.

The school should let parents know that if it is discovered that students are bullying others or being bullied, the school will contact the parents concerned and ask for their cooperation in bringing about change. They should meet together to discuss the situation with them and collaboratively arrive at a plan for solving the problem. Parents who suspect their children are bullying can help by coaching and praising their children for cooperative behavior, setting up reward systems for good behavior and setting up rules that make it clear that they take the bullying seriously. If both the school and parents are responding with a consistent message, bullying is less likely to reoccur. For the family who is chaotic and disorganized, teachers can help parents define a few family rules which are written down and displayed and plan a set of consequences for violations of those rules. They can encourage parents

If both the school and parents are responding with a consistent message, bullying is less likely to reoccur.

to coach and praise their child when he or she follows the rules and is friendly with others. Parents should be urged to spend time engaged in child-directed play with their child and get to know their child's friends. Schools can offer parent training groups where parents are taught how to use social and emotion coaching methods in their play interactions with children individually or in groups.

Parents who suspect that their child is being bullied should let their child's teacher know as soon as possible. They can also try to increase the self-confidence of the victimized child by helping him or her establish friendships and stand up for himself or herself assertively. Although it is understandable to want to protect a child who has been bullied, parents should avoid being overprotective, as this attitude on the part of parents can increase a child's sense of isolation from peers and thus exacerbate the problem. When parents and teachers collaborate regarding solutions without blaming each other, they can bring about significant reductions in bullying.

CONCLUSION

Taking Charge

Violence and aggression in young children is escalating around the world. As the intensity of the problem increases, the age of the offender decreases. Families and educators struggle to maintain hope in the face of grim forecasts by news reporters and statisticians. But instead of getting caught up in feeling powerless, teachers and parents can 'take charge' by supporting one another and creating an emotional and social teaching approach that will both prevent and reduce aggression in young children as well as build their social competence, emotional regulation and empathy. Starting early is the key to helping 'immunize' children again bullying, peer rejection, and violence.

There is no one-way to begin this process. Each early childhood program and school will have its own resources. Each teacher will have his or her own unique situation. But as you take responsibility for your part in this effort, you will find you will connect with other teachers, parents and mental health providers interested in this endeavor and will begin to create a strong network of support for your creative initiatives. By taking action and using some of the teaching tools suggested in this book combined with your own practical wisdom, you can make a positive difference and encourage optimal growth in the lives of many children.

TO SUM UP...

- Recognize early signs of bullying in schools and/or children who are in victim roles.
- Scaffold unstructured settings and occasions such as cafeterias, playgrounds, bathrooms and buses with adults who are trained to coach and reward friendly social skills, prevent bullying and help children problem solve conflict situations.
- Help children from establishing negative school reputations by teaching them social skills, emotion regulation, problem solving and highlighting their special talents.
- Help victims to be comfortable asking for help when feeling bullied and to stand up assertively to stay safe.

REFERENCES

Cook, C. R., Williams, K. R., Guerra, N. G., Kim, T. E., & Sadek, S. (2010). Predictors of Bullying and Victimizatin in Childhool and Adolescence: A Meta-analytic Investigation. *School Psychology* 25(2), 65-83.

Dodge, K. A., Coie, J. D., Pettit, G. S., & Price, J. M. (1990). Peer status and aggression in boys' groups: Developmental and contextual analyses. *Child Development, 61*(5), 1289-1309.

Farrington, D. P. (1992). Explaining the beginning, progress and ending of antisocial behavior problems: Stability and factors accounting for change. *Journal of Child Psychology and Psychiatry, 31,* 891-909.

Farrington, D. P., & Welsh, B. C. (2003). Family-based prevention of offending: A meta-analysis. *The Australian and New Zealand Journal of Criminology, 36*(2), 127-151.

Fox, C. L., & Boulton, M. J. (2005). The social skills problems of victims of bullying: Self, peer and teacher perceptions. *British Journal of Educational Psychology, 75*(2), 313-328.

Loeber, R., & Farrington, D. P. (2001). *Child Delinquents: Development, Intervention and Service Needs.* Thousand Oaks, CA: Sage Publications.

Loeber, R., & Schmaling, K. B. (1985). Empirical evidence for overt and covert patterns of antisocial conduct problems: a metaanalysis. *Journal of Abnormal Child Psychology, 13*(2), 337-353.

Olweus, D. (1978). *Aggression in the schools. Bullies and whipping boys.* Washington, DC: Hemisphere Press.

Olweus, D. (1989). Bully/Victim problems among school children: Basic facts and effects fo a school-based intervention program. In K. Rubin & D. Pepler (Eds.), *The development and treatment of childhood aggression.* Hillsdale New Jersey: Erlbaum.

Olweus, D. (1993). *Bullying at school: What we know and what we can do.* Oxford: Blackwell Press.

Pulkkinen, L., & Tremblay, R. E. (1992). Patterns of boys' social adjustment in two cultures and at different ages: A longtitudinal perspective. *International Journal of Behavioral Development, 15,* 527-553.

Smith, J. D., Schneider, H., B., Smith, P. K., & Ananiadou, K. (2004). The effectiveness of whole-school antibullying programs: A synthesis of evaluation research. *School Psychology Review, 33,* 547-560.

Snyder, H. (2001). Child delinquents. In R. Loeber & D. P. Farrington (Eds.), *Risk factors and successful interventions.* Thousand Oaks, CA: Sage.

Tremblay, R. E., Japel, C., Perusse, D., Boivin, M., Zoccolillo, M., Montplaisir, J., et al. (2000). The search for the age of "onset" of physical aggression: Rousseau and Bandura revisited. *Criminal Behavior and Mental Health, 24*(2), 129-141.

Tremblay, R. E., Mass, L. C., Pagani, L., & Vitaro, F. (1996). From childhood physical aggression to adolescent maladjustment: The Montreal Prevention Experiment. In R. D. Peters & R. J. MacMahon (Eds.), *Preventing childhood disorders, substance abuse and delinquency* (pp. 268-298). Thousand Oaks, CA: Sage.